Through Silent Country

Through Silent Country is a journey of discovery and testimony which began when Carolyn Wadley Dowley stumbled upon a small reference to a remarkable escape story. Although at first it seemed faint, she set out to follow the trace of the narrative back to its origins, in the remote area around Laverton, north-east of Kalgoorlie — Wongutha Country. There, the people she met not only confirmed details of the story, but revealed how it was a part of the many stories which are their history. 'They were keen to speak of the past, to teach me what had occurred and how it still affects them.'

The stories of the Wongutha people, and careful archival research, enable Carolyn Wadley Dowley to traverse the historical silence and piece together a remarkable story of injustice, survival and triumph.

Cover photograph: Lake Moore, *Richard Woldendorp.*

Carolyn Wadley Dowley has a passion for narrative exploration of the past in the present. 'My hope is that "new" historical knowledge will promote deeper understanding amongst and between all Australians.' *Through Silent Country* is her first book.

She holds a Master of Philosophy in Australian Studies, and is occasionally an architect. She has worked for the United Nations Centre for Human Settlements in Nairobi, and is currently writing a commissioned work on East Perth which links her interests in narrative history and architectural design.

Carolyn currently lives in Perth with her husband, Ian, and her baby daughter, Ellen.

CAROLYN WADLEY DOWLEY

Through Silent Country

FREMANTLE ARTS CENTRE PRESS

First published 2000 by
FREMANTLE ARTS CENTRE PRESS
25 Quarry Street, Fremantle
(PO Box 158, North Fremantle, 6159)
Western Australia.
www.facp.@iinet.net.au

Copyright © Carolyn Wadley Dowley, 2000.

This book is copyright. Apart from any fair dealing for the purpose of private study, research, criticism or review, as permitted under the Copyright Act, no part may be reproduced by any process without written permission. Enquiries should be made to the publisher.

Consultant Editor Ray Coffey.
Production Coordinator Cate Sutherland.
Cover Designer Marion Duke.

Typeset by Fremantle Arts Centre Press
and printed by Success Print, Western Australia.

National Library of Australia
Cataloguing-in-publication data

Wadley Dowley, Carolyn, 1971– .
    Through silent country.

    ISBN 1 86368 281 3.

    1. Moore River Native Settlement (W.A.) — History.
    2. Wongai (Australian people). 3. Aborigines, Australian —
    Western Australia — Moore River Region — Reserves — History.
    I. Title.

994.120049915

The State of Western Australia has made an investment in this project through ArtsWA in association with the Lotteries Commission.

Publication of this title was assisted by the Commonwealth Government through the Australia Council, its arts funding and advisory body.

This work is dedicated to my Gran,
Lydia Gronow.

Acknowledgements

My thanks go to all those who have contributed to the process that has resulted in this book.

Thanks to the Wongutha people who so generously shared with me aspects of their past and their present. Heartfelt thanks to those who encouraged me to record the histories they told me: Auntie Wyallie, Auntie May, Auntie Sadie, Auntie Rosie, Auntie Ngunnu, Auntie Queenie, Ranji McIntyre, and the uncles who have since passed on. To Auntie Dora and to Claude, to Cheryl, Gayle, Sonia, and especially to Miriam Brownley and Jane Beasley, thanks for your support and enthusiasm.

Additional thanks are extended to May O'Brien and Sadie Canning for editorial advice relating to Wongutha matters.

Thanks to Auntie Rosie and her family for access to and permission to use extracts from personal file documentation relating to escapes from the Moore River Settlement in the 1940s.

Thanks to Margaret Morgan for access to and permission to use the letters, diary, archival records and photos of Rod Schenk.

Through Silent Country started life as a research thesis — my sincere thanks to Professor Tom Stannage for taking on the supervision of that work, and for wise counsel, visionary guidance and scholarly insight.

My thanks to Ray Coffey for perceptive editorial comment.

Thanks to my family and friends — and in particular to Ian Dowley, Rosalie and Lynn Wadley, and Ian Wadley — for your unfailing support, sustained enthusiasm, inspired comments and all your practical assistance.

Thanks to my beloved husband Ian for journeying with me.

Contents

Foreword	9
Introduction	13
1. Journeying	17
2. Speakings	69
2.0 Introduction to the Speakings	70
2.1 Reg Johnston	72
2.2 Ranji McIntyre (First conversation)	75
2.3 Ranji McIntyre (Second conversation)	95
2.4 Queenie Donaldson	105
2.5 Rosie Meredith	108
2.6 Wyallie and Ngunnu	140
2.7 May O'Brien	172
2.8 Sadie Canning	192
2.9 Margaret Morgan	204
3. Writings	221
3.0 Introduction to the Writings	222
3.1 Laverton Police Records	224
3.2 R S Schenk's Letters and Diary	236
3.3 Moore River Native Settlement Records	248
3.4 William Harris, Letter to the *Sunday Times*	264
3.5 Absences in Contemporary Writings	267
3.6 Interpretive Accounts and Absences in Recent Writings	281
4. A New Account	317

MAPS
  Western Australia   9
  Laverton Area   10
  The Journeys   347

APPENDICES   365
  Notes and Glossary
    A1. Notes on Transcripts   366
    A2. Glossary of Wongutha Words   367
    A3. Explanations of Process   368
  Supplementary Text
    A4. Escape and Pursuit   373
    A5. 1921 People: Who were exiled? Who escaped?   379
    A6. William Harris' Evidence   385
    A7. Notes from A O Neville's Files   387
    A8. Rosie Green — Escape Documentation   402
    A9. Notes on Cosmo Newbery   411
    A10. Notes on Mt Margaret Goldfields Contact History   416
    A11. Review of Legislation in Western Australia
         Affecting Aboriginal People in 1921   425

ENDNOTES   429

FIGURES AND ILLUSTRATIONS   447

BIBLIOGRAPHY   449

INDEX   457

Foreword

In 1997 Carolyn began work on an M.Phil thesis at the University of Western Australia. It was a new departure for her. She was a trained architect, but in 1997 she wanted to learn more about Australian Studies. She also wanted to tell a Westralian story. It was a story already told, not often by 'historians' and not well; but it was a story known to and shared by Aboriginal families since 1921.

Carolyn and the Wongutha people would talk and walk the story through the silent country, and offer it to all Australia in the year 2000, the year of renewal. The year of peace. Their story is also a story of Christianity, both in its wide social darwinian expression and in its caring, supporting, loving expression. To tell the story, Carolyn had to revitalise historical presentation, to move beyond us as it were. She was also inspired by a great teacher, Diane Barwick, a courage-maker, whose articles and books on Aboriginal history were based on unconditional love and respect.

Carolyn journeyed with her subject and with those whose lives contained the story. Her diary of the journey was as poignant as it was brilliantly written. Here was a new voice for history in this State, so her supervisor believed. And then an examiner and a publisher agreed. And the owners of the story were happy to see it told in a very public way.

Western Australia is richly blessed with fine young writers, artists, actors, singers, musicians and composers. Their themes are as wide as human experience. Their gifts are prodigious. We celebrate their presence and wish them a profound influence on our society and beyond. I welcome Carolyn Wadley Dowley's 'arrival' among them, after her profound journey through silent country with the Wongutha people whose generosity of spirit made the book possible.

TOM STANNAGE

Cautionary note: This book contains, with permission, names and photographs of people who have now passed on. Any person to whom this may cause distress should exercise care in reading this book.

Western Australia

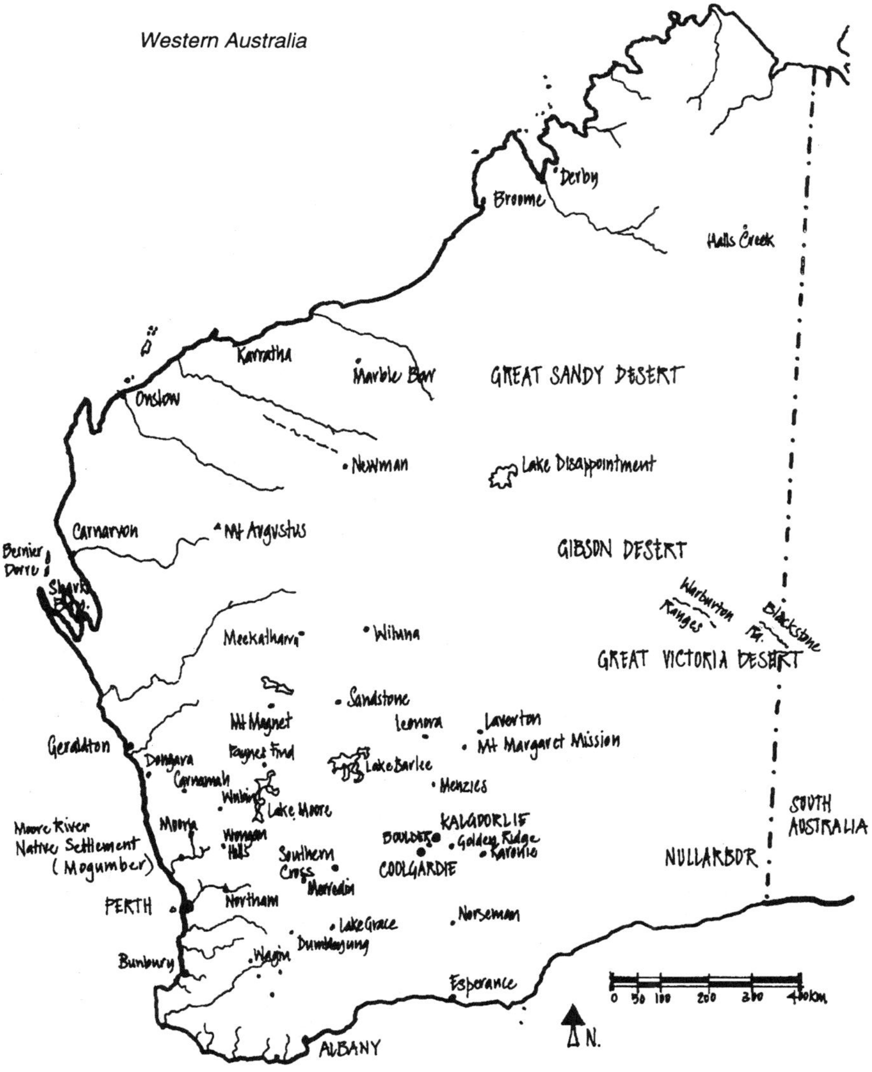

The Laverton Area

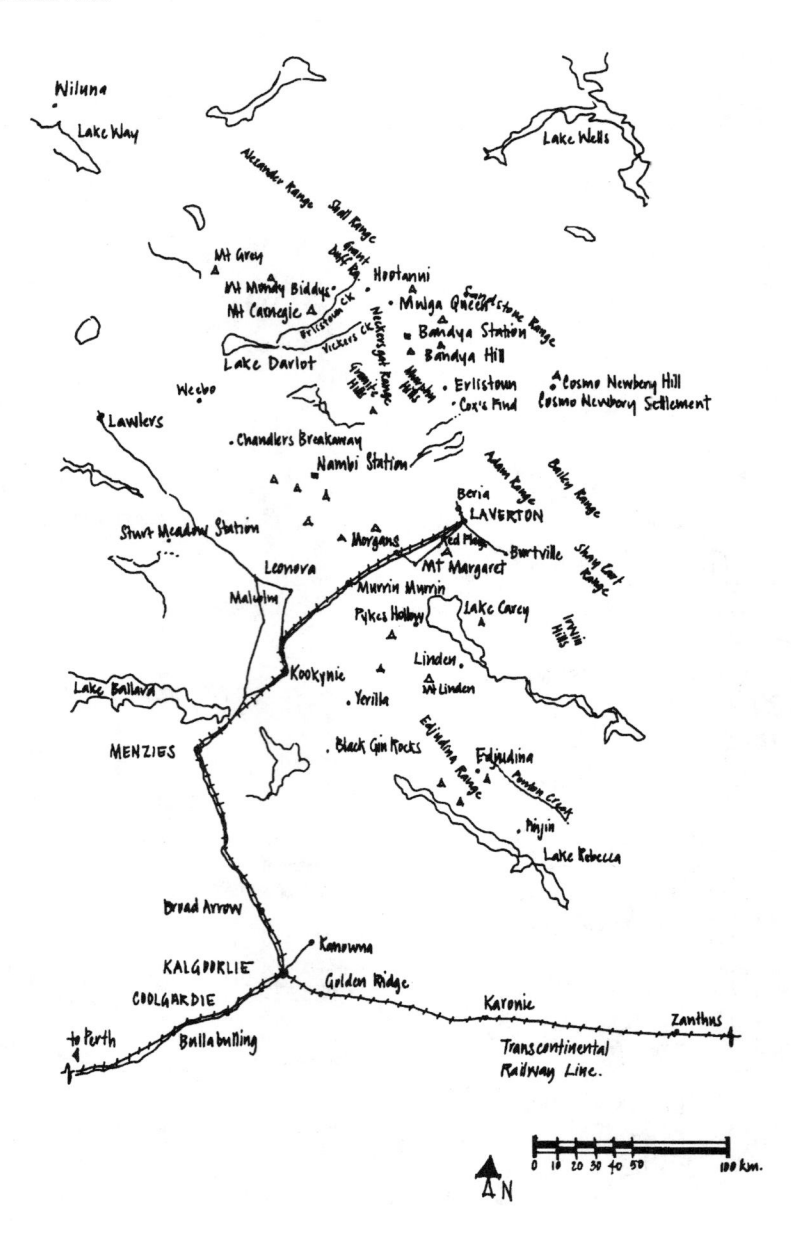

Introduction

We were standing in the doorway, on the threshold, looking out at a million desert stars. I was with a Wongutha woman. We had been talking for only about half an hour when she took my hand, and I was invited to call her 'Auntie'. Even at the time I knew it was a turning point. Looking back, that was when this book began.

We sat around kitchen tables in the heat of the day and on verandahs in the cool of the evening and talked of the possibility of a book. I was tentative. But the people I talked with were enthusiastic, they were firm believers that there would be a 'real' book. When I went back to Kalgoorlie for the second trip, this time with tape recorder in hand, these people told me their stories again, for the sole purpose of this book.

In the morning I would go over to Auntie Wyallie's place, and sitting around the table, drinking cups of tea, those people who gathered there would make suggestions as to whom I should talk to that day. When I returned at the end of the day they would check that I had been told the good stories.

They have told me of the history of the area around Laverton. And the story telling goes on. Each time I have visited, they have told me more detail of the stories they first told me, and also new stories. 'Write it down, write it all down,' I have been told, again and again. The willingness of people to talk to me — a stranger — of aspects of their past, astounded me. I am honoured to have been told these Wongutha stories, to have been encouraged to pass the stories on even as they were passed on to me. This book would not have been written without the interest, support and contribution of the expert knowledge of the Wongutha people.

There are many more stories to be told, to be heard, to be passed on.

Some stories have been told to me that I will not pass on. For some elderly Wongutha, there is intense pain in the past. This pain is not confined to the past, but continues into the present. For some individuals, the pain is carried in silence. I have respected requests to maintain silence on certain aspects of the history they have endured.

These Wongutha people have taught me many things; they have also taught me of 'the importance of being able to live with, rather than simply accumulate knowledge about, the past in the present'.[1]

One day, a few years ago, I walked into Fremantle and bought a book. The journey of discovery that took me to Wongutha Country began with a reference in that book to a story set in Laverton in the 1920s — the story was arresting.

It was a story of exile and escape. The people in this story were from a part of Western Australia that is practically on the edge of the Great Victoria Desert, closer by road to Uluru than to the capital of Western Australia, Perth. On the whim of the government authorities of the day, eighteen people were exiled away from their country and their people, sent a thousand kilometres away, almost to Perth. They were seemingly powerless. They were locked up, trucked off, given inmate numbers in a government compound — their fate was sealed. And then they escaped. It was perhaps the largest escape bid in the history of that place of exile. They escaped, and walked home to their country. All but one arrived home safely. It was an astounding journey to undertake on foot, through inhospitable and potentially waterless landscapes, unknown terrain.

I couldn't find any mention of this story in other history books I looked into. No one I talked to had heard of the story, and the one person who knew the story — Bill Bunbury, the author of the book[2] I had bought — told me there was nothing more to find out than what he had written, that the story was effectively lost.

I couldn't quite believe that the story was lost — seventy years or so wasn't that long ago. I was hopeful that the story might still be within living memory of someone, somewhere.

The people in the story were from around Laverton. They were Wongutha people.

I wanted to travel across the land that the 1920s people had walked over, measuring its distance with my eyes and my soul.* I wanted to know the physical reality of the places in which the events occurred. I was also, against hope, hoping to perhaps cross the path of some people who might know the reality of the story.

Part one — Journeying — is a collection of journal extracts, impulsively written thoughts and impressions arising from encountering people and places on my travels through the land.

While travelling, I met some Wongutha people in a little church in Leonora, near Laverton, and I was welcomed, generously and unexpectedly. The senior women invited me to address them as Aunties; they introduced me over the next months and years to their husbands, cousins, sisters and brothers, children and grandchildren. They instructed me to write down the things that they told me. They were keen to speak of the past, to teach me what had occurred and how it still affects them.

The words they spoke for this book, powerful and poignant accounts of the past, are presented in part two — Speakings.

Previously I had been unsure as to whether I could, as a non-Aboriginal person, attempt to research and write about Aboriginal experience of Western Australian history. It was a complex ethical and moral issue — would the Wongutha people want this history written down? And by me? Could I tell these histories, their stories? I did not want to do it if the people whose past it was did not want it done. My problem was resolved by the people.

I undertook archival research, a long process of seemingly fruitless searching. I began to doubt that the old files of government

---

* *I had planned to walk some of it, to know the distance with my feet also, but when I called in to the Wongan Hills Hospital with a strangely sore throat before embarking the next day for Southern Cross, I was sent home to Perth. A day later I was diagnosed with glandular fever — this turn of events rather conclusively put an end to my walking plans. My deferred journeys were, of necessity, by car.*

departments and agencies would ever reveal evidence of this 'lost', not-so-long-ago history. But in time I came across a document which referred to the story. More followed. The archival evidence that I collected, over a long period of time, is presented in part three — Writings. More recent, interpretive written accounts of the story are also included in Writings.

I have tried to minimise explanations which might detract from the process of interpreting the evidence or interrupt intuitive understanding. Comparative analysis of evidence, and explanatory and supplementary material to parts two and three has been placed at the back of the book in the Appendices.

Part four, the final part of the book, is what I have called 'A New Account' — this is my account of the story of the 1921 events. I have woven this version of the story together using all the evidence uncovered in my searching. The New Account presents all that I have learnt of the elusive truth of the story. The 'whole truth' of the story is perhaps impossible for any individual to tell. Not even the original participants in the story could have told the 'whole truth' of the story — they would have told of their personal experience of the events, and their stories would have made sense of and interpreted the events in different ways according to their individual perspective. My account is my attempt to make sense of, to bring together, all that I know of the story. This New Account of the events is not definitive; it is one interpretative narrative.

I invite you to develop your own interpretation of the material presented in this book.

CAROLYN WADLEY DOWLEY

1

Journeying

Journal Notes

The following notes are taken from thoughts and impressions that I recorded in journal form during two (of five) journeys through the country that the 1921 exiles walked across — from the coastal plains north of Perth out into the very edge of the desert country. The text, extracted from a journal, communicates a highly personal and immediate response. It is not written with the detachment of distance, nor after careful reflection, and is not intended to be interpreted as analysis, nor to convey a considered academic or philosophical position.

The journal sets out to communicate the non-tangible moments of the journeying, and the reality of the experience of encountering places and people.

First Trip, 3–10 October 1997

Friday 3/10/97

As Ian* and I drive out of the last lingering edges of Perth, the sky is shiningly blue, holding out the promise of a wider, more expansive sky to come, and the road ahead stretching towards the edge of that sky. We are setting out on a holiday into the wonderful inland red country; part two of our honeymoon. Additionally, for me, it is part of my search to develop an understanding of the land in which the events I have been researching took place. I am also maintaining the hope of meeting the people who have always loved this land, who know its stories and who speak its language. This long-planned and much anticipated journey is beginning, and we

---

* Ian — Ian Dowley

are ready to look in wonder at all we see.

We don't find anything wonderful for a long time.

We see signs directing the tourist to a 'Pioneer Park' in almost every town, we see the treelessness the pioneers wrought. We come to one town which declares itself the land-care centre of the state; the sign proclaiming it is on the edge of a barren saltlake; it seems ironic.

We drive on and on through the farmland and the towns, and I am struck by how little we know, driving through, of who the 'pioneers' were and who the people they displaced were, or anything of their personal triumphs and tragedies. The land is silent.

Wongan Hills.

After about three hours, just before Kellerberrin, we come across a hint of the past. A small brown sign (tourist information — do the locals see it?) informs us briefly that we are, at that moment in time, crossing the 'York–Goldfields Heritage Trail'. Then it is gone. We don't see much of the trail, we are reading the sign. The silence swallows us up again. The people who walked it were colonial men, primarily, and I wonder when 'heritage' will celebrate the activities of women and Aboriginal people. I wonder if any of the people driving along this road know about those people who walked to the goldfields, not seeking riches and adventure, but escaping oppression and returning against all odds to their home.

At Kellerberrin, turning north, we leave the highway and its tourist information. We set out to pick up the railway line and the most likely line of travel for the group of Wongutha escapees who walked this most

Looking east from Kellerberrin.

southerly route. I check their names as we head towards their path — this is the party* that included Jidu, the King of the people. I wonder about how the escapees decided which party to align themselves with.

We round a bend in the road and suddenly, away from the highway, the country springs to life. The air is full of a hazy late-afternoon light, and the road has become lined with glorious old eucalypts, their smooth bark radiant.

I am driving; I pull over and stop the car. We jump out, feel the dust settle on us, hear the birds, see the light change minute by minute, watch the trees and wonder how old they are and what they have seen. It takes a long time to cover the sixty-one kilometres to Trayning — we keep stopping. It is too beautiful. But how would you feel if you were from a place with small desert trees, mulga trees, I wonder? How would you feel about these large solid trees, blocking out the sky, reaching over your path? How much was cleared then?

We reach Trayning, the railway, and the path of their travel. I am feeling exhilarated by the beauty of the land and, somehow, suddenly tired at the thought of how far we have yet to go. I am more than glad that we have a car, that no one is pursuing us, that we have a map, and food.

Road-side vegetation and pipeline between Kellerberrin and Trayning.

We drive along next to the railway; there is a small reserve of bush left along the line.

When the railway heads off to the north, we take a back-road, the

---

　　* *The escapees had split into three small groups, each taking different routes back to their Country.*

Salmon Gums, east of Nungarin.

most likely direction of travel, and despite having an inadequate map, we expect to find our way. There are no signposts at the intersections we come to, just dirt roads stretching away in every direction. The sun is setting; it sets, and we are out under the stars in an unknown place. We keep driving, we think we remember where the sun went down, we can see the stars of the Southern Cross. I think of the people, steering their way by the stars, not knowing how far they have come and how far they have to go; not knowing the countryside they are passing through, where the next house might be, the next person who might see them; being afraid of being apprehended, re-exiled. The petrol gauge runs lower and lower and I think of the people and their water supply.

Margaret Morgan told me that they 'begged bread' along the way and no one refused. They must have been encouraged. And then, they were given eggs by a friendly farmer's wife, along here somewhere. Perhaps at this stage they were getting so tired that they had no choice but to stop and eat, whereas before they had kept on pressing on despite the hunger and exhaustion. After a while the road we are on starts veering the 'wrong' way, we decide to head south at the next chance and to see where we come out on the highway ... We re-join the highway not far from the town of Southern Cross — we are pleased. And hungry. And tired.

Southern Cross is where the 1921 people rested for a while. It is late. We stop for the night.

Saturday 4/10/97

Southern Cross main street has an old general store building; the bricks are painted out on one side with the slogan 'genuine pioneer store'. I don't photograph it, I am getting annoyed by the all too frequent pioneer references. I wonder whether any of the 'pioneers' in this town gave the escapees food, water, whether anyone was kind. I wonder if anyone took any notice of a group of five or so

Aboriginal people who were not speaking the local language.

From Southern Cross, they followed the pipeline, on and on, eventually to Coolgardie. The pipeline and the railway run parallel to our road, and we understand the fears of the two other groups of the escaping Wongutha who thought that this route was too open, too easily watched.

Rainwater collected on granite outcrop, with pipeline in the distance. East of Southern Cross.

We drive on and on, observing the bush, looking for landmarks that might have interested the travellers. A large rock, a very large rock, appears above the endless scrub and we pull over — rocks are good for catching water, rock-holes/gnamma-holes for storing water. We walk through the bush to have a look at this rock. It turns out to be a very big rock, and there is water collected in pools on it, and there are lizards sunning themselves. Food and water if you wanted it, and no doubt other animals would come here for the water too. A good place. But rather open, and, we find out, rather near an old town. There is a man-made water catchment system around the base of this rock, and it is channelled, we find, into two good sized dams, which are both full of water. Enough water to service a sizeable population. As we come down one side of the rock, we see the old railway line and the old pipeline arriving at an old town. We poke around on the mound of earth that was the railway line, finding old sleepers and old tins and old iron bolts — they seem to be

Remains of water catchment system, Yellowdine.

tangible representations of the way things were when the people walked through. The culvert for the old water pipeline runs near this bushed-over railway, and there is an inspection point which is still intact and recognisable near the townsite.

Only remnants of the town remain; a few old stone/mudbrick houses in various stages of decay, lots of cleared space where the timber/hessian houses would have been, some fence posts, the railway siding, some old rusting sheets of iron roofing ... We find out later that it was the gold-mining town of Yellowdine. Were its people generous to the fugitives? Did they see them?

Remnants of a mudbrick house, Yellowdine.

We drive on to Bullabulling, where Margaret Morgan has told me that they caught rabbits, ate and camped. Perhaps this is on the border of country they were familiar with; perhaps from here they were more confident of how much further there was still to go. Perhaps it is because here they met up with the other half of their own party who had forged ahead ... Perhaps the ones who went ahead would have had time to catch some food and prepare it by the time the rest of the group arrived. There is another large rock here, with another water catchment system.

They stopped here, and ate, and camped.

We have a late lunch here, having wanted to rest and eat in this same place. There are shady acacias around the edge of the rock, and we are glad for their protection from the sun. It is hot, and after lunch, I lie down in the shade of a desert sheoak and sleep briefly, being wakened by the sound of bird wings close to my head, the sound of the wind in the grasses around me, the sound of the wind in the spindly leaves above me.

We go on, on, away from the afternoon sun.

At Coolgardie we stop, and find the railway station. Jidu and the people with him didn't catch the train until Kalgoorlie, but I expect that the Kalgoorlie railway station would have changed more in the last seventy-five years than the Coolgardie one, and that in 1921 they may have been quite similar. So, therefore, we stop here. I imagine a place like this full of people; I wonder how a group of Aboriginal people would blend into the crowd ... There is an old passenger train, a museum exhibit, at the platform ... They rode on the cattle trucks though, and for free — perhaps they jumped on when the train was about to leave; perhaps they jumped on immediately it pulled in and so somehow escaped notice; perhaps it was a very usual thing for Aboriginal people to travel that way from Kalgoorlie and therefore unremarkable to the other passengers and to railway officials alike. I expect that it still would have taken a lot of courage to approach a place full of white people, an institution of colonial expansion; to be so visible in a large town. Perhaps the land around Kalgoorlie was almost like home, perhaps this gave them confidence.

Coolgardie Railway Station with steam passenger train.

Coolgardie has another museum, which has been recommended to us — we decide to have a look at it. It's quite impressive. It even mentions that Aboriginal people existed — some of the time. There is one objectionable display chart showing the rapid population growth in the goldfields due to the goldrushes — the 1890 population is declared as nil. It is an old looking chart; it looks as if it was made in a time when Aboriginal people seemingly did not exist. Things have (perhaps) changed. We find, after wandering through two rooms of stories about the glory of gold and the hardships of life on the goldfields, two rooms entitled 'Aboriginal Artefacts'. Are artefacts the things left behind by a passed race/group of people — or can they also be things which have been left behind by a continuing group of people which have been collected by another group of people? Perhaps Coolgardie is willing to acknowledge, now, that Aboriginal people did live here, once upon a time, a long time ago … There are some great photographic portraits on the walls in these two back rooms. But the faces are nameless. There is no mention of the history of first contact, no explanatory panels on the walls to tell us the great names of the old heroes, of the hardships of life, of conflicts or treaties with the goldmining community over use of land, water, game; no mention of Aboriginal women in either community. There is nothing to suggest that Coolgardie was once a gathering place for Aboriginal people from as far away as the Nullarbor, a place of corroborees.

There are no 'donated by' tags on these 'artefacts' — spears are carefully strung with fishing wire from the ceiling, spear throwers and food carrying implements are tucked under bushes or prominently displayed on a red dust (or was it yellow sand?) exhibition piece. I wonder who looks at this museum. I wonder what impression the tourists who find their way to these back rooms, and the local schoolchildren who presumably come here, carry away with them.

Kalgoorlie we drive straight through, and we turn north. The sky is suddenly empty of clouds, the air is hazy and warm and the late afternoon light is washing over the salmon gum trunks and the gimlets. I am feeling as if I too am returning to a place that I love. I rejoice in the colour of the earth and the trees and the sky. I drive on, on and on until the salmon gums fade almost imperceptibly away into a lower acacia and mulga bushland, and the sun slowly sets over a distant, distant, smooth horizon. The colours linger in the sky for a long, long time, and all is peaceful.

We stop in Menzies.

We arrive after dark and stay in the old pub, (blackboards on the facade advertise the special of the day as corned beef: $6) and as the evening wears on the bar fills up with the local mining blokes. They all come driving in to 'town' in their white four-wheel drive mining company vehicles. There are no Aboriginal people to be seen in this one street town, let alone in the pub. I know Reggie Johnston used to live here, but where?

Sunday 5/10/97

Early Sunday daylight reveals another street, parallel to but quite a long way from the highway/town strip. Run down cottages are spaced along it; there are no mining company vehicles at any of these places. Some are boarded up, empty. Perhaps Reggie Johnston used to live in one of those.

Menzies is where the group that walked due east across the roadless, un-settled country arrived at the north/south railway line. Gadajilbi was one of them.

I go out early in the morning and stand in the middle of the empty town, under a wide sky, looking across a wide and open landscape, looking across a wide and free land. I look towards the west, where they would have come from; I can imagine them, tired and bone-weary, walking jubilantly in to Menzies. They would have had little indication, out there amongst the vast salt lakes, of the distance they had covered and how far there was still to go. They could have watched the vegetation slowly changing, and known that they were getting closer to familiar country as the vegetation became slowly more identifiable. Here, though, they would have known for sure that they were close to home. How would they have felt, coming home; coming home to this known country; to this country they loved?

It is dry and dusty as I look west. I am amazed, awed, at the thought of them walking through kilometres and kilometres of this landmark-less land and coming out 'dead on target' to Menzies.

I wonder if they were cautious, coming into town, because of the settlement and all it represented, or confident, being so close, in their own country, almost invincible.

We drive to Leonora feeling as if tomorrow might be the beginning of something remarkable. If I am to meet people who may know some of the stories, it is likely to be here. Reggie Johnston, so the lady in the Post Office in Menzies told me when I rang a few weeks ago, now lives in Leonora. And other people? Margaret Morgan told me, twice, that probably no one except Reggie Johnston and herself knows these stories now.

Sadie Canning, who was the Co-Commissioner for Western Australia in the Stolen Children National Inquiry, also lives in Leonora, some of the time. I met her at the Commission's community feedback meeting held in Perth in July this year. She may not remember me — but I will try to contact her tomorrow.

We pull over near a small rocky hill and my thoughts swing onto a different tangent. A fence is running parallel to the road, fencing us off from the hill. I am a little resentful. Whose hill is it? What if this was your country, and someone fenced your hill off? This is the only hill on the whole horizon! Back in 1921, the fences would have only just been appearing — how must it have been to watch the enclosure of your land? Now, under the hot sun, the reality of lost access to land is strong. This fence

Near Menzies, looking to the east.

becomes a tangible reminder of the dispossession of the people from their land. We climb through the fence, deliberately, and we climb the hill. I weep for the people, the land, the exiled people and the taken land; those people who never returned and those who returned to watch the changes; those who are still watching, those who are bereft.

> a captured people
> I sat on that stony hill and wept
> I heard the wind
> the grasses
> the soft grey mulla mulla leaves

Laverton railway line, near Kookynie, looking north.

We arrive in Leonora in the middle of the hot, still, Sunday afternoon.

I am somehow emotionally exhausted, and sleep until the evening.

We go out walking around the town in the last of the sunlight — I am still tired, weary. We are out to find a church to see if there are any services on tonight.

As we walk around I feel conspicuous. I am worried about appearances, I don't want to look like a tourist out to observe the locals. No one meets our eye as we walk. There are families in their gardens, and other people out for a stroll, but no one looks at us. We try to chat to some little kids who are walking home with a parcel of chips; they say hello and talk for a while as we all walk along, then suddenly take off. I feel distinctly out of place, alien.

On another silent street we find a pale green corrugated iron building which turns out to be the church. The notice board says there is a service in two hours time.

We come back to the church at the specified time, feeling hesitant after the afternoon's experiences.

Sadie Canning arrives as we do! She hands us hymn books and makes us welcome, introducing us to the handful of people already gathered in the building as if we are old friends. My anxieties evaporate. Sadie and I have a church-whispered chat about why I have come to Leonora, and Sadie half-turns to the man sitting behind us.

'Cyril,' she says to me, 'Cyril is a good source of information.' She asks him where Reggie is.

'Reggie?' he says.

'Our Reggie,' Sadie responds, and that 'our' seems to explain it all.

'In Kalgoorlie with Christopher,' is the ready answer.

After a few moments he asks me why I want to know. I start explaining why it is that I want to meet Reggie Johnston, and he looks up quickly.

'My grandparents were part of that group,' he says, proudly.

I find, to my surprise, that I am awed, lost for words, taken completely by surprise at the immediacy of this direct link.

I search for words, trying to contain my elation at finding someone who knows the reality of the story. I manage to ask him whether he knows any of the stories of the journey. His face grows sad, suddenly, and I feel his sorrow. I feel that I should not have asked — some painful memory has been called forth by my question, and he is suffering.

'To tell the truth, I don't know,' he says, slowly. 'It's a long time ago now.'

'It is,' I agree, quickly. My heart is aching for this elderly man who doesn't know this story about his grandparents.

What can I say? What can I possibly say to acknowledge his past and his losses?

How am I to keep asking people questions, reminding them of their losses — lost people whom they loved, lost stories due to separation of families, lost histories, so much evident pain.

The service begins, and I am left wondering whether I will try to ask Cyril who his grandparents were, later. I am doubly hesitant; firstly, there is his pain, and then there is also the issue of naming the names of people who have died.

But he leaves straight after the service, and the decision is made for me.

I think also of the time I rang up Doris, a Mt Margaret woman who now lives in Queensland, whose grandmother was 'old Mudarn', one of the exiles. She was interested, pleased to talk about Mt Margaret. I asked about her grandmother. And even by phone it was evident that she was devastatingly grieved that she could not remember anything about her grandmother, except that the missionaries took her to visit when her grandmother was dying.

After the service, various people come up to chat to us, to see what we are doing in Leonora, and how long we are staying for. There seems to be an increase in acceptance and friendliness when Ian announces that we are travelling around on our honeymoon. It is a matter of course that people travel when they are on their honeymoon, and they seem pleased that we have chosen to come to Leonora. And then I talk a little about hoping to find out about the stories, but it seems to be of secondary importance in everyone's classification of us. Ian is volunteered by Claude to help shift some heavy thing into someone's ute, and I meet May, and Dora, and Cheryl.

Cheryl and I chat, and when we talk about my hopes for finding out about people escaping from Mogumber, she calls Wyallie over. I talk to Wyallie about the story I am hoping to find out about, and she tells me, seriously, confidentially, that I should come down to Kalgoorlie in a few days and meet her cousin Rosie, who has some good stories to tell about running away from Mogumber. She looks around often, to make sure that no one except Cheryl is listening, and the others laugh when she tells them not to listen. We are standing in the doorway, they keep their distance, outside under the stars. She tells me that she only escaped being caught because she is a fast runner, and again, that I should come to Kalgoorlie and she will tell me the rest of the story at her house.

I agree to come.

Wyallie smiles, and takes my hand.

'Call her 'Auntie Wyallie',' says May, coming over.

And all the elderly ladies smile, and they all become Aunties, and Ian and I are invited to Auntie Dora's for fruit cake and tea.

We are given a lift to Auntie Dora's place, just on the edge of town, where the trees are. The night has become clear and cool. Stars are out in great glory, the tree shapes show up darkly against the brilliant sky.

Auntie Sadie is already sitting on the verandah when we get there. She calls us over to meet the dingo pup. Claude, Dora's husband, comes out on to the verandah and takes on the role of storyteller, telling us stories about dingos, and the Rawlinson Ranges, and the Warburton Ranges. Sadie interjects, wistfully, that you have to register all dogs in town and that dingos aren't classified as dogs, they're classified as vermin. She laughs and tells us the story of someone who took one on a plane to Perth and called it an Asian Wolf; Claude tells us of a fellow they know who registered one as a Rawlinson Terrier because it was from the Rawlinson Ranges. Sadie makes some remarks about the vicious imported dogs which are allowed, they both sound sad at the exclusion of the dingo. It's something I hadn't ever thought about before. I wonder how many instances there are where the imported culture's expectations and objects still displace the indigenous, where the indigenous is still outlawed. And where perhaps only the indigenous people know and mourn their loss.

I stop listening to Claude; I am thinking about all the changes which these people have seen and experienced.

Frank, another guest, joins us, and the dynamics change, leaving Sadie and me free to start another conversation. We chat about Mt Margaret and the old days; Sadie grew up there and knows all of the people to be known. During the course of the conversation I ask her whether Lampi Turner is still living in the district. She looks suddenly sad, and I instantly regret the question. I wonder how often my questions will be touching raw nerves, drawing forth pain. How can I know, how can I avoid doing so? She tells me that he passed on, (not passed away, I note) a year or so ago, and abruptly gets up and goes inside.

I sit on the verandah feeling terrible. He has died, and I should not have mentioned his name. What am I to do? I stay on the verandah, half listening to Claude, and his stories of trackers, and a man who identified the footprints of his brother-in-law from the back of a moving ute when Claude couldn't even see the prints ... I can't concentrate, I am anxious, grieving, uncertain as to how to approach the subject of the past when talking to these lovely people.

We are called inside when the cake has been cut and sandwiches made and the tea is ready to be poured; I am greatly relieved when Auntie Sadie beckons me over to where the women are gathered in the kitchen. She tells me, in a whisper, that Auntie Wyallie knows lots of stories about Lampi. Auntie Wyallie chooses the places at the table where she and I will sit, and then reconsiders as the other eight or so people gather round. Auntie May and Auntie Wyallie decide that Auntie Wyallie and I will sit apart from the others, at the kitchen table, with our own supply of food, and where we can 'talk' without being overheard. We are in the same room, we can see them, but they cannot hear us. Auntie Wyallie leans over the table towards me, confidentially, and starts telling me stories about Lampi.

They are great stories. We laugh a lot, and the others sometimes all look around, at which point Auntie Wyallie will stop talking and wave them all away.

'They're trying to listen to me,' she whispers to me, and laughs. The others laugh too, and start up their own conversation again. I wonder whether the stories are secrets.

She tells story after story about old Lampi, full of humour and love and respect. I ask her after a while if it was all right for me to have named a person who had died — I wonder if she is whispering because of this reason. She thinks for a while, and says yes, it is all right.

Auntie Wyallie asks me about my family ... She tells me again some pieces of her story of how she came to be at Mt Margaret, but when I ask a question, she won't say any more. She winks and nods at me and reminds me that I should come to visit her in Kalgoorlie.

I am very aware of the wonder of the situation. I am sitting happily, comfortably, at a kitchen table with this lovely elderly Wongutha woman, and she is warmly accepting and loving towards me, telling me stories, inviting me to her home, welcoming me. She is sharing her past and her memories with me to an extent which I had not dreamed possible. There seems no rational reason for her to welcome me in this way. We have little in common — but

I am hardly conscious of the differences between us — in some respects we have everything in common. There is a trust, a meeting of the spirits, which transcends the potential barriers and differences. It is in the back of my mind: the gospel of Jesus sets us free. It is such a contrast from the no-eye-contact of the afternoon.

Auntie Wyallie and Auntie May are leaving Leonora tomorrow (the timing astounds me), and as I say goodnight to the women, Auntie Wyallie is keen to ensure that I am coming to see her in Kalgoorlie. She decides that Wednesday would be a good day to meet Auntie Rosie. I hope Ian doesn't mind back-tracking two hundred and thirty kilometres ...

Auntie Dora invites us to come back for tea tomorrow night, and we are sent on our way with singing hearts.

Monday 6/10/97

Clouds appear, surprising me after two days of cloudless blue stretching from one horizon to the other — streaky clouds, forming lines, lines running parallel to our direction of travel, leading us on and on and on to Laverton, and lines radiating out from a distant place yet unseen, slightly to the south and east of our road.

We pass unmarked tracks leading out into the bush; where do they go?

There is a feeling of being 'new' to this country rather than alien in it. The clouds are somehow like a blessing.

Mulga and Mulla Mulla, west of Laverton.

And then, marvelling at the clouds, we find that there is one which is more like a spiral than a streak, and then, astoundingly, at the next glance, there are bright orange colours appearing in this one cloud. The colours spread as the cloud moves, I pull over and stop the car and stand under the sky, my head thrown back and arms outstretched — a few vehicles go by, no one stops. The colours are making a rainbow formation, a big arc swinging around the sun. Is this rainbow without rain commonplace? Can the passing drivers not see it? Do they see the beauty of the land? The cloud expands, and the rainbow expands with it, it almost circles the sun. The blessing is confirmed.

I watch the mulga bushland suddenly change to open spinifex country, feeling as if we are crossing an edge ... We cross it, and I drive on and on under the midday sun. There are a few hills to the south, and all else seems flat, stretching on to the horizon, stretching on to eternity. We wonder where Mt Margaret might be, relative to the few landmarks. Then we pass a track, signposted 'Mt Margaret', and I am struck by the reality of the place. It seems unreal, impossible, unlikely that I should be driving so comfortably along this highway, so rapidly and smoothly and quietly. (It seems likely that the drivers who missed the rainbow will miss the Mt Margaret sign, and that those who miss the visible present will miss the invisible past. How could a passer-by know the history?) The track is perpendicular to our road, and is gone in an instant. We have only a short time, a small opportunity, to see it ...

Country near Laverton.

We stop for lunch, and the sun is too hot to be in for long — we find a rocky outcrop with some shady acacias and a good view. Sitting in the quietness, looking around at the beauty, again I am struck by the loss of this land to the people. We had to climb over a loosely-wired fence to reach this resting place — again, what if your family had always walked this land and then suddenly-arriving-strangers started putting up fences, fencing your land and calling it theirs, fencing off your water supply and calling it theirs, attempting to keep you out, off, away from the places that you know and cherish and have always known and cherished? What if they introduced sheep which ate your bushes and fruits and muddied your water supplies? What if they threatened to shoot you for frightening their sheep when you attempted to walk through the land, or to obtain some water? What if they did shoot you?

Approaching Laverton I feel the heaviness and the sadness of the events which took place here. I think of the people coming in from the bush during the drought to get water from the town dam, their water supplies exhausted by the sheep. I think of the people coming in to town to beg for food scraps after the miners and woodcutters and pastoralists had shot the local game supply into scarcity. The white newcomers had used, without compunction, all the Wongutha sources of food and water and yet were unwilling to see Wongutha people use the town water and gather town food; were aggrieved when the people turned to them for assistance; were seemingly un-compassionate, heartless, ruthless. Forced by the white newcomers to find alternative sources of food and water, the Wongutha people had little choice. I think of the appalling treatment dealt to them by the police, of the horsewhips flying through the air and into flesh as the Wongutha once again were driven forcefully out of Laverton. I try not to think of the horror of each moment, the confusion of stumbling and crying as they fled, once again. I think of old Mudarn and the scars she bore. How they must have despaired at the inexorable power of the white police. I think of the daily desperation, the hopelessness of the situation.

Spinifex country, north-west of Laverton.

I think of the archived letters of the police constable which I have found, of his uncertainty in how to best manage the interactions between whites and Wongutha at first, his responses to the white townspeople when they complained about people begging at their doors and drinking at their dam, of his gradual hardening of heart. I think of his treachery in capturing the people on the day that they could apply for and receive government rations from their Protector, the policeman, at the police station. I think of his letter that 'the problem' was solved by the exiling of some people; of the fact that he must have deliberated over how best to scare the people into staying out of town — I don't like the thought of him and his colleagues sitting there working out the most efficient and effective way of terrifying the people, deciding on their plan and working out how to carry it out …

We arrive in Laverton and the train of thought grinds to a halt as we come slowly into the ex-goldrush, ex-Western-Mining town, still street-tree planted and with the usual 'welcome, keep our town tidy' sign. We are struck by the security-grilled windows, and the lack of a main street feel to the main street. There is a new police station opposite an old hotel. I am almost glad that the old police station is not here. There is one other old building, it seems, and I photograph it and the Desert Hotel for the record. These two buildings are as close to the old Laverton as I want to get. While I am lining up clouds and the buildings, Ian sets off to buy a paper to check the weather forecast for the next few days.

In the papers that day, the *West Australian* had a front page full colour article about City Beach students waving flags for racial harmony; it seemed totally irrelevant in a town of barred windows and flagons on the street. The *Kalgoorlie Miner* was full of the wedding photos of persons of Anglo-Celtic descent.

Ian comes back excitedly, with the news that there are some old photos of old Laverton on a wall of the shop. We both go back to the shop and look at the photos, and chat to the lady behind the counter who volunteers information about the building and the photos. We ask where the old police station is in the photo, and she comes out from behind the counter.

'I can show you,' she says, and walks past us to the door. 'It's still here. See over there, the yellow building …' She points over some fences, and tells us that the yellow building is the old gaol, and that the police station is just next door. I start to go numb. She continues, cheerily, telling us that the buildings could be locked up and that if we want to have a look around inside, the Shire might have the keys.

We say goodbye and follow the direction of her pointing to the Shire Office.

36 Journeying

The receptionist is busy, she smiles cheerily at us and goes on talking. Eventually she looks up and I make our request. She looks mildly surprised and mildly interested, and thinks for a minute.

'I don't think we've ever had anyone ask that before,' she says, and goes off to ask someone else. He comes back, looks us over, and declaring that we look like trustworthy individuals, announces his decision that we can have the keys if the receptionist can find them. The keys, he tells her, are on the same keyring as the toy library keys; one tag says 'Old Gaol' and the other says 'Toy Library'. It is unfortunately likely, he tells us, that someone else might have them. But the keys are found in a drawer, and along with a few curious glances, we are given the keys. The secretary says cheerily that she's been here a few years and has been meaning to go down herself and have a look at the Old Gaol. We'll have to tell her about it, she says enthusiastically, as I sign the book, and her tone of voice perturbs me — I'm not expecting it to be a happy experience, and I find myself wondering how such a place can be spoken of so lightheartedly. Is the past so invisible?

The barbed wire fence* around the two old buildings is like a sign, like a portent. We go through the gate, it closes behind us. The buildings are very small. One is timber clad, has a window, two blue doors and a verandah all around; the other has spikes on its iron wall, no windows, and a heavy metal door with a large rusting bolt.

I take my time photographing details of the buildings while I prepare myself to enter this place. After driving through the open sun-flooded country around Laverton, even the main street felt oppressively restricting, claustrophobic. How much more so here! These buildings represent fully the

---

* *'barbed wire fence'* — *obviously recently constructed, it would not have been there in 1921.*

fearful aspects of closing in and locking away. And they are more than representation. I think of the people from the immense desert being brought in here, being locked in this tight space — it is too much — I turn my back on the gaol building and photograph the police station.

Inside the yard, old Laverton Lockup.

I try not to think of Margaret Morgan's story about the captured women screaming from terror all night in the lockup, about the policemen who worked from this office horsewhipping the people out of town, about the policeman known to the people as the evil one. I don't like this place at all.

I line up the little one-roomed timber office in my lens and think of the people waiting to receive the government handout through that very window, of their confusion and anxiety when they were suddenly surrounded and roughly taken around to the back of the office, of their increasing horror as they were pushed towards and into the tight confines of the lockup yard. I absurdly hope, as I see the three tiny, windowless cells of the lockup, that they were allowed to stay out in the yard under the stars for that awful night.

The front of the old Laverton Police Station, showing the rations window.

A cell is overwhelmingly dark.

I try to record the feel of the place in the photographs. It feels terrible, my emotions are wordless. I am freezing up inside. The sun is beating down on my head.

We take the keys back to the Shire, and I wonder how to answer the receptionist when she asks what it was like.

She asks whether it was good, and I tell her it was distressing.

She looks surprised. 'What they had to put up with, you mean?' she asks.

I say yes, although it is not entirely what I meant.

She looks at me for a moment, then says politely, 'Well, I'm married to a policeman so I suppose I would see the other side.' She smiles and looks away. We leave.

Inside a prison cell of the old Laverton Lockup, looking out to the Lockup yard.

We have to ask for directions to Mt Margaret as the gravel roads out of Laverton are not signposted. We set off, hoping that the woman in the petrol station has remembered the right set of turns; she called it the back way. It is the most direct way, and we take it.

It is hot in the car, and I am still frozen inside.

It stays hot and becomes dusty as we drive towards Mt Margaret. We are both silent for a long time. What words can we use to express our grief and horror? And how small our experience, how remote our connection to the place and the people who suffered in it. The past is visible, tangible here. If we can see, can feel, how must others feel? How must they have felt? I wonder how people can live next to those buildings, can walk near them every day and remain unaffected by their presence and their past.

It takes us an hour or so to reach Mt Margaret. My soul is

gradually restored by the sun and the sky and the open land stretching away on all sides as we drive.

I think of the advice of an anthropologist who told me that you can't just turn up at Mt Margaret, that he lived there for a few years and he wouldn't advise me going there. I remember him saying that the people there were not easily approachable. I am not as uneasy as his words once made me; when I mentioned our plan to visit the Community to Sadie and Dora last night there was no recommendation not to do it. The Mt Margaret Community Officer I rang this morning was friendly and welcoming. My overall feeling is one of incredulity, that this place that I have heard so much of, and talked of, is going to suddenly appear from over the horizon and we will be there, in a real place. The phrase 'Mt Margaret people', I realise, which I have often used to describe the escapee travellers, in reality covers a huge number of people. Mt Margaret is not a description, it is a place, and we are driving there.

We arrive, and the anthropologist's words fall out of my consciousness. A young Wongutha woman sends us up to a new brick house on the side of the hill to see Marjory. Marjory and Ron greet us very warmly; once again, I am overwhelmed by the unexpected generosity of the welcome. Ron asks if we will stay for a night or two; Marjory tells us that she knew in her spirit that we were Christians too.

Marjory shows us around, down to the old dining room and the old dormitories, which are being refurbished under a training program. One dormitory has been converted to an arts centre and short-stay accommodation; the dining hall is being refurbished to become a meeting place, where conventions and functions can be held. Marjory tells us of the annual convention, which was last weekend, and how they had hoped that Margaret Morgan could officially open the new arts building, but that the Laverton plumber hadn't finished his work on time. We are asked if we know the Morgans — it is obvious that Marjory holds them in high regard.

She shows us where the kindergarten used to be; she shows us the tree under which she was born. Clearly, for this woman, this place is home, and has been a safe place. Her voice is full of pride as she describes various events and points out places of significance. She cannot speak highly enough of what the Schenks did in establishing Mt Margaret for her people.

The afternoon slips by, and we say our goodbyes. We are invited to come back and stay in the new building next time we are up.

The directions for driving out to the main road towards Leonora are slightly more complex than those to get here from Laverton, but we recite them until we have them right. We are fine to get out of Mt Margaret itself, yes. Then, we are to go left, and keep turning left at every intersection until we come to one where there is a sweep this way in the road first, then we go over a cattle grid, there is a windmill to one side, and lots of incoming roads; a messy intersection. At that point we are to go right, and we'll turn north and reach the highway near the new Anaconda mine. That way, we can't go wrong, Marjory assures us. We set off confidently, and happily.

We come to the sweep in the road and the grid and the messy intersection much more quickly than we had thought we would. Is this the one Marjory meant, or is this only the turn onto the 'main' dirt road again from the Mt Margaret Road? We have no concept of distances from her description. We think it can't be, it is too soon, and turn left. After a few minutes, we change our minds, we think it must be — it fulfils all the criteria. So we turn around and go the other way. After driving for about fifteen minutes we come to a T-junction with the road on which we drove in from Laverton. We must have taken a wrong turn! We remember, too late, the windmill that was supposed to be at the intersection where we turned right. We turn in the opposite direction from Laverton; we guess that this unmarked road might be the one shown on our map as running parallel to the highway, and we decide to take it until we come to the next road north. We are driving in a direction just south of the setting sun, and we feel as if it will still work out. It does in the end.

I realise that the sun is a strong navigation reference point no matter whether you know the country or not.

Around the dining table that night at Auntie Dora's we are told that many people have got lost coming out that way.

We speak of the old gaol at Laverton — we are told about someone who dug his way out of that lockup in the early days; they tell us story after story of people escaping from imprisonment, and gradually the terribleness of the Laverton lockup is reduced. The power is not all one way, the people are not broken.

Sadie asks me, across the conversation, whether I am going to write a book ...

We all wash the dishes, then Claude asks Ian to give him a hand with some more heavy lifting outside, and they leave. I wonder briefly what effect the teatime talk about a possible book will have on the trust and acceptance that has been extended to me. But, if anything, these women are now more keen to tell me their recollections. Auntie Sadie and Auntie Dora and I sit down around the kitchen table and they start telling me detailed stories. Stories about Lampi escaping from Rottnest by swimming, stories about Lampi's brother. 'If he'd had education he would have been someone,' Sadie tells me. Lampi was a cousin of Happy-Land Joe's.* We speak of them both.

They tell me a little of Dora's history. Dora's mother Lily escaped from Mogumber and walked home to Laverton with Dora when Dora was only a baby. Dora is silently weeping as she talks. Her mother took her to Mount Margaret, a place of safety, so that Dora wouldn't be taken away by the police. And Dora's mother left her at Mount Margaret. I don't ask any questions, I just listen. Sadie and Dora talk about growing up at Mount Margaret.

Sadie remarks, with a sigh, that it is good to talk about the old days.

They move on, they talk about the transmission of language, about skin groups, and Dora finds a language book which I might like to try and buy in Kalgoorlie. Sadie tells me the names of some people in Kalgoorlie who might know the stories that I'm looking for. I try hard to hold the names in my head, but some of them are unfamiliar sounding and they slip through.

I am also given instructions about how to find Reggie in Kalgoorlie, how to get to Auntie Wyallie's place — all spoken rapidly and with the assurance that I will remember — but I can only remember a sequence of about four directions. The difference between an oral and a written tradition of conveying knowledge and information is very apparent! I find I am much better at remembering a sequence if it is drawn in the dust for me. I am no good at following if the directions are illustrated with finger movements on a table-top. I need to see the

---

*   *Happy-Land Joe — Mulgathunoo Joe.*

connections to fix them in my head.

Auntie Sadie goes back to revise the suggested names, and then tells me that Auntie Wyallie will know who I should talk to in Kalgoorlie, and will probably take me around to visit people. She mentions a lot more names, and I remember some of them: Doolkie, Auntie Queenie, Auntie Violet.

'Lean on Wyallie,' she says.

I like the expression.

Claude and Ian come back and sit at the other table, the dining table, and the two groups continue their separate conversations.

It gets late, and we prepare to leave our new friends in Leonora under a moonless, star-filled desert sky.

Tuesday 7/10/97

We drive south again, feeling as if the road is familiar, arriving in Kalgoorlie in about three hours. We had rung Auntie Wyallie earlier to say that we are arriving today; she said to come over at four o'clock.

We find a backpackers' hostel to stay in; we seem to be the only travellers. We find ourselves in the midst of a work-booted, loud-mouthed, brash young male population.

We look at the map on the wall by the front door to locate Auntie Wyallie's street, as the directions we were given for the best way of getting there have become vaguely confused with the directions for getting there if we were going to take the second best route. The chap behind the desk asks what we're looking for and starts to tell us that everything we want to see will be on the main street. We tell him we're in Kal to catch up with some friends and he wants to know where they live. He gives us a funny look when we say the name of the street. We smile at him and leave.

Auntie Wyallie's front garden has a little child playing in it. He turns and runs back up onto the safety of the verandah when we emerge from our car.

A woman who looks to be his mother comes out and ushers us and the child inside. Auntie Wyallie comes out to greet us and, taking my hand, leads me in to the kitchen and meals area. We stand in the doorway and she introduces me to her cousins Fred and Rosie, to her daughters Miriam and Jenny, to her various grandchildren as they come in and out. She tells me she can't remember our names, we introduce ourselves. In another situation I might feel awkward, an intruder, if my name was unknown to everyone there, but Auntie Wyallie's hand-clasp is strong and warm and welcoming and I am put at ease.

Uncle Fred tells us we'd better sit down, and we do, and Auntie Wyallie pours the tea. We admire the family photos, trying to commit to memory the names of her children and grandchildren. We hear about Fred and Rosie's family from Wyallie; Uncle Fred asks us how many children we have and is delighted to hear that we've only been married for two weeks. He chuckles for a while, and tells all subsequently arriving visitors of the new story — we feel as if we've suddenly and unexpectedly been absorbed into the story repertoire of this family. It's a lovely feeling. Uncle Fred asks more questions, about where our families live and how many brothers and sisters we have (given the lack of children, siblings are the next best thing it seems) and where they live.

Auntie Wyallie tells us that we should come back to Kalgoorlie in August and we'll go out in the bush, all of us, and dig for bardi grubs.

Uncle Fred looks at me and says, 'You dig.'

He pauses and adds, 'I eat,' and I laugh.

'It sounds like a good system,' I say, 'for you.' And everyone laughs. I feel as if we are somehow embraced within the circle of this family.

Cheryl, Auntie Wyallie's daughter whom we met in Leonora, arrives with her four children, and the house seems full to overflowing. Cheryl leans on the kitchen bench between the kitchen and the meals area — there is no more room around the table. We all talk for a while, and when all the family-related talk seems to have been covered, Auntie Wyallie makes a comment about how I should hear some of Rosie's stories. Auntie Rosie smiles and makes an off-handed gesture of dismissal. I wait for a second to see what will happen, but there is a gap — I lean forward and look down the table to Auntie Rosie, 'I'd love to hear some of your stories, Auntie Rosie,' I say, hoping that I'm doing the right thing, wondering whether it is presumptuous of me. Auntie Wyallie leans back and smiles, Auntie Rosie leans forward and begins her story.

She is a great storyteller, we are caught up, taken along.

Auntie Rosie escaped from Mogumber and walked back to

Nambi Station, near Laverton, when she was a girl. She was taken three times to Mogumber, and escaped twice. The first time, Rosie and a friend from Carnamah escaped but Rosie turned back and turned herself in at New Norcia — the journey to Laverton was too far to tackle on her own. The second time, three girls made the escape; two from Laverton and the same one from Carnamah. The journey home took them about six weeks; they walked day and night, resting only for a short while during the night. They followed the Geraldton railway line to Carnamah, (the Kalgoorlie line had a road alongside it all the way, Rosie commented, it was too open, so they went north) and then followed the roads out to Wubin, then Mt Magnet, then Sandstone, then home. The three young girls walked on the road at night, and off to the side of the road, 'where it was thicker', in the bush, during the day. They escaped in the summer, when water was scarce, when they could safely cross the waters of the Moore River.

Country north of New Norcia.

Beside the Mt Magnet–Sandstone Road.

Most of the pieces of the story are about how they eluded their pursuers, tricked the trackers, found food and water, avoided people along the way, and what they said to those they couldn't avoid. Auntie Rosie and her two girl companions are triumphant. She doesn't speak much of the exhaustion or fear or other things she must have endured. I don't ask. She doesn't mention anything to do with her time at Mogumber before escaping, or what happened when she was taken back after turning herself in on the first escape. Again, I don't feel as if I can ask.

There are stories of limited food and water; of running out of water and having to approach a station homestead, risking recapture, to ask permission to get water from a dam; of carrying water in drums; of being worried about frightening sheep when trying to get water from troughs; of running and running and running; of avoiding towns where there was a police station; of taking some flour from an unoccupied campsite and of anxiously keeping watch; of the huge risk of digging up a goanna by the roadside on the Sandstone road; of getting water from a dry creek bed by digging a hole and letting the water seep in.

There are stories about trying to negotiate their way around the spiritual places along the way — they are going through 'other' country, it is not known, and a number of times the Wongutha girls are frightened by events which Rosie attributes to spirits. I expect that the 1921 Wongutha walkers would have had similar experiences.

There is a deep sadness when she tells about having just got home and the police coming out to take her away again — 'someone pimped' — and she notes that she could have run again, but there was no point. We don't hear the story of how she got home again — people are coming and going and being introduced in the middle of the stories and Rosie and Fred decide that it's almost time to leave. 'You can hear more next time,' says Auntie Wyallie, with a nod of her head at me, and Auntie Rosie tells me it's a long, long story, that we need more time.

I realise with a start that nearly all of the stories are in the present tense, that conversations are remembered and presented verbatim. And that although Auntie Rosie is prompted every now and then by Uncle Fred, he didn't ever tell any of the story himself. 'What about the mysteries along the way?' he asks her at one stage, then he turns to me and says, 'Some of things Rosie's seen you wouldn't believe.' And Auntie Rosie then begins the story about the wind and the little brown bird, or the motorbike sound.

It's obvious that Uncle Fred knows the story well, almost word for word; he corrects her every now and then, when she says the stars were shining at one stage, he interjects, strongly,

'No, it was early morning when you were there.'

Auntie Wyallie, too, supports Rosie's story with sound effects, or little remarks to us — she knows it well — but she too calls it Rosie's story, and Rosie is the only one who tells any of it. Do people's stories belong to them? Are there protocols about who can tell a story and who can't?

Auntie Wyallie tells me that her daughter Jenny has all the old photos, she'll find them for me for Next Time I come up. I'll be here for a few days, I say, but she simply repeats the phrase 'Next Time'.

I start to wonder about all the references to Next Time. I like the idea of a Next Time. It implies a continuing friendship, a steady building up of trust between us, a gradual sharing of experience. Perhaps my willingness to make multiple journeys to visit them is taken as a measure of my sincerity? This slow friendship and revelation seems right. A quick glimpse of a lifetime of memories would be less than right.

The house is full of people and kids and babies; Auntie Wyallie gives me Tarquin to hold for a while. Auntie Ngunnu calls in, joining Cheryl in the kitchen, leaning over the bench towards us. She comes over, every day, after work to see Auntie Wyallie.

When Auntie Rosie finishes telling the part of her story where she is recaptured, Auntie Wyallie launches into the story of how she narrowly avoided being caught and sent to Mogumber. She tells us of how she had charcoal rubbed over her skin, of how she would sit with her back to the fire at night in case anyone saw that she had light skin. She talks of how she and her mother left their home country and went out to Karonie on the Trans-line (Transcontinental Railway Line) to be away from the police, so that Wyallie would not be caught. After a close call with a policeman, when the risk of being caught even at Karonie seemed to be getting dangerously high, her mother and Auntie decided to take her to Mount Margaret. They walked there, and when they finally came to Mt Margaret it was bright moonlight ...

They all talk for a while about the sadness of growing up in buildings instead of the bush, of how they were locked in at night ...

Uncle Fred and Auntie Rosie leave, and Ngunnu sits down in Uncle Fred's chair, and brings Auntie Wyallie up to date on who has been brought in to the hospital today. They both start telling us stories about the old people brought in from Warburton Ranges who can still sing the English hymns Mr Wade taught them. And then continue on with the stories of growing up at Mt Margaret. Ngunnu tells us that she used to cry herself to sleep, that Auntie Dora came over to her the first night and said, 'Don't cry, we're all here.' They talk about the pain of separation from their families, offset with continual reference to the formation of deep friendships amongst each other. 'We're all Mt Margaret people, Sadie, Dora, Wyallie, Ngunnu, May ...'

Auntie Ngunnu tells us how when she was little, a bit bigger than Tarquin, who is not yet one year old, she had to be ready to run into a sugar bag if the policeman was coming. The people kept watch, but she had to play close by so that she could run for that bag. One time the policeman came, unexpectedly. She ran, she got in to it, she was shaking all over after running for that sugar bag. The people were all making a commotion, lots of noise, to distract the policeman, and all the dogs were yapping.

The policeman said to her mum, 'What's in that bag?'

And her mum said, 'Only tucker!' and all the people said, 'Tucker! Only tucker!' And they threw the bag around in the air to each other to show it was only tucker.

And the policeman left.

Then Auntie Wyallie tells us she remembers being out in the bush one day with a group of people, when they suddenly heard this strange noise all around them. It was bullets flying all around them, there was a group of white men shooting at them. Auntie Wyallie hunches her shoulders in and tucks her arms in as she shows us how she hid behind a tree, trembling. Then, she says, they just stopped shooting, and rode away. All the people ran away in different directions. She reminds Auntie Ngunnu that that's when one girl went 'funny', twitching all the time.

'They probably did it for fun,' says Auntie Ngunnu, the pain evident in her voice.

I am speechless by this time. I had read of Aboriginal children being hidden in flour-bags so that they would not be taken away from their families, and I was deeply grieved, but this, this is a soul-racking thing to have someone tell you such a story with first-hand experience. I had read, and been appalled and horrified, that the white people at Laverton used to go out shooting the Aboriginal people, but the fact that it is one of Wyallie's childhood memories is almost too much to comprehend.

The memories that these people have, the pain and suffering, the injustice — I am shocked, filled with grief. And I am awed that they will receive, with graciousness and generosity, a white stranger into their homes, into their lives.

There is no sense of 'interviewing' these people. There is no way that I can view these stories as good information, these people as contacts; they have gifted me with their memories, they are drawing me into their experiences. I have had the tape recorder in my bag, to be brought out and talked about and turned on if the right situation arose, but I leave it in the bag. Later, I will ask about bringing it next time.

Auntie Ngunnu tells us that it's only recently that she can be with white people, and I am suddenly acutely aware of the magnitude of the graciousness and forgiveness of which I have been conscious. The Mount Margaret people, she says, don't have that bitterness and hardness to white people.

Auntie Wyallie nods. 'Thank the Lord for the missionaries,' she says, with feeling. Ngunnu declares that it's only the Lord who can bring peace and healing.

So many memories; so many things seen and remembered, so many things experienced and remembered.

So many of the experiences are ongoing.

Auntie Wyallie wraps up the discussion by remarking that it's good to talk about the old things. I suddenly remember that Auntie Sadie said the same thing last night. I am gladdened, encouraged. This revisiting of the past is not too much to ask.

I ask Auntie Ngunnu about visiting her brother Reggie Johnston tomorrow. She tells me that he has been sick, he may get tired quickly, but that she'll call Marjory and let her know that we'll be coming. We are given directions to get to Marjory's house; it seems that Reggie is no longer with Christopher. I am glad that we can go to visit Reggie with Ngunnu's blessing, to the right place. Auntie Wyallie tells me to write down everything Reggie says, because you never know when someone will be taken. She hugs us goodbye, and remarks that she might see us at Reggie's house.

Wednesday 8/10/97

I ring Auntie Wyallie in the morning to talk about all going together to Reggie's house, but she is no longer able to come, having been ill during the night. You'll be right, she tells me. I ask her about visiting Ranji McIntyre too, and she tells me that he is at the Little Sisters of the Poor Nursing Home. And that it would be fine to visit him, that he has some Good Stories to tell.

We look up the address of the Little Sisters of the Poor Nursing Home before leaving. We cannot see it on the town map, and while I look up the phone book for Catholic Church nursing homes, the inquisitive man behind the desk asks us what we're looking for this time. We tell him. He's never heard of it. I find something which could be it in the phone book, and we look for the street. The man looks up in surprise.

'There's an Aboriginal place down there, I think,' he says, as if warning us.

'That would be it, then,' I say, and we smile and leave him looking confused, again.

It is the right place. The Sister who answers the gate tells us that Ranji can receive visitors. I arrange to come back at three o'clock.

We have some spare time before our visit to Reggie, so we set off to find the language book which Dora showed me. It is still published by Kalgoorlie College, and the bookshop there still sells it. I ask about local Aboriginal authors or poets, and where I could find their work. The young sales assistant looks blank.

Marjory is not home when we get to her house, but a woman called Joanna welcomes us in, and tells us that Uncle is in the living room. We walk in to where Uncle Reggie Johnston is sitting in his wheelchair, and we sit down around the table. I feel terribly sad, I wonder how I can ask a man with so little strength and life left in him to summon up his memories for me.

There are a lot of happy, and very noisy, children running through the house — 'They're not all mine,' Joanna says a few times, as we sit down and get settled. Reggie has been silent ever since we have come in, he does not seem to be noticing our conversation or presence until Joanna tells him that he has some visitors. It is a prompt, Reggie looks up briefly at us. I tell him who we are and where we are from, and how we met Ngunnu yesterday at Auntie Wyallie's house. He makes no response for what feels like a long time. I feel out of my depth. His silence is in stark contrast to the noise of the children. I wish Auntie Wyallie could have come. And then he asks about our families, and we tell him where they are from, and then there is more silence.

I ask him if we can talk to him about the old days at Mount Margaret, and, keeping in mind Auntie Wyallie's instructions, whether I can tape-record the conversation so that I can write it all down later, for a book. He nods, with little hesitation, as if it is unimportant, and asks if we know Mrs Morgan or her sister Esther. This makes me wonder: why does everyone call her Mrs Morgan when she is younger than they are? Why is Esther on a first name basis?

He looks very weary. He starts to talk about how Mount Margaret Mission was founded by Mr Schenk. He tells us that Mr Schenk was living in Victoria, and that the Lord called him to come to the Wongutha people. We hear the details of how Mr Schenk bought a motorbike, and the details of his travelling to Laverton. This man has a great memory, most of the details collaborate exactly with Margaret Morgan's book about Schenk and Mount Margaret. He wants to tell us about how he became a Christian, and about how a great many people became Christians. I tell him that Ian and I are Christians too; I am hoping that he will realise that he doesn't have to convert us. Perhaps he does realise; perhaps he is deliberately telling us these things knowing that we will understand them. It seems that all he wants to talk about is the Lord. He tells us that the Lord is coming soon, that all the old ones have gone, that soon he will go too.

I sit back and listen, I find it impossible to contemplate interrupting his thinking and re-directing his thoughts on to topics that are more 'useful' to me. It would be unthinkable to press this man in failing health for a particular memory, of less significance to him than the ones he is already sharing with us. I sit and listen as he slowly speaks.

After a while he begins to speak of the fact that lots of the young ones were taken away and never came back. I ask him if he remembers the story from the 1920s about Jidu and the other people walking home from Mogumber, and he does. But he is not really interested in telling it. He responds to my questions about navigation, and sources of food, patiently. I ask him about the different paths taken and he simply agrees that there were three different ways. He asks Marjory, who has come home and is now on the telephone, to give us a certain man's name and phone number. Reggie doesn't say why he is giving us this contact. I wonder if Reggie has told this man the story, and is referring us on.

Reggie's story of the 1921 events, as made more widely known by Bill Bunbury's book, is the story on which my interest is founded. Reggie is said to be the most knowledgeable person about this story — it was he and Lampi who told Margaret Morgan the stories which she wrote into her book. The possibility of talking to Reggie Johnston has been one of the impelling factors in making this trip. And here he is, knowing all these things, and too tired to talk of them. His remaining energy is focused on the next world, his faith and his Lord, he speaks of little else.

He goes back to telling us that he had travelled all around the state, preaching and translating, and that he went to Sydney on what he called 'the Minstrel tour'. Reggie has been described to me as a great singer, a great conductor, a leader of the singing at Mt Margaret. He talks for some time about those singing days.

And then he says that it was a pleasure to meet us, and we take the hint and say goodbye, wondering whether there have been other hints, more subtle, which we have missed. We head out into the back yard where Marjory and Joanna are sitting in the shade of a tree, watching the ten or so children playing. I sit and chat with them; Ian plays basketball with the kids. Marjory remarks that some people were supposed to come and borrow her ute and take Uncle out for a day in the bush, but they never came. They draw a map in the dust to show me where they go when they go out bush. We talk for about an hour; it is a happy time, and when we say goodbye the children enthusiastically invite us back again, any time.

But I feel extremely sad as we drive away. I have no words to express the pain, my grief; it is for Reggie's weariness, it is for imminent death, it is for sickness, it is for all the sorrowful memories of these proud elderly Wongutha people, it is for all the ones who were taken away and never came back, it is for the many losses, for all the unkept promises and unfulfilled hopes.

We drive slowly back into the centre of Kalgoorlie. My tears for

Reggie are only just below the surface. I need some non-emotional activity. We decide to continue our search for some literary works by local Aboriginal people for a while.

I am pleased to see three bookshops on the main street. But there appear to be no books of Aboriginal poetry at all, let alone locally written works, in any of them. I ask the sales-assistant in one shop whether they have any books by local Aboriginal authors. 'Oh yes', the young woman says, looking as if she is sensing a good sale, 'this way.' At last, I think! We follow, and she flourishes a glossy book of Sally Morgan's paintings towards us. 'I mean a local writer,' I explain, patiently. She looks annoyed. She looks pityingly at me, as if I am terribly naïve. She points us towards the 'Goldfields' display stands, and walks off without saying anything more.

We have a careful hunt through the 'Local History' and 'Goldfields General' display stands. Not only is there a lack of material written by Aboriginal people, there seems to be a lack of anything that mentions the existence of Aboriginal people. There are plenty of books about explorers, gold-seekers, the perils of the goldfields, a history of the hospital and all the nurses, plenty of voyeuristic material about old Kalgoorlie's women, a few editions of the recollections of 'pioneering' women.

We leave, and try the last shop. Here I find a book by Aboriginal author Doris Pilkington about some girls from Jigalong and their escape from Mogumber, as well as a book by a South Australian author about a Wongutha woman who is hounded by the Department for Aboriginal Affairs. I already have both books. And they are not written by local authors. But I am relieved to see that these books about Aboriginal experience appear in at least one shop in Kalgoorlie.

The dictionary of Wongutha language which we purchased at the College appears on none of the bookshops' shelves.

We try the tourist bureau, as a last hope. Perhaps they could tell us where we might find a place that sells the books I am hoping to find. They have nothing to say to us. In fact, they too seem defensive, threatened by our questions.

Perhaps there are no such books after all ...

We find a quiet place to have lunch and then stop to have a rest; we are both feeling exhausted after the morning's experiences.

When I wake, I try ringing the number that Reggie gave me this morning. The man, Greg, turns out to be the director of a large and very busy Aboriginal Health Service in Kalgoorlie. I don't get to speak to him in person; his secretary answers the phone. I explain my purpose for calling, and she tells me that he is very busy for the next two days. She offers to tell him that I called and to see what he says about talking to me; I should then ring her back later in the afternoon for the answer.

I head off to see Mr Ranji McIntyre. I brace myself for a similar experience to that of talking with Reggie; there are lots of silent people sitting on the verandah in chairs and wheelchairs, watching me as I walk up from the gate behind the Sister. She shows me into a foyer with a few chairs around its walls, and I sit down and smile at the two men already sitting there. One smiles back.

Ranji walks out to meet me, looking alert and tall and proud.

We start off, as usual, with an exchange of details about where our families are from. I am expecting it by now. I have found that the most interest is shown in the connections to the wheatbelt district where my mother was born; it seems that Perth doesn't really count.

We have a great talk, and we laugh a lot. It is entirely unlike the pain-filled conversation of this morning.

Ranji has a strong sense of humour; perhaps this is how he has remained so unbent and so unwearied by all he must have seen and known and suffered in his lifetime.

He is an excellent storyteller. I remember Auntie Wyallie's comment about the old people's passing, that Ranji is the oldest. Ranji is happy for me to tape our conversation and to write it down for other people to see. Perhaps it is a consciousness of the tape which prompts him to start off with a dramatic story. Perhaps it is the presence of the other listeners in the room — they seem to know the story; they laugh in the right places (most of the time), startling me by their sudden participation. Ranji is unperturbed by their interruptions, and by the noisy flow of people and wheelchairs through the foyer in front of us.

He doesn't know the story of the 1921 escape, but he knows about some of the people. And he tells me of a journey that he made along the Kalgoorlie pipeline in the 1920s.

He tells me, 'Come again, sister,' when I say goodbye. I remind him that I live in Perth, and so it might be a while before I'm back in Kalgoorlie.

'When you come back,' he says, as if he'll be there for a long time and anytime will do. I say that I will go and see him, when I come back, and I carry a chair out on to the verandah for him.

'Thank you, sister. Goodbye, sister,' he says.

Does he think I'm one of the Sisters? Are the only white women who come to this place Sisters? Or are all women sisters?

A smiling Sister lets me out and I walk out of the Nursing Home into the hot bright sunshine. I feel as if the world is all right again, as if there is still hope.

I call the secretary back, and she tells me that unfortunately Greg is too busy to talk to me this time. Perhaps I can contact him by fax from Perth. Maybe I'll catch up with him next time.

I head off to visit Auntie Wyallie.

She is feeling a little better; I have just missed Auntie Ngunnu and Auntie Rosie.

She wants to hear about what has happened, and whether Reggie and Ranji told me the stories about that escape. I hesitate, and tell her that they told me lots of great stories, but, no, not much about that story.

She sighs, and tells me that they know the stories...

> '15 niggers, it had
> on the side,' she says.
> 'They send them
> right to Perth,
> and ... I think they,'

She pauses for a while, as if deciding how much to say,

> 'They walked back
> — the right way —
> in two weeks they were back
> only one died in the bush.
> Ranji know that story.
> Reggie too.'

She pauses, and I wait, I hold my breath. Auntie Wyallie knows the story! But she is sounding uncertain, perhaps she is not sure about telling it to me. She has known it, and yet she has sent me to other people to hear it. I wonder if, perhaps, as with Rosie's story, it belongs to certain people to tell. Her direct quote from Margaret Morgan's book *A Drop in a Bucket* takes me by surprise.

Auntie Wyallie begins again, but she has changed stories:

> 'Dora
> was with her mother,
> she was baby.
> They came round this way
> following the railway line
> through Kalgoorlie.
> Walked back
> this way.
> Dora tell you?'

And Dora had.

I ask Auntie Wyallie if it would be all right if later I write down some of the things we are talking about. Auntie May, I remember told me to write down what Auntie Wyallie said on the first night I met her, and Auntie Wyallie told me to write down what Reggie and Ranji said to me. It seems that these people have a strong sense of the importance of writing down the memories of their lives. She nods, 'Write it all down.' She signals to me to get some paper and a pen, now, and slows her speech so that I can write the things she says.

I ask her if I could write down what I remember of what Auntie Ngunnu and Auntie Rosie had said the day before, and whether I could see them again to ask them about bringing a tape recorder next time. Auntie Wyallie says that it is a good idea to write everything down, and to print it all in a book. 'Write it all down,' she says again. 'It's all part of the story, isn't it?' Her comment surprises me. 'Even about the fruit cake and cups of tea?' I ask, 'Even what we said then?' She says yes, all of it. And that next time, we can tape the whole of Auntie Rosie's story. She tells me that I should tape that story in this house, so that she (Auntie Wyallie) can be there when Auntie Rosie is telling it.

We talk for a bit longer about who might tell me more of the 1921 story.

Auntie Rosie wouldn't know, Auntie Wyallie thinks, because

she is from Darlot way. Uncle Fred would know. I ask her how he would have heard the story, wondering if this is how she knows, too. 'Heard Wongai's talkin',' is the answer.*

I wonder why it is that Fred would be able to tell me, but that Auntie Wyallie won't.

She asks me if Cyril told me much.

And I say that he told me that his grandparents were part of the group, but not who they were, and that he said he didn't know the stories. Auntie Wyallie sighs.

'Cyril Barnes, his grandfather was the one who died out there. Very sad.'

She starts running through a list of who I could talk to next time I come:

Auntie Queenie at Kurrawang, Auntie Violet at Kurrawang,
Ranji and Reggie, Auntie Bessie, Auntie Doolkie.
Auntie May might know.
Jessie Evans, at Leonora, is a good storyteller.
Isobel Brand, at Leonora, and my sister June. She'll make you laugh.
If my husband was here he'd tell all the stories, but he's gone.
They're all passing away.
Then there's Jim Brennan at Menzies. He's one of them. His wife got sent to Mogumber too, she's from Wiluna way. They're old, Fred and Rosie's age.

It's good to talk about what's been happening, a long time ago. Some sad, sad stories. Some happy stories.

Auntie Wyallie's daughter Miriam has been part of the discussion for much of the time, and now she talks about when I might come back to hear the stories. I suggest December. Auntie Wyallie says in August, when it's cooler, and that in August we'll all go out in the bush. I say that I'd love to come back in August and go out in the bush. But could I come back sooner than that to hear the stories?

Auntie Wyallie is determined that I should come back when it is cooler. Otherwise, it is too hot for talking.

I suggest March or April next year.

Auntie Wyallie thinks that March would be all right; Miriam

---

* *Wongai — abbreviation of Wongutha, very frequently used in speech. I was advised to use 'Wongutha' in preference when writing and have done so, except with direct quotation.*

reminds her that it's hot in March. I suggest that maybe November, before it gets too hot, might be good. Miriam agrees, and persuades Auntie Wyallie that November is cooler than March.

Auntie Wyallie tells me to come back in November, in six weeks.

As I am leaving, she tells me that she will have her old photos of Mt Margaret people ready in six weeks.

And she says that I could go and visit Fred and Rosie in the morning if I want to ask Fred about the 1921 story, but that they might be going out bush.

Auntie Wyallie walks me out to the car. 'Will you be all right to come all this way by yourself when you come back?' she asks. My feelings of great joy overflow.

I drive away from a grandmother, waving until the end of the road. The elderly woman standing on the dusty verge waves, and turns away into her garden.

Thursday 9/10/97 and Friday 10/10/97

We are up early and out at Kurrawang Christian Community at the time Auntie Wyallie suggested. We ask around and eventually find Fred and Rosie's place. It starts to rain. We knock, a little hesitantly. Auntie Rosie answers the door and her face lights up, we are ushered in. I'm not so certain that Uncle Fred is happy to see us. He sits at the table looking rather fierce.

We chat for a while; they ask if Auntie Wyallie is better today. Auntie Rosie starts to tell us some of her stories again — 'What about that motorbike?!' but Uncle Fred cuts her off. He tells Auntie Rosie to keep the stories in the right order and tell them, properly, when there is more time. Auntie Rosie says nothing. Uncle Fred looks at me. I, for something to say, mention that Auntie Wyallie thought he might be able to tell me some stories about the old times when Jidu and some others walked back from Mogumber. Fred says something about how that story is in his file.

He tells us that he is not very impressed with people who come looking for their stories. Someone else — he remembers her by name — came here once with a tape recorder and recorded Rosie's story. She said that she would come back, but she never did.

She didn't send them the tape, like she said she would. She didn't send them anything.

He sounds angry.

Rosie says that she thinks that the woman might be coming back today.

Uncle Fred asks her what day it is, patiently, as if that will settle the matter, and she replies, Thursday, and then she says, hopefully, that maybe the woman will come tomorrow.

Fred says nothing.

Auntie Rosie quickly begins to talk to us about her children.

I mention that Auntie Wyallie thought they might be going out in the bush today.

Auntie Rosie tells us that they are going prospecting. She talks about some of the finds they have had, and where they have been. Uncle Fred corrects the details of whether it was morning or night-time.

We don't stay for long, it seems as if Uncle Fred is keen to get going, and we set off, with the agreement that when I come back next time it will be a good time to sit down and talk about all the stories. And that I can perhaps bring a tape recorder, we will see, we will talk about that when I come back.

We leave Kurrawang and head back into Kalgoorlie, then drive north again, back to Leonora, and beyond. We are on the homeward stretch of our trip, travelling over parts of the northern route taken by the group which included Ngada and Jinera. We drive from Leonora to Leinster. There is a darkly threatening storm out

The country near Leinster.

to the west, the early winds of the gale buffet the car and huge sheets of rain are sweeping towards us, grey and cold-looking, impenetrable, blocking the view of what is behind them. It looks very wet. We stop at the police station in Leinster to ask whether the dirt road across to Mount Magnet is still open to two-wheel drives. The officer there puts through a radio-call to Sandstone and says, yes, if we hurry we might just make it. There's a big

The road to Sandstone.

storm out there ...

At the petrol station someone has just driven across from Mount Magnet and the proprietor laughs and tell us he doesn't like our chances.

When the escapees walked through this country it was the middle of winter. There was a lot of rain while they were walking, enough to flood the roads to Laverton. They wouldn't have stopped for the rain, they would have been glad that it would wash away their tracks, would provide them with drinking water. I wonder if they stayed warm because of the speed at which they were walking. I wonder if they stayed warm at night when they stopped.

We drive westwards on the dirt track out to Sandstone, amazed at the number of emus and emu chicks we see, the track edged by emu-high hakeas and grevilleas flowering a brilliant orange under a storm-luminous sky. We are watching the sky and wondering whether we will get through to Mount Magnet, watching the light fade, imagining the small party of Wongutha walking fast and looking anxiously around them for different signs of danger. Imagining this endless countryside dry and dusty in the summer, we think of Auntie Rosie walking through this way when she was a young girl and are astounded. We marvel as we think of all the people who have walked home to Laverton, despite all odds.

The storm goes to the south of us and the sky opens out once more.

We camp out under the stars, in

Near Lake Moore, looking east.

the spinifex, somewhere between Sandstone and Mt Magnet. It is very quiet.

> they walked across strange landscapes
> unfamiliar country,
> unknown terrain
> silent country
>
> walk where they walked
> what you will see?
> no trace of their journeying
> what will you hear?
> silent country

I am no longer in silent country, the stories are now ringing in my mind.

More Journal Notes

I ring Auntie Wyallie often in early November, but no one answers the phone.

Monday 17/11/97

I guess that they must have gone away somewhere; I ring Auntie Wyallie's daughter in Leonora on the off-chance that they are all there. I am a little anxious that they won't remember who I am, but when Auntie Wyallie comes to the phone, she says 'Hello!! You came back!!!'

She sounds very surprised, and very pleased. A phone call is enough to 'be back', as if I by phoning I have suddenly re-appeared from a doubtful existence. As if she wasn't really expecting me to keep my word, to come back. (That well-remembered woman who never came back, what has she done? More worthless agreements, the taking away of their memories as well as their land and their people. I am suddenly very, very glad that I didn't talk about tape recording the stories of the younger people on the first trip.)

Auntie Wyallie is staying in Leonora for a while, it's too hot in

Kalgoorlie. She suggests I come up to Kalgoorlie in December sometime; I should ring in the first week of December to see if they are back there yet and then we can arrange a time for me to visit.

Second Trip, 9 to 12 December 1997

Tuesday 9/12/97

I call in to visit Auntie Wyallie when I arrive in Kalgoorlie, at around sunset. The heat of the day is still radiating from the roads. The car that I've borrowed from friends in Kalgoorlie is like an oven. We sit on the couch in the twilight, with Miriam sitting on the old TV, and Auntie Wyallie teaches me some Wongutha words, and a song. We sing it for a while, Miriam joins in. Auntie Wyallie patiently corrects my pronunciation. I try to picture the words in my head so that I can remember them and am again conscious of how much my knowledge base depends on written words.

Auntie Wyallie rings various people to track down Auntie Rosie to check that tomorrow morning will still be suitable to record some stories. It seems to be not suitable anymore. Auntie Wyallie breaks into language. I am obviously not intended to understand; I am very conscious of their courteousness in so often speaking in English when I am there.

Rosie and Fred have to go out to a site tomorrow, the land claim processes are progressing slowly, they call it the 'land title business'. We arrange that I will come in the morning to record Auntie Wyallie's story anyway, and that Auntie Wyallie will try to contact Ngunnu and invite her over.

Wednesday 10/12/97

Auntie Rosie and Uncle Fred appear at Auntie Wyallie's house in the morning, to the surprise and delight of everyone. We sit around drinking tea at the kitchen table.

Land title talk again, pain and angry talking about the people putting claims on top of claims. 'They not from that country! We know where they from. They not from there. We know where they born. They not even born in the bush!' (Fred)

'We the ones who had all that hardship.' (Wyallie)

Fred is angry. He looks at me, I am sure that he is angry with me, too. He speaks again of that woman who never came back.

Auntie Rosie gets up and goes into the other room, Auntie Wyallie follows her. They sit and look out the window, not talking.

Uncle Fred is looking at me still. I say something about just wanting to hear Auntie Rosie's story about Mogumber, and after a long pause, he starts to tell me that he wanted to write his story once, when he lived in South Australia, he wanted his relatives to write it for him but they didn't have time.

He calls Auntie Rosie back and tells her it's only her Mogumber story I want. There seems to be a change; Auntie Wyallie comes and sits down again too, and everyone looks at me expectantly.

We sit around the table, and we talk again about why I want to tape the stories, why I want to try and write about the history.

Auntie Rosie agrees to start, and we turn the tape player on. Uncle Fred is surprisingly keen to make sure that the tape player really is working. We check it, and then rewind it, and then Auntie Rosie begins again. The formality takes me by surprise; this time, there are fewer interruptions and contributions from her family, only Rosie makes the sound effects that go with the events, people who are coming and going whisper in the background, even the children are hushed. The story is less vividly told, some details are omitted. I don't mind, I am happy for Auntie Rosie to tell whichever version she likes, it is her choice, she can freely construct the story and the telling of it for the wider, unknown audience. It is right that she should modify the telling if she wants to.

After a while, Fred joins in a little more, Rosie keeps asking him questions. And when she comes to the part where she runs away, she mentions another lot who also ran away, and to my delight, Uncle Fred tells a small part of the 1921 story. Just a small part; the rest of the story, he says, is in *A Drop in a Bucket*. Rosie picks up her story again and continues.

Auntie Wyallie, when she records her story, does not want her English name known, not spoken on the tape, not written down. She says she doesn't want people to know that it's her story. I guess she means that she doesn't want white people to know; her family and friends will recognise her Aboriginal name but white people will not. Ngunnu, too, doesn't want her English name recorded on the tape. Their need for anonymity makes me suddenly, painfully, joltingly aware that their wariness in speaking about the past comes from a lifetime of not being able to do so without fear.

Uncle Fred and Auntie Rosie and Auntie Wyallie sit around the table after we have turned off the tape recorder, and the conversation goes back to normal. It is definitely not for taping. They talk of a man called Donegan; these people, and others I've spoken to, make the comment that he was 'a bit rough'. One of the women starts to say that when Donegan took all the Wongutha off to Cosmo Newbery — and someone interrupts. 'Is he still alive? Maybe we …'

'No,' says Uncle Fred, 'he's gone, but his widow is still alive. She still remembers.' The talk continues, and I am left wondering if it might have been stopped if Donegan was still alive to inflict more pain on these people.

They are still not free to talk openly about what has happened in the past.

Later, Uncle Fred sits at the table reading, Miriam is in the kitchen smiling at me, I am at the table. I ask Uncle Fred again, a little hesitantly, about the story of the 1921 mob.

That story is in *A Drop in a Bucket*, Uncle Fred says. It's already written.

I say that I want to hear what Wongai people say about this story; that it's Wongutha history, that I want to make sure I get the story right.

He doesn't answer for a while. But then he looks straight at me. Uncle Fred tells me that, about that story, he only knows the bit about Joe going out first to have a look around, and what he read in *A Drop in a Bucket*. He says he has a draft copy of the book in his file which I can maybe have a look at sometime.

He goes back to his reading, but he doesn't look so angry.

THURSDAY 11/12/97

Auntie Wyallie tells me that tomorrow all the people are going up to Leonora for another Land Meeting. We talk about whether I should go too; everyone will be there, I am wondering if it might be a good time to hear some stories. But they will be busy talking about Land. I change my train ticket back to Perth from the Friday night train to the day train.

I visit Ranji McIntyre again, and he too looks pleased that I've come back. He tells me more stories, he tells me one story again. In the middle of the day I drive out to Kurrawang to try to find Auntie Queenie and Auntie Violet. Auntie Violet is away, staying with family who have a cooler house. I find Auntie Queenie's place; it is 43 degrees in the shade on her verandah, we sit in front of a fan and chat for a while. It is too hot to talk much. I head back into Kalgoorlie.

When the light starts changing and the heat begins to drop a little, I go over to Auntie Wyallie's place again.

'You see Auntie Queenie today?' Auntie Wyallie asks me.

'Yes,' I reply, wondering what Uncle Fred will say, think, about me asking more people for stories. I look over at him, warily.

'What stories she tell you?' he says.

I wonder briefly if I am supposed to keep secret what people tell me, whether he is testing me; not that there was anything that seemed like it should be secret, and not that these people haven't already shown that they know everyone's stories. And not that stories told for a taperecorder and a book would be at all secret.

I say that she told me how she came from Karonie — I mispronounce it several times and it takes them a while to work out what I am trying to say — and that she went to Mt Margaret when she was small.

'She tell you about her brother, what he was doing around that time?' Fred asks.

'No,' I say.

Auntie Wyallie and Auntie Rosie interject, 'She didn't tell you that story?' and Uncle Fred begins to tell it.

I am amazed; I had been expecting him to be closing down on all the stories which the others might begin, to be saying that the stories have to be told right. But he is telling me this story, with great enthusiasm, he is an excellent storyteller:

> He was with Carlisle.*
> They wanted a criminal, they pick him out for a
>   criminal.
> The policeman pick him up
> and they on the train to Perth.

---

* Carlisle — a police officer.

Iron ball on his leg.
Handcuffed.

Well, he tell the policeman he want to go to the toilet.
The policeman sitting outside the toilet, waiting.

He break that window with that iron ball,
he wait 'til they passing some sand-dunes,
he jump out the window onto that sand.

Rosie: The train moving, he jump out!

Wyallie: He still got that handcuff on.

Rosie: The policeman still waiting.

Fred: Well, the policeman, he get tired of waiting,
he go in
and he's gone.

Well, he know the police will be coming after him.
He gets that ball off
[hand hitting movements, like a rock in the hand being used to smash the chain].

He goes to a farm and the farmer gives him a feed.
That farmer's a pimp, he rings the police.

He knows the police will be coming after him,
he's still got that chain on.
He takes off, running.
He see a motor coming, way back,
the policeman.

The policeman send a dog after him,
that dog coming for him.

Rosie: The dog comes up,
and wham, he finished.
He used that iron, wham, on the dog, maybe his

head,
when he comes close to his legs to bite him.
Him finish.

Fred: Then he took off, running.
The policeman couldn't do nothing without his dog.

Rosie: Those sand-dunes not far from Coolgardie?

Fred: They almost to Perth.

Did he walk back again? I ask.

Fred: They pick him up again near Coolgardie.
They put him in the lockup.
He tells the policeman he want to go to the toilet
he never come out, he hiding.

Well, they go looking out in the bush for him, but he go around to the motor. Keys still in the ignition. He drives off in the motor while they out looking for him.

And the story abruptly stops there. I imagine that the ending is not triumphant.*

Uncle Fred starts telling a new story, the story of Bluegum, and Mick.

They brothers, and they look the same.
Policeman ride up to the camp,

---

* *Perhaps he was triumphant after all — over the next few years, Auntie Queenie told me a number of stories about her brother, his ongoing ability to attract police attention, and his numerous successes in outwitting police who attempted to lock him up. I also found a reference in the* West Australian *in 1938 to a story of an Aboriginal prisoner who, under police escort from the Goldfields to Perth, jumped out of a moving train and got away — the public were alerted.*

>   he say to the man, 'Where's Bluegum? You
>   Bluegum?'
>   He say, 'He must be somewhere else!
>   Out that way!'
>
>   Telling lies! [Aside to me]
>
>   He throw a boomerang, and the policeman
>   watching it.
>   He run for the thicket!
>
>   He get in that thicket!
>   Policeman look around, and he gone! He off!
>
>   It was him,
>   but he gone!
>   They can't get him.
>
> Wyallie: They can't catch Wongais.

Another story follows. One leads to another, there are many to be told. The past is full of stories, the present is full of the past.

So many stories, so much history, so much pride in enduring the history.

'Next time we'll go out in the bush and show you some places, out in the bush. Come back in August when it's cooler.'

Friday 12/12/97

I catch the slow train back to distant Perth. It takes all day.

All day I am thinking of when I might next come back, I will not ever be the same.

2

Speakings

2.0

Introduction to the Speakings

The Speakings declare that the past is not lost.

These voices are not from the long distant past. The experiences related are within living memory. This history is still with the speakers, with us all.

The speakers took me in, trusted me with their words, entrusted me with their words.

The older speakers tell of the anguish of experiencing early Goldfields contact with white people and the resulting breakdown of family, separation from country, white people taking their people away, white people taking their children away, white people taking their land, sheep trampling their land, white people shooting each other, rough policemen executing a rough justice, policemen chaining up Wongutha people and sending them away to Perth, ever-increasing uncertainty and a newly precarious existence. They speak of journeying to distant places, and of no place to go but the mission. One man remembers back to when local men enlisted for the First World War; he remembers the people who escaped.

The younger speakers tell of ongoing injustice and uncertainty, of fear and good reason for fear, of childhood memories that include instructions on how to skin a kangaroo, how to stay warm at night, how to listen for attackers; experiences that include being shot at, being hidden, being silent, being disguised, running from the police. Some recall being given up to the mission as the only hope of staying in their country and close to their family, having new names, being locked in, abiding by unfathomable rules, longing for family and acceptance. One remembers being handed over to the police by the station owner, being jailed, being sent away to Mogumber, and running away to try to get home to her family, being jailed again, being sent to Mogumber again, running away again, being jailed again.

One speaker is non-Aboriginal. She speaks the Wongutha language and has been told elements of the 1921 story — stories of the group of people deported from Laverton, their escape from Mogumber and their return home — by Wongutha people who have since passed away. She expected that no one else would accurately remember this story.

The Speakings presented in this book are personal, individual recollections of events. The knowledge they present is sometimes seemingly unrelated to the 1921 events, and yet, all the Speakings are representative of, and give glimpses into, the daily experiences that make up the shared, diverse history of the Wongutha people.

The transcribed stories are deliberately constructed by the speakers for the purpose of this book.[1] The speakers have chosen their histories and retain authority over their stories.

The Speakings contain much pain; they also contain much triumph. Endurance and survival are celebrated.

This history is not lost.

Reg Johnston

(Spoken on 8 October 1997)

The conversation* with Mr Reginald Carmichael Johnston (now passed on), took place in his home in Kalgoorlie.
  Mr Johnston's mother was a relative of Jidu's.

...†

Mr Johnston: Then the government took all the kids away.
               Took them,
               took them down to Perth,
               give them education, took them to Perth.
               And, some of them never returned.
               They went away and got married, and never returned.
               Settled.
                 ...

               __ __ [But we were safe at]‡ Mt Margaret Mission.

Carolyn: We heard that some of the first people to stop at Mt

---

* *The conversation did not run with rapidity — the formatting is intended to make the speaker's pauses and breaks obvious to the reader, and so, if possible, to communicate some of the rhythm and nuance of the spoken conversation.*

† *The symbol '...' is used to mark places where sections of the taped conversation have been omitted from this text.*

‡ *The symbol '__' is used to mark places where I have been unable to decipher words or sentences from the taped conversation. The man who spoke these words has passed away and so the text could not be clarified. (His sister has kindly given permission for this text to be included in the book and for his name to be used.)*

  The symbol '[ ]' is used to contain my best guess at inaudible words, for example [But we were safe at] Mt Margaret Mission.

Margaret were the ones who had been taken
down to Mogumber, and who had escaped and
walked home ...
Can you tell me some of that
story about the people who escaped and walked
back again?

Mr Johnston: They didn't know how to swim back ...
They couldn't get over the river.
So they had to cut the big long tree down,
and climb up the tree and go,
go over the river.
Over the tree.
And, and come all the way to Mt Margaret
Mission.

They walked.

__ __ [They caught] wild food.
They hit him with a wooden stick.
Knock him on the head.
Kangaroo, and emu and goanna.
Oh, they eat up everything!
Wild cat.

And all the farmer gave them eggs and bread, you
know.

Oh, they can find the water.

They find a tree, __ __ water there.

They left in the middle of the year __ __.

...

They went the long way round.
They don't want to get caught by police.

...

Oh, they keep on the north.

They keep on the north side.
...

Carolyn: I heard that one group went straight
through the middle to Menzies;
one group went north,
one went to Menzies and one went along the
pipeline.

Yeah.
Yeah. Three, three ways.
...
We heard when, the people, they came
back.

Carolyn: Can you tell me any stories about Jidu?
He was one of the people who walked
back from Mogumber ...?

Mr Johnston: He, he our, our king.
Mm. He went down there __ __ to
Mogumber, then he come back.

... He was pretty old when he died.
He was our king.
...

Lot of them people died when they went
away.
There's no people left now.

Carolyn: Those people who got taken down to
Perth, it must have been hard for
them. It must have been hard to be
taken away from this country.

Mr Johnston: Yeah! Lot of them never returned.
Lot of them went down there and got
married and never came back.

Ranji McIntyre

(Spoken on 8 October 1997)

The first of two conversations with Mr Ranji McIntyre, recorded at the Little Sisters of the Poor Home for the Aged, in Kalgoorlie.

Mr Ranji McIntyre remembers the years before the First World War. He is in his nineties, or possibly one hundred years old. He knew many of the people who had been taken to Mogumber in 1921. He did not know the story of their deportation as he had arrived in the Mount Margaret community some years after 1921. Ranji McIntyre's wife, now passed on, was the sister of the baby sent away in the 1921 deportation, Elyon.

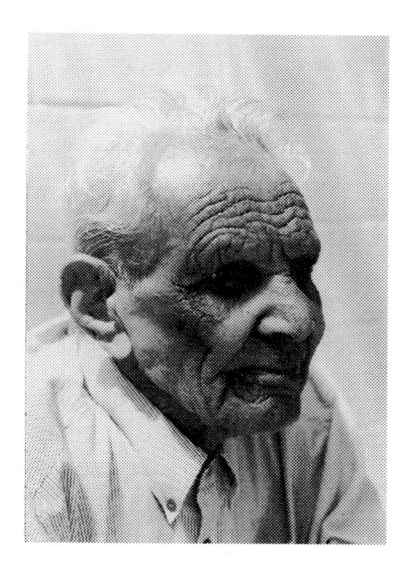

Carolyn:	So the people who got taken to Mogumber,
Ranji:	Yeah,
Carolyn:	lots of them didn't come back,
Ranji:	No.
Carolyn:	but some of them did come back?
Ranji:	Some of them come back and some of them didn't.
Carolyn:	Do you know the stories about the people who

76 Speakings

                walked back?

Ranji: Some of them old people they walked back, and,
they come through the bush, I think.
Yeah. I don't know how they get on for tucker and things, but,
I s'pose they get plenty of meat,
you know, rabbits,
and things like that and the __ and all that.

No trouble there, be able to get them rabbits.

Ah, you know, my place,
home,
before I come to Mt Margaret Mission,
my place called Burtville
...
I grow there, and I born there.
The first year, of the first war, 1915, I was about then.
I remember everything, people called up for war, that year.
They went away,
they fight war, overseas somewhere.
Gallipoli's war.

Yeah.
They fight,
and when they finish fighting,
some of them didn't come back,
but some of them come back.
Yeah.

Yeah.
I worked there, when I was growing up.

And I worked there on a cattle station.
I working there all the time.

Two blokes, they was a good friend one time.

And then, they went and got so many head of
    cattle, you see?

And half of them —
and they're not too, they're not too good friends,
    see?
They fight it out, like, he take his half of the cattle.
The other fellow took his half.
They split up.

And the bloke send us out to go and get some,
to have a look in the breakaways,
and have a look any, his cow that got calf.
And,
'You see any my cow that got calf, you just drive it
    away steady,
but as long as you don't 'sturb Tom James' cattle.'

Yeah. We went, we went, we done that job.
We come back with about thirty, forty head of
    cattle.

We come back, passing this Tom James' property,
    see?

And he just happened to come along on the horse,
and he had somebody with him,
he come along and he asked us,
'What you boys doing with the cattle?'
I said,
I said, 'Jack, sent us out to get some cattle, that he
    wanted in the yard.' You see?
And, he stand there for a while,
and he say,
and he say, 'You boys leave that cattle here! And
    you go and tell Jack to come and get it himself.'

Yeah.
Well, as soon as we let the cattle go, the cattle were
    all mixed up with the others! They were keen

cattle, you see, they knew a favourite spot.
There were a lot of cattle sitting in the dump there,
in the shady trees,
along side of the well, you see?
Soon as you let them go, they all turn around and were all mixed up!

So, we went to tell him.
He asked me, 'How you boys going with the cattle?'
I said, 'We, we brought across quite a few cattle there and Tom James come along and put a stop to us.'

Yeah.
And, old __ [Jack], he come up, he was doing a bit of mining there, __ __ his place. So he come up the ladder.
And he went down, and changed his shoes, put on his other little light shirt, and said, 'Can I borrow your horse, do you reckon, and I'll go down there and see old Willie Burton.'

And then he went up there.
He went up there, having an argument.

Yeah.
He had an argument there, and,
and, he argued this bloke to,
he wanted this bloke to get off the horse,
and told him to have a fight, you see.
But the other fellow was still sitting on top of horse.

Yeah.
And, the bloke gets,
an old __ [scratchy?] spanner, a big one,
and while he not looking,
he, he hit him in the back!!

Yeah.
Hit him in the back.

And so this fellow,
spur his horse and gallop back to his place and got
  the gun and come out.
Got the gun,
come out,
went and over and shot him!
Yeah.

He was lighting fires of foliage, and see a
  horseman come along with a gun!
He should have gone and hide somewhere!
  [Laughs]

Yeah.
Anyway, he put three shot in him,
Bang. Bang. Bang.
He drop him.

And he gallop back to the home, and he pull up
  there,
and he says, 'Eh,' he says, 'I want you boys to let
  all the cattle go and let all the horse out o' yard,
  and,
and, I'll take this message up the house.'
'Cause he's going to tell him that he's finished up
  the bloke, you see.

We let all the cattle go and we let the horse go,
and we, we got going too!

So, they rang through Laverton Police.
Come out
and went up to his place and pick him up
and then take him down to where he shot him
and picked the dead body up, and thought, take it
  together.

	Yeah. And we, we got going, anyway! After when that, that was all settled down, we come back later on, you see. Well, we just go in two at a time, you see.
	The policeman is, Dave Hunter. Dave Hunter and Tommy Thompson. Yeah. That's the, that's the old day police, they driving with a horse and truck, or else they'll ride the horse. There's no motor cars in this time. Yeah. It's all sulky jobs.
Carolyn:	They used to give the Aboriginal people a hard time, in Laverton, did they, those police?
Ranji:	Yeah. Yeah. Yeah. They might steal something, they might have gone to another place, and they'll follow it up, follow him up, and then, they chain all up, and put him in the train, and send him to Perth.
Carolyn:	Those people that got sent to Perth and then they escaped — and walked home again, how would they know which way to walk?
Ranji:	Oh, well, they, they would, they just read the stars! So when they watch the sun rise that way, they got go __ __. See? Travel from Perth, to east! You get to Laverton.
	I went, one day, I come down from Burtville, a horse and cart, me 'n' a white bloke.

Take us, take us nine days to get to Kalgoorlie!
We left Burtville there,
and come all the way down the line, and got here,
 nine days.
We come in the town here, at the Boulder Oak, we
 stopped in there.
And we give the horses __. [a barrow?]
And from there,
And we started again from, went through
 Coolgardie and all round,
and through to, to Southern Cross.
From Southern Cross to Merredin,
from Merredin to — been south that way,
then to Bruce Rock.
Bruce Rock we went on to place called
 Dumbleyung.

And, been there for a couple of years, working
 with that bloke,
and, I got sick of the place,
and I come back!

Got there,
I only just went for him, with him, for company,
 you see.
Then when I don' like it, well, I can come back, you
 see.

I didn't come back in the train, I come back on the
 pushbike!
Settled this pushbike for, for, for twelve quid.
Yeah.
Brand new, brand new bike,
and name o' the bike is 'Wes'.
Wes.

I leave Dumbleyung straight after dinner.
I travel that afternoon about sunset, from sunset 'til
 midnight.

I, I got off the road,
and I, sleep place, and I made a bed and went to
  sleep.

I get up daylight again, I hope for Merredin.
I got Merredin just around about sunrise.

I waited there,
round about, just after, seven o'clock when the cafe
  opened.
I went and had a bit of tea, and got a bit of
  sandwich.

I got on the bike,
and I off to
Southern Cross.
In a day.
I rode it telegraph, you can't ride him in the main
  road 'cause it's too sandy.
They all gravel, you see.

I keep going,
and the pipeline, they got a path there.
People looking after pipe, you know. Water pipe.
And they got a bike path, you know.
I ride along on my little bike, you know.

I travel from after breakfast,
I travel to Southern Cross,
I get there around half past four, nearly five
  o'clock.

I didn't went to town,
I went down the railway station,
and the old goods train was hooked up on
  Coolgardie line!
Ready to go on to Coolgardie!
I went round the other side.

I went to another side, and,

the guard blows the whistle and the train was
   getting ready,
and the train started moving.
I lifted bike on the __ [low? slow?] train,
I lifted bike on the __ [seat?],
and I got on and made a bed and went to sleep.
I woke up, next morning, Coolgardie,
daylight, and the morning star was up.

Yeah.
I took me bike off,
and rolled up my skinny swag,
and I off to Kalgoorlie for breakfast.
Yeah.

And, I came __ __ near the railway station,
butcher's shop there, old butcher's shop there.
Horne brothers' butchers shop.
And, back of that, a couple of fellows was a
   camping there.
I went and had a break with them,
and I had two days rest with them.

And I started from there to Menzies.
Camped a while in Menzies.

Then to Malcolm.
I got to Laverton around about the afternoon.
I was home and dry!

Well, that's the, the end of story anyway ...
All the __ [people] glad to see, I come back and all
   that!

Carolyn: How did you find water along the way?

Ranji: Oh, water! Just riding along side the pipeline.
Had, water-tap everywhere!
All along! *[Laughs.]*
Yeah.

84 Speakings

Carolyn: When would that have been? Do you know about what year that would have been, or how old you were then?

Ranji: Oh, I was, I was, I was old, a good size.
But, I really can't tell you time, but it's —
and after that, when,
and when the town was, Burtville town was closing up, see,
and we don' know where to go,
and so we come down and made a home at Mt Margaret Mission, you see. About nineteen, you know.
I might have been there, twenty to twenty-four.

Working with all them
— _ in the *Drop in a Bucket* —
building houses as a teenager there.
That was, some of my job there.
Mr Schenk, he teach me how to build, build a house, you see.

So, when they,
I left Mt Margaret Mission about four or five years ago, and I come down and stop in Coolgardie for a while, and I stop in Kurrawang.*

And I, I started getting blind.
So they, come and put me in the Sister Poor, you know.

Sister Poor took me down to Perth and we, got the eye fixed up.
Yeah.
They give me, they give me five months here, in

---

* *Kurrawang — Kurrawang Christian Community, located between Kalgoorlie and Coolgardie.*

	the, in the Sister Poor. 'Cause they, they, they didn't come for me yet. *[Laughs.]* So I had to stop a bit longer.
Carolyn:	I was wondering if you can tell me some stories about some people. Do you remember Mulga Joe?
Ranji:	Mulga Joe, yes!
Carolyn:	Yeah? Can you tell me any stories about him?
Ranji:	Oh yes. Yeah. He go out, and picking up bits of gold here, and give them to Mr Schenk, and he, he get a nugget there and he give it to Mr Schenk. And Mr Schenk went and bought a two-room house for him! Yeah. Yeah. Mulga Joe. A lot of the people there, they all, they all passed away, you see, now. I'm the only, the oldest, oldest people here. But the others, the old people what I know, just all finish!
Carolyn:	What about a man called Wawuja, or Ginger? Do you —
Ranji:	Who?
Carolyn:	Wawuja, or Ginger? He was at Moore River too. I

don't think he was from Mt Margaret, I think he was from somewhere else.

Ranji: Oh yeah.
Yeah.

Carolyn: He helped those people escape. You don't know him?

Ranji: No.
But, but what his name?

Carolyn: Ginger was his nickname.

Ranji: Old Ginger, yeah!!
Yeah.
Yeah. Well, and see, a ___ of the old blokes, are all called aroun' here, Ginger Stoke.
Ginger Stoke.
Yeah. He used to, used to work around here.

Who was the other one?

Carolyn: Oh, there was Jinera — what about a blind man called Jinera?

Ranji: Old Jinera. Yes.
Yeah.
I see him in, in early part of the Mt Margaret Mission, old Jinera, yeah.
The others there, they'd lead him.
Lead him with a, with a, with a stick, you see?
He'd carry a stick, and he'd, he'd come along behind there.
Yeah.
I had, I had, my mother, blind like that.
Yeah. My other step-brother used to carry around with a stick, you see.

Yeah, yeah.
They used to come along behind there, holding the

	stick there. And you go along in front of him, you see for him, you know. ...
Carolyn:	Is it all right for me to say these people's names, now they've passed on? Is it okay for me to ask you about them?
Ranji:	Yeah, yeah! No problem.
Carolyn:	There was an old lady called Mudarn ... Do you remember her? Old Mudarn?
Ranji:	Old Mudarn? Mmm. [Long pause.]
Carolyn:	What about Jidu?
Ranji:	Old Jidu, yes! They call him, old King Jidu. Yeah. He used to, he was in Mt Margaret Mission, early time. Yeah. Mr Schenk pick him up in Laverton, and took him to Mt Margaret Mission. Old Jidu. He got two sons. Yeah. Kunjil, and, the other one was deaf and dumb.* And, old Jidu, he was, the first wife, he called her old man Jolbadgeri. Any more?

---

*   'one was deaf and dumb' — Dion Dirk.

Carolyn: There was someone called Moongoodie.

Ranji: Who?

Carolyn: Moongoodie, and his wife was Thalbin. Thalbin.

Ranji: Thalbin, Moongoodie!
Yeah, yeah.
They call him old, old George Moongoodie.
Yeah. George Moongoodie.
Yeah.

Carolyn: Then there was another one, whose nickname was Gadajilbi.

Ranji: Gadajilbi, yeah.
Yeah.
Yeah.
Gadajilbli, that's —
Gadajilbi, old Gadajilbi, that's —
I think,
I think he got a son.
Old Gadajilbi.
Oh, I can't think of it.
Gadajilbi, old Gadajilbi.
I can't think this —

He always belonged to Laverton.
I don't know where he come from, though.
I don't know where he come from. He come from bush, I think.
And, he, he settled in Laverton.

Oh, old Gadajilbi.
Old Gadajilbi, he was a __.

Where did you get that old Gadajilbi —
you get, he got, he got Mrs with him?

Carolyn: Yes. Tharnmoon.

Ranji:	Old Tharnmoon! Yeah, yeah. Old Tharnmoon! Gadajilbi and Tharnmoon. That's — that's old Tharnmoon, he* got a, he got a son. I can't think of — yeah, Gadajilbi.
Carolyn:	What about old Wunu? Wunu, and Biyuwarra?
Ranji:	Who?
Carolyn:	There was a man called Wunu, and his wife was Biyuwarra, and they had a baby called Elyon. Old Wunu.
Ranji:	Old Wunu! Yeah, and Biyuwarra!
Carolyn:	Yeah, they were walking back from Mogumber too.
Ranji:	Oh yeah.
Carolyn:	Do you know any stories about them?
Ranji:	No.
Carolyn:	Okay. How about a man called Bill Carrigg? I don't know how to pronounce his Wongai name Nganjur?
Ranji:	Who?
Carolyn:	Nganjur? I don't think I can say this name properly! Nganjur, he was known as Bill Carrigg.

---

* *Tharnmoon, he — he/she is used interchangeably. Tharnmoon is a woman.*

Ranji: Mmm.

Carolyn: What about Tom Harris? Bithulyi?

Ranji: Tom who?

Carolyn: Harris.

Ranji: Tom Harris!
Yeah, yeah!

Carolyn: You remember him?

Ranji: Yeah.

Old Tom Harris. Yeah.
He's, he's been ta'en down too?

Carolyn: He was sent down to Mogumber

Ranji: Oh yeah,

Carolyn: and he walked back to Mt Margaret, as well.

Ranji: Yeah?
Mmm.

[Long pause.]

Carolyn: What about any other old stories from the beginning of Mt Margaret. Can you tell me any other stories about what happened in those days?

Ranji: Well, there was a lot of people, but some of them, they all pass away.

Yeah, there,
Old Tharnmoon, yeah, I'm trying to find his son.
Old, old Gadajilbi.
Gadajilbi and old Tharnmoon.
Yeah.

Sister:*   Do you want a cup of tea Ranji?

Ranji: Yes please, Sister.

[Tape is paused.]

                Yeah, well, I've done a lot of work for Mr Schenk
                    when I come down there in Mt Margaret Mission.
                I sank about four, four wells for him!
                There's one near to the kitchen house,
                and another one up the back of that hill there,
                at the battery there, where we __ __, you see,
                another one near the tennis club there,
                and another __ __ down there.
                Only one well down the Mt Margaret Mission, and
                    they couldn't keep the water up, you see.

Carolyn: Yeah. What about in the bush, how would you
                    find, how would people find water in the bush?

Ranji: Oh, water.
                They got to go, they got to find water and have a
                    look in the rockholes.
                Yeah. Some, you get water in the rockhole,
                the hole might be about three four depth you see.
                Yeah. So you have plenty water.
                And sometime you, might be soak,
                you got to dig the soak out and get the water, you
                    see.

Carolyn: Yeah, like in a dry river?

Ranji: Yeah.
                Some, if you going to another water rockhole,
                some of them, a little bit, little bit, you know,

---

   *   *Sister* — One of the Staff at the Nursing Home, whom Ranji addressed as Sister, came through the hallway/sitting area with a tea trolley and the conversation turned to other matters for a while. The tape was paused while the Sister had a chat.

a bit too far to get to in one day.
You, you'll have to,
you'll have to leave, aft'noon or something,
you, you go along and you camp, dry camp in the night,
and you get up early in morning,
and you'll be there dinner time,
the next water.

Yeah, you got to work it that way, you see.

If you, if you close up to there, you might just go,
just get up in the morning and go,
you get there aft'noon, about three or four o'clock,
and you'll get there.

Yeah, some of them little bit,
long, long,
far apart, and long way.

Yeah,
You got to, you got to camp halfway or something,
and make a early start, and you'll be there.
Yeah. [Laughs.]

Carolyn: Say the people who got taken down to Perth — when they were around Perth, they wouldn't know the bush very well. It wouldn't be like up here, they wouldn't know where all the water was. So they would just have to guess, wouldn't they?

Ranji: Yeah, yeah.
Yeah, yeah.
They got to,
they mightn't be, they mightn't be they know the, you know,
the gnamma hole or something,
the rockhole or something.

They might keep going to rock, to a granite rock.
They might get some water there, you see.
...
But if you go along, go along the pipeline, you get
   plenty of water!
[Laughs.]

Yeah, well when I finish at Dumbleyung,
and I come back, and,
I come back, went back to Burtville,
and Burtville finish.
And, the squatter said, 'Put them, put the sheep in
   the paddock,' in that Burtville town, you see!

That's, the town always all full, of everything,
and they had the sheep, the sheep take it.
We had to, we had to make a home in Mt Margaret
   Mission, see.

Carolyn: And at Mt Margaret, the police couldn't come and
   take you away to Perth?

Ranji: Oh no. No.
Yeah, they won't come there
   when Mr Schenk there.
'Cause he, he,
he the boss of the, Aborigine people, you see.

Yeah, so,
Old Gadajilbi.
His __ name —
Gadajilbi.
Eldangwyn!

Carolyn: Ah, you got it!
You've remembered it!

Ranji: Yeah!
Eldangwyn.

Carolyn: Eldangwyn?

Ranji:	Yeah. He's gone, a long time ago. When the mission was started, they all finish. Yeah, somewhere, 1924, somewhere around there. 'Cause I come there myself in 1924. To Mt Margaret Mission from, back from Burtville. Yeah. Old Jidu, old Jidu, he had two sons, one's deaf and dumb, another one, the other one's all right. Yeah.
Carolyn:	Do you know why the police took Jidu when they took him away in 1921?
Ranji:	I don't know! But, but, they took Jidu, they took Jidu too?
Carolyn:	Yeah, they took him too. But he escaped as well and they all —
Ranji:	They all come back?
Carolyn:	Yeah, they nearly all come back.
Ranji:	Yeah! Yes, that's right, a lot of people they go away and they, they — some to Mogumber, and when they grow big, and they get a job there, and then then they can't come back to see father and mother. Yeah! We can't see 'em. I know a bloke, who went there. Jack McKay ... He, he passed away now, but he, he, passed away too.

Mr Ranji McIntyre

(Spoken on 11 December 1997)

The second conversation with Mr Ranji McIntyre, also recorded at the Little Sisters of the Poor Home for the Aged, in Kalgoorlie.

...

Carolyn:	You went there when you were quite young didn't you, to Mt Margaret?
Ranji:	Yeah. Yeah, I born in Burtville for a long time, in the first war.
Carolyn:	You were born around the first war?
Ranji:	Yes, before the first war. Yeah, because I remember all those people who were called up to the war. I was a goodsized kid then! I had a playmate then, he was Tommy Lowe. He's somewhere around, in 1908. ... And, you went right back, Perth, and you come back?
Carolyn:	Yeah. I went right back down to Perth again,
Ranji:	Yeah,
Carolyn:	and then I came back up here again, just for a few days.

Ranji: Oh yeah.
And how'd you get on with them there family trees?

Carolyn: The family trees? Going well — I'm getting it sorted out.

Ranji: You got it all fixed yet, or?

Carolyn: No, no not all fixed yet. I'm still, still trying to find out about some of those people. Yeah, I was asking you about old Jidu and people like that last time.

Ranji: Old Jidu, yeah.
Yeah.
I was, when I met him at the start,
he was the first old bloke, sitting down at Mt Margaret Mission!
Yeah, he's the one, Mr Schenk picked him up.
Took him up this place there,
when the Mission started, he was right there.

He had two sons,
one deaf and dumb, he couldn't talk.
The other one all right, his name, Kunjil.
...
Well there, Mr Schenk went there and got that Mt Margaret Mission
in Morgans* one time, Mt Margaret Mission.

And he put up the Mission place.
For all the people.
Go out and gather all the people,
and bring up, and learn them in the school, you see.

He learned me how to build a house.
And, I can build a house!
When I first come there, I don't know how to build

---

*   *Morgans — old mining town (near Mt Morgan) on the Kalgoorlie–Laverton railway line.*

a house.
'Oh,' he said, 'I'll, I'll learn you every day,' he reckons.
So he learned me, and I can build a house myself.
[Laughs.]

Carolyn: Did you learn English when you got there to Mt Margaret, or somewhere else?

Ranji: I, I learn English from the old prospector.
Us, before, we couldn't go to school then,
they won't allow nothing.
No, no Aborigines go to school.

Only one bloke, Jimmy Brennan.
Yeah. When his mother passed away,
and, and the white people, they claimed that boy, you see.
They kept him,
kept him, and,
grow him up and send him to Laverton school.
He's the only one boy been in school.
Nobody else.
And the kids there,
send him away to Laverton,
send him down to Mogumber.

Some of them come back,
and some of them didn't come back.
They stay there and they're all finish.

But, us, we, we never picked up.*
We lived, working Burtville,
working for this bloke, Jack O'Loughlan.
He's been a policeman one time,
and then, when you finish the police job,
he and another mate

---

* *'we never picked up' — we never got picked up by the police and sent away.*

went and got so many head o' cattle.

And, keep the cattle out there.
And, we work with him.

Yeah.
Looking after the cattle.
And after that, when they not too good a friends.
So they, they split up.
He took his half of cattle,
and, and, old Tom Jame took his half.
They kept them in a different place, you see?

The other one gets a windmill, to pump the water for the cattle.
The other one get a fire, going to light the, the old battle __, all this, with a steamroller, everything.
To pull the water.
With a steam roller.
So he pumped water up, out o' the bottom of that there well.
__ __ pumping water for him.
And then, __ __, he shot his mate!
Yeah.

Carolyn: Rough times!

Ranji: Yes it is!

We went out and get,
that morning, we went out and got them cattle for him.
You know, his cows and his calves, we bring them in, just so long as we don' touch Tom James', see.
Well, we done that.

And we, was bringing the cattle in to put it in the yard, and Tom James come along, and put a stop to it!
He said, what we doing with the cattle?

I said, 'Oh, well, they Jack's cattle.'
'I think you better leave it here,' he reckons, 'and
 go and tell Jack to get it himself!'
You see?

So we let the cattle go,
and all the cattle were all mixed up with the others,
 see?
'Cause, a lot of them were sitting in the sand dump
 there
Where there's all these shady tree.
Soon as we let him go, the cattle's all mixed up!

Well, __ __ we went to tell him: 'He said, "You go
 and tell Jack to come and get it himself!"'
Well, that's what he said to us,
and we, and we went.
And Jack's at __ __ [Major Stream] see?

And, he asks me 'Why'd he want to stop you for?'
And I said, 'I don't know!'
'He said, he told me to tell you that you've got to
 go down and get your cattle yourself.'

Yeah. Well, he don't like it, you see.

Yeah.
Load up gun, left him,
and got on his horse and had a row down there.
And the bloke hit him,
got a __ __ [cross-bar] spanner and hit him in the
 back, you see.

And, spur his horse, he gallop back to the house and,
break in the door and grab the gun,
and got on the horse and went,
and shot him!
Put three —
Put three shot in him!

	Yeah. He went, he went and got the cattle, got the cattle all on his own!
	…
Carolyn:	What about those prospectors who you used to go and talk to when you were young — can you tell me some stories about those prospectors?
Ranji:	Oh, yeah. We go there every Sunday, because one of them, he's the old Christian people, you see? Yeah, well we go there, and he shown to me, about Jesus. Preacher, you know? And he played the organ, and he played the tin whistle, and we all sit down and listen. Yeah. Yeah, every Sunday. He was, in Burtville. Yeah. We used to go out in the bush and pull sandalwood for him, too, out in the bush. Camping out for, might be, months, or anything like that. Horse and cart, go out and pull some wood. You pull it for him, and then, he clean it. When you get, get a truck o' wood, you finish and you come home. And the people go out, and pick the wood up, and take it to Laverton. __ __ in the train, and sell it. First to Kalgoorlie, here.

Carolyn: Yeah.
And they used to give you some pay for doing that work?

Ranji: No, you don't get, you don't get much.
Yeah. Might get a
pair of suit, a suit of clothes.

Carolyn: Would it take many days to cut enough wood for a truck load?

Ranji: No, might be little bit, might be, say, four weeks or something.
They're not, they're not, they're not too <u>easy</u>,*
anyway!
It's <u>hard</u> work.
Yeah.
...
When I was working, I'd set the camps on my own.
— —
Might have to, go to another rockhole,
and we might have stopped,
and did a bit more around there, see?

Carolyn: At another rockhole?

Ranji: Yeah.

Carolyn: You had to go where there was water?

Ranji: Oh yeah!
Could be,
you've got a, you've got a two hundred gallon tank.
Well, you could take the horse and cart and go and get a load of wood, you see? Might be, might be a

---

* '<u>easy</u>' — underlined words are words on which the speaker placed strong emphasis; such words were also elongated.

week, or more.

Go out there.
You might be out in the bush,
and the rain come along and fill the rockholes up
    and you're, you're right for water, you see. Yeah.
Yeah.
You go out and do that, wintertime, while it's cool.
Not summertime.

Summertime, he works in the mine.
A bit cooler.

Cut sandalwood in wintertime, while there's
    everything cool.

Carolyn: And what about food?
What about getting a feed, when you're out there
    in the bush?

Ranji: Oh, well, be short of tucker,
you've, you've got to go to town to get some, you
    see.
Might take a day to get to town, to get them stores
    and come back.
Get something that would last you
'til you get a truck of wood, you see.

Carolyn: Yes.
Did you used to catch goannas and kangaroos — ?

Ranji: Oh yeah! Yeah, plenty!
Plenty kangaroos.
That old prospector, he always got a gun.
Yeah, we go and shoot rabbits, or kangaroo. Yeah.
...

Carolyn: Do you know any stories about people who went
    down to Mogumber, down to Perth, and who
    came back again?

Ranji: Yeah.
I think there's some people come back,
but there's some of them didn't come back.

Well, they didn't come back on the train, they, they
  cut across the bush.
From Perth to somewhere.
They cut across to Laverton.

Yeah.
See, night time, they look to where the stars
  coming from.
See all the stars.
Don't know what to have a look, you better to read
  the star, where you going.

Of course, there's some of them come back all right,
and some of them didn't.
Don't know what happened.
Might have stayed there, and might have finished
  there.
Don't know.

Carolyn: What about those old policeman in Laverton?

Ranji: Oh, they a bit rough!
Yeah.
There's a bloke come there,
this, this bloke,
his name's
Donegan.

He come up there and he took half,
half the people from Laverton to,
to Cosmo Newbery.*

---

* *Cosmo Newbery* — Cosmo Newbery Native Settlement, established in January 1940 by the Department of Native Affairs under A O Neville, managed by AJ Donegan. Refer to Appendix A9 for additional notes on Cosmo Newbery.

And Schenk took half,
and he took half.*

Yeah.
He took them up there,
and he's treating them Wongais a bit rough.
Makes them __ __, brushwood fences. Yeah.

Carolyn: That's Mr Donegan, he used to do that?

Ranji: Yeah.
But he, he didn't stay there too long because he finished with them,
and he got going,
and all the people come back to, to Laverton.

Carolyn: They had a rough time with Donegan.

Ranji: Yeah! Because he's calling all the peoples there, names.
'Quot-bot', and 'dolly-pot', and 'pannikins' and all.

...

---

* 'Schenk took half, and he took half' — Donegan, empowered as local Protector of Aborigines, forcibly removed people from Mt Margaret Mission and took them to Cosmo Newbery.

Queenie Donaldson

(Spoken on 11 December 1997.)

The conversation was recorded at Auntie Queenie Donaldson's home in the Kurrawang Christian Community, near Kalgoorlie.

Auntie Queenie is one of the most senior Wongutha women living in the area.

Carolyn: Shall we start the tape at Karonie?*

Queenie: Yeah.
We was there.
No school or anything.
No home.
Just stay in the bush.

Oh, so, we gather in Mr Neville time.
He sent me out to go to Mt Margaret Mission.
School there.
So, he, they got a turn-out for us to go Mt Margaret.
So we went then.
They took us there.
I remember, one night, we camped __ __ then the afternoon we got to Mt Margaret.

Carolyn: You were walking all that way?

Queenie: No. They had a camel team. They arranged it for us.

Carolyn: They arranged it all for you?

---

* *Karonie — area around a Government ration depot of the same name on the 'Transline' (Transcontinental Railway Line).*

Queenie: Yeah.

Carolyn: Is that your families, who had —?

Queenie: No, the government.

They take us.

Went to Mt Margaret, __ __ we and children, __ __ more people.

When we got to Mission, Mt Margaret Mission,
we got in the dark place —
when we in the dormitories.
Mt Margaret.
The dark room, we went straight in there.

So the parents what took us there, they went back to Karonie.

Carolyn: And that would have been a strange thing, being in a dormitory, when you were used to being in the bush.

Queenie: Yeah. Yeah.
But we was all right.
Some, all the girls who know us, they was there.

Carolyn: Yeah.
Do you know why the government wanted you to go there?

Queenie: 'Cause there's no school in Karonie.
You been there, to Karonie?

Carolyn: No, I haven't been to Karonie. I went to —

Queenie: Oh, oh, it's just like a desert.
Just a __ __.
...

Carolyn: I heard from Mr Johnston some stories about some

people from around the Laverton area who went, who got taken by the police, down to Mogumber.

And they walked home. Do you know the —?

Queenie: To Mission?

Carolyn: Yeah, they walked back and that started the Mission.

Queenie: Yes, some come there.
Well. It's a slow journey from Mogumber.
...
Taken away down there.

Carolyn: So, those people that went to Mogumber, in the very early days, did they often come back?

Queenie: Oh, one did.
I never heard of any one else.
Mrs Taylor, Ada. She came back. They sent her back.

Some of them run away!

Carolyn: Do you know about those ones who ran away?

Queenie: Oh, no.

But they were saved. A lot of people ___ ___.

Carolyn: Yes. They were brave people, the ones who ran away.

Queenie: Yeah.
They know where to go!
I reckon I'd get lost!

Carolyn: It's a long way to walk!
And they didn't know where the water was, or anything like that?

Queenie: They know where they going though.
Yeah. Some of them older ones, with them.

That's all.

Rosie Meredith

(Spoken on 10 December 1997)

A conversation with Auntie Rosie Meredith (Green), Uncle Fred Meredith, Jane Beasley (Meredith), Auntie Wyallie and Miriam Brownley at Auntie Wyallie's house in Kalgoorlie.

Auntie Rosie was born in the 1920s in the Darlot area. Her youth was spent in the bush, successfully avoiding the police and others who might send her away, but in 1940 the Minister for Native Affairs issued a warrant for Rosie's removal to the Moore River Settlement. Later that year, Auntie Rosie successfully eluded a party of trackers, the Laverton policeman and Native Affairs employee Donegan, only to be handed over to the Leonora police by a station owner. She was transported to Mogumber. Auntie Rosie made a number of successful escapes from Mogumber in an attempt to get home to her family and her country.[1]

Rosie: I born in Darlot.
    I grew up round Mulga Queen, and Bandya Station,
    'cause my Mum always work on the Station.
    You know, clearing,
    on the mine,
    or fencing,
    or something, you know.

And, the other side of Mulga Queen,
Oodnooi,*
these people came up for looking for someone, and I was frightened.
I was younger than you!
Policeman were there too
but he wasn't looking for me; he was looking for the other troubles.

Yeah. And later on, we went away,
to Darlot, and left the families.
And then we went to Biddie's Patch,
not all of us, but my mother and father, went there.

And Donegan came up,
Donegan looking there.

Fred: Protector, of Native kids!

Rosie: He never found me anyway, I got going!

Carolyn: He was looking for
children?

Rosie, Wyallie, Fred: Yeah!

Rosie: Anybody, not only children.
Anybody.
I took off! He's not going to catch me!

Old Mr Donegan,
I don't know whether he took a policeman or not, looking for me.
I run away,
with no blankets, nothing.
When I run away, they pick my mother up,
took her away,

---

* Oodnooi — *Wongutha name for a place called Hutnooi in English.*

             took her to Cosmo,
             Cosmo Newbery.

Fred: And even think, the policeman! <u>Disgraceful</u>.

Rosie: They know I was there, at the Station,
             but they never say nothing, 'til later.
             When Donegan started off.

             They had to say it, they didn't want to get in
                 trouble.

             And the Station owner, Mr Warren,
             took me to Leonora.
             Drive me right to the police station!
             I was in the gaolhouse for a couple of days.
             There's a little room for the prisoners;
             they put me in there and locked the door.
             I just kept quiet — it's not going to help me if I
                 make a noise.

             Next day I was going on the train.
             They didn't put the handcuffs on me;
             they locked the door.
             The police worker and his wife,
             Mr and Mrs Mohr,
             and a daughter, took me to Perth.
             They take me to the lockup in Perth.
             And I stayed some nights there too.
             Perth.
             We had to sleep on the floor.

             I can't <u>sleep</u> at night!
             The policeman was walking 'round with all them
                 <u>keys</u> rattling.
             Looking through the little pigeon-hole, in the door.
             See if I'm still there!!

             You'd think I was a criminal, killed somebody,
             the way they was carrying on!

I was about fifteen!

I'd, I'd make up sleep, shut my eyes
when they come around looking, but I'm awake,
   right up to the morning.

The morning — breakfast, I can't eat it.
It's only a rough one, really.

And then, the policeman took me to Moore River
   Settlement.
What's the name of that — Mogumber, now.
And I got off, at Mogumber.
Yeah.

They had all the people waiting there, them girls,
   to see this new girl come in. *[Laughs.]*
When I got there, <u>big mob of people</u>!
They were all watching me, staring.
I don't know <u>any</u> of them!
I was frightened!
But one girl comes along.
Belinda Jacob. She comes along and makes friends.
'Come on, they're always staring at anybody new.'
I was happy for one friend anyway!

And from there, I stayed there.
And another girl settle, same place!
Bessie Carnamah.
From Carnamah Station,
Mt Magnet way, somewhere.

We stayed there for a while.
Maybe one year or something like that.

Wyallie: One year.

Rosie: 'Cause I had no friend, to go with!

   Bessie Carnamah comes there.
   Then, we took off!

In the afternoon, every day,
they let us go and walk around anywhere we like,
we can sit down anywhere.
We made our minds up
to run away!
We take a blanket,
we're sitting under that tree.
In the afternoon, about four or five,
we cross that river — <u>deep one</u> too, but we wait 'til
    there's no water.

They have the roll call at night.
When we're climbing up the other side of the river,
crossing the river, going away,
they call the roll,
singing out for me,
'Rosie Green!'
We're off!

It's not dark yet.
We head off, we come to a big hill, near that Mission.
We wait 'til dark, and then we cross the road.
It's a busy road,
the main road for Geraldton.
We don't want to be seen!

We went away, we had nothing for dinner, went
    right up to — what's that mission?

Fred: New Norcia.

Rosie: Yeah. There.
    We had that, the other side, nothing.

Then,
'Oh look, Bessie,' I said, 'I can't go! See, when you
    go home, you got to go on your own, to
    Carnamah, to your people,
and I got to go on my own, to Laverton, to my
    people.

It'll be too far for me on my own, you know!'

Travelling, too far!
It's a long way to walk!

So, I said, 'I'll go back.'
She's a brave girl!
She said, 'Good bye, and maybe we might meet
    again!'
We did meet again, and we run away again!

I went to that mission. *[Laughs.]*
All the other people there.
Noongars.

So, I ran away from that Mogumber.
And they took me to the Moora Police Station and
    they put me in the gaolhouse.
You know, while they waiting for court, ten o'clock
    court.
They come up and pick me up, went over there.

But I never done no talking.
The policeman talking.

Saying it, you know:
'No wonder, that's why they running away,' he
    said.
'She has to go back home.'

I didn't talk there.
They done the talking.

Yeah. Yeah.
They saying:
'Missing their family,' and that.
He told them: 'She has to go home to her parents
    and her country.'

Never mind.

This bloke Wandan, he's going to that Mogumber.
So,
they send me there,
and they took me there,
and I stay there for a while then.
Waiting, *[laughs]* for somebody else to turn up!
   [Laughs.]
Yeah.
Waiting in that one place.

Me and that girl, Bessie Carnamah, at night-time,
at night-time, before the roll called, we go.
See, we ran off when there's no <u>water</u>; the river's
   too <u>deep</u>!
So anyway, then I come back, and she went on.

And later on, maybe a month, or maybe earlier, she
   turned up again!
They sent her back!

We sitting there worrying,
we're worrying about running away!
'One day we'll get going!'

They got a fireplace at Mogumber.
We call it the police station.
The trackers sit around there.
We got to sit with them.
Us girls got to sit down there.

We're thinking, 'We're still going to run away!
I don't care what you lot say,
We're not going to stay here!'

And, another girl turned up,
my mob, my family, of my Auntie,
and we all, we stayed there.

Fred: You say the name.

Rosie: Ivy.

Fred: Patterson.

Rosie: Yeah.

Jane: She was also called Ivy of Wiluna.

Rosie: Yeah.

    Yeah.
So, I went back again,
at Mogumber again, wait for some more girls.

When Auntie Ivy come along, we three, you know,
    we talk it over for a long time, you know.
We asking one another, 'You like it here?'
'Nuh!'
'All right, there's two of you, one day we'll have to
    leave this!'
Get going.

One afternoon, we ready!
You know, we can walk around anywhere we want.
This time, all the other girls coming back.
Us three, and blanket, we gone!
We took our blankets with us! To run away with!
We been gone for long — nobody knows.
Then there was roll call there.

Line all the girls up:
Name,
Name,
Name.
Come to these <u>three names</u> — no answer!!

Nothing.
We gone!
Running away!
Well, you know, when you're in
place like that, you don't know anyone there!

And, anyway, we gone then, when that Bessie come back.
'Cause she know the way,
until we get to the other side, where we'll know where to go.
We're going to travel along to where she come from, and then we two got to travel together.

We gone, the three of us.

And later on, we went to this big hill, waited there!
Got to wait a bit, you know, they been looking for us.
So we stayed there in the bush, right up to dark.
Then we, crossed this <u>big main</u> road, with car coming, one after another, too. When there's a gap there, we <u>quickly</u> run across.

Anyway, going along, along,
away from the road, we walked.
Going along — we see this cat, 'hsss!'
coming out of a burrow.
This cat dragging a rabbit along!

Ohh! See that poor cat drop the rabbit,
and see it move a bit, the rabbit!
Cat only bite him up here in the throat, not the whole bit.
Good one, too!
We get that rabbit!
Poor cat! Never mind — he can get another one.
Took the rabbit a long way.
Make a fire, clean it all out and everything.
We cook him and have a feed!

So we go along.
We find little creeks, you know.
I say: 'Somebody been looking for us here!'
'See this track here!'

Jane: Trackers!

Rosie:	It made us move __ away from the road. Going along, and we come to — What's that, Wongan Hills? What's that place? Miling there somewhere too, ___ up that way there, too. We walked along, went to this, what's that place I said?
Fred:	Wongan Hills?
Rosie:	What's that other town? Can't think of that town now! Wubin! That one. We seen this bloke outside the town. Ivy went along, up to the house, for water. This car pulled in, this truck, you know! We got on the back, they're drunk, too. That bloke's drunk. And he might go telling the Police! We got onto this truck, he took us five miles. 'You girls wait here!' I said 'Yeah, we'll wait here.' This is the five mile from Wubin, the big dam. He said, 'Wait here, I'll come back.' And first, he going the right way where we want to go. Now, he want to go back there! 'Right. We'll wait here!' The three of us said it. We not waiting! We gone! On that same road where he going! Going along, see that light coming back. We <u>hide</u> in the bush. Gone past and we go on.

When he coming back, we off again!
He might be telling the police!

Long way! That's the only ride we had, that five
   mile ride.
We're thinking — if we get too many rides, they
   might have the police waiting for us!

And, we have a little sleep. I'm not laying down
   long!

Something making noise!
'What's that?'
A <u>chain</u>, you know! That dray, or whatever, you
   got to go before cars, when you've got horse.
   Making a <u>noise</u>, that chain.
We walking off the side of the road 'til it's gone
   past.
Laying down quiet, so quiet.
When it gone, we go on.

Travelling.
No breakfast.
We got no food!

So, we going along, __ __ __ __.

And this ... bloke, when we go through, he's seen us
   run to the tree,
but this was, we was away from the road,
and we still going along.
And, we hear that same hooves, going back that way.
Going back to town, must be!
Them two want food now, __.
They going to have a look; that bloke's got feed
   there!
I said, 'Hey, don't take the lot! You better hurry up,
   you might get caught!'
Them two got a bit of the flour and a bit of each
   thing, you know.

'Little bit, little bit, don't take the lot!'
And so, we got it, from __ that bloke!
So, we got it, and we off!

We going along the fence there, the netting fence.
Road there too.
A car turn off, coming along, and we got ourselves seen.
And this bloke: 'What are you lot doing there? Where are you going?'
'We going *that* way. I'm going to see my brother,' Bessie saying this!
We show him the other way to where we going, back to front!
But we really going *that* way, north.
'Yes. Well, get out of here. I don't want you lot frightening the sheep!'
'We not killing your sheep or chasing 'em or anything! We just going! That's all.'
'Well, get out quick as you can!'
Ohh, so take off the other side into the bush.
We going on the other side of the netting fence, the rabbit proof fence.
He might get the police!

Bessie said, 'I'm going to see my brother, working on the station out here.' Telling lies!

We're too cunning!
We're off!!

'Hey! Where we going to get our water?'
When we went bush, see an old windmill there, got no windmill top.
'We got to try!' I said.
'We got a wire? Put it down.' Billy-can, you know.
Vvm, vvm, vvm, long way, we got it!
Pull it up, have a drink!
Taste it.

'Hey! Good water!'
So we got it and fill it right up!

We can't drink it all at once.
We don't know where the next water is!

And night-time comes, we go on the road,
and then daytime, we off in the bush.

We going along, we come to this __ end of billy.*
Like it or not, we just tried it. Went to a farmer's
   house.
Somebody asked, 'Can we get our water out of a
   dam now?'
'You not getting water out of the dam, you can get
   your water here!' the lady said. 'I give you water,
   rainwater.'
And, she give us some food.
So we got going, thanked them and the whole lot,
   and went away.

One morning we come to another station.
And one bloke there, Wongai, you know, he's a
   police pimp! He'll go and tell the police!
So, we got to go right around!
We didn't come into there, we swerved around.

Well, going along, we come to this rockhole here.
We're looking for water,
we didn't look on the other side — someone there!
Somebody up there waving, shouting from the
   thicket, 'Ahh, wait!'
So we, 'What are we going to do now?' we said.
Nothing we can do,
we have to stand and wait, see what they're going
   to say!

---

*   'end of billy' — they ran out of water; the billy that they carried
     water in was empty.

Lady came: 'You got any feed?'
'No, we're travelling.'
'Come along! Come up to my place along here.'
Good people, mother lives in Mt Magnet.
So, we have a bit of a spell, staying there with
  them, all afternoon.
'Don't say anything you're going, to this old man,
  one bloke there. He'll be telling the police!' Or,
  maybe not police, but the station owner.
When he rode back to the station, we off!

They give us some food and another little drum,
  about that big *[indicates twenty centimetre
  diametre]*, for carrying water along.
We gone!
They make the damper, and they give us that,
send us on the road with that.
We off, yeah.

Long, long. We come to this place.
'Go along', she said.
I looking at her hair.
When first I met that girl, you know, Bessie, 'What
  happened to your hair?'
'Oh, I born like that,' she said. Green, <u>all colours</u>,
  they're pretty!
When I first seen that, I said, 'What happened to
  your hair?'

But anyway, she said, 'When you come to this mill,
  this is the place. You know you been asking
  about my hair? Well, this is the place,' she
  reckoned, 'my father used to shoot a lot of
  pigeons here! We used to eat a lot. That's how I get
  this hair here.'
You know, __ in the mother, you know, pregnant?
When they shooting, that's the one that put that
  kid there, that hair there.
I never seen anybody's hair like that! All those

<u>colours</u>, like <u>pigeons</u>!
Yeah, lovely.

Ah, my friend, she passed away now.
Two gone, two, the other one, my aunt.

Anyway, 'This is the place, you know you talking about my hair,' she said, 'this is the place where my father shoot a lot of pigeons.'
In the afternoon, when they come in for water.
They eat 'em.

It's still a long way from Mt Magnet.

Yeah. Long way yet. Yeah. I don't know what that place.

We come this one station now *[claps]*.
That's where she got to walk, split up with us.
Early in the morning, at that place.
She said, 'I'm going back that way now, to Carnamah Station! Follow the fence.'
<u>All along</u> to her place ground.
'I have to leave you two friends,' she reckons. 'I have to go back on this road home. I hope you get there safely.'

That's the last time I seen her, my friend.

We going along.
'Now, don't lose that road, there.
Remember: along that road,
follow that road,
all the way to this, this station,' she said.
'Big,' she said, 'big station there! And they pimp too!
So you just
go around, or, go the other way,
and follow that road <u>all</u> the way to Mt Magnet.'
So we did!

And then, rain come too!
But we had, picked up a — Road Boards, you know when they do the roads? They camp, and they left a bit of canvas. Like this table, you see? When this rain come, we got to get under that!

Long, long time.
And we looking at it too.

This mob of <u>dogs</u>,
and one man walking.
Talk about I don't know how many dogs!
I say, 'We got to go steady now, they might want to kill us!'
Dogs, you know!
So many dogs!
He been at that station...
Sitting there at the other station, you know.
And then he going back to Mt Magnet with a <u>mob of dogs</u>.
All tracks, all kinds of tracks, all sorts of colours, and sizes!
All along.
We going, must be day behind or two days behind. That's good! I wouldn't have wanted to met those dogs!

Come to that station.
Cheeky one: ask for way, but we knew!
We want <u>that</u> way, but we ask back the other way.
Yeah. We going <u>that</u> way!

She said, 'Follow that <u>big main</u> road all the way to Mt Magnet.'

Going along.
At night-time we travel on the road!

After the rain though, we seen a big goanna track going along.

We got to kill this!
He, it ran, standing up, <u>big</u> one too!
We got a long stick, that big *[indicates approximately
   one metre]*, tied it on here, __ __,
   __ march far away!*
So we went in the bush and made a fire, and
   cooked it.
Waited.
A <u>big</u> one! Not really big, but big enough!!
Waited there ...
When he's cooked we pull him out.
We had a feed, and take some on.

Going on the road,
we finish that meat,
it's gone now.

Seen a <u>light</u>, when we come up the rise.
That's that Mt Magnet!!
And that daughter back there, where we meet
   them, said, 'Go, you see one light, in the creek.'
That's the killing place, the slaughter yard.
'Go a bit further, follow that long, that creek, you
   see my mother's house.'
Lonely, one house.
They've a dog, two kangaroo dog, they heard us
   coming!
Oh, they come out chasing the dog around, seen
   us!
'Oh, come in!'
They might have ring them up, or something, I
   don't know, the daughter.

And they told them, anyway, they made a big feed
   for us.

---

* *'got a long stick, that big, tied it on here... march far away'* — *They caught the goanna and tied it to a long stick which they carried between them; they walked a long way carrying it.*

And she said, 'You be careful. You want to go
   tonight, all the way?'
'Yeah.'
'Well, you better be careful, this part of the hill,' she
   said.
Hill, something bad, she reckon.
'Hey, what we gunna do now?'
Us two, by ourself, walking!
'Oh, we better camp here! And get up <u>early</u> in the
   morning, and get going!!'

Got up early, walking up that hill, and eating.
And we heard that motorbike going! ...

And, you know, there's a road right there, you can
   see the <u>dust flying</u> —
But nothing!!
We can hear the noise, but we can't see him!
'Never mind' — we didn't notice.
'Quickly! We better get going!'

Run, run, into that road there, we're looking:
   'Where is that motorbike?!'
He sort of was on us now.

And we looking for the road, or the line, going to
   Sandstone.
When we passed that road, we gunna cross across
   the other way.
This motorbike come along — I can't even see!
Gee whiz! Come along, frightening!
BBRRRM, come along one side of me, then go
   round to her.
You can't see!!

BBRRM, like this big flash motorbike noise!!
BRRRM!

We running up a rough creek — big holes in that
   creek!

Wheels — it still follows! The motorbike is still
   with us!
Over to that other side, to the hill.
Went up to that hill — nothing.
Motorbike — BRRM, BRRM!
Just like — standing there, and took off!
BRRRM,
   going back!

He chase us a long way;
then he gone back.

That's the Wongai site or something, I don't know
   how to explain. They do that to the stranger.

That lady said it:
I thought about it then, just like that lady said, told
   us.
'Cause she said, 'That's the Wongai things there, on
   that hill.'
It's a wonder they never drive us into the —
   somewhere else!!

But we, away we're going that time!!
We went down to that creek, and have a _good sleep_.

And then that, _whatever_, going back. BRRM.
That motor noise going back!

Course, you wouldn't have want to have been at
   night!
Hey, that lady said it, you know!
The Wongai call it the Mungun, you know.
That hill there, _something_ in there,
Mungun country.
That's the _thing_ there!

Drive us away, because we was a stranger!
If you belong to them, they don't frighten you.
   Only the strangers!

Because you're the stranger here.

Mmm.
It went back, <u>big motorbike</u>, flash one!
Making noise, couldn't be someone doing noise
   like that noise!! BBRRM!

Gone, and we gone!

Now, we never had tea and __ __ we don' have any
   fire!
We got to go anyway now!
'We'll have to go this way!'
'Not that way, if we go that way, we'll hit the road!'
Come to the fence, the telephone wire running
   along that fence too!

Going along.
Come to this road.
'Well, this the road!'

Going along now, we going along.
Here comes a <u>little bird</u> now!!
Oh gosh, <u>everything</u> was wrong!

Little <u>brown</u> bird, little one, would be about that
   high.
Comes to where she walking, you know, Bessie.*
Lay down on road, you know!
There's the middle part of the road, there's the
   other one. I'm on this and she's on that.
Come, lay down in front of me, Vrrr, and then go
   back in front.
'Huh! We can kill that bird!'
'Don't do that!' I said. 'We'll be — you know
   what's going to happen to us? We'll be, end up
   that hill back there, you know where we were

---

* *Bessie — This is a slip. Rosie means Ivy as Bessie is no longer with them.*

running? Don't do it! Any animal, don't hit him! Just let him go!'
Well, we keep walking all the way over there.
Vrrr, vrrr.

'Hey, I'm having a rest now,' Bessie __ __.
'There's a road there and a line there!'
'Never mind! We, if we get caught, we get caught.'

And this, <u>bird</u>, still sitting there: Vrrr, Vrrr!
And then there comes a, <u>wind</u>.
Hey, mark that, talk about dust!
Vrrr!
Night-time. We got up and off!! *[Laughs.]*

We think everything been, frightening us <u>all</u> the way!
We off!

Going along.

Got to get a water.
Just this windmill here, and a station there.
station away from that windmill, away from the road, a bit.
We went there, got a bit of water. We pressed it down, see, and the water run.
'Hey, __ __ we don't want __ __, we better go!'

Going along,
on the road there.

And when we went there and seen this little mound, a goanna, we knew!
'Hey, we got to get that!' she reckoned.
'Yeah!'
'And what we gunna do now?'
We have to get a stick.
'I'll dig first, and you dig next. You stand up there at the corner —'

See, the road comes like this, to a corner.
So, she standing there.
That goanna's right on the corner too, you know, that goanna.
A big goanna in there, not <u>really</u> big one, but <u>big enough</u>!

I'm digging, digging. 'Your turn now!'
She digging now.
On, she can see that <u>tail</u> now!
'All right! When I call on you, you got to lift up, break that back!'
So, we killed it.
Just killed that, and got away from the road there, and <u>car</u> comes!
We just behind the <u>little tree</u>!
I don' think they seen 'em!

So, we going along.

And we had to have a rest somewhere, to cook the goanna.
That one too, I hate the fat — I chuck away, too fat!
Only have the tail part of that.

We come to this, <u>windmill</u>.
Got some water, and went on.

One part of it, we walking along the road too!
This <u>car</u> come along!!
But they didn' take any notice, you know.
Went on,
we get off the road now!
We don't come this far and get caught again!

We come to this Hotel there.

Sandstone Road, and the mine there, it was running then.
She went up to get a water! Someone was up there,

but he was drunk!
'Hey, __ don't mess around, we better go!'
'Cause can't get a water!
'Never mind, we'll, find a water somewhere.
    There's plenty of places!'

Never got a ride, nothing! Only that five mile ride!
Yeah.

Still we walking.
Not too many cars run there.

Come to this government well,
a bloke there.
'Hey, what we gunna do now? He might go tell on
    us!'
But he didn't!
He was a'right.
We left there, and went on to Sandstone.
He went and got the feed for us, and sent us on,
    you know.
Said, 'Go on, go right away. There's a rubbish tip
    there, but, go over that, right round that, and hit
    the road on the other side.'
The Lawlers Road.

We going along
and we got to the wrong road.
On this road, <u>nobody's</u> up and down here!
So, 'What are we going to do?'
'Eh, we going on the wrong road!'

There's a creek there.
Kangaroos have been digging around for <u>water</u>.
Water, you know, in the sand.
'I'm going to dig this creek.'
I dig in the sand — good water.

Follow this road a bit, still nobody on it!
'This must be the wrong road!'

Oh, 'We not going down this road, we going this way!'
'Never mind where this road going. __ __ by myself', I said, 'we going that way.'
We leave that road, cut off in the bush.

Going along,
we come to this, big hill.
<u>Hot</u> day!
We come up the valley, you see, there's a <u>windmill</u> down the bottom!
Big mob of sheep there too!
We went and got the water out of where they pumping the water!

Getting it out, we're getting it out.
We've got a cheek too, we sitting down under the tree!
Never mind, we went just like we <u>owned</u> the place, we sitting down by the tree there, big mob of sheep there!

Big dark clouds coming.
Rain!
And the <u>rain</u> came <u>pouring</u> down,
lightning too — I hate lightning.
Before, the ground was hard, now it's all soft!
There's lots of water laying around on the ground, here and there.
We got to get moving!
When we got to the higher ground — 'It's no good walking! We got to camp!'
We make a fire and that, __ __, we got the fire going.
We're not worried about that fire — nobody will be looking in the rain for us!!
I wonder if the musterer seen that place: 'Ashes, must have died'!!

Next morning, we off!

I went along,
Went along.

Camp another place.

It's too far to go.

'Hey,' and she reckoned,
'Hey, what about we kill one of these, lamb?'
'Ah! No way I killing any animal! If you want to
   kill him, you kill him! I don't want to be, in strife
   now!'
Running away!!

I mean, I don't like that __ __ rabbit. She getting
   hungry for feed!

And when we run into this road, she said,
'What, this must be the Lawlers Road, Leonora
   Road.'
From Sandstone.

Well, we going along.
She said, 'We got to be careful in Lawlers, there's a
   policeman there.'
So, we going along.
'Now which side we going to cross?'

__ that policeman, in that open place too.
police station, __ __ there's a policeman there.
'We better go across that way, then.'
We went around, a longer way around.
When no car coming, we cross.
Out of that creek and gone.
Gone to Darlot Road then.

All the way,
we only had that five mile ride.
That's all the ride we had, no more.

Only that five mile.

Walking!
Might have been, I don't know,
walk from this —
we don't __
we don't sit down, we going!
And might have a five minute spell and off.
Some time we keep going!

Nothing much load to carry.
We want to get there!

When we get to Weebo Station,
at the wool shed,
now, nobody there!

Walk across other way.

We got to, near, Darlot, we looking that way.
They been camping around here,
all around here,
somewhere.
When they seen us coming,
the dog barked, they all <u>crying</u>, them people.
Seen us coming!

Yeah! Everybody.
Yeah.
'Have a look!'
'You there?!'

Got there, and everybody there happy!
Everybody made the damper, so many we can't eat!

Two days, and I go on again.
That's the time I seen her last.
I'm moving on to __ station to see my people, she
   stay there with her people.
My uncle, and, Auntie, them two. Horse, and the

134 *Speakings*

> camel.
> We gone, where my mother and brothers.
>
> Got there,
> went to the station,

Fred: Tell her what station.

Rosie: Nambi!
> Uncle Jumbo, and my Mum, and all them lot were fencing, for Fitzgerald.

Fred: They fencing, there.

Rosie: You know, fencing, that bit, new country __ __ .
> Mother and father and all that.
> My three brother there, too!
> They were sitting down there,* working.
> A lot of people working there then,
> miners, and all of that, at Nambi.
>
> And the station owner
> Mr Fitzgerald
> went and call the cops!
>
> I was going to run, and,
> I'm a good runner!
> Get going — up to the hills!
>
> Oh, 'Never mind.'
>
> I was going to make them run, and chase me
> but I changed my mind.
> Too much running. I'd better stop. No more running.
>
> They been chasing me around the bush.
> They chasing kids around, any kid.
> That's the Government.

---

* 'sitting down there' — living or staying there.

What's that man — Mr Neville — he's a cruel man,
    taking all the kids away.

I made up my mind — no more running.

They send me <u>back</u>!
I went to the gaol house in Leonora,
and wait there for the night.
I couldn't sleep.
Just wait. Been there a couple of days.
The next morning on the train with the policeman
    and his wife and a daughter.
Going back, same way!
Mmm.
Oh gosh, everything wrong!

Anybody,
doesn't matter what colour,
the kids,
got to send 'em away, or something.
Now, nothing doing now. Finish!

Mmm. Good time, now. We don't __ __ chasing
    people about.
We remember this, you know.

Oh, 'Where you fellow come from?'
Some reckon I come from north.
Kids from everywhere.
'And where you come from?'
'I come from up north!'
And all them all from different country, different
    places.
Lot of Noongars there.

Carolyn: At Mogumber?

Rosie: Yeah.
Another lot been there before, isn't it?
They all run away!

	I run away too!
Fred:	But her run away, and Mulgathunoo Joe he run too! He tried to __.
	He didn't know which way to go.
	So, he ran away. He just went around to get the lay of the country. And that's in the *Drop in a Bucket*. …
	Yeah, he know where he come from, but he want to see country.
Rosie:	See where the road was, or what?
Fred:	Well, where the farms are, and all this.
Rosie:	Too many farm!
Fred:	So when he went back the second time, he grabbed the whole lot and went away. …
Rosie:	Sent me away, Took me to Perth. They took me round to this Girls' Home* and left me there. Then, after putting the cops on, Fitzgerald asked them if I can go and work with them. … My brother asked him to talk for me. So Fitzgerald talked for me. I went back up and worked for Mrs Fitzgerald,

---

Girls' Home — in East Perth, probably Bennett House.

with them, the Fitzgerald families.

That's the finish of them police chasing around.
Oh, Donegan used to, he still.
He sent my mother too, took her away. Took her to
   Cosmo.

Now everyone free walking.
Nobody chasing. No police chasing.
Then, before, one little noise — we're <u>gone</u>!

Any kind of kids — not just half-castes, dark ones
   too —
they not allowed to stay with their mothers.
Put them in the Home, or send them away.
When I'm at Mogumber, there's lots of girls there,
and boys, too, not just girls,
boys and girls there from everywhere, all over the
   place,
up north
and from the South-west.

The Government cruel, taking the kids away.
My mother, she didn't want us taken away.
She wanted me to be close, by her.

Not chasing no one around. Finish!
Everybody, now, walking around anywhere now!
   Not like before!
Good thing too!

Run out of stories!

Carolyn:	So, when you were walking, that time, do you know, would it be a couple of weeks, or months, that you were walking for?
Rosie:	Mmm. <u>Long way</u>, no rides!
Fred:	No. Six, six weeks, I s'pose?

	Seven weeks?
Rosie:	Could be, could be six. Might be, maybe less. 'Cause we walk all day, and half of the night. Yeah. Get up early and off!
Carolyn:	Yeah. And it was the summer when you were walking?
Rosie:	Oh, we went from the summer, and some of it, and when we were travelling, winter time! Cold, you know, when that <u>big rain</u> came too. Pouring down.
Carolyn:	So you had to carry that canvas to keep warm at night?
Rosie:	Mmm, yeah! That blanket, we took one of the blanket away from that Home! [*Laughs.*] …
Carolyn:	And when you lit fires, to cook your goanna and things, were you worried about people seeing the smoke?
Rosie:	No, we got off the road.
Carolyn:	Ah, far enough away.
Rosie:	Yeah.
Carolyn:	And, you would you have been about fifteen?
Fred:	Be about that.
Rosie:	Mmm. Something like that.
Fred:	Thirteen?
Carolyn:	And, Ivy? Ivy was about that age too?

Rosie:	She a bit younger than me.
	Well, it was a long way to walk.
	Long walk.
	That's good that you're going to write it. About time too!
Jane:	Are you going to tell her your name?
Rosie:	Tharan.
Carolyn:	Shall I write that too?
Rosie:	Yeah.
Jane:	And her mother was Annie. And her real name was — you say it.
Rosie:	Dootharra.
Carolyn:	Thank you!

Wyallie and Ngunnu

(Spoken on 10 December 1997)

The conversation with Auntie Wyallie and Auntie Ngunnu was recorded at Auntie Wyallie's house in Kalgoorlie. Other family members were also present and contributed details to the stories.

Wyallie was born about ten years after the deportation of Jidu and the other Wongutha people to Mogumber; Ngunnu about twenty years after. They speak, in this conversation, of childhood in the bush with their families, of the daily concern of avoiding being seen and captured by the police, and of being taken to the relative safety of Mount Margaret Mission when they had grown too old to be successfully hidden by their families in the bush.

Wyallie and Ngunnu each requested that only their Wongutha names were recorded in connection with their stories.

Wyallie.

...

Wyallie: I'm Wyallie
and, I was born at
Mt Margaret Mission.
In nineteen, nineteen thirty. March the eighth, nineteen thirty.
Then from there, my mother took me to

Burtville.
There used to be a lot of people there, gold mining.
   When our people — Wongais — find gold they
   take it there, get food and some money.
Finish now. It's all long gone.

Then from there we
used to go out in the bush and all that.
And, I was a baby there.

And, from bush, we go walkabout to,
— what's that place, Ngunnu? Other side Cosmo?
Minnie Creek.
Minnie Creek and
all around there.
We run around —
We had, I had friends, other children there too.
   With me.
We used to go out there, and some __, and we
   come back to, Burtville,
with our people with us,
and we, do some jobs for
white people and get some feed.

And <u>then</u>, from there, we went across, we go to __.

My Country, Burtville, all around Burtville.
Down to Karonie, all that way.
Right around there,
and we go out hunting and all.

Afghans used to be there too!
They, have, all the, horse and cart.
They went around selling things all the time.
And our people, they always, you know, do some
   prospecting,
on the ground they look and find some gold.
And they save it for these Afghan people, go to
   them.

Then, they carried that gold,
and they buy us some lovely dress, or little bangle
   and all that.
They go off to Edjudina way,
they go to Edjudina then come back to Linden.

And we,
and we, us,
you know, we half-caste kids,
we never go into town.
We just stay out in the bush.
When the police come, off we go! And hide!
Because they're sending some children to Perth.
We took to the hills, because,
the police don't go the hills.
In those days they haven't got four-wheel drives!
[Laughs.]

Carolyn: Ah! Did they used to come on horses?

Wyallie: Yeah. But we just go, and hide!
They don't go to the hills.
They don't know where all the hiding places are!

Then,
then from Linden, to Edjudina we went.
There's a station there.
Some of our people worked there too.
I was round about, five.
Five or getting on to six.
That's when our people had a <u>big corroboree</u> there.
Yeah. They'd be dancing and all that.
And we sit up all night
watching.

Towards the morning,
we all go home.

We go home.
Have a feed, and then we go out again

looking for bardi.*
This is the right time for bardi.†
And all these station people
　— bardi and goannas —
the people get them and they kill it and they show
　us how to get it ready.
And, and cook the kangaroo with the dirt.
You know, they dig the hole.
Ashes.
And light the big fire.
And they put the kangaroo and singe that,
the fur, the hair.
And they put it in the fire.
Then they cover it up.
Wait.
Some people take it out too quick.
And our, our mothers they make damper
and put a billy of tea on.

And when time to come out
father comes,
— I call him my father, he's the one, my full blood
　father, he's the one that looked after me.
cut it up the right way, show us how to do it.
Not just any way, you got to do it the right way.
Cut it up.
It's <u>really cooked</u> too!
Not half raw.

The kangaroo — men cook that.

Women cook the goanna:
light the big fire,
put it in the fire, cover it up.
Wait.

---

*　*bardi* — *larvae of a grub which lives underground; the Wongutha word is* maku.

†　*'the right time for bardi'* — *September, October.*

When it's ready,
get the branches, clean ones, put them on the
   ground.
Put the goanna on the branches,
cut it up,
and share it around with all the people.
The tail's the best part!

We had a good feed, with the damper.
They make good damper, our people.
We watched how they do it, so we make it too.

Have it with honey
— from honey ants, you know honey ants?
You got to dig a long way.
Dig, dig, dig.
Then you see them all sitting there in the hole.
You get a soft stick and push the ants away,
<u>gently</u>,
then you can get the honey out and put it in the tin.
   It's good, too!

So, have a good feed!

Then we'd go round, looking for
gold and all that.
When we find gold, we sell it to the prospectors.
They take the gold and they give us food, some
   money.
They was good to us,
they didn't tell the police.
Some prospectors, they feel sorry for us.
When they see the police coming,
they hide us kids in their huts.
The police, if they saw you, they send you to Perth,
   to Mogumber.
Especially girls.
The boys were all right,
the girls got sent away. Not me!!

Then one day
my father, taking us to, oh, Edjudina.
That's the one I coming to __
I was there.
'Bout, six year old then.
And, we was in this bush, sitting down,
under the tree.

And our mothers, our aunties and their children,
— three, three kids was there, two girls, Thelma, Isobel and,
that Maisie; they was in a bag, they was carried around, you know?

Carolyn: Oh, when they very small they were carried in a bag on the back?

Wyallie: Yeah. On the back.

And anyhow, I was playing around and
my cousin, Ben was there too. *[Hand motions to indicate height.]*
He was about three years older than me anyway.
He was there.

We was playing around, then,
next minute
I heard this <u>shooting</u>!

Chttoow, chttoow, chttoow!!

Then I looked,
ooh,
these <u>white blokes</u>
all on the horse, three!
Shooting!
Then I heard these __
<u>screaming</u> and all that, <u>shouting</u>!
So I went,
we ran for our dear lives!

And hide!
I was standing one side of a tree so they won't see
  me.
<u>Shooting</u>!
And <u>then,</u> after that, they went away!

And, after that, Isobel you know, she get that
  rickets?
Isobel __ she go to school like that, she and
Thelma.

Ngunnu: Yeah, Thelma got it too, eh?

Wyallie: Yeah, Thelma was like that [shows shaking
  movement of shoulders].

And from there, we, we [bangs table]
left Thelma and Isobel.

Us lot, we went to
— my father and all that, some of the other people,
  we went to,
we had to walk from Edjudina right to,
right through the bush.
And we had our camel with us, Kana.
You got the camel's name?
Kana, that's the one that's been carrying me
  around.

I don't know, must have been two weeks …
I think we were out there two weeks.

We travelled day,
all day we're travelling!

Then maybe we go stay the night,
camp for the night,
then next morning,
— you know how Wongais, they get up early?
Off we go again!

	Then my father would carry me on his neck.
Carolyn:	Ah. So you didn't have to walk all that way?
Wyallie:	Yeah. Carry me on the neck and my mother carried me on her back. My auntie growling, 'She's big now!' All the way, then, have another sleep. Then travelling all the time. <u>All the way</u>, 'til we came, — it must have been two weeks. Travelling. Then, then we had to stop and make our camps because our people got to go and have a look at this place, Karonie. They went along, showed themself first. And we all sitting down waiting. Go to town, have a <u>look</u>. Then they came back. Everything okay. Then we went to Karonie!
Carolyn:	When they went to see if it was okay, what were they looking for?
Wyallie:	They looking for all that, you know.
Ngunnu:	No fights, and all that.
Carolyn:	Oh yeah, check if it was a safe place —
Wyallie:	Yeah, yeah.
Carolyn:	for Wongai people to go?
Wyallie:	Yeah.

There were other Wongais there too.
Stayed there for, almost a month I think.
Then met up with all other boys and girls there.
Jack Ridley was there.
'nowy Livingstone was there.
But they got those names later, didn't they, when
 they went in the Home?

Ngunnu: Yeah.

Wyallie: And,
and then,
one day,
we all got on that truck,
they put us on the truck
and they cover us,
— gee Ngunnu, you'd better tell your story!!
Got on the truck,
and they covered the half-caste children,
or else they'd put a, you know, bit of charcoal,
and rub it on my face and hands and leg.
So the policeman, they think 'Oh, there is a full
 blood there.'

Then, laying down,
covered up with a blanket.
Laying down there,
they say, 'Don't move!'
We're travelling to Kalgoorlie.

Went <u>along</u>,
then we came to
— what's that place not far from Kalgoorlie?

Ngunnu: The Lake?

Wyallie: There, where they come and pull up.
— That's where Henry was working.
I forgot that name.
Not far from Kalgoorlie anyway.

...

Miriam: Oh, Golden Ridge!

Wyallie: Golden Ridge, we pulled up there!

Anyway, they all <u>throwing</u> everything,
us
all out!
All the Wongais, stand there,
catch us.
And they take us in the bush and take these bags off.
They say 'Bagula! Get up!'
And they wash the charcoal all off.

Carolyn: That was in case anybody stopped the truck and —

Ngunnu: Yeah.

Wyallie: Yeah, there might be policeman there.
Got to have that.
From there, we went to this Lake.
__ lake, not sure of that place.
Went to that lake
Look at this little one! *[Her baby grandchild wakes up.]*
Lake Wood, yeah. Lakewood.
Lakewood.
We went there
in the bush.

And we all there, we camped there.
When the people see us, they all crying! That's the Wongai way.
And they gave us tea and damper.
Then they had a <u>big corroboree</u> there.

— — —

[Crying child makes it hard to decipher tape!]

Oh, ninu, what's the matter?

[Tape is stopped and child is quieted and then the speaking resumes ...]

> Next day
> in the morning, all the mothers and aunties,
> and,
> they go out
> for to see all the old white people.
> 'Cause they make them do some work,
> clean the yard and all that.
> That's how they get clothes,
> they just tell them, 'Oh, I've got a little piccaninny
>   over there!'
> And they give some clothes.
> And I remember my mother brought these,
>   sandshoes.
> Do you know the pretty ones, pretty ones? Early
>   day one, all different colours.
> She brought me these sandshoes.
> Yeah, pretty colour ones.
> And dress.
>
> While they was out there, you know, with these old
>   ladies,
> my father was looking after me at the lake.
> Next minute we saw this motor coming!
> This white man was going out to work!
> He thought that was a policeman!
> We was running round and round this tree!
> <u>Round</u> and <u>round</u>!
> Then when that motor went past, then we *[laughs]*,
>   then he took me over this way!
>
> He thought that was a policeman!
> He thought, 'Oh, no, he might grab her now!'
>
> So anyway,
> sat and waited for Mum,
> mother and all my aunties and grannies to come
>   home.

And it was getting dark too!
Then they came.
I thought they got, you know, put in gaol!
'Cause they been away for a good while!

Waited there,
and they had this, another corroboree.
Dancing and all.
Good too!
Good to see, you know,
our people dancing and singing and all.

Then, later on, from there, I went back to Karonie.

Carolyn: Went back on that truck again?

Wyallie: Yeah! [*Laughs.*]
They did the same thing!

Got off the truck, went back to Karonie.
Not into the town — we've got to be in the bush,
   sitting down with our grandmothers watching us.
Went and stayed there for a, what was it, a month.
They had rations there, too.
For old people.
  __ __ and go on and talk to some old people.
And they get biscuit and all for the kids.

While I was there, I, __ got to meet this woman
  there, Miss Lockhart.
She a <u>Christian woman</u>!
We go there, have meetings there.
Singalongs.
That's the time I heard that hymn,
'When the trumpet.'
'When the trumpet of the Lord shall sound and
  time shall be no more'
and we were all singing!
We had a hymn book.
She gave us a hymn book, but I don't know how to

read!
Just holding it, watching everybody! *[Laughs.]*

When the 'Tea and Sugar', they call it the 'Tea and
   Sugar Train',
comes in, from Kalgoorlie,
we're all standing there, cadging.
'Drop the penny! Drop the penny!'
They're throwing it down to us.

Then, one day, we went to, this passenger train,
a passenger train.
People with a lot of money all sitting there!
So, one lady gave me, two shilling! Two shilling!
I said, 'What's this big one? __ __, you know!'
<u>Big money</u>!

Anyhow, then,
when I got that two shilling,
I looked
a policeman came!
Came around.
Somebody pimped, you know!
Came around,
but I went in and went through the
culvert, and ran!
He couldn't come in!
He couldn't get into there!
Ran for my dear life!

Went along,
and climbed this tree.
Wait.

Heard my mother whistling.
When I hear that, when she whistles,
I know that everything's okay,
it's safe!

There were other girls running away from the police.

Running! I'm a good runner!

I've got no people up there!
I don't want to be sent up there!

I was sitting there.
Waiting.
Heard the whistle,
she was looking for me.
Then I got down
came down, and saw her,
and she said 'Well,'
In Wongai, she said, 'We going to take you to Mt Margaret.'
Reg's mother, she said, 'Right, we going to take you <u>right</u> to Mt Margaret.'
And put me in the Home.
I thought I got to go in the Home, and <u>come out</u>!
Went and stayed there 'til I got married!

And so, we travelled,
I remember,
it was bright, moonlight, that night.
Bright!
You could see, you know, where you're walking!

So she went and got our camel, Kana.
And we travelled, night-time.
She said, 'We've got to go as far as we can go!'
'Cause of the policeman who saw me,
'cause they been after me all the time!

Anyway
We <u>walked</u>.
<u>Walked</u>!
My father was carrying me on his back.
And my mother carries me on the back
when he gets tired.

<u>Going along</u>

| | Camp halfway.
| | Camp there.
| | Some of our people go in front,
| | go kill a kangaroo,
| | cook it
| | and while we were coming along, by the time we get there,
| | that kangaroo's cooked!
| | And we have a feed.
| |
| | And then, travelled.
| |
| | Travelling all the way.
| | — What's that place, we've got to go? __ __ that boy got shot?
| Miriam: | Oh, Pinjin.
| Wyallie: | Pinjin, yeah.
| | And when we came to that place, Pinjin,
| | we went
| | — There's a lot of people used to be there, white people. There's a mine there.
| | Went round!
| | Stayed there for a, must have been a week, or two weeks.
| | 'Cause they wanted to, stay there for a while.
| |
| | Then, from there, we went <u>right</u> back to Edjudina,
| | Edjudina to Linden.
| | Went through the bush again,
| | not where, where all the white people living,
| | through the bush.
| | Went <u>back</u>
| | to, Pyke Hollow, Pyke Hollow we went.
| | Then we came to this water, Muggan.
| | We call that place Muggan.
| |
| | That was Sunday, too, it was Sunday.
| | We camped there.

No more water there you know!
It used to be <u>good, cool water</u>!
I hope they didn't blow that up!

Went <u>there</u>!
Late afternoon,
late in the afternoon, we climbed that hill, you know
— do you remember that hill? Mt Margaret, beside
__ __.

Miriam: Oh, Golden Ridge?*

Wyallie: Yeah, Golden Ridge, we climbed that.
And then we went over
— there's some houses there of old prospectors.

Miriam: Oh yeah.

Wyallie: We <u>looking</u>.
And we went down
and came to the Boys' Home.
Boys' Home was down, but we was on the side of the hill.

But my Auntie said, 'Right, we've got to camp here.'
So we camped there.

…

And a bell rang that night!
While I was sitting there!
And I asked Mum, Auntie, 'What's that bell ringing for?'
And she said ' Oh, they got to doolgoor† again.'
— Singing. Going to church.

---

* *Golden Ridge — possibly a local name for the hill near Mt Margaret, or perhaps mistakenly used here (elsewhere in the story reference is made to the mining town of the same name near Kalgoorlie).*

† *doolgoor — singing.*

156 Speakings

>
> I saw a lantern, you know, the children all going to the church.
>
> Then, in the morning, got up.
> Then my mother said, 'Well, going to take you, and stay with this place 'til ration day.'
> They all get in for flour and sugar and all that.
>
> And when I got there, and —
> No, my mother took me to all of those people that they saw me when I was a little girl.
> They all, she took me round, they all <u>cried</u>!
> To see her come back!
> <u>Crying</u>!
> Cry for me!
> Then my mother came and took me to the hospital, give me drops, I had a very bad eye.
> And then, as I was coming, I look at all these girls, playing.
> I'm asking Mum if they were 'Mithithi'* — I thought they were white kids!!
> [Laughs.]
> And, __ I'm part myself!
> And she said, 'No, __ '.

Ngunnu: We never realised our colour!

Wyallie: Yeah!
> Went along!
> Then, she went and showed me to those people, and then,
> I went in the Home then!
> Then I thought I'm going to come <u>out</u>!
> But I stayed there 'til I got married!
>
> I'm glad I went in the Home, because, because,

---

*   *mithithi* — *white person.*

	you know, they might find me, they was after me, all right.* They was going to send me to Mogumber. But, the missionaries prayed for me. They got that that verse in Psalm, — what is it? 'He shall love thee, and God shall save her, and that right early.'† So I praise the Lord, you know!
Carolyn:	You never had to worry about being taken to Mogumber again, or were you still thinking about it sometimes?
Wyallie:	Yeah. Still do. But that time, safe. I was happy to be there with our people there, too. Mona Burton, Linda Barnes; they saw me when I was a baby. They know me. They was happy to see me when I got put in the Home. My cousin Sadie was there before me. I didn't want to go, leave my Country, leave my Mother. I didn't want to go that strange Country. I stayed in Mt Margaret. It was good to be there, anyway. Yeah. Your story now, Ngunnu. The one about the bag, sugar bag!
Ngunnu:	Already my story in a book.

---

* 'they was after me' — the police, the local Protectors of Aborigines.

† 'He shall love thee ...' — a personalised paraphrase of a verse from Psalms.

158 Speakings

Wyallie: But __ she want it herself!

[Tape is stopped while consultation occurs.]

Ngunnu: I'm Ngunnu.

Wyallie: Yeah, put her name.

Ngunnu: I was born at the mission, Mt Margaret. Ngunnu.
That's the real way, but people call me Ngannga.
   You can call Ngannga if you want to.
   ...

Wyallie: Ngunnu, that's her real name.

Ngunnu: Her grandmother give me that name! *[Laughs.]*
She's my cousin.
Yeah, my family, you know.
She reckons I used to be a little boss, when I was a
   little girl!
Boss of them all! Yeah!

Carolyn: You'd get everybody organised?

[All laugh.]

Ngunnu: You put that tape on again, didn't you?*

Carolyn: Yeah, it's on, ready to go whenever.

Ngunnu: What did I —

Wyallie: Ngunnu.

Ngunnu: start from?
'My name is Ngunnu.'
I told you I was born at Mt Margaret?
My mother's name was Kath Yuramu

---

*   'You put that tape on again ...?' — *the tape had been turned off while Ngunnu decided whether or not to record her story.*

and my father is Dawy.
See why, I think why I was born at the mission
was because my mother knew that I was a half-caste
  child.
And I went there more or less for protection.
And they put me, like,
they didn't know how my father would take it, see?

And he was very good about it when I was born,
you know.
...

After that, my mum could travel around. I was too
  small to remember that ...
First we went to, back to Burtville and, Cox's New
  Find, and King's.
King's. All of those little places, you know! We
  travelled around.
My area was in the Murrin Murrin area.

That is __ __ when I tell my story because it is
  really, you know, hard.

Later on as I got a bit bigger,
we used to help our
mothers in that family to find gold.
And there is a big creek, United Creek.
And, all the family would be sitting in the creek
and all doing their little bit with the pipe, you
  know?
With a pipe.
All blowing the pipe.
And I said to my mother, 'Move away!' you know!
'Move away, I'm going to work here!'
And my mother moved away
and I was blowing and I found a big gold!
Next minute they shouted, '<u>Hey</u>, this little kid
  found a big gold.'
Oh! All the <u>family</u> was <u>happy</u>.

All of them saying, 'Eh, that little girl, __ got a big
  gold!' [Laughs.]

That's the story they told me,
and I can remember being in that creek!
'Cause they
repeat it over and over.
They like, you know,
— it's history to them
and they like to know that you're part of the history.

When I was in the bush,
I don't know where this place was, it was out of
  town somewhere, not far from town.
And we were all there.
My mother said, 'Ngunnu, don't go too far away
  from the camp because the policeman might
  come out and the horses.'
And, 'If you see the white horse,' she said, 'you run
  and get in the sugar bag.'

So, I used to play,
not very far,
<u>play round</u>,
and then,
one day, I saw the four legs of the horse come!
Oh, I was just <u>shaking</u>!
I ran <u>flat out</u> and into <u>that bag</u>!
My heart must have been <u>pumping</u> there!
And my mother made it, and she was sitting on
  that bag!
And the police,
I heard the policeman saying, 'Any half-caste kids
  here?'

'Any kids here?'
'None at all!'

All the people were making a big noise! All of

them! 'Oh yary yah!'
And <u>all</u> talking the <u>language</u>!
And we __ __ __ and <u>all shouting</u>!

And he said, 'What's going on?'

Anyway, he said 'What's in that bag?'
Oh, if he opened that bag I would have been gone!

But the Lord had His hand on that bag, and said
  'You're not touching that bag.'

And my mother said, 'Nothing, nothing!'
'Tucker! Tucker!' she was saying!
And all the people were still making a <u>big noise</u>
  there, you know.
'Wa one!' Making all this noise, so,
to distract him.

And, anyway,
he got going then.
He got going.

Oh! __ __ and I was so happy.
So happy.

Later on, see, when my mother
she got civilised a little bit
and we used to go to this town, Murrin Murrin,
and we used to go to do shopping.
— But I still can't go to the town! We were so used
  to being in the bush.
My mum went and bought this boot polish.
The boot polish! She had seen the white man
  polishing shoes, you know?
And come back with this boot polish!
And they're all helping — put it all on,
talking,
we're all happy, we're putting it all on!

And then, later, when it all
dried,
all peeling off!
That didn't work.

They put me —
they lit a big fire,
and trying to smoke that fire,
make that smoke come and make me burn a little
  bit, you know.
That didn't work.

Everything they tried, couldn't, didn't do any
  good! *[Laughs.]*

So, I was —
But they were so smart, that they kept right away
  from the town.

And we knew, we, got to be,
quiet
and we knew we had to be obedient,
when they tell us, we've got to be obedient!
We listen, because our lives —

Wyallie: Ngunnu was a good girl!

Ngunnu: My mum used to look after Wyallie.
She said 'Oh, Wyallie was the best girl! She is a
  <u>good girl</u>, not like you!'

Carolyn: It would be hard for a little kid to understand why
  you had to be so, careful.

Ngunnu: Mmm.
Today, I always tell my grandchildren when we go
  in the bush,
at night time,
really listen!
Because any little thing, you know somebody's

around!
Even a little twig!
Wongai pick that up!

__ little twig! Or stone roll.
You know somebody's around.
Those are the little things that we were taught.
  To be quiet at the right time.

There's times, they let us play.
We have our time playing,
but there's times,
most of the time they'd be on the alert,
watching out for any,
people coming, you know.

Raiding, or,
maybe spies, or maybe someone to,
come and cause trouble with the family.
All those little things.

My nephew had a dog called Rocky, and when he
  had to go to the Mission —
we know we've got to go.
If we don't go,
— 'cause we're getting bigger —
if we don't go, sooner or later, we will be caught
  and sent away.
So that's how families know, 'Oh, these kids are
  getting big now! We can't cover them up
  anymore!'
Hide us!
But they tried to keep us out of town.

And when my nephew went, he said to me, 'Oh,
  you look after my dog?!'
And he said, 'I got to go!'
And, I was looking after that dog, you know.
When <u>my</u> time came, I had to leave that dog!

And I was crying too!
You know, when I went in that Mission,
I was crying.
My parents!
'<u>Rocky</u>!'
'You aren't here!'
Crying for my home,
that place near United Creek
in the Murrin Murrin area.
Can't get it, get it out of my head.
Then they asked me, 'What are you crying for?'
and I was, 'Rocky, Rocky, Rocky!'
'What you crying for?'
And I was crying and see if I could see the dog.

So those are the little things, you know, that are
   still in our hearts,
and in our minds, you know.
It's hard to get rid of it.
We could try all day
and then it's still in my heart, you know.
They were happy times for us,
and it still remains with us.
History, you know.

When the time came for me to go in the Mission
   there —

Wyallie: Why did they take us? __ __ old men!

Ngunnu: Our people used to give us,
when we were little kids, we've got to have, we
   were given a man.
When we grow up, we've got to marry him.
And by the time, that man is old, we might be just
   children, __, we've got to marry that man!
But the idea is that he's got to look after the family.
Our mothers and that.

Carolyn:	Yeah. While you're growing up?
Ngunnu:	Yeah. And when I was little, I had to go every day and sit along with this man.
Wyallie:	[Laughs.]
Ngunnu:	I don't want to sit over there, and I would say 'Why? Oh!' And she would say, 'Oh, you got to go and sit over there!' Every day I got to sit over with that man and make sure that, you know, he's going to look after him.*
Wyallie:	[Laughs.]
Ngunnu:	Yeah. And, I want to go and play! But I get an earful!
Wyallie:	___ <u>looking</u>! He's coming in from the shop! You used to get that __, that fence. And would <u>lay down</u>! <u>Lay down</u>! So then he won't see you!! When he died I was happy! But, I shouldn't be!
Wyallie, Ngunnu:	[Both laugh.]
Wyallie:	I was happy that he died!
Ngunnu:	We never told our friends, we had, a given man. We never told our __ __. Kept it quiet because I didn't want them to tease me!

---

* *'he's going to look after him' — he's going to look after the family.*

	And then I went in the Mission and that was it.
Carolyn:	Were many children taken away?*
Ngunnu:	Oh yes.
Wyallie:	Yeah, before us.
Carolyn:	That's why everyone was taking so much care?
Ngunnu:	Some of the people used to kill them, too, you know. Because, they're like a burden, so they kill them. And Wyallie's got a mark there,† and I have too. June, her sister, has got a mark there. Mrs Rundell has got a mark there, Violet has got a mark there. We've all got marks there! I'd like to know what happened. We're all half-caste girls. We all got that. They tried to kill us, maybe?
Wyallie:	Tried to kill us.
Ngunnu:	We never found out. Maybe they branded us? I did ask my mother, one day. I said, 'Did you want to kill me when I was born?' 'Oh, no!' See? She said, 'No, I never! I didn't want to kill you.' …
Ngunnu:	But we all grew up together, and happy… I'm thankful. When I think,

---

* 'taken away' — *by the police, on behalf of the Aborigines Department, taken from their families and sent away to Perth/ Mogumber.*

† 'got a mark there' — *a small scar at the base of the neck.*

when I think of the time that the police could have
    picked that bag up!

I could have been gone!
Taken away and never,
probably never heard of,
never heard of the Lord.

Wyallie: Never heard of.

Ngunnu: You know?

Wyallie: Some children was a baby.

Ngunnu: Some children, some children was a baby.
They don't know who they are.

I met a, couple of twins, son and daughter.
Her name was Joan Laverton, and I forget the
    brother's name.
They're named after the town they were in.
That's all they know.
Lost their __

Wyallie: Yes.

Ngunnu: So sad, you know, what they've done to us.

Wyallie: It's very sad.

Ngunnu: They could have been more, kind.

Carolyn: Oh! They could have been a lot kinder.

Ngunnu: Yeah.

Carolyn: They, they were awful …
The police would strike fear in you, wouldn't they?
    Every time you saw the police coming you had to
    be so —

Wyallie: Scared!

Ngunnu: You know what?
Not very long ago, oh, last year, I got caught for —
I'd just come around the corner from my son's place, but I didn't have a belt on.
I just pulled in —
and he saw me.*
Pulled me up,
and he fined me.
But do you know what? After he left, I shook and I trembled.
Really <u>frightened</u>.
You know, after all these years!
And I went home, and I said, 'I'm feeling sick.'
And you know, my cousin Jessie said, 'Look, we'll pray.'
So she, we prayed together, to make me feel better.

It was still — I didn't realise — it was still inside!
Yeah. And every time I see them coming,
I just
shake!

Wyallie: I don't like to talk to people __ talking.
Nervous!
Police, you know,
went all over the place,
looking for
half-caste kids, you know.

Carolyn: And they said —

Ngunnu: And they said, 'Oh, reconciliation!'
but the damage has already been done.
It's in us. Until we die out.
That's a __ thing.
But while we're still alive, the hurt is still there,

---

* 'he saw me' — *a policeman saw Ngunnu.*

	and that, fear. I can shake like that when __ white people. —.
Wyallie:	White people. When I see policeman, or white men, just coming, I get frightened. Want to hide! We're still frightened of policemen. Can't trust them. Now, some policemen are good. Some white people can be selfish.
Carolyn:	Which is why I want to write down these stories, so that people know and understand —
Ngunnu:	Yeah. Good, too! Look at us in a different light.
Wyallie:	Yeah. That's what we need. …
Ngunnu:	Just imagine somebody come and take your little child, take it away. And, if they, policeman didn't take us, if mothers didn't put them in, they would come and take us by force!
Wyallie:	By force! Yeah.
Ngunnu:	Our people kept us, took us to the only place where they can visit. And they can come and visit us. Otherwise, we'd be gone just like sheep. On the truck and gone to Perth.

170 *Speakings*

Wyallie: 'Fifteen niggers to Mogumber.'*

Ngunnu: Mogumber, on the train, you know.

Wyallie: 'Fifteen niggers to Mogumber.'

Ngunnu: 'Fifteen niggers to Mogumber,'
on the truck.
Just like a little flock of sheep, or goats.
Truck them off.

Carolyn: They were brave, those people who walked back,
who escaped and got back again.

Ngunnu: Auntie Rosie.

Wyallie: Auntie Rosie — they sent her to Mogumber. All
those strangers there!
But they never caught me anyway!

Ngunnu: We were lucky, we had our
mothers
who were very, very careful!
They kept us right in the bush!
We'd never been to a town!

You know, one hill there,
out of Laverton, there is a big hill there.
One of the ladies showed me __, you know.
She showed me this big hill.
She said 'Ngunnu, all you half-caste kids,'
— not all at the same time, but it's a big hill.
Whenever there's half-caste children around,
our grandfathers and that, they sat down there
with us.
Watching!

---

* 'Fifteen niggers to Mogumber' — *A direct quote from Rod Schenk's diary (quoting the label on the train cattle-truck) referring to the fifteen Wongutha people sent to Mogumber in 1921, as published in Margaret Morgan's* Mt Margaret: A Drop in the Bucket. *1986.*

	Overlooked.
Wyallie:	Horse!
Ngunnu:	'A horse coming!'
	Policeman always come in the bush, too.
	__ coming, come along.
	Just sat.
	<u>Right up</u>.
	Watching.
	So our people were cunning too!
	They were more,
	clever than the policeman,
	because __ __ we still here today.
	[*Both laugh.*]
	To tell the tale!
	…
	Another thing, was that the Lord was behind all this.
Wyallie:	Yeah.
Ngunnu:	The Lord had his hand on all of us, you know.
Carolyn:	Keeping you safe?
Ngunnu:	Yeah.
	…

May O'Brien
(Spoken on 30 December 1997)

A conversation recorded with May O'Brien at King's Park, Perth. May now lives in Perth; she regularly returns to her home Country.

May O'Brien's memories of childhood begin in the bush, living with her people. She was taken to the Mt Margaret Mission as a small child.

...

May: Mr Schenk, and the mission, was never, ever given
 permission from the Native Welfare Department
to take me in, at all.
Because I was supposed to go to the Moore River
 Settlement.
My sister and I,
and Auntie Amy were all listed to go to the Moore
 River Settlement, near Perth.
...
When we went to the mission, we had to adhere to
 strict rules!
And when we did anything
in a way that was different to the non-Aboriginal
 culture,
one of the missionaries' girls would say 'Oh!
 You're behaving like a Wongai!'
I used to say, 'Well, I am Wongai. I'm not a
 mithithi!'

Mithithi means white woman or white girl.
Mind you I muttered this under my breath!
We weren't allowed to answer back. But sometimes we got away with it.
'Yes! I'm a Wongai. And there's nothing wrong with being one!'
This girl everlastingly made us feel that it was a big shame to be a Wongai!
But we weren't ashamed of being a Wongai — Aboriginal — at all.

Carolyn: You managed to preserve that pride despite all the things they —

May: Yes. That's right — we all thought that this missionary girl didn't want us to be like that, she wanted us to adopt a non-Aboriginal culture.
We're Wongais.
We're Aboriginal people.
There are similarities but there are also differences between cultures.
Anyhow, why should we be ashamed of how God made us?
But that's how it was at the mission.

Carolyn: Before we turned the tape on you started telling me a story about the time that you and Phyllis ran away from the mission — can you tell me again now?

May: Well, firstly, I'll tell you where Mt Margaret is and how we came to have the idea of running away, and then I'll tell you the story.

Mt Margaret Mission was situated eight miles east of Morgans.
And twenty miles west of Laverton.
So we were stuck there in between!
Twenty miles to Laverton, eight miles to Morgans.

The main road was north of the mission, but there
    was a detour from Laverton and one from
    Morgans. Mr Schenk and the Aboriginal men
    made that road from Morgans to Mt Margaret
    and Mt Margaret to Laverton, to meet up with
    the main road.
People in spanky new cars rarely came to the
    mission in those days
but some of them made this detour.
They wanted to see Aboriginal people.
They wanted to know what made us tick!
Sticky-beaks they were!
But at the same time, we loved them coming!
Because it was a <u>change</u> from seeing the
    missionaries all the time!
And we wanted them to see the work we did at
    school — we were proud of our school and our
    schoolwork.

Women with rosy red cheeks, wearing high-heeled
    shoes and carrying fancy little handbags always
    stepped out of these cars.
Their children looked different to us — they had
    long noses and white skin and beautiful blond
    hair! And bright blue eyes.
Of course, we had brown eyes or hazel eyes
and they all had blue eyes.

And whenever there was a car approaching
we'd see the dust on the horizon.
Then as the car came over the rise we'd all yell out
    in Aboriginal English, 'Mootooga, mootooga!'
    meaning 'motor car, motor car'.
We'd run across the creek and over to the petrol
    bowser at the shop — flat out — the <u>dust flying</u>
    behind us,
right up to the shop, just by the side of Mr Schenk's
    house.

And we'd all stand there, goggly-eyed, looking at them,
all these women with their red cheeks and high heel shoes and handbags.
And Phyllis and I stood there looking too.
We'd be looking and I'd say,
'When I grow up, I'm going to be just like those mithithis. With lots of money.'
And Phyllis would say, 'Me too.'

It was about the time we were reading the story of Dick Whittington and his cat at school.
I was sitting next to Phyllis, and we talked about that story, and the way Dick Whittington became rich. We were so envious of him!
He sold his cat to a man who had a plague of rats and mice in his town, and in the end he made a lot of money!
We got excited _every_ time we read that story. One day I whispered to Phyllis, 'You know, there's lots of wild cats in the bush — we can become rich too if we catch a cat from the bush!'
'It's so easy,' Phyllis said to me. 'We'll go and catch one next time we go on a picnic.'
We were only about eight or nine years old! We had this great idea of being dressed up like the visitors that used to come to the mission.

We'd wear high heel shoes and carry handbags,
wear rouge and paint our lips red and wear pretty dangling earrings! We would look ever so grand!
Just like those ladies.

It was about this same time that we'd visit the Mission Library. Every girl our age wanted to borrow this book about Shirley Temple. She had all these different seasonal outfits. Beautiful they were to us kids in the home.
There were also cardboard cut-outs of her clothes

as well.

We'd say, 'Look at Shirley Temple with her curly blond hair!'

And we'd make a wish that we could be just as rich too!

'Look at us! We wear these government dresses!'

'Tuff-nuts', they were called. They were dresses made out of jeans material, all stiff and starchy.

So, Phyllis and I would sit and day-dream, and talk a lot about how we could we leave the mission and make our fortune!

'We can go away and, like Dick Whittington, we can become rich! We'll have plenty of money! We'll drive to the mission, and when they see us coming down the rise they'll be yelling out 'Mootooga, mootooga!'

The kids would run up and say 'Oh, two Wongai ladies! Phyllis and May!' and goggle at us like we did at the visitors.

We'd be wearing our jeans and our slacks — this will give them a shock, we thought! We weren't allowed to wear jeans, slacks or shorts at the mission because the missionaries said it was an abomination unto the Lord. We thought, we're going to come back and do all these things we weren't allowed to do.

'We're our own bosses,' we'd say, and we'd wear our hair behind our ears! (Mrs Jackson often told us that if we did that we were just like Jezebel in the Bible!) Mind you, we always did this when we wanted to annoy her. To make it worse we'd stick huge safety pins into our ears and let them dangle right down. Never worried about our ears getting infected — never gave it a thought back then.

And all the kids would yell out, 'May and Phyllis

being walji, walji.'
Walji means being wicked girls — and we loved it, you know.
Mrs Jackson would say, 'Oh, don't they look like Jezebel.'

We said, 'Who's this Jezebel?' We asked the senior girls, and they said, 'You're too young to know about her.'

Mrs Jackson was a hard-working lady — worked night and day! We really loved her and Pop Jackson — they looked after us well. Now that we're older we realise how much they loved us and cared for us, and we can appreciate how much work they did. They never seemed to stop!

Anyhow, Phyllis and I thought we could come back to the mission
in a big, red, flash car.
We'd drive <u>slowly</u> up to the petrol bowser so <u>everyone</u> could see us. We'd take our time getting out and all the boys and girls would yell, 'Oh, Phyllis and May are in that car!'
We'd have money to spend! And we'd give out lollies and chocolates and chewing gums just like those visitors did when they came to the mission.
We had all these ideas in our heads — we really thought it would happen for us! We really did!

So one day when we were reading about Dick Whittington, I nudged Phyllis and flicked the page with my hand and went thump, thump, thump with my pointed finger! 'Read that!!' I whispered.

Phyllis read it.
Phyllis's eyes went big.
And I nodded my head, 'You and me!' I said in

sign language. (We couldn't talk much in school
  because we had work to do.)

For weeks we planned on running away, and what
  we should do.
We said, 'The time must be just right!' and no one
  must know.
As each day came,
and the next day,
'No, today's not right.'
Sometimes we'd hear the people say, 'Oh, the
  featherfoot man's been aroound in the bush.'*
They'd come around to get people that broke
  Wogai Law.
We'd be too frightened to go!
  When we got up one morning, Phyllis said,
  'Tonight's the night we're going to run away and
  get this wild cat from the bush! Then we can go
  far away and sell it and then we'll be rich!'

Phyllis's job was to make a damper during our
  lunch break.
She made the damper, and I kept watch
because if the girls found out what we were up to,
  we'd be in trouble!
they'd yell out, 'Phyllis is making a damper!'

We had to be quiet about it, or everyone would
  shout it out at the top of their voices, then Mrs
  Jackson would blow her whistle, and that meant
  if you were causing trouble you had to go to her
  and explain.

Phyllis made two dampers. One for her and one for
  me.
She cooked under the laundry copper fire, which

---

* *featherfoot man — person with special powers, often used for purposes of retribution.*

they used to boil the sheets to make them white.

I went and stole some salt and some dripping, and wrapped it up in brown paper.

All the time, I was watching to make sure that nobody would come, or find out what we were doing!

And I made a billy can — put a wire through it so we could have a handle.
We put everything in it, and said, 'Today's the day!' Then we waited for the bell to ring for tea.

We looked at all the kids as we sat at tea — big long tables — boys on one side, girls on the other side. All the time Phyllis and I were making eyes at each other, swinging our eyes around and pouting our lips and muttering to each other, '<u>Poor things</u>. This is the <u>la-a-a-ast</u> meal we're going to have with everybody.'

We always had our tea at four o'clock and by five, the girls were locked up in our dormitory. The boys stayed out 'til later.

So after tea was over, Phyllis and I volunteered to help with the washing up!
'It's not your turn!' someone shouted.
'We know that! We just want to help out so you can finish early.'
In fact we weren't much help at all! We were a real <u>nuisance</u>. We kept walking back and forth and back and forth to the door to see how dark it was outside.
We were waiting, and the sun was going down, down, down.
We were waiting and waiting, and it was getting dark.

At last Phyllis nudged me and whispered, 'Quick, get your billy and <u>run</u>.'
So I scurried off to the toilets. They seemed so far away!
And next door to the toilets was a big chook yard!
When they heard me coming, the chooks went 'Yahk, Yahkyahk yahk!' as loudly as they could! They're making all this noise, because no one ran up to the toilets at that time of the night, so the chooks are wondering what's going on.

Soon after, Phyllis joined me. And all this time the chooks went on and on and on!
We knew if they kept this up, Mrs Jackson would send out a whole army of girls to find out what was wrong with the chooks. Then we'd be in <u>more</u> trouble!
We started throwing sand at the chooks to shut them up, but the more we threw the sand the more they jumped up, going 'Bwak! Bwakbwakbwak!!!'
'Shut up! Shut up!!' we called out.

We were also afraid the noise would bring Matron Murray outdoors. She lived just across the road, not far from the chooks.
She used to tell on us when we were riding the goats behind the toilets. The younger girls called her a 'tell-tale', but we wouldn't dare say that to her face or to the senior girls. Oh no! We knew better than to do that!
If Matron Murray knew we were up at the toilets at this time, she'd ring Mrs Jackson up on the missionaries' intercom line, and then we'd be in <u>serious</u> trouble.

We waited for it to get darker.
We could still hear the girls in the dining room, you know, rattling the dishes as they set the

tables, ready for breakfast the next day.

'<u>We</u> won't be there for breakfast! We'll be gone, right up to Laverton — twenty miles away.'

When we thought it was dark enough, we made our next move.
We made a dash for the ditch behind the chook yard.
There were these big culverts there, to stop the water overflowing to the school and the chook yard when it rained.

We hid there, and we stayed still, just in case Matron Murray might have seen us.
It was pitch dark now.
We were just going to make our next move when we heard this, 'Whoo-whoo-whowhowhowhoo!'
It sounded scary!
Phyllis and I moved closer to each other.
'Featherfoot man,' we whispered at the same time.

Just then we heard the sound again, 'Whoo-whoo-whoo-whoo-whoo-whoooo!'
It sounded much closer to us now.
'It's only a night owl, you know it won't hurt us.'
I only said that to stop Phyllis from making me scared!
'We're not going to stop now we've made it this far!'

Our hearts were thumping as we sat still. When we heard the sound again we were scared out of our wits!

'Mamoo, mamoo!' (which means 'Devil, devil'), we whispered to each other.

We were petrified!

We sat there in the ditch, not knowing what to do!
It was <u>dark</u> all around us and we couldn't even see the one tree hill in front of us.
'The featherfoot man must still be behind that tree waiting for us!'

Now Phyllis said, 'I don't want to run away any more.'
And I said, 'Come on then, let's get back quickly before the others miss us!'
I was pretending to be brave!

We scrambled out of the ditch and made the dash back. The chooks were still kicking up a fuss!
'Shut up!! Shut up you stupid old things!' we muttered as we ran by.

We didn't stop until we reached the kitchen.
The girls were just closing the doors when they saw us and asked, 'What are you two girls doing out there?! Up to no good by the look of it!'
'Oh, we just thought you might still need some help.'
'We <u>finished</u> now! You two were here before! What are you coming back for? You two are up to something.'

'Come on, Phyllis, we gotta go back to the dormitory.'
We went back in, pretending nothing had happened.

Quick smart we pulled off our play clothes and jumped in the bath. We all had to share that same bath water, all of the junior girls. Water was precious, see?

We were still giggling to ourselves when we hopped into bed.
And all the time we were whispering, making all

these cryptic remarks, you know, so the girls wouldn't know what we were talking about.
We were laughing and giggling so much that one of the senior girls came by and asked, 'Are you two making fun of someone?'
'<u>No</u>! We're not poking fun at anyone. We're just laughing about nothing!' we said.

When the girl had disappeared we started singing at the top of our voices, 'Turn again Whittington,' then ducked under the blankets and kept on singing that song: 'Thou worthy citizen, Lord Mayor of London' and we'd pop our heads out again and crack up laughing, thinking about what we'd been up to.

We nearly became rich!
We nearly had beautiful clothes!
So, yeah.

Carolyn: Yeah. So you nearly ran away!

May: Nearly ran away — nearly became rich — nearly came back to the mission with high-heeled shoes and bags and make-up on our faces and lipstick and earrings and permed hair and all that stuff — so we thought!

Carolyn: Yeah. Ideal dream things! Did many people try to run away from…?

May: Some of the time — <u>excitement</u>!
The senior girls who ran away were our role-models. They were our idols!
Oh, these girls were brave. Yeah. Very brave, we thought, to run away in the dark.
It caused excitement
because they knew they couldn't go far, and they would be found and brought back. They all came back. They jolly well made sure they did!

	At that time we were very unhappy about the freedom the boys were allowed. Girls were chaperoned and had a big fence around our home. We could only play in the creek bed in front of our yard. I suppose when we got older we realised why. Yeah, but we hated it!
Carolyn:	Yeah. Apart from Auntie Rosie running away from the Moore River Settlement, do you know of any other people who did that?
May:	Yes. There's a few of them — Margaret Morgan's book, *A Drop in a Bucket*, can tell you about some of the older people who tried to run away from the Moore River Settlement. That happened long before I went to the Mission.
Carolyn:	Was the Mt Margaret situation as bad as the Moore River situation?
May:	No, no. It wasn't that bad, because our people could come and see us any time. The Moore River experience was much more serious. At Moore River you are in another person's country — that's not our country. Your heart would be in your own country and yet your physical being would be at the Moore River Settlement. You'd be a broken person — broken in spirit and shattered. You're not a whole person — you'd be miserable and <u>sad</u>. At least we were still in our own country.
Carolyn:	So for the people who did walk back to Moore River, they had to walk through country they didn't know.
May:	Yes, this is it!!! No one liked walking through

someone else's country.
Gosh, you'd get frightened when it's not your own country because you didn't have permission to walk there. Each group was possessive of their country.
Noongar and Yamathee country, they were walking through!
Yeah. And Country is important!
Your own Country is very important.

Carolyn: Yeah. Because you don't know the physical land, but you don't know all the other things as well — all the spiritual things?

May: Yes — that's right. Yes. Yes.
That's it. Each group has a special spiritual attachment to their land.

Carolyn: And, all the things like water and food, and where the houses are?

May: And that too.
You know where the water is in your area.
The finches flying around would tell you that.
And you know where the water holes are too, and what type of bush food grows in your country.
Whereas in Noongar country, if you don't belong you don't know that country very well at all.
So, Auntie Rosie was brave and clever.

Carolyn: You wouldn't know which farmers were likely to —

May: No. That's right. Some of them would ring the police and tell them, and they'd get punishment worse than ever.
And if you're halfway to Mt Margaret, your own Country, you wouldn't want to get caught halfway. You'd be devastated. All that planning for nothing.

...

Carolyn: When you went to Mt Margaret, you were quite small then?

May: Yes, I was about six — the mission records differ about my age.
I think I was turning six in the year I went to Mt Margaret.
Eva and Norman Forrest took me there.
They took me over to the Home and tried to hand me over to Mrs Jackson who looked after the girls.
When I saw all these girls and Mrs Jackson who was trying to grab me,
I cried and yelled and screamed.
I got hold of Eva's skirt — and I ran round and round her. Her skirt was creeping up higher and higher and all the time she was growling at me.
I didn't care — I was worrying about this other woman wanting to take me!

The next minute they took me away from the mission and we were back on the road to Laverton.

But when I woke up in the morning I was in a <u>big</u> dormitory.
Eva and Norman had brought me back to the mission when I was <u>asleep</u>.
And when I woke up in this big dormitory I was bewildered and shocked.

I'd never been in a big house like that before.
I either lived in a tent, or out in the open, or in a wilja,* or in a hut with hessian lining. This place was different. It was <u>huge</u> and full of girls my age.

Norman and Eva were always on the move.

---

* *wilja* — A simple shelter constructed from branches and leaves of the natural vegetation.

Norman was a prospector and he also put down
   wells, so he was always on the move.
And, life was free and easy.
You were travelling around
and there were no rules
and no big buildings like this one.

When the door opened, and the girls piled out, I
   ran out screaming.
I looked out and I could see a gate, right in front of
   me, so I made a <u>mad dash</u> for it! Everyone was
   yelling, 'Grab her! Grab her!'
When one of the girls grabbed me, I was
   screaming, and stamping my foot, and my
   sinews were all out in full.
I was shouting on top voice, yelling and crying out!
   'Eva! Norman!'
I cried and cried and cried! ... Oh, it was terrible.

'Where are Norman and Eva? Where have they
   gone? They left me in this place!'
Next day they never came.
The day after, nothing happened.
For a whole week I was looking, looking from
   behind a high fence.
Thinking, 'Norman and Eva, where are you?'
My eyes were wandering around, looking.
'Where, where are they?'
I'd see people come down from the hill to the shop.
I'd think, 'Norman and Eva might be with them.'
I'd be on the look out for them — nothing.

They took me out for Christmas in 1938, but after
   that I never saw them again.
And I was so disappointed and hurt.
Firstly my mother appeared not to want me,
and now Eva and Norman.
Now I am stuck in this mission.
I didn't like the mission much at first.

But I got to like it.

...

Sometimes when I got into trouble I'd say, 'I hate this mission.'
Mrs Jackson would say, 'You'd better go to the Moore River Settlement then.'
Well, that's the worst thing she could have said to me.
No one wanted to go to that place!

...

Carolyn: Earlier you were saying that your mother left you with Eva and Norman because the police were always after her?

May: Yes, and the police were after me!
I was one of a lot of children listed to go to the Moore River Settlement.

The police really didn't know who I belonged to.
All they knew, I was wandering and running around in the bush.
They knew that Dinah was my mother and that I was always running around in the bush.

And when anyone came into camp, we were warned to run for the trees.
'Run for the trees, hide!'
We'd hide behind a tree — stiff as a poker!

Or we'd run for the culverts, and hide there 'til it was safe to move.
We didn't know why we had to do that.

Carolyn: It'd be a hard thing for a little kid to understand.

May: We were taught to fear white men we didn't know, and we lived in fear of the police. Every white man we saw we thought was a policeman

	coming to take us away.
Carolyn:	Yeah. That was because there was a very real danger?
May:	That's right. They were trying to keep us from being caught and sent away to the Moore River Settlement. They'd never see us again.

But then I went with my mother. She would come and get me periodically and take me to places on the Trans-line, like Zanthus, and on to Ooldea, and Loongana and all of those places.

There was a drought there, big drought there when I was born.
In those years — for the first eight years of my life there was a drought. And we were starving.

Each day we'd climb the trees, mulga trees, and collect these caterpillars, you know, these green ones?
We'd put them in a little Lifeguard milk tin — you weren't born so you won't remember that! Lifeguard, with the British Grenadier on it — it's like Tongala, or condensed milk. There was a Lifeguard Soap as well.
We used to fill the tin up with the caterpillars, and we'd chew them! At least they were moist.

At that time I had to beg on the Trans-line, and people would throw food and we'd race around, scratching around on the ground. People used to laugh and carry on, take our photos.

I haven't told you yet about the Italians who lived and mined in the area. When we were in that drought time, they were very helpful to us. They were very kind in giving us food.

...

There were lots of happy days at Mt Margaret as well.
But life was different there from when I was in the bush.
It was mainly the regimentation — so many rules. Sometimes we didn't understand the rules, but we got punished by those rules if we broke them.
As you got older — that's a different story.
But when you're little, you don't know what you are getting hit for.

Once Mrs Schenk growled at me,
'What's this I hear about you crying because you don't want to be at the mission? You should be grateful for what we have done for you! We have given you clothes — you would have been out there in the bush naked!'
I would be muttering, 'If I was with Eva I wouldn't be naked.'
(When I was with my mother I never had sets of clothes.)
Often we slept in a creek bed.
And in winter they would get the fire and warm up the earth, and you would sleep in that, and it would keep you warmer.

Carolyn: Earth, I suppose, stays warm for a long time with the fire?

May: For a while.

Sometimes we'd put down a bush or a fresh branch of a tree to make a bed. Some of the wattle trees around the place are lovely and soft.

...

Carolyn: I'm wondering whether some of the stories which

people told me are like secrets — is that why sometimes people wouldn't want other people to hear them telling me a story?

May: No, they're not secrets. It's because people interrupt the story, they query what you are saying,
'Oh, is that really what happened?'
'I know my story! You must all stick to your own story!'

What happened is that, for so long, we've kept our feelings about our personal past to ourselves and haven't really spoken about it.

And then if people start questioning your story it takes away from the experience of saying it. You're getting it out of your system; it's been bottled up for too long. You don't want other people interrupting when you're getting it off your chest.

And really, no one else knows your own feelings. Each person has their own story, their own experience, and they should not feel guilty about it.
We all had different experiences. We need to get it off our chests. It's good to tell you about it. It becomes easier to tell each time.

Sadie Canning

(Spoken on 10 September 1999)

A conversation recorded at Sadie Canning's home in Perth. Sadie divides her time between living in, and working out of, Perth and living and working near Leonora.

Sadie Canning's childhood in the bush with her people was short-lived; she was taken to the Mount Margaret Mission as a small child.

Sadie: Because of the 1905 Act and the White Australia Policy, all part Aboriginal children had to go into an institution of some sort.
I was with my mother until I was four
at Laverton, I was born at Laverton.
I wasn't born in hospital, but just on the edge of town.
We were in the bush near Laverton
and my mother hid me in the creek bed with blankets over me whenever government officials came, or anyone that looked like an official.

I didn't know what kind of officials, but,
one day these officials came along and they were standing around the campfire
and I'm supposed to be under the blankets.
I peeped out and saw my sister standing there.
So I just got out and walked over to be with my

sister.
So that's how I came to be at Mt Margaret.
I was four years old.

Carolyn: Four years old!

Sadie: Four years old, yes.

Well, they took my sister into the Home as well.
That's where I ended up from 1934 to 1948, fourteen years I think.

Being taken away from my parents at an early age and put in the Home was cruel.
That was a terrible piece of legislation
to take children away from their parents.
It was because they wanted
everybody to be white really.
It was a genocide policy.

I look at it in two lights:
I missed out on having the mother love
which is the right of every child.
Education is _never_ better than mother love!
But, I look at it — I was given opportunities
to be able to mix in the world today.
The other factor, the main factor, is
that's where I found Christ as my Saviour.

And if it wasn't for the Missionaries
I don't know where I would have been!
I praise God for them.

Carolyn: There's not a lot of hope in the world apart from Christ?

Sadie: There wasn't any hope.
There wasn't any hope for Aboriginal people then.
Nor is there any hope for anybody right now
unless, you know, you have Christ.

So, with having been at Mt Margaret I had the
  education
and I wanted to be a nurse.
Perth hospitals wouldn't have Aboriginal girls at
  that time,
that's 1948,
so I went over to Melbourne.
I did my nursing training in Melbourne.
I graduated in general nursing, midwifery and
  infant health — that was a triple certificate.
I did some work around Perth,
and Melbourne
but I decided where I'd be best used would be
  amongst my own people. So I applied for a
  position at Leonora Hospital.
And I got the position
as a Sister
then a year later
the position for Matron came up
and I got that position as well.
I felt there was a call,
a call to work amongst my people.
That was part of my mission.

Carolyn: The' good works prepared for us before the
  beginning of time'?*

Sadie: Yes, that's right.
So, I was there for thirty-four years.
Thirty-four years.
Aboriginal health improved for that time, as far as
  the town Aboriginal people went, because they
  learnt to bring up their babies to the Hospital a
  lot earlier than they had previously.
I saw a big drop in infant mortality rate and so on.
They started learning, as I say, to come up earlier

---

*   *'good works ...'* — *paraphrase of Ephesians, Chapter 2, Verse 10.*

and ask for medical help instead of waiting until the babies were dehydrated and then come up for help; coming up as soon as they were getting sick.
Quite a lot of Aboriginal girls worked there, we employed Aboriginal people there as well.
Only one or two would be employed at the hospital before I got there.
I think the relationships between the Aboriginal and white people sort of improved as well, and people started to come to live in town too.

Carolyn: That must have been inspiring for people to see you making such big changes from the times when Aboriginal people weren't very welcome for treatment at Leonora Hospital. It must have made a big difference!

Sadie: Yeah, it did, it did give the Aboriginal people help, because, they knew that they could come up to the Hospital
and that I'd see them and look after them.
And then I retired in 1990.

Carolyn: And you've been very busy ever since!

Sadie: Yes! Very busy since, yeah.
There are a lot of other experiences I've had.
The Royal Flying Doctor Service
— there was a Sadie Canning plane named after me.
Too many stories, so many!

Carolyn: Another time!

Sadie: Yeah.

Carolyn: One story I've heard mentioned — can you tell me about the awards that you have received for your nursing and community work?

Sadie: I never talk about it.

[Pause]
In 1964, I was awarded the MBE — Member of the British Empire.
Also, the Queen's Silver Jubilee Medal in 1977.

Carolyn: That must have been exciting! Exciting times, and hard times.

...

When you went to Melbourne it must have been hard, being on your own over there.

Sadie: It was hard!
It was, you know, it's that homesickness
for my Country
for the Country.
...

Carolyn: Can you tell me any stories about people getting out of the lockup in Laverton?

Sadie: How long ago?

Carolyn: As long ago as you like!!

Sadie: I don't know that many!
There was one in the early seventies, I think.
An Aboriginal guy from Warburton area, his name was Dthubinna.
And he managed to get out of the lockup,
I don't know how he did it.
This policeman was a bit lenient and this time he had to go somewhere
so he locked him up.
But he managed to get the flooring boards up,
— and there's not much,
not much area between the ground and lockup floor
but he managed to get out.
Just about that much space! [Indicates with hands.]

Carolyn:	So there was about fifteen centimetres of space under the floor?
Sadie:	Yeah, yeah. He managed to get out of that! He took the floorboards up and then he managed to get out!
Carolyn:	Did he stay out, or was he caught again?
Sadie:	Oh, he stayed out for a couple of days. They know he's too far from his home already. They said, 'Oh, he'll turn up anyway.' No point making a big fuss about it. They said, 'Oh, you know, he'll turn up.' And he turned up all right, the only one I know who turned up again. It's a wonder there's not been more people running away! Today, even, today. 'Cause you go to Leonora, you go to Laverton, most of them sit down on the lawn. You've seen them?
Carolyn:	No, I didn't see them.
Sadie:	You have the court house, police station there *[drawing sketch plan]*. And you have the court house here and there's a sort of lawn around like that and they just sit there during the day.
Carolyn:	I guess, in the old days, the police were quite a lot more —
Sadie:	In the old days they were, more harsh. Now it's different.
Carolyn:	And there's more strict laws now about what police can and can't do?
Sadie:	Yes, that's right.

| | And they just tell them, 'You're trusted to sit down.'
They just sit out there
and then they go in at night.
Much better than the old lockups!
Things are so much better, yes, much better for them that way. |
|------------|---|
| Carolyn: | I saw that, in the records from Mogumber, the Moore River Settlement, that Mulga Joe was sent there three times and twice he escaped and walked home to Laverton. He must have been pretty brave? |
| Sadie: | Yes! And they cut through the farming areas and along the pipeline. |
| Carolyn: | It's a long way! |
| Sadie: | A long way, yes!
But they knew which way to go.
Could find their way home.
I'd be lost somewhere!
Unless I had something to follow. |
| Carolyn: | Would they have known about the pipeline, do you think, in the 1920s? |
| Sadie: | Yeah, they would have, yeah.
Some went along the pipeline, because that's a straight line east.
Some of them went through <u>that</u> way.
And then the others cut across farm country. |
| Carolyn: | And some of them went right up, north, and around past Mt Magnet and around that way? |
| Sadie: | Yes. |
| Carolyn: | Would they have known Mt Magnet when they saw it,
or would they have just said, 'We've got to go this |

	way until the land gets like this and then we'll go East?'
Sadie:	I don't think they would known Mt Magnet as Mt Magnet.
Carolyn:	No. They wouldn't have thought, 'Right, we've got to walk until we get to Mt Magnet and then turn East.'?
Sadie:	No, no, no, no. No, they just followed the stars and the sun.
Carolyn:	I guess when they got far enough north some of the stars would have got closer to where they should be in the sky —
Sadie:	Yeah.
Carolyn:	if you were looking at them from Laverton.
Sadie:	Yeah.
Carolyn:	They could match the stars up or something?
Sadie:	Yeah, yeah. They know the stars.
Carolyn:	Because I was unconsciously thinking about it in terms of how Margaret Morgan described it, that they walked north to Mt Magnet and then they did this and then —
Sadie:	No. No navigation aids, no maps.
Carolyn:	They might not have even heard of Mt Magnet!
Sadie:	No, no they wouldn't have. Because that was out of their Country. Magnet was out of their Country.

Carolyn: Is that Darlot Country, Mt Magnet?

Sadie: No.
Mt Magnet would be, I suppose, that's, Yamathee Country.

Carolyn: Would the people have known it was Yamathee Country?

Sadie: Yes. These ones called themselves the Yamathee. But that's become ___.

Carolyn: So the Wongutha people back in 1921 would have known.

Sadie: Yes, they'd know that <u>that</u> was Yamathee country, they'd know <u>this</u> was Wunmala country.
And Wunmalas used to fight the Wongutha.
Wunmalas — they're the Wiluna ones.
They used to come down and fight.
Fight, around, not far from Mt Margaret, near Laverton, around that area
and they'd run off with their wives!

Carolyn: I think I read something about that,
and I think the writer called them the Darlots. Are they the same?

Sadie: Yes, they're the Darlots, they're the Wunmalas.

Carolyn: Wunmala.
Does that have a meaning that can be translated?

Sadie: Well, Wunmala in our language is, they're the killers.

Carolyn: The killers!

Sadie: Mmm! Wunmala is also 'featherfoot'.
(Wongutha can be featherfoot too.)
Wunmala came from around Darlot and all that —

	and they call them the Darlot mob as well.
Carolyn:	So 'Wunmala' is what you called them?
Sadie:	They called, they called themselves that in the Native Title Tribunal. Yeah, Wunmala.
Carolyn:	And what about Yamathee — what does that mean?
Sadie:	Yamathee means friend.
Carolyn:	Friend. Did the Yamathee have much to do —
Sadie:	No. Yamathee's didn't have much contact with the Wongutha ones, but that's because of the tribal Laws. But the war was always with the Wunmalas which is the Darlot mob. Conflict.
Carolyn:	Would there have been any exchange of —
Sadie:	They must have had some sort of exchange to the coastal areas because, we've got those pearl shells. You know those pearl shells? Our people always wore them during the ceremonies and so on, they wore those pearl shells. So they must have had some connection with the coastal people through ceremony.
Carolyn:	So those pearls shells would be very precious items, to have travelled so far from the coast!
Sadie:	Big shells, too.

From the coast.
Because there's nothing in our area except some,
in the middle,
in the middle of some bush area, you know,
these little shells,
tiny little shells.
You can find them.
They must have been left over from Noah's time!
[Laughing.]

Carolyn: Right!
[Laughing.]
But not the pearl shells!

Sadie: No, not the pearl shells, the pearl shells are —
they must have had some connection
with the coastal people.
It could have been the Geraldton mob, or further north.
They must have had connection.

Carolyn: Is that connection what people also call Songlines?

Sadie: Yeah. There's a Songline that people have with different areas.
We didn't have the opportunity to go deeply into the storytelling.
Having gone in at four to Mt Margaret
and coming out to study nursing,
I didn't have much opportunity to mix
or to listen to the old people.
It was twenty-four hours, seven days a week, at Leonora Hospital.
We hardly had any staff, then, when I first went there.
We were very busy!

So you didn't have much time.
It's only in the latter years

that you've gone home.
Go to the places.

The history books need to be changed to tell the truth of what's happened.
It's the truth that has to be told.
That's what I'm advocating in the Reconciliation process.
So the kids in school can learn the truth,
from school age,
learn about the truth of what happened.
I don't think half the people really know;
the general run of the Australian people don't know what happened.
People don't appreciate the Stolen Generation mob.
People are still hurting today;
Aboriginal people haven't come to grips with things;
some of them are still searching for their roots.

Carolyn: We all have to come to grips with the past.

Sadie: You have to know the past to move on to the future.
I think you have to know the past in any walk of life.

Margaret Morgan

(Spoken on 22 March 1997)

A converation recorded at Margaret Morgan's home in Perth.

Margaret Morgan grew up at the Mt Margaret Mission, not far from Laverton. She is the first daughter of Rod and Mysie Schenk, founders of the Mission; she has written an account of the history of the Mt Margaret Mission, 1921–1953. Her book, *Mt Margaret: A Drop in a Bucket*[1] quotes Schenk's diary entries and letters relating to the sending of the fifteen Wongutha people from Laverton to the Moore River Native Settlement in 1921, lists the names of the people, details some of the events of the escape and return journey, and outlines the various routes taken.

Carolyn: ... we're talking about the people who escaped from the Moore River Native Settlement and walked back to Laverton. Margaret, you were just talking about how you found out these people's names.

Margaret: Yes, because I wanted to put their names in, and you know when my father was writing things, letters to his friends, he wouldn't mention their names because they meant nothing to the readers, and being in Aboriginal language,

people just skip over them.
So they were never really written down, who they were.
Except that I did know that Jidu, that was Dad's best friend there, he's the old bloke, he was one, I knew that.
So, when I went up to Mt Margaret,
— I made three trips up there with my tape recorder, and nobody would understand what we were talking about, for most of it was half Language,* half English. *[Laughs.]*
And we'd be talking about the dogs and the children and all sorts of things, whatever interrupted, I didn't want them to feel, to have anything off-putting, because they didn't like the look of the tape recorder for a start, that you were taking everything down that they said, and so I used to have to just leave it kind of obliquely on the side of me, and hope I've got everything, which meant that sometimes I didn't.
And sometimes I didn't have it on, and all this sort of thing. *[Laughs.]*
Oh dear, I was really quite a new chum at it.
So, I had to ask them their names:
'__, who were these people who went to Moore River?'
There was fifteen of them — I think there was fifteen, I've even forgotten that.

Carolyn: And two there already.

Margaret: Fifteen, two there already, yes, that's right.
And oh, they didn't want to cough up about the names, because you never mention the name of somebody deceased. You talk about, oh his uncle,

---

* 'Language'— Wongutha language.

his uncle pass away, or that was his auntie, gone.
So that's the way you know.
...
You'll never mention — you'll talk about their sister or their auntie, or your little ones, or something like that.
So they weren't going to tell me any names.
So I sat there and looked quite sad.
I said, 'Oh, that's a shame you know, because all this wonderful story about how they got back. In fourteen days, they got back again! How did they get back from Moore River, in fourteen days?'
— Except for one old man, he was blind, he didn't get back 'til — oh, he was the last one to get back.
And I said, 'How did that happen?'
And I said, 'You know, if you don't tell me any names, I'm sorry for the kids' sake.'
I said, 'Look at them, your grandchildren playing around here. They won't know anything about these wonderful people and what they did. They won't know how clever they were getting back.'
Well. After that I had no trouble.
I had great cooperation.

Well, Elyon was the baby,
and her mother was Biyuwarra, and she was one, she was the wife of —

Some of them I knew.
Some of them I knew.

Old Jidu I knew, I remember him.

And I remember quite a few.
Jinera, I remember old blind Jinera.
That story is absolutely fascinating, I think, how he was sitting in the middle of the paddock, yelling his head off, and the station owner, took him up, right up there to Yalgoo!

And then he meets his sister up there.

Now that's been documented — that massacre —
the Darlots, they came down, now that was
where that sister came from!
I think Daisy Bates tells the story of it, I haven't got
any of her books, but I believe that she talks
about that massacre. So that will be a good one
for you.

And, how they got back! I couldn't get over it!
His sister took him
from Yalgoo,
right up there!
Right up to Wiluna! She'd have contacts up there.
Walking all that way!
I don't think Dad ever knew how he got back — all
he knew was that this blind man turned up on
his own!

Now, see this part of the story here, *[points to map]*
old Lampi Turner, he told me this part.
See, that's old Jinera and this is the party he was
supposed to be with.

Carolyn:	This is the northern party?
Margaret:	Yes. See, they plug across here, they knew what they were doing. See, Laverton's — where is it? — there. They knew what they were doing. Had no trouble at all. And he, his sister, took him around to here. *[Pointing from Cue to Laverton on map.]* I said to Lampi, I said, 'How come his sister didn't come to the mission?'

Well, she had to go home, you see she had a
   husband back there.
And so she walked,
she put him on the train,
and back she went.
Walking, just walking.
Just walking.

And this here, if you look at the map, you'll see
   that this is just arid, there's no habitation around
   there. *[Central route.]*
And they just cut across — now, who told me that?
Reggie Johnston told me that.
They just cut across there, and they hit,
they hit Menzies, spot on,
and they finished on the train. *[Laughs.]*

The trains back in those days; they
   had goods trains, lots of goods trains — I think
   they used to have a train a day before my father
   came there. A third of the population of WA
   lived up there in the Goldfields. Every town, had
   their — not pub — pubs, and even their own
   brewery.
They were well and truly inhabited, all those
   places.

So the trains, they used to have one a day,
   and then later they got to every second day,
   and one a week by the time I was a little girl, it
   was one a week.
So it was train day, we used to talk about
   train days.

And when they were talking, when they gave
   times, my mother used to ask them, 'When was
   your baby born?' because she kept a births and
   deaths, birth book. Because, they were not
   registered in those days, nobody cared whether

they were alive or dead, they never told anyone.
But my mother kept a record of all the babies that were born, and those that died.

And she'd say, 'Oh, you've got a baby!' when they'd come.

'Cause they always went walkabout, they went walkabout from right up here *[points to map — Balgo Hills area!]*
right down to Kalgoorlie, not past Kalgoorlie maybe,
and they didn't go to Esperance.
Our lot, they went to Linden and they'd go down to Karonie, which is down on the Trans-line.
That was all their area.

Yes, so she'd say, 'Where was your baby born, what place?'
And they'd tell her. And she'd say, 'What time?'
Oh, she'd look at the baby and she'd think 'new born,'
and they'd say, 'Oh, three train days.' Three weeks ago.
Or they'd say 'Oh, before Christmas, the other side of Christmas.'
Or they'd say two Christmases.
So there was Christmas, and train days.
Or moons, the month. The months. Two moons would be two months.
So she wrote down the date, what she reckoned the date was by what they told her.

Carolyn: Yes. So, when they were catching the trains, how did they avoid people saying, 'These might be the people who escaped?'
Were people on the lookout for them, do you know?

Margaret:	I don't think so. The police might have been, but they wouldn't come down. See, they were stationed at Laverton. They wouldn't come down looking. … They described to me this tree that they went up. There was a young fellow who really helped them all over, a young fellow who was already there. They told me his name, Wawuja. I don't know about him. I don't know him. He might have gone somewhere else before I was the age to remember him. I don't remember him. When did that happen?
Carolyn:	1921.
Margaret:	Well, yes, I was born in 1924.
Carolyn:	Right, Wawuja, he was twenty already, in his twenties.
Margaret:	I don't remember him at all. Who was the other one? I know the other one, I knew the second one.
Carolyn:	Joe Mulga–
Margaret:	Joe, yes. Yes, I knew him well, that one. He's a wonderful old man. He really loved the Lord, that man. There was a Sister Eileen at Moore River, she was an Anglican Sister and she loved the Lord — that's where Joe Mulgathunoo first heard the gospel, at Moore River.
Carolyn:	Do you know why he was there already, in the first place?

Margaret: Well, I don't know. I never asked him you see.
He was gone before I had the chance. When I thought of it later on, when I'm writing this book, he wasn't around.
I don't know why.
Generally it was some misdemeanour, if you stole things from white people, for instance, you'd be caught.
And if you came around the homesteads of the whites, and frightened them, you'd be caught and sent down there.
They didn't want trouble around towns.
In fact, that's what the townspeople used to say, they'd tell the police, tell the Native Affairs, 'Get rid of these people.'
And they used to tell them to go out bush.

...

Carolyn: Do you think that the police perhaps didn't even know whom they had sent to Mogumber?

Margaret: I don't think they knew.
I don't think my father would let on.

Carolyn: I was wondering whether it would have been widely known at the time that they'd come back, or —

Margaret: No, I don't think so.
My father, of course, was well aware, but he wouldn't tell them.

Let sleeping dogs lie.

And ah, they all started to creep back again, he used to call it 'creep',
they'd creep back again to the backs of the township, that's were they could get food.

And that's where they used to beg around the
   backs of the township.
And they would creep in,
they'd creep in, and then out, as fast as they could
   go.
So they didn't get into trouble.
If they didn't, if they hung around town too much,
   well, then they got whipped out of town.

Carolyn: Was the escape widely known amongst the
   Aboriginal people though?

Margaret: Oh, I would think so, I would think so.
That was a new thing at that particular time, I
   think it was because of what was happening
   around the district.
It was drought, and they were stealing food.

They were stealing food and killing sheep.

And because of that, it was punitive:
'Send them off, get them out of the way.'
And if they took one lot, it would speak to the rest.
And, that's exactly what happened.
They all just vanished.

But I think he
says in his little book here*
that after a while they began to creep back again.
But he was very, he felt very stirred within himself
   at what had happened,
and he thought 'I must do something, get a place
   where they can feel safe.'
That's what he felt.
It's not that he was wanting to start up a settlement,
but he just wanted somewhere where they could
   feel safe.

---

*   '*he says in his little book*' — *Schenk records in his diary.*

Carolyn:	The attitude at the time was pretty hostile towards Aboriginal people, and I guess also towards anyone who started to question the status quo —
Margaret:	That's right, they wanted to keep the status quo where they could just have them do jobs without paying them for it, just give them a shirt or some old bit of clothing.
They were never paid, nobody ever paid.
So they never had any money to go and buy anything.
They were dirty and dusty
and they had things wrong with them, health-wise, too, so they were a poor bedraggled lot.
They really were.

...

I said 'How did you get stuff to eat?'
Because when you look at the map, it's all a really dry area.
'Oh,' they said, 'they'd find things.'
Little animals, little reptiles, green stuff here and there, and, as you say, it had rained.
I've got this story about the eggs here *[points to* A Drop in a Bucket*]*.

...

Just somebody, un-named, who was kind.
They met kind people.

And that Mitchell family, they used to run to him when they'd had a whipping, and he would bathe their wounds. There was no good going to the hospital. |
| Carolyn: | When you went back to talk to the people about the walking and the journey, what sort of — after their initial reluctance to talk about the people because of the names of the dead issue — what sort of things did they mention most? What was |

the hierarchy of the importance of the events?

Margaret: Doris, Doris wasn't an __.
Doris is this one here [points to photo].
She gave me this part here [points to map].

Carolyn: That's the Southern Cross route?

Margaret: Yes ...
Now Doris, she was the one, she married Bert Thomas.
__ __ She was very knowledgeable about the Aboriginal ways and methods and all their doings.
Very knowledgeable. About the language and everything. I used to ask her things about the language. And she knew.

Doris gave me the story about the eggs.
And the bit about the bald hill — you can see that hill when you're travelling along — they stopped on that hill just out of Bullabulling. They found plenty of rabbits running around that hill! She told me about what they caught.
And I asked her questions: 'Did they go along the roads?'
'No, they didn't. They walked along the side, in the bush.'

She told me how they cooked things.
They made a fire, in a hole in the ground and cooked in it, and huddled around the fire.
And then they covered it up and went on their way.

She always — she lived in Laverton — she was always, she was like a mother to all ... Doris was like that.
So I used to ask her about everything.
She knew all about this lot. [Southern Cross route.]

She didn't know about <u>this</u> lot, I got that from Reggie. *[Northern route.]*

And <u>this</u> one here, who gave me this *[Northern route]*, was sitting in the Leonora hospital, up in bed …

And when I went up there, I said, 'Who can tell me about Jinera and —'

So what I did was, when I went up, I'd ask, 'Who knew about that?' and I'd ask around.

Ngada's party… Ngada's party met with trouble.

I said, 'Who knows anything about Ngada? And who was with him and all that?'

So, I said, 'I'll go and see what Lampi knows.'

He couldn't see too well, Lampi, but he had a loud voice …

Anyway, this Lampi. He sat up in bed, and he, we sat at court, my sister and I. And he sat up like King Farouk or something, and in his bed…

Oh yes, yes, he'd tell me this — so I'm trying to write it all down, trying to get it on that tape recorder.

Sometimes, I wasn't too good. I didn't want to put them off when they were in midstream. So, I'd quickly make notes in case I didn't put it on right, I didn't want to frighten him off.

Well, he told me this wonderful story, about Ngada's lot, what they did, how they went straight through, they reached Mt Magnet, that's right, and then they turned eastwards, and walked downwards from Mulga Queen, and walked down in to Laverton, that's right.

And they walked a distance of well over 800 k's,

I worked that out, and it was eighteen days from the time they'd been trucked out of Laverton.

And then he told me this absolutely marvellous story of Jinera!

You see, my father never knew that. He just knew
    that this blind man came back on his own, he
    didn't know where he came from! I thought that
    was absolutely wonderful ...

And, that's what I asked him: 'How come his
    sister's up there?'
And that's when they told me: She was one of the
    Darlots, that they caught; they killed all the men
    off, and took the women off.
And I thought to myself, 'I wonder when that
    happened?'
And I noticed in some book since, Daisy Bates
    wrote about it ...

Carolyn: The people that you talked to about the stories,
    Lampi and Reggie and Doris — did they have
    family members who were involved in the escape
    or did they have the story passed on to them
    generally, do you think?

Margaret: Passed on to them. Reggie Johnston, he was related
    to this one.

Carolyn: Jidu?

Margaret: Yes, Jidu, two generations back, his mother I think.
    His mother was related to Jidu.
But Reggie Johnson's my age, and he is a full
    blood. Went to school, very clever, but because he
    had a black skin he never had a chance to get
    anywhere in life, but he had a great personality, a
    great personality. He was a great person.
He, oh — getting everybody singing. He was
    wonderful. He was an inspiration to me when I
    was up there.

Carolyn: So he would have heard the story from his family?

Margaret: Oh yes, from his relations, it would have been

talked about.
It would have been talked about among his people, his relations.
And Doris, she's up in Laverton, now she heard from — who were hers?

Carolyn: The Southern Cross people.

Margaret: Yes, I think they were <u>Jidu's</u> lot.
Jidu's lot as well.

But, Reggie knew about <u>this</u> lot, he knew about them.
'Cause I said about them, 'Who was in this lot?'
They gave me the names.

Carolyn: In the Menzies lot?

Margaret: Yes.
I don't think I've got Ngada's lot.
There were some I think that they couldn't tell me, but they told me everyone who went.

Carolyn: They *[Ngada's group]* had someone called 'Old Wunu'?

Margaret: Old Wunu, yes.

Carolyn: Who didn't make it, but apart from that, you don't know the rest of their names?

Margaret: Yes, that's right.
Dad said there was only one who didn't come back.
So, his records, are what they said.
And they told me what happened. I couldn't get over it.
But it's just what they do; when they're out walkabout, if somebody gets too sick, and they're going to die anyway, they just leave them. They don't see it as being cruel.

	It's a fact of life. It's a fact of life in a subsistence society, and a walkabout society.
Carolyn:	What about Lampi, how would he have known, do you think, about these northern stories?
Margaret:	Well. I don't know. He was tribal. Whereas these two were educated, who told me the other stories.* He was tribal, he was the one sitting up in the hospital, and we just didn't interrupt the flow. I don't think I asked him any questions at all! He just went for his life, told me all about it. I don't know how he was related — he might have told me, I might have not got it down. Anyway.
Carolyn:	Do you still have the notes or the transcripts you made —?
Margaret:	Well I should have, but I think they must be down, my brother must have some. Goldfields interviews — see, I've got that down; 'Margaret's interviews with Goldfields people in the early days.' I've got it marked GI. But I can't find it amongst the archives that I've got here, so my brother must still have it down at Esperance, I think … I just brought these up last time I went down, that's why I've got them here. See, I sent them all down to him, thinking that I would go first … Most of them are probably illegible __ are half, half shorthand, half other.

---

*   'these two … who told me the other stories' — *Mr Reggie Johnston and Mrs Doris Thomas.*

	... When I did this — before I got this all done — it was '78. That's right.
Carolyn:	When did you go and do the interviewing in the Goldfields about this story? What year would that have been?
Margaret:	Oh, it was after Mum went, and she died when she was eighty-two and she died in '80. She died in '80 and she was eighty-two. Dad died ten years before then.
Carolyn:	So it was some time after that when you did the interviewing?
Margaret:	Yes, because what I did was, I thought I'd just collate all the material first ...
Carolyn:	Are Doris Thomas and Reg Johnston still alive?
Margaret:	Doris has gone. Reg Johnston is, but he's not quite with it now. He used to be very articulate. Very, very articulate. ... You could, you could try and ask him if you went on a little visit up there.
Carolyn:	I'd love to go and try and talk to some people... Would any of the people still up there know the story, do you think? Would it have been passed on?
Margaret:	I wouldn't think so. If they did, they wouldn't have the facts. I wouldn't think so.
Carolyn:	So, Reg Johnston is probably the last one?
Margaret:	Yes. Yes, yes I would say he was. See, I'm seventy-

three, he'd be seventy-five.
...
It had to go down in writing.
You know, I had people say, 'You shouldn't put
these things in. It's only going to stir things up.'
And I said, 'It's history.'

Carolyn: We need to face up to it.

Margaret: It's history.
It happened.
And I'm glad I did.
...

3

Writings

Introduction to the Writings

The discovery of the written evidence of the 1921 exile and escape was not straightforward nor linear. Government department archives were restricted; letters-of-application-and-permission later I sat down in the silent State Records researcher's room and began, gingerly, to turn the pages of the old ledgers which had been retrieved for me. I spent a long silent summer looking for archival sources that verified the facts of the 1921 story. I had not yet met the people whose testimonies you have already read in the previous chapter; at the time my single source of information about this story suggested that the events took place in 1926. Searches through records about Laverton and the Moore River Settlement in 1926 proved fruitless, frustrating. The silence was heavy.

Perhaps, as many people had told me, it was impossible to find the story without a more informed starting position. Maybe this piece of history was, after all, lost.

I had requested the Laverton Police Files dating from 1915 in order to place the '1926 events' in context, and while sifting painstakingly through these early records I stumbled upon references to a story that seemed surprisingly similar to the one for which I was searching. The Police Files dated the deportation of a group of Wongutha as occurring in 1921.[1]

Now that I knew the correct date of the events, I found more evidence of the story in the Laverton Police Letter Book and in various parts of the Moore River Settlement archives. The silence began breaking up. Fading ink-penned scripts testified to the reality of this story, and a hundred other stories waiting to be told. Reading the handwritten 'Register of Inmates' of the Moore River Settlement was a numbing experience. Real people had written these names, real people had owned these names, real lives had been often irrevocably altered by admission to this Settlement.

There were many admissions listed, and very few departures — I was overjoyed, triumphant from seventy-six years away, startling the other researchers, when I found the records documenting the Laverton people's escape.

Writings presents documents that provide written evidence of this deportation, escape and return home. Documents that illuminate the social and political structure of the Laverton society at the time are also presented in order to provide a contextual framework in which the events may be understood.[2] I have decided not to duplicate contextual material that is readily available in other published works.[3]

The first five sections of Writings were all written around the time of the 1921 events — they are contemporaneous to the events. Material written since 1945 I have categorised separately, considering that the accounts of recent writers are essentially interpretive and should be read and understood differently to the accounts of writers who were contemporay to the events. Recent writings are presented in the final section of Writings.

The written evidence of this history is primarily constructed by people of European descent, with the exception of the newspaper-published letter of William Harris, a prominent Aboriginal spokesman at the time and the founder of the Native Union in Western Australia.

Writings documents all the available written sources of evidence. Other sources identified remain unavailable — in my archival searches through the government department indexes I came across many interesting file-titles, but the files themselves are 'closed', unavailable for research, containing restricted material. The correspondence between the Chief Protector (A O Neville) and the Local Protector of Aborigines (Police Constable Thompson in Laverton) is one such file. Undoubtedly, additional evidence remains to be found in these archival files at such a time as they become 'open'. Other potentially revelatory archival files are 'missing' from the State Archives. The picture is not complete, the whole truth eludes discovery.

Laverton Police Records

The Laverton Police Letter-Book[1] records a copy of letters and reports sent from the Laverton Police Office, supplemented by some, but not all, of the incoming correspondence. The letters and reports give a clear indication of the attitudes of the police officer in charge at Laverton towards the Wongutha people. His reports to higher authorities and his replies to official telegrams and letters from the Kalgoorlie police, the Commissioner of Police in Perth and the Chief Protector of Aborigines in Perth, provide an indication of the policy and priorities of these authorities also.

Constable E P Thompson's police duties were complicated by his extra duty as the local Protector of Aborigines.

In his various roles, he was to patrol, control, and sometimes assist the Wongutha. He was to issue food rations and other government supplies to the people; he was also to keep the people away from his office and out of town.

> Police officers and justices of the peace were also granted special powers over Aborigines ... They could order 'loitering' or 'indecently dressed' Aborigines to leave the vicinity of towns. The police were to lay charges against persons offending against the Act ... In the case of Aborigines offending against the Act, police did not require a warrant to make an arrest. Obviously, the Act left the Police with very special powers. Given existing Departmental practice, there was every likelihood of police being appointed as honorary protectors and, combined with existing powers as police officers, this was to give them unprecedented power over Aborigines.[2]

Thompson was answerable to his superior police officers, stationed in Kalgoorlie, for enforcing law and order; he was also answerable to the Aborigines and Fisheries Department, in distant Perth, for 'protection' of the very people who experienced the roughest application of white man's law and order.

More immediate than either of these authorities was the concerned and vocal white community living in Laverton; he saw them in his lounge, in the pub, at the store, station, post office, and further afield in the mining and woodline camps scattered through the extensive Laverton Police District. Many of them could remember only too well the twenty or so years back to the aggressive times[3] when the Mt Margaret goldfields were first entered by white men. Thompson, in their eyes, was personally accountable for preserving peace and safety in his remote 'outpost of civilisation.'[4] They encouraged him to use every effort to ensure their comfort and security.

The change in the Laverton officer's descriptions of Wongutha people over the years to 1921 is particularly interesting. In January 1915, his first year of Protectorship, he states that they 'behave themselves well', and later in the same year, that they 'do not give any annoyance that I know of.' He then moves, by 1919, to a position in which he describes 'hordes of natives infesting the towns', and gradually between 1919 and 1921 the situation becomes more and more 'troublesome'.

Convictions of Aboriginal people rise markedly for this time span. Only one Wongutha person is sentenced,[5] to a term of six months, in the year covered by the July 1917 annual report. In July 1919 Thompson records the conviction of twelve Wongutha offenders over the previous year; their sentence terms have increased in length to two and a half years. In the first three months alone of 1921 he records convictions and sentences for six Wongutha offenders.

Thompson consistently defends his sympathetic actions in allowing the Wongutha to gather near the town (contrary to the 1905 Act) from 1915 until 1921, despite increasing political pressure levied on him. He refuses to exercise his power to expel the Wongutha until April 1921, when he is compelled by orders from the Commissioner of Police in Perth to deal 'stringently' with the people; he carries out the instructions to drive them out of the town. But they return. A few months later, in a bid to strike a proper respect for the law into the defiant Wongutha, the Laverton police deport some of the Wongutha people to Mogumber, as reported in Thompson's letter of October 1921.

After this letter, Thompson makes no further mention of the deported Wongutha in his records.[6]

Note: The following extracts are presented verbatim. The original grammatical and spelling errors of the archival record remain.

Extracts: Laverton Police to Kalgoorlie Police. Report on the Wongutha,1915

<u>Annual Report on Aborigines 25.1.15</u>

Sub Insp O'Halloran,

I respectfully report that on the 30/6/1914, there were approximately 400 Natives in the Laverton police dist.
Of that number 30 at Laverton and about 40 at Erlistoun were receiving Govt rations ... Native game and food is not plentiful but should be better than it has been for a good number of years, as there has been good rains ...
  Drunkenness was very rare amongst them. One white was fined £10 for supplying liquor to them.
  The Natives give a good deal of trouble to the police in having to remove them from town sites and mines where they congregate from time to time, but taken on the whole behave themselves well.
  At the present time I do not think any improvement can be made on the treatment they receive.

25.1.15 E P Thompson 292

(AN5/Laverton ACC3354/1 p159,167)

Letter to the Sub-Inspector at Kalgoorlie, responding to complaints, 1915

<u>Complaints re Natives at Laverton</u>

Sub-Inspt O'Halloran

I respectfully report, that there are always a large Camp of Natives a few miles out of Laverton, and on most days a number of the old Men and Women come to the town to get scraps of food from the inhabitants.

They are not diseased and do not give any annoyance that I know of ...

The position in the Laverton district, as regards the Natives, is a very hard one to deal satisfactorily with.

In the first place there are in the Laverton Police district, some 400 Natives, only 15 are receiving Government rations. Native game is very scarce, in fact practically extinct, and they have water in the bush only when it rains and for a few weeks after, the consequence is they flock to the towns to beg food and water.

If they are dealt harshly with, driven away & kept strictly out of the town, they must either starve or steal, and naturally prefer the latter which is only instinct, it is then they give the Police no end of trouble, they will rob Prospectors and Woodcutters camps, with no impunity.

When they pilfer in outlying places it is in most instances difficult for the Police to effect early arrest and put a stop to the crime.

Some few years back the Natives were harassed & driven into the Bush by the Police at Laverton & the result was, they robbed camps to such an extent in the outlying parts that the Prospectors & Woodcutters threatened to deal with them themselves in a drastic manner, and in one instance the Natives were shot at by the latter.

By allowing the large camp of Natives near Laverton they are practically under Police supervision & give little trouble. I have interviewed Mr W. Mackey JP the Secretary & Inspector to the Laverton Board of Health, and he has no complaints to make against the Natives.

5/6/15 292

(AN5/Laverton ACC3354/1 p174)

Laverton Police General Report, 1917
(Extracts related to dealings with the Wongutha.)

General Report as Required
(File 777/16 1 July 1917)

...

(2) Approximately 410, condition fairly good, 11 employed under permits on cattle stations, Rations at present to 52 old & indigent (20 at Laverton, 12 at Burtville, 20 at Erlistoun) Natives have not given so much trouble as in past years. 1 Native sentenced to 6 mths during this year.

...

(AN5/Laverton ACC3354/1 p201)

Laverton Police General Reports, 1919
(Extracts related to dealings with the Wongutha.)

General Report as Required
(File 776/16 2 July 1919)

...

(2) approximately 500, condition good, 7 employed on cattle stations under permits, 15 old are receiving rations at Laverton. Have been very troublesome this last 12 months, a large influx of Spinifex Natives took place and will not leave the district, 26 offences were listed against Natives, mostly all stealing. 12 Natives were convicted and sentenced to terms from 6 Mths to $2 \, ^1/_2$ years.

...

(9) The prospects of the dist are not over bright ...
The Native question here is becoming acute, hordes of Natives keep infesting the towns & when removed either go to another place or come back as soon as police have gone an hour or two, they are also continually thieving from isolated places, a constable could be kept with horses doing

nothing else but keeping Natives in check and following up Native offenders.

Const 292.

(AN5/Laverton ACC3354/1 p214)

Letter to the Inspector after receiving Instructions from the Commissioner of Police to deal stringently with the Wongutha, April 1921

Inspt Duncan,

I respectfully report that on receipt of the attached telegram from the Commissioner of Police in Perth, stringent steps were taken against the Natives who were in the vicinity of Laverton, Mt Crawford and Beria, with the exception of a number of old ones, they were dispersed into the Spinifex, & although small parties of them keep coming back, they are again driven out.

The native question in this district is anything but a small matter, there are approximately 450 of them throughout the police district, the majority being born and reared here.

The getting the whole of them out into the Spinifex is nearly impossible, some of them are semi-civilised & others purely wild. They cannot be got together & driven out like sheep, as soon as a move is made against them by the police they scatter like rabbits through the bush and camp in small parties of twenty's & thirty's.

The present difficulty with them has arisen through two causes principally — such as the decline of the small mining settlements throughout the district and the absence of native waters, there has been no rain for practically 12 months & the natives have been dependent on the towns for water, native game is not plentiful as stated by the Chief Protector.

In dealing with the natives in the past, a number of things had to be taken into consideration, when they were driven out relentlessly, the camps of Prospectors & Woodcutters in the outlying parts were robbed with impunity & by the time the police were informed, the offenders were days & miles away or they would go and camp near the windmills on the pastoral stations & disturb the stock, with the result that the station owners would complain and request the immediate removal.

The natives in the district are born thieves. It is nature to them, the past records of convictions against them will bear this out, from the 1/1/21 to the 17/3/21 six male natives have been convicted of offences against the property & person, 2 received 12 mths each, 4 received 6 mths each.

It would be of great assistance to the police here & have a good effect on the natives throughout the district, if the Natives who are convicted & sentenced to gaol, were on the completion of their sentence kept away and sent to other parts.

Through the closing down of Beria, the local police should have plenty of time to deal with the natives, as I have already mentioned the chief difficulty in keeping the natives well out is the absence of water.

Laverton 11/4/21
Const 292.

(AN5/Laverton ACC3354/1 inserted at p226, not fixed, no telegram attached)

Annual Report, date obliterated (July 1921)[7]

<u>Annual Report (File no. obliterated)</u>

(1) Approximately 400
(2) Approximately 475, condition only fair, 4 employed on cattle stations, 15 old ones rationed at Laverton, 100 received clothing and blankets in May last. They have been very troublesome during the past 6 mths, thieving from camps and infesting the towns begging, this has been brought on by the recent drought, absence of water & native game, also the closing of the Woodline & the Beria mine where the native obtained a large quantity of waste food for doing odd jobs. During the past yr 13 natives were convicted of various offences (principally stealing 6 received 6 months each, three

received 12 mths each, 2 received 7 months each & one native youth was sent to an aboriginal home.
...
(9) The prospects of the district are anything but bright & the future looks dismal, all the principal mines throughout the district are shut down ... The population during the last 6 months has been reduced by about 600 persons.
...

Const 292

(AN5/Laverton ACC3354/1 p226)

Letter to the Deputy Chief Protector of Aborigines, 1921

<u>The Deputy Chief Protector of Aborigines. Perth</u>
Re the attached application of R S Schenk for land for Mission purposes:-

Providing the lands dept have no uses for the Commonage, I see no objection to the same being granted to 'Schenk' personally, to conduct on his own responsibility.

The land applied for is fully 18 miles from Laverton, & if he could get the Natives down there (& to remain) it would be a great relief to the residents of this district.

At the same time I would strongly urge upon your dept, the necessity of not committing itself with 'Schenk' otherwise they will be deluded with applications (endless) for assistance on a large scale from him.

Personally I do not think 'Schenk' can make a success of the land he proposes to take up, it will require a good deal of capital (which he has not got) & further the Natives will not stay in that part of the Country for any length of time.

The Natives about here, have always been a source of trouble, and the advent of 'Schenk' to the district, did anything but improve matters with them, this man has endeavoured to take upon himself duties with the Natives, other than teaching them the gospel, he is also obsessed with the imaginary importance of bringing the standard of the

Natives to the same level as the 'Whites'.

The Natives here at the present time, are giving no trouble & keeping themselves fairly scarce, this is principally through the recent deportation of a number of them to the Coast,* this deportation, I might state is greatly resented by 'Schenk' and in consequence, I know he bears the Aborigines Dept and the Police no good will.

There is now plenty of native game and water, available, & no occasion for any Natives, outside a few old ones, to loiter in the vicinity of towns.

I interviewed 'Schenk' on the matter and he states if the land is granted to him, he is going in for goat farming, collecting Sandalwood & growing vegetables & is quite confident the natives will go on the land with him.

Laverton. 1/10/21
Protector of Aborigines

(AN5/Laverton ACC3354/1 p227)

Telegram from the Inspector of Police at the Kalgoorlie District Office requesting a list of all 'indigent natives' in the Laverton District, 1922

Jan 26 1922
The Officer in charge of Police,
Laverton,

Please forward as early as possible a list of all indigent natives in your District.

DO Kal 21/1/22
Inspector of Police.

(AN5/Laverton ACC3354/1 p228)

---

* 'deportation ... to the Coast' — deportation to Mogumber. Neville also referred to Mogumber as the settlement on the coast. Refer to Neville's letter to Mrs Boxall in Appendix A7.

Record of request from the Aborigines Department, Perth, for a list of all 'indigent natives' in the Laverton District, and the reply from Laverton Police, 1922

> Aborigines Department
> Perth
> 24th January 1922
> Circular (CSO 173/21)
>
> Constable EP Thompson
> Police Station,
> Laverton.
>
> Will you please let me have, as early as possible, a list of all indigent natives in your district.
> For secretary
>
>
> Copy
> Laverton Police Station
> February 6th 1922
>
> Sent Inspt Duncan & Aborigines dept.
>
> I respectfully report the indigent natives in the district are as follows,
> Laverton about 15, Ida H 3, Burtville 6, Beria 5, Erlistoun 7.
>
> Laverton 6/2/22
> Const 292
>
> *(AN5/Laverton ACC3354/1 p228)*

Annual Report Laverton Police, 1922

> Annual report 'file 776/16'
> Laverton Station July 1st 1922
>
> ...
> (2) Approximately 400, condition only fair, 11 employed on

cattle stations, 15 old ones rationed at Laverton. 100 received clothing and blankets in May & June last. They have been for the past 12 months rather troublesome as regards stealing from the prospectors' camps, this can be accounted for owing to a number of bush natives coming in from the Spinifex and mixing with the thieving natives here. During the past 12 mths, 9 natives have been convicted of various offences (principally stealing). 1 received 3 yrs, 1 recd 2 yrs, 2 recd 1 yrs each, & 5 recd 6 mths each.

...

(9) This district is having an exceptionally good season, feed & water is plentiful, & from a grazing point of view the district never looked better.

Laverton 1/7/22
Const 292

(AN5/Laverton ACC3354/1 insert, not attached)

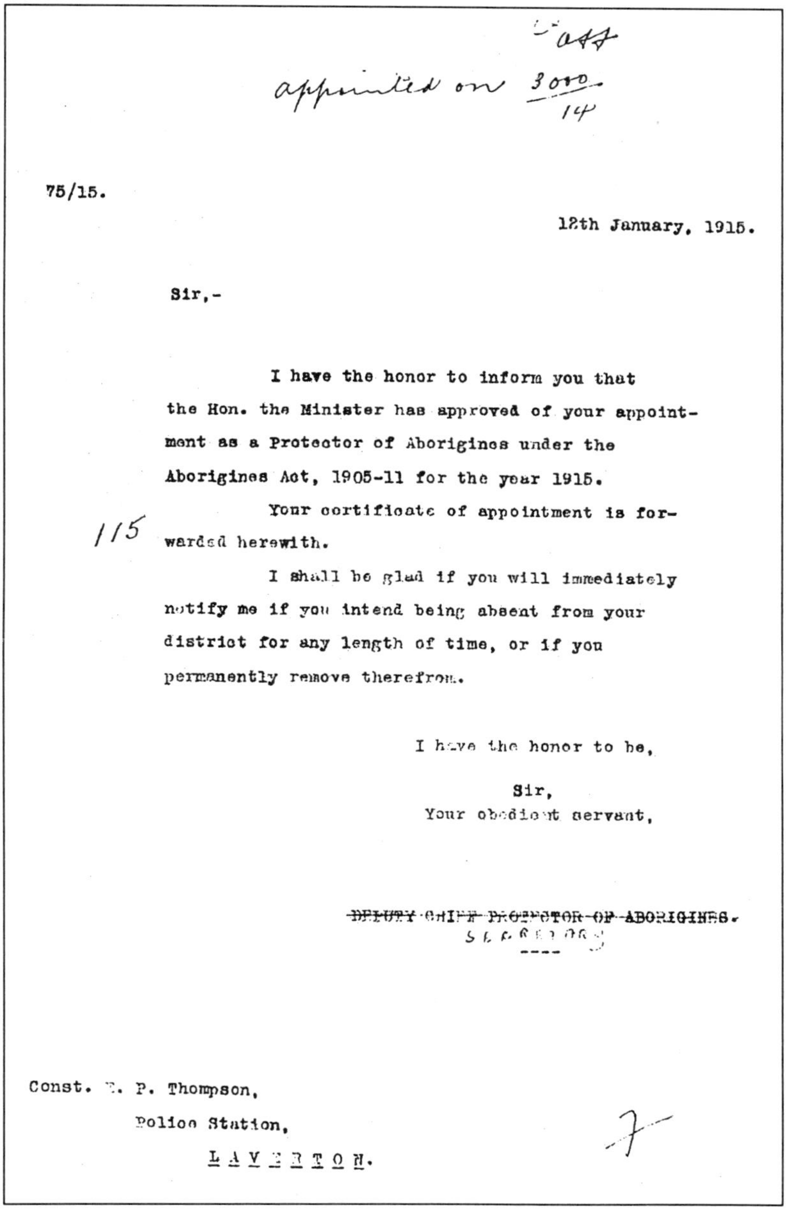

75/15.

12th January, 1915.

Sir,-

I have the honor to inform you that the Hon. the Minister has approved of your appointment as a Protector of Aborigines under the Aborigines Act, 1905-11 for the year 1915.

Your certificate of appointment is forwarded herewith.

I shall be glad if you will immediately notify me if you intend being absent from your district for any length of time, or if you permanently remove therefrom.

I have the honor to be,

Sir,
Your obedient servant,

~~DEPUTY CHIEF PROTECTOR OF ABORIGINES.~~

Const. E. P. Thompson,
    Police Station,
        L A V E R T O N.

Figure 3.1-A
E P Thompson's original letter of appointment as Protector of Aborigines in 1915.

R S Schenk's Letters and Diary

In June 1920, Rod (Rodolphe Samuel) Schenk wrote from Victoria to the Chief Protector of Aborigines for Western Australia, asking for statistics on the Aboriginal people of Western Australia and requesting information on the best means of travelling in the north-west of the State.[1] He arrived in Perth in March 1921 and immediately met with the Chief Protector, Neville, in order to continue the dialogue about mission work with Aboriginal people in the north. Neville persuaded Schenk to take his zeal instead to the Laverton Goldfields, a particularly 'troublesome' area[2] that had been the subject of police/protector communication since 1915. Schenk lost no time, and set off to the edge of the desert as soon as he had gathered supplies, arriving in Laverton three weeks later. He was shocked by his impressions of the community in which he found himself, and he recorded these impressions in letters to his friends and supporters in Victoria. The local contemporary attitudes towards and treatment of Aboriginal people, as well as other happenings and events of interest, are succinctly documented in Schenk's letters.

Schenk's letters and diary record a uniquely sympathetic voice:

Extracts from a Letter to Friends, Perth, March 1921

> I have been to see Mr Neville (Chief Protector of Abor.) and I find that the Govt. here is not so amicably disposed to Gospel mission work as would appear by correspondence ... As regards Moola Bulla and Violet Valley Cattle Stations — Mr Neville says that they would not allow a Missionary to go there at present under any circumstance ... I am told by them (Mr Neville and Mr Copping) that the Laverton and Wiluna district is the best for pioneering work but it must be pioneering. If I collect them near a town and they become a

nuisance to the white people then they will shift both the Aborigines and me ... The Govt here make a practice of periodically thrusting the Aborigines out of the towns so that they will go out in hunting bands through the country.

(30/3/1921. Private Collection)

Schenk's diary records that he arrived in Laverton on 22 April 1921. A letter written on 24 April indicates that he had already begun to seek out Aboriginal people and to speak with them. The white community did not regard this as socially acceptable behaviour; Schenk's diary entry for 7 May notes that his communication with and sympathetic interest in the Aboriginal people was resulting in 'opposition from whites'.

Extracts from a Letter to Friends, Laverton, 1921

Laverton, WA,
24/4/1921

In the train to Laverton a long discussion took place with my fellow passenger. He is well known as Brother John and is the Anglican Lay-Reader for the district. He said that except for Leonora the whole district from Broad Arrow is worked by him. He journeys up and down on the train and visits the different station townships en route. One or two Methodist parsons came to Laverton but I understand were starved out. But Brother John is not averse to his glass of wine or game of cards etc, and so he gets along alright ...

He left the train at Mt Morgans and said he was pleased to have met me. His hope for the Aborigines is 'nil'.

... All these dear folk use emphatic terms about the unstable Aborigine ... The Aboriginal problem is a very 'vexed' one here. There has been a severe drought and together with the mine closing down things are in a bad way. The mine employed hundreds of men and the Aborigines being short of game relied upon the dry bread etc thrown away by the big wood cutting camps and also a little they could beg from the settlers nearby. They began to beg more around Beria and Laverton when these camps closed down. The police took action to expel them and used stock whips to flog them away with. One Aboriginal woman had her arm broken through forcible expulsion. Mr Thompson, and his colleague, Mr Hunter, are the two police in charge. Mr Thompson is also Protector (?) of Aborigines for the district. The dark people became vindictive and are now robbing huts and homes of prospectors of their food. The police are now after one Aborigine who robbed a prospector of food, a revolver and cartridges. They say they must have [indistinguishable]1* firearms amongst them in the bush now. I have heard of about 200 natives some miles out, demanding food from settlers ... From what I see and hear there is no work for the Aborigines and just now there is no game. They are truly very wild here. About twenty of them are allowed rations and they come in from the scrub and vanish into it again as soon they get their flour. Mr Thompson says that they have no camp — not even a collection of bough gunyahs. He does not allow them to congregate anywhere. They can be seen in ones and twos creeping around the houses on the outskirts to beg food. I have been speaking to many but they don't understand even the simplest of English except 'bacca', 'flour', 'sugar' ...

[Only page one of the original letter still exists, but M Morgan has a typed copy of a second page, which follows.]

Mr Thompson advised me not to go too far into the bush lest I be speared. He says that they are very wild and that he would not think of entering in amongst them without being armed and mounted. I would feel the same if I were a policeman.

Farther north is a still more hostile tribe called the Darlo natives. These natives visit Wiluna. Some weeks ago they made war on the Laverton natives, leaving 8 dead and many wounded just outside the town.

---

* *The number is perhaps 11, 21 or 31 — the first numeral is obliterated in the original.*

An official in Perth who says 'he knows', believes that Mr Neville wanted me to come here rather than to the Kimberleys where some of his pet schemes might be upset (Moola Bulla and Violet Valley Cattle Stations.) ...

(Private Collection)

Extracts from a Letter to Friends, Laverton, 1921

Laverton, W.A.
2/5/1921

Dear Friends

...

Since last writing I have had the pleasure of the first meeting with a congregation of Aborigines. I met them about two miles out ... Of course they have no idea of a meeting and they simply laugh, talk or scream in the middle of one's well prepared address. Some are still a little suspicious and in the middle of the meeting the word 'Cooeyanbah' acted like a magic wand in a vanishing movement. 'Cooeyanbah' means Hunter the P.C. or any other bad man. My young native friend told me that there were several half-caste children in the bush near by but they were afraid that I might be working in collusion with Hunter to have them snapped up and taken away as others have been taken south before. 'Cooeyanbah' proved to be a false alarm and they soon came back ...

Water is one of the difficulties here ... Most of the lakes here are brackish and even fresh water lakes are not good enough for drinking purposes ...

An old prospector with two others has just left Laverton with 10 camels and £125 worth of provisions to try a certain range of hills 400 miles out for gold. The last party which went out had 2 of their number speared by natives ...

(Private Collection)

Extracts from a Letter to Friends, Laverton, 1921

9:5:21

Dear friends ...

The police have successfully caused a general migration of the natives. There are still about 100 natives around Laverton and Berea and as these are likely to remain, there will be scope for work in the meantime. Regarding the drastic measures taken by police. They act under orders of the A.P.B.* and if I cause a stir about it then it would only boomerang back on my own head.

    A Mrs Bates I understand came over to Western Australia to reveal certain facts but she soon found that it was better for her to retire to SA. ...

    One item of food 'til lately, were the rabbits. Where rabbits disappear to in drought time is a standing mystery. Especially here as the desert is on the East and the two WA rabbit proof fences are on the West.

(Private Collection)

Extracts from a Letter to Friends, Laverton, 1921

Laverton, W. AUS.
1 August, 1921

Dear Friends

It has been my joy to win more of the confidence of the natives ... In doing work among them one has to go from

---

*   APB — *Aborigine's Protection Board. Schenk applies the term to the Western Australian Aborigines Department, headed by the Chief Protector of Aborigines. (In Western Australia the APB was in fact abolished in 1898, at which time the reponsibility for Aboriginal affairs was transferred by the British Government to the Australian State Government. In 1921 A O Neville was the administrative head of the Aborigines Department.)*

group to group as a general assembly is forbidden ...

One night they sprang to their feet, grabbed their spears, and with fire flashing from their eyes rushed forward. They thought the 'Darlos' (another tribe from the North) had come, but it was a false alarm ... I was nearly speared another night on entering the camp because, unwittingly, I did not answer a sentry call. The white folk are astonished to think that one goes out to them at night time. The white folks and natives have a wholesome fear of each other. Six native outlaws have been deported since I came here and to these poor souls the message of life was given ere they departed ...

(Private Collection)

Diary Entry, Laverton, 1921

Aug 15 Natives (15) sent away, others fled and I left alone ... Never more discouraged.

Extracts from a Letter to Friends, Laverton, 1921

September, 1921

Dear Friends

I am writing early this month ... The A.P.B. has seen fit to remove some of the natives from here, and the rest, fearing a general deportation, fled to the bush. The natives miss the white man's food and some are creeping back. I cannot find out what is determined concerning them, but perhaps another scatter will be made. It now seems to me that from the time when one decided to settle here, a definite movement was set on foot to have them sent to a settlement down South ...

(Private Collection)

Diary Entries, Laverton, 1921

Aug 30 Some natives back from Moore River.

Sept 2 Nearly all natives back.

Sept 13 ... Often walk 5, 6 and 7 miles to find the natives but the weather is cool and I enjoy the walks.

Extracts from a Letter to Friends, Laverton, 1921

26th September, 1921.
Laverton. W. AUST.

... the news, now to hand, that the natives are to stay, makes me decided to inaugurate a settlement. I have applied for the lease of a common about twenty miles out ... I find that goats are a payable proposition ... they are the best investment to supply the natives with meat — their staple item of diet ...

By the way, the natives eat dingo. My, they are tough! Both the eater and the eaten. Wild cat is another toothsome dish ... They miss the turkeys so much. The white folk tell how they once could take a day off and bag two or three turkeys — they can't bag one now. If a native kills a sheep, he pays dearly for it; but he has to silently watch the mileoo (kangaroo) and the nunoody (turkey) shot away from him, with no redress.

... my heart aches for the distressed natives. 'Something big' and 'something quick' should be done.

(Private Collection)

Extracts from a Letter to Friends, Laverton, 1921

Laverton W Aust,
30/12/21

... Some of the natives were taken to Moore River ... I thought of the distance, and I thought of the APB allowing their plan to be thwarted ... The natives sent to Moore River escaped and are back in the bush here (intended re-capture is reported but I am believing otherwise) ... I feel that the first victory of a long battle has been won.

(Private Collection)

Diary Entries, Laverton, 1921-1922

Dec 16 Came to Mount Margaret.[3]

Jan 9 Mr Mitchell from Carrolup visited us as Inspector of APB to see what we were doing.

Jan 12 Received lease of land.[4]

Mar 31 Nunjoor and Kardatilbe* come out, our first two natives.

April 2 Nunjoor and Kardatilbe go back to Morgans and the white people laugh and challenge us to get the natives here under any arrangement.

April 20 APB say won't give us the rationing here. Natives say this is stinking country when I asked them in Laverton to come.

---

* 'Nunjoor and Kardatilbe' — Nunjoor/Nganjur, also known as Bill Carrigg; Kardatilbe/Gadajilbi. They are two of the 1921 deportees.

Extracts from a Letter to Friends, Laverton, July 1922

... Our first old man, who has come back five times now, has six relations here with him, and all desire to settle. This is their first desire of settling ...

Joe, our youngest, has been on a settlement down south, and understands 'English' fairly well. He is very anxious to keep his job of shepherding the goats, so we are glad, as he is just the one we need. He says, 'by-and-by a lot of fellas are coming to sit down at Margaret.' 'By-and-by' may mean next week or next year. To 'sit down' anywhere means to work or abide at such a place.

[handwritten notes on Morgan's photocopied version:
1. the 'six': Jumbo, Nardie, Faldool, Lame Charlie Gooran, Mardigal, and Peter, Moongoodie and Dalphin, Geelul, Kitty, Bingie and Kunjel.*
2. Joe — Joe Mulgasunnoo, Joe Mulgathunoo or Mulga Joe.]

(01/07/1922. Private Collection)

Extracts from a Letter to Friends, Laverton, October 1922

... We have up to 50 natives here at a time ...

(07/10/1922. Private Collection)

Diary Entries, Laverton, 1922

Nov 19 No natives here.

Dec 2 Dalphin, Kitty, Kardatilbe, Mick, Tommy and Terry arrived.

Dec 4 Nunjoor and Lame Charlie come.

---

*   *Jumbo/Jidu; Lame Charlie Gooran/Grarn; Dalphin/Thalbin; with Moongoodie, all 1921 deportees.*

Extracts from Annual Report to the Australian Aborigines Mission. 1922

I went to Laverton, and after being there a very short time some of the natives were removed to a settlement near the coast as the authorities thought the natives were too many and too troublesome around the township ...

We were told that the natives here were the wildest ... tribe in W.A.

The Inspector of the Aborigines Protection Board classed this tribe of natives as being the most reticent and most difficult. They certainly have reason to be reticent because of the treatment meted out to them. Personally, I have seen them chased by the constable with a stock whip. On two or three occasions they have even been shot at and wounded by the constable. The natives in turn get vindictive — one stole a gun and held up a white man for food, another was sent to gaol for also having a gun and just before I came one native nearly flogged a white man to death with a waddy. Two natives made a daring escape from the Laverton platform, handcuffed and ready to be entrained for gaol. They are still at large but in their own clever way have succeeded in taking the handcuffs off ...

(Private Collection)

Diary Entries, Laverton, 1923

Jan 8   All men gone to Linden for a fight. Left all old and children with us. This is the first big step of confidence in us.

[handwritten note on Morgan's photocopied version:
60 miles away. Used to walk backwards and forward to Linden just as though they were walking up and down the street.]

Feb 7 ... Natives arrived from Linden.

Extracts from a Letter to Friends, Laverton, 1923

February 1923

... We are receiving great encouragement from the natives and have about 70 here just now ... Another encouragement is that the natives now hold their biggest corroborees here, instead of at Laverton as hitherto. The most influential native in the district has made his home with us, and intends to stay.

[Handwritten note on Morgan's photocopied version: 'The most influential native' is Jumbo/Jidu.]

(Private Collection)

Diary Entry, Laverton, 1923

Mar 10 White people tell natives lies and tell them that the police will remove them from here. But Jumbo says he wants to sit down here 'til he dies.

Notes from Speeches to Australian Aborigines Mission Meetings, Victoria, undated (c 1923)

... A large band of 40 natives came to stay. Found out that white people who were exploiting the natives had told them all kinds of lies: that we were trying to gather the natives for the Government to snatch them away (a truckload of natives having already been caught by the police at Laverton and sent away). Other white people said the Government would send along an aeroplane and get them if they came here to Mt Margaret ...

Extracts from a Letter to Friends, Laverton, 1923

April 1923.

... Jumbo, the King of the whole district, now asserts, after living here for several months, that he intends to stay here till he dies ... Speaking of the Laverton natives, we had a joyful surprise to find that about 50 here object to that term applied to them. They say, 'us nothing Laverton blackfella, us sit down along Mission, us Margaret blackfella.' The first six months of my sojourn here, not one native would abide at Margaret ...

*[Handwritten note on Morgan's photocopied version:
Jidu was known as Jumbo.]*

Diary Entry, Laverton, 1923

May 5 Big crowd natives here — fight again tonight. about 200 natives here.

Mt Margaret Mission became well established over the years; many Wongutha made their homes there. It became widely known in the region as a place of freedom from police harassment, and, in time, somewhere which offered the Aboriginal people employment, education and health care.

Schenk, disregarding censure from Neville, the local police and some local pastoralists, continued until his retirement to protest against the harsh treatment of Aborigines.[5]

Moore River Native Settlement Records

Archival records of the Moore River Native Settlement[1] document the arrival at the Settlement of a party of people from Laverton in 1921. Records also show that they escaped.

As seen in the Speakings, the Moore River Settlement, or Mogumber as it was often called, was fearfully regarded by Laverton Aboriginal people from the 1930s onwards. In the 1920s it was just beginning to earn notoriety.

Bolton notes that the importance of the Moore River Settlement to the Aborigines Department increased from around 1921:

> Under Neville ... by 1921 ... Moore River was not simply a place of compulsory reception for south-west Aborigines allegedly in need of care and protection, but was receiving inmates from every part of Western Australia. Those sent from the goldfields and pastoral districts tended to be individuals whose behaviour or circumstances were thought in some way to constitute a social problem.[2]

The arrival of these 'social problem' inmates may have prompted the Department's desire for an increase in their knowledge about and tighter control of the happenings at Moore River. The Aborigines Department focused much administrative energy towards this fast-growing settlement during 1921; the administrative standards demanded of Superintendent Campbell increased markedly.

Communication in 1921 between the Secretary of the Department and John Campbell, the Superintendent of the Moore River Native Settlement seems to have been unsatisfactory to the Secretary. The Moore River Letter Book contains many requests from the Secretary for information, for registers, for neat memos, and for efficiency. In March, and then again in April, the Superintendent is requested to kindly update the 'register of inmates' and forward this register immediately to the Perth Department Office so that 'cards' and 'office records' can be checked and updated.[3] Perhaps the administration system was still in a formative stage — the Settlement at Moore River had only recently been opened in 1918. And John Campbell was a new Superintendent. He had been appointed in February of 1921; in his letter of application he described himself as a 'Veteran Returned Soldier' seconded to the Harbour Lights Department in Derby. His career had included an administrative position as the Military Paymaster in Perth, followed by Camp Commandant positions at various Military Camps; at Geraldton, Rockingham and Blackboy Hill Military camps he had supervised capital works programs. Perhaps the Department chose him as Superintendent for the ill-equipped fledgling settlement due to his expertise in overseeing the design, construction and maintenance of buildings, drains and water supplies. In Campbell's first nine months at the Settlement in 1921, a dining room, store and office were successfully constructed.[4]

Campbell's less than perfect paperwork was to the advantage of some of the Settlement's inmates. He had another characteristic, unusual in Superintendents: an inmate of Moore River who experienced a succession of Superintendents distinguished Campbell as being kindly.[5] His influence for kindness at Moore River ended in 1924 when he was killed in a car accident.

On 22 April 1921, the Secretary sends instructions to Campbell regarding a new method for regularly updating the central records system, requiring an exchange of information about inmates each month. At the end of April, a list of admissions and departures for the month is duly compiled by Campbell and returned to Perth. (See Figure 3.3-A)

Campbell records the arrival of nineteen new 'admissions' from Laverton amongst the twenty-one admissions for the month of August; the letter is signed off in September. See Figure 3.3-B.

This letter is received on 6 September 1921, stamped, signed, and admonishment is meted to Campbell for 'incomplete' information about inmates; Campbell had been reprimanded for a similar lack of detail in June 1921.[6]

250 Writings

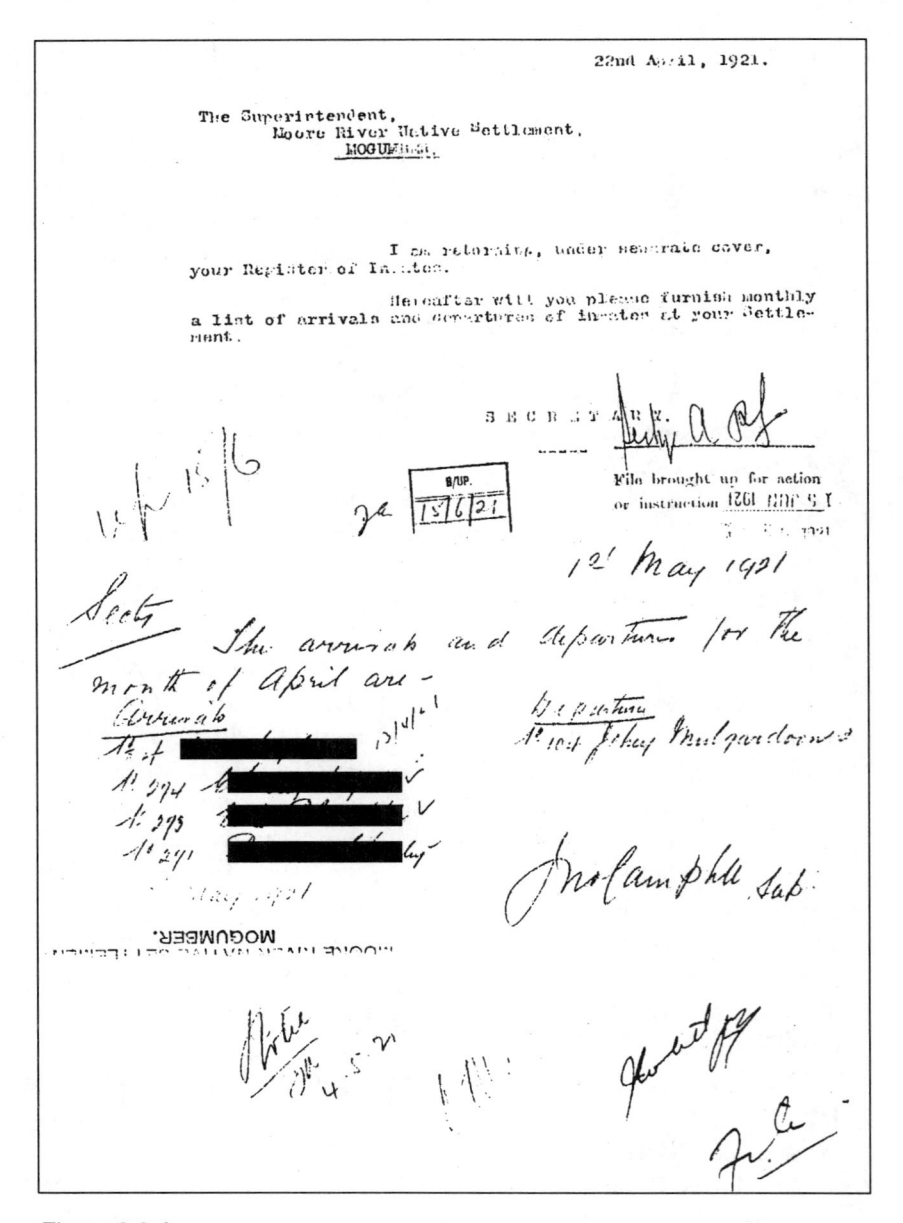

Figure 3.3-A
April/May 1921. Correspondence, Superintendent of the Moore River Native Settlement and Secretary of the Aborigines Department.
(AN 1/6 Acc 1326 p64 State Records Office, Western Australia)

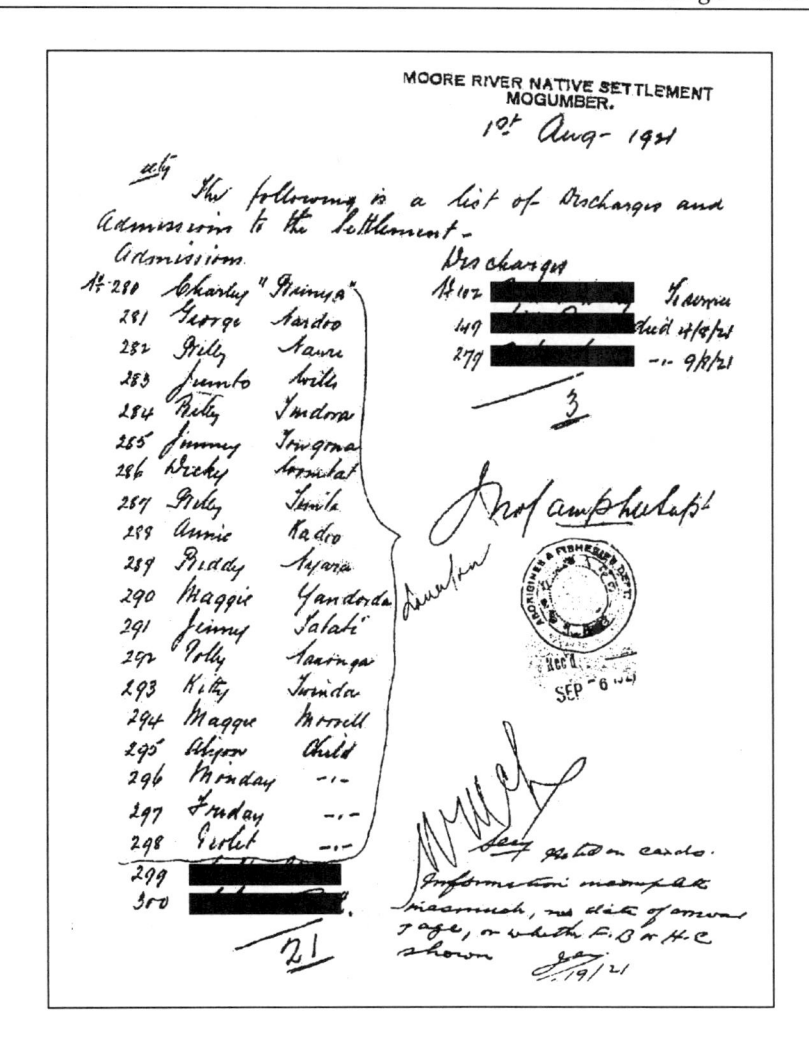

Figure 3.3-B
August 1921, Admissions & Departures List. Correspondence, Superintendent of the Moore River Native Settlement and Secretary of the Aborigines Department
(AN 1/6 ACC 1326 p 71 State Records Office, Western Australia)

NOTE: Names obscured for reasons of privacy.

Campbell's September list of admissions and discharges duly shows dates of arrivals and departures, in addition to classificatory information based on a guess at parental lineage. In a break from the usual practice, the 'Discharges' list is instead under the heading of 'Departures', and the list is sizeable. The total number of newly departed is twenty-one; sixteen of these are marked as 'deserters'. The names of the escapees include thirteen of of the Laverton people admitted in August, plus a few extra.[7] Their date of desertion is recorded as 18 September. (See Figure 3.3-C)

August and September appear to have been difficult months for the staff, and more particularly, the 'inmates' of the Settlement, due to what the *West Australian* described as an influenza epidemic. It seems likely that the Superintendent and his matron wife would have been busy coping with the epidemic and that the Superintentent might have wished to avoid the creation of additional paperwork about escapees (that might then also result in a Department directive to immediately retrieve the escapees) at this time. The ever efficient Secretary, on 19 August 1921, requests Campbell to 'Please certify as to the correctness of the attached account for 19/- (1 doz. Germicidal Soap) in favour of Messrs F.H. Faulding & Co., Perth.' (Acc 1326 AN1/6 File 622, 1921.) But despite the Secretary's usual vigilance in dealing with the Settlement's paperwork, no further correspondence relating to this large escape could be found.

Polly Tarnuga, 292, one of those admitted as part of the Laverton group in August, is not recorded in this letter as one of the group of escapees. Her name, however, is crossed off the Settlement's Inmates Register with the note: 'Deserted 18/9/21'. (See Figure 3.3-D) Obviously Campbell's recording system was not yet flawless.[8] So fourteen of the nineteen who arrived in August escaped almost immediately. Of the five who remained at Mogumber, four are recorded as escaping in November 1921. (See Figure 3,3-D.)

Three of the main party of September were not part of the group admitted in August 1921. Their allotted admission numbers indicate that they were admitted prior to the main Laverton

Writings 253

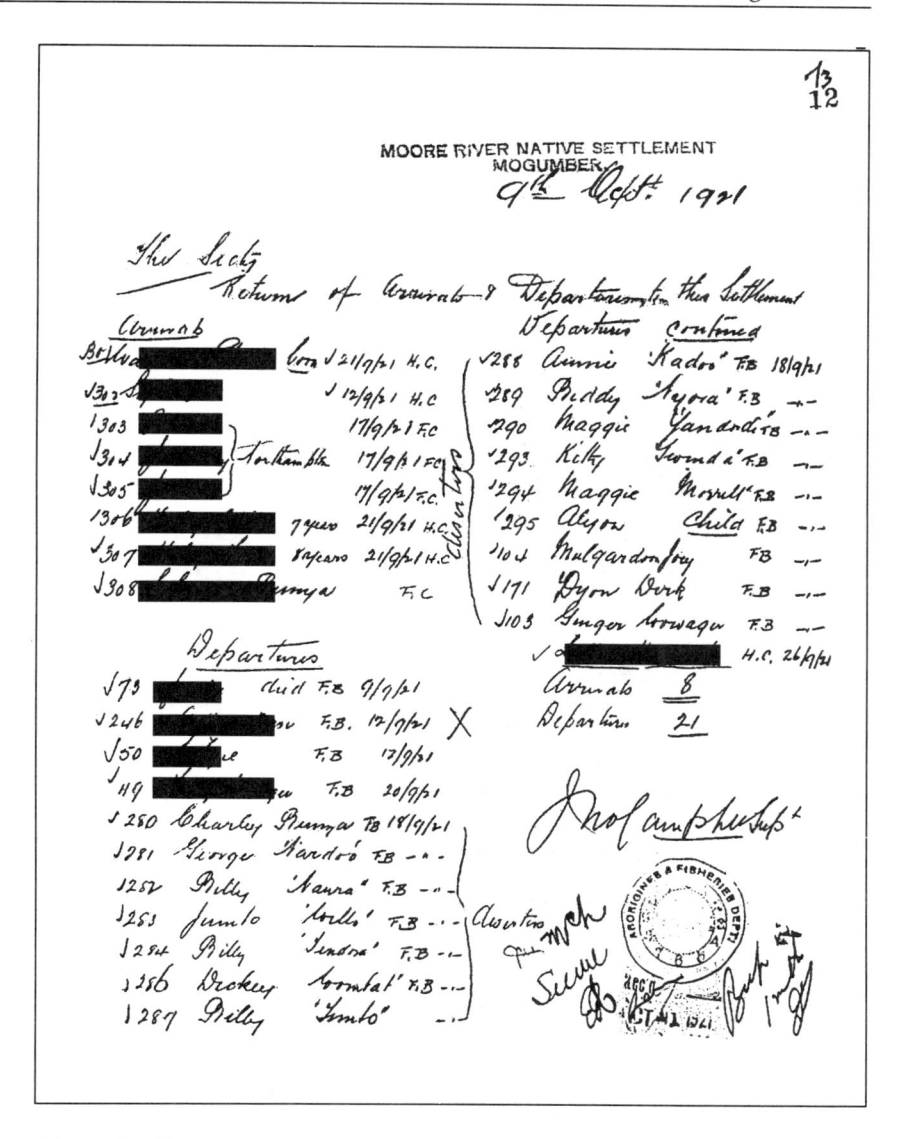

Figure 3.3-C
September 1921, Admissions and Departures List. Correspondence, Superintendent of the Moore River Native Settlement and Secretary of the Aborigines Department.

(AN 1/6 Acc 1326 State Records Office, Western Australia)

254 Writings

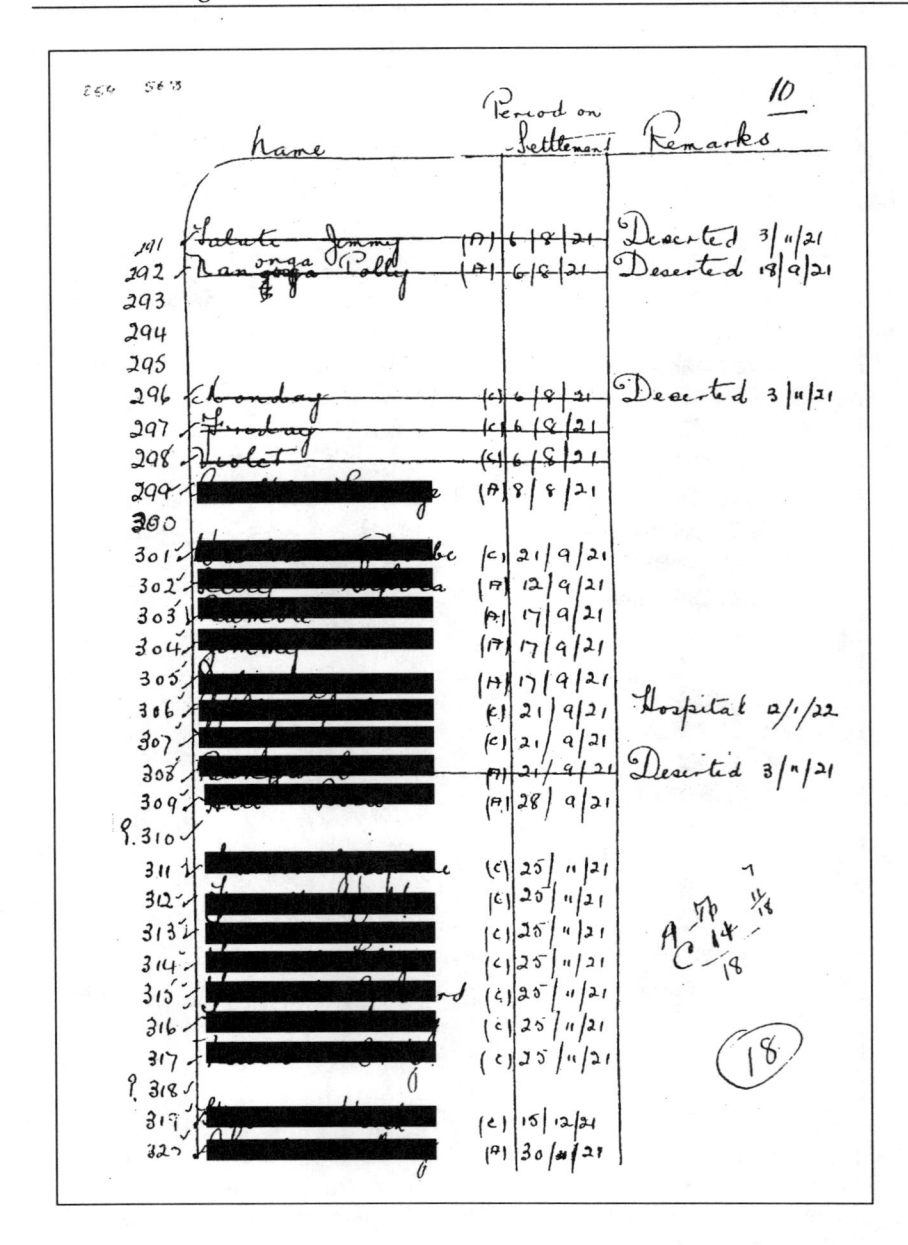

Figure 3.3-D
Register of Inmates, Moore River Native Settlement, 1921.
(AN 1/6 Acc 1326 State Records Office, Western Australia)

group, almost two hundred names earlier in the case of Mulgardoon Joey (Mulga Joe or Mulgathunoo Joe) and Ginger (Wawuja), and about one hundred names earlier for Dyon (Dion) Dirk.

These three were also Laverton people. Dion Dirk was the deaf and dumb son of Jidu, the King, and was possibly in his early teens.[9] Mulga Joe was a 'fiery fighter' in his teens. Ginger was from Cox's Find, just north of Laverton, he was in his early twenties and regarded as an 'accomplished horseman'.[10]

From the Laverton Police Records it is clear that Wongutha people were frequently sentenced to imprisonment away from Laverton for various unspecified offences (noted as 'principally stealing' in most reports.[11]) It is likely that Ginger and Joe were being held at Moore River because of a stealing offence.[12]

Wongutha offenders, in the period between 1915 and 1921, were sentenced to exile and imprisonment ranging in duration from six months (most commonly) to two and a half years. An unspecified number received two-and-a-half year sentences in 1919. Archives record the admission of Joe and Ginger to the Moore River Settlement on 6 May 1919. (See Figure 3.3-E)

So, Ginger was initially admitted to Mogumber in May 1919. He then escaped in August 1921. Apart from these two occasions, records of other admissions to and departures from the Settlement were not found. It therefore seems most likely that, at the time of his escape with the large group from Laverton in August 1921, Ginger was completing a two-and-a-half-year sentence dating from May 1919.

Dion Dirk's arrival at the Moore River Settlement was on 11 October 1919. (Refer to Figure 3.3-F.) The Superintendent notes beside Dion's name 'deaf and dumb from Swan Mission'. In his youth Dion had suffered severe burns and had lost his right arm as a result of the burns[13] — perhaps the local Protector had assumed custody of Dion at the time of the burning and sent him away to Perth and the care of the Anglican Home for children. It is possible that Dion's transfer to Mogumber was due to the imminent closure of the Swan Mission.[14] The Superintendent's comment that 'these people have been isolated in two of the

256   Writings

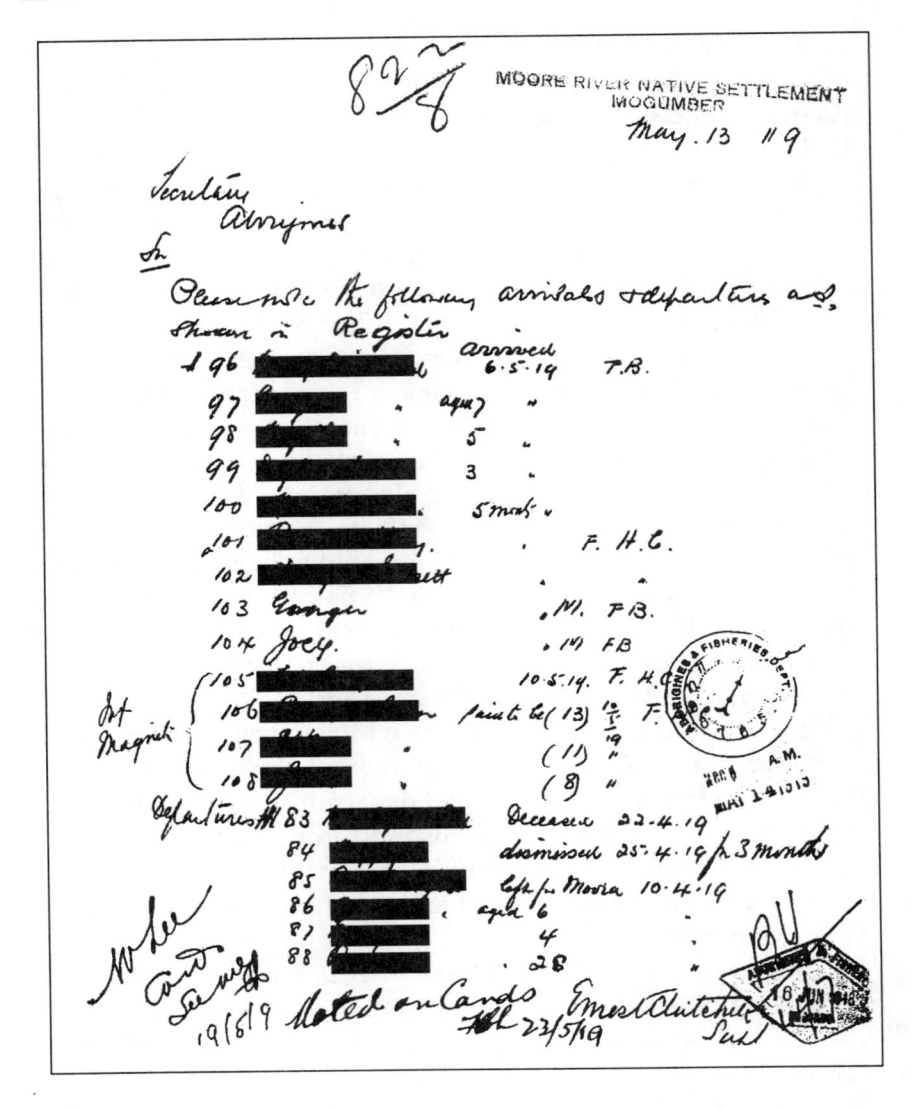

Figure 3.3-E
May 1919, List of Admissions and Departures. Correspondence, Superintendent of the Moore River Native Settlement and Secretary of the Aborigines Department.
(AN 1/6 Acc 1326 State Records Office, Western Australia)

borrowed tents' could possibly imply that the people admitted on 11 October were ill and contagious — perhaps Dion was sent to the settlement after contacting a serious illness. In any case, his transfer to the Settlement worked in his favour in August 1921 when he was reunited with immediate family members and then made his successful escape with the entire Laverton group after at least two years of exile in various institutions.

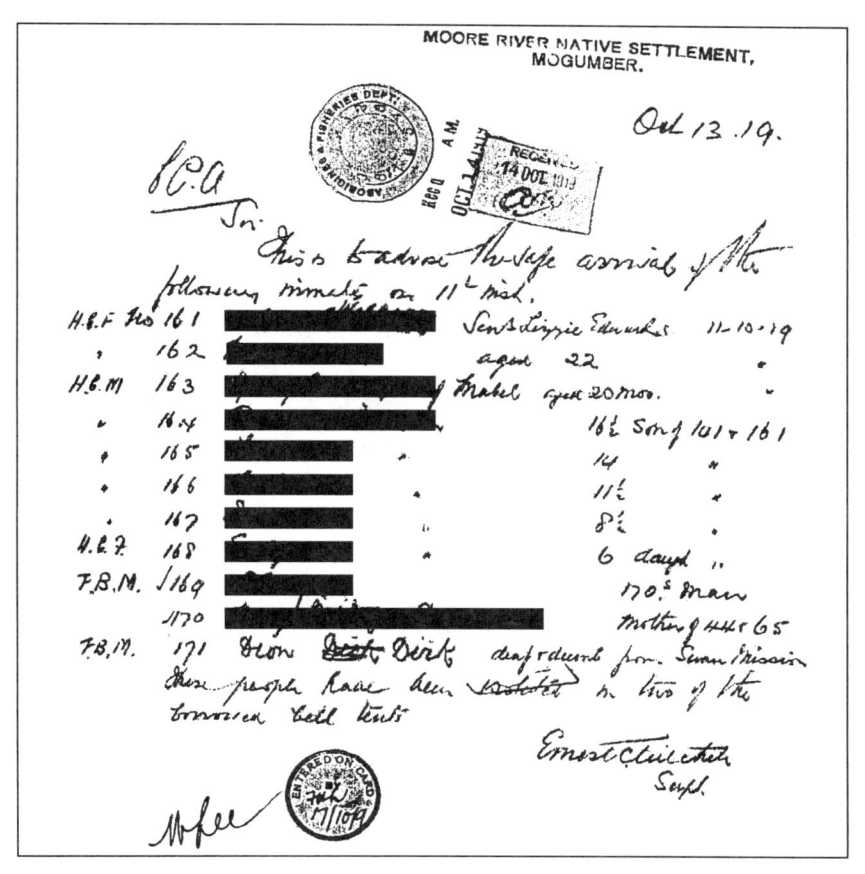

Figure 3.3-F
October 1921, Admissions and Departures List. Correspondence, Superintendent of Moore River Native Settlement and Secretary of the Aborigines Department.
(AN 1/6 Acc 1326 p51 State Records Office, Western Australia)

Mulga Joe was admitted three times to Mogumber; he made two documented escapes, and one apparently legal departure.

He was first admitted with Ginger in May 1919 (See Figure 3.3-E). He then departed from the Settlement in April 1921, two years after his initial arrival. (See Figure 3.3-A) It is probable that he had completed a two-year sentence and was now legally free to return to his Country. The following month the Laverton police officer wrote:

> It would be of great assistance to the police here & have a good effect on the Natives throughout the district, if the Natives who are convicted and sentenced to gaol, were on the completion of their sentences kept away and sent to other parts.[15]

A few months later the Laverton police send Joe Mulgathunoo back to Mogumber again. The list which records his arrival is undated (See Figure 3.3-G), but the Department Secretary signs and dates the record as received on 16 June 1921, noting to Campbell that, 'The actual date of arrival and departure would be handy'. Given that Joe's departure from Mogumber occurred in April 1921, he must have been re-admitted in either May or early June 1921.

Joe then escaped with the group of Laverton people. Their desertion date is recorded as 18 September 1921. (See Figure 3.3-C)

Joe reappears in the Moore River records five months later; he is re-admitted on 6 February 1922 as 'Mulgadoon Joe', age seventeen. This time the details are archived only in the Settlement's Register of Inmates; (see Figure 3.3-H). Campbell seems not to notify the Department of Joe's arrival.

Joe's name is crossed out of the Register — the 'remark' column notes that Joe 'deserted', or escaped, on 30 March 1922. He remained at the Settlement for less than two months before escaping. Perhaps he was waiting for the end of summer and cooling of the weather, or for good rain, before leaving.

In his required report for March, submitted on 4 April, Superintendent Campbell does not notify the Department that Joe has 'deserted'. Campbell's letter to the Secretary instead records that Joe has been 'discharged'. (See Figure 3.3-I) Perhaps Campbell was tired of being reprimanded for his inadequacies by the

Secretary. Or perhaps he liked young Joey and decided against alerting the Department to Joe's unlawful freedom. In any case, the change in description from 'desertion' in his own record system to that of 'discharge' in the records being sent to the Secretary effectively ensures that Joe Mulgathunoo becomes, in the eyes of the Department, a man who has served his time and is now entitled to freedom.

Joe is free once more, and he does not return to the Moore River Settlement.

Mulga Joe again successfully makes the long journey back to the Laverton district; three months later he is working as a goat herder at the new Mt Margaret Mission.[16]

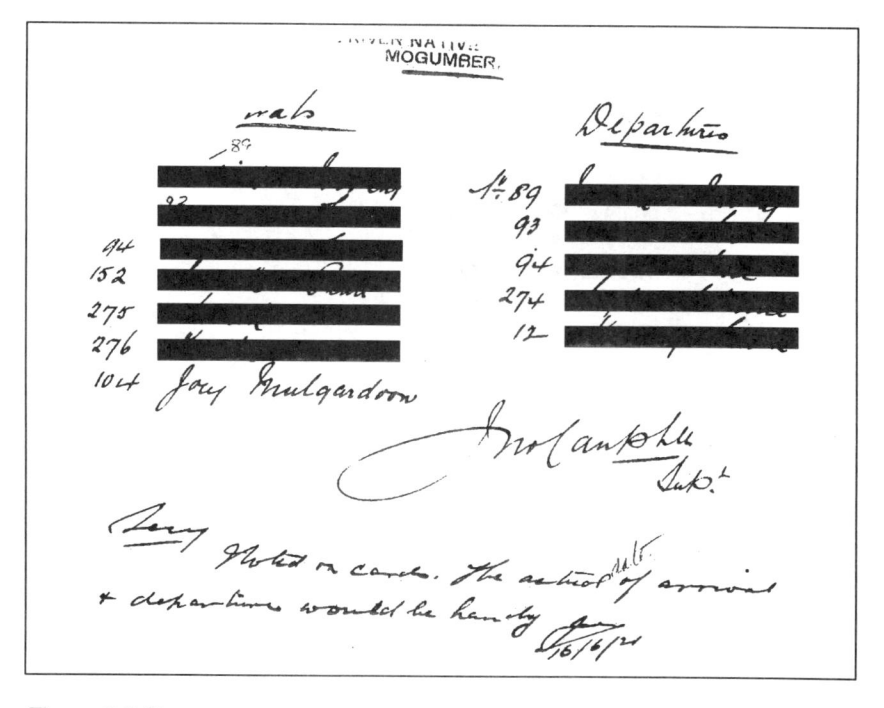

Figure 3.3-G
Admissions and Departures List, 1921 (prior to 16/6/1921). Correspondence, Superintendent of Moore River Native Settlement and Secretary of the Aborigines Department.
(AN 1/6 Acc 1326 p80 State Records Office, Western Australia)

260 Writings

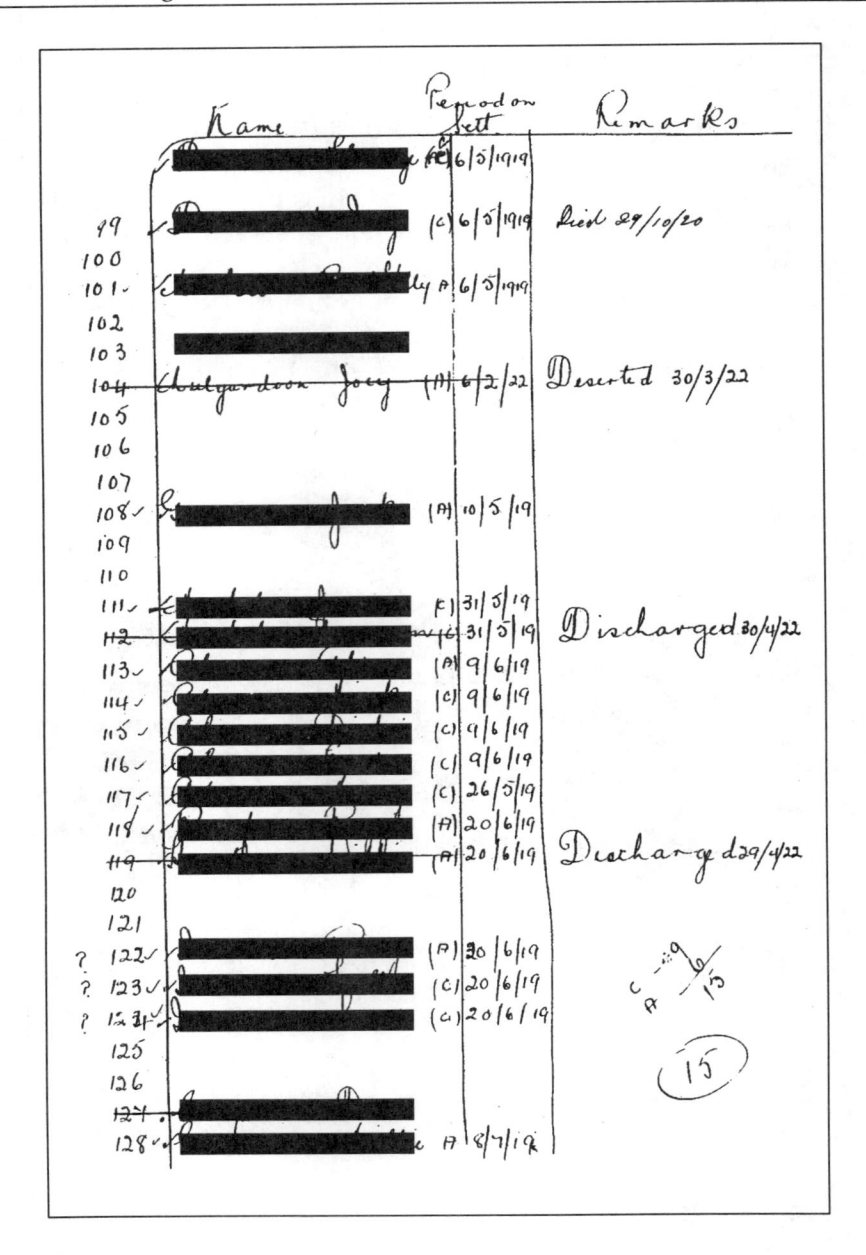

Figure 3.3-H
Register of Inmates, Moore River Native Settlement.
(AN 1/6 Acc 1326 State Records Office, Western Australia)

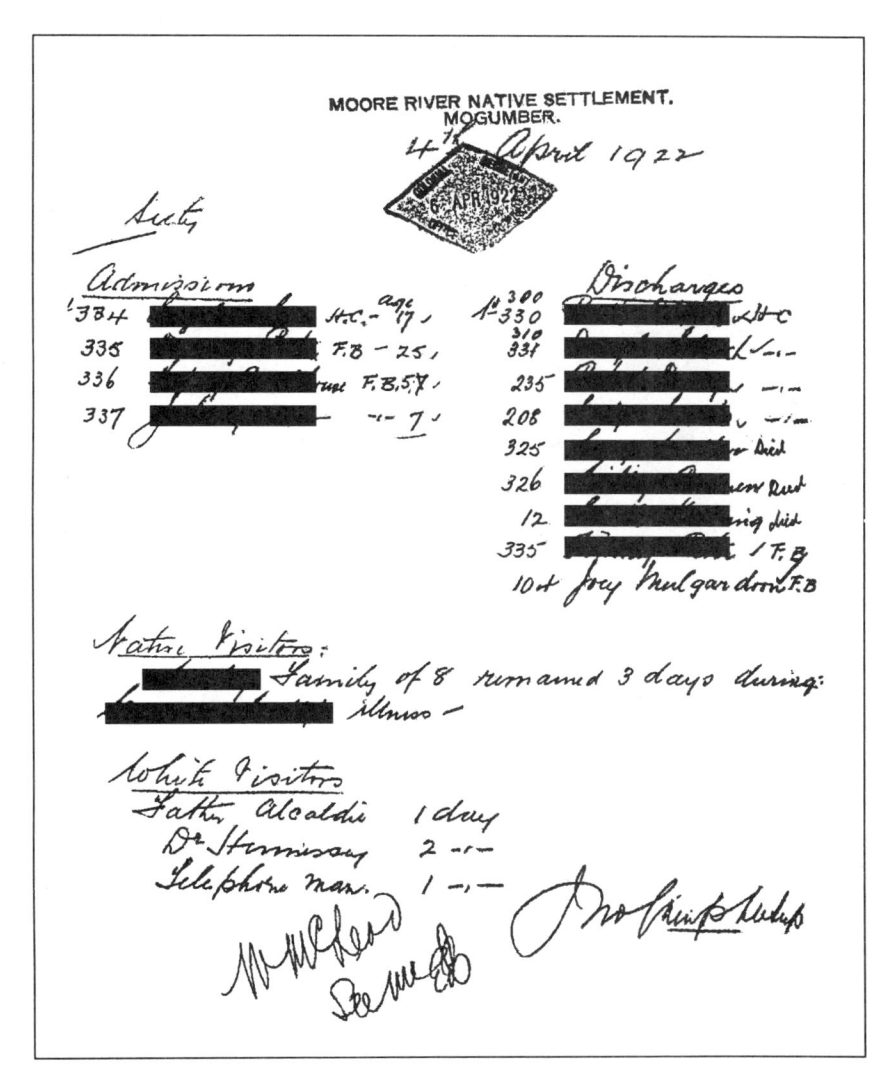

Figure 3.3-I
March 1922, Admissions and Departures List. Correspondence, Superintendent of Moore River Native Settlement and Secretary of the Aborigines Department.

(AN 1/6 Acc 1326 State Records Office, Western Australia)

Moore River Native Settlement, c 1920s. Part of the camp compound is in the foreground, with the institutional buildings on the ridge above. (Courtesy Battye Library 12227P)

The Moore River, c1920s. (Courtesy Battye Library 12222P)

Moore River trackers, c.1920s.
(Courtesy Battye Library 12238P)

The Moore River in flood (c1920s), as it perhaps was at the time of the escape by the Wongutha group in 1921.
(Courtesy Battye Library 12246P)

William Harris, Letter

A significant reference to the Laverton people's escape from Mogumber was made by prominent Aboriginal spokesman William Harris in 1926. His letter to the editor of the *Sunday Times* was published with an accompanying explanatory note from the editor. The editor's patronising introduction is indicative of the views of the society for whom the paper was published.

From the *Sunday Times*, 14 November 1926:

NATIVE QUESTION

TREATMENT OF ABORIGINES
THE STORY FROM THEIR SIDE

William Harris, an educated man despite his colour, seeks permission to publicly view the matter of the treatment of aborigines in the light in which it is regarded by his own people. Many of his statements lack the essential of proof, but the presentation of his side of the story may lead to a more sympathetic handling of a problem in whose satisfactory solution the credit of the State is at stake. This earnest champion of the natives and half-castes writes:

> Ever since the whites settled in Western Australia the aborigines have not lived in a more cruel and lawless state than they are living today. Since the inauguration of Responsible Government their condition has gone from bad to worse, and has now become unbearable. For hundreds of years, in song and story, it has been Britain's boast that under her flag was found justice and fair dealing for all. But in dealing with the aborigines it has been reserved for Western Australia to overturn British law and justice and that consideration for the weak and helpless that are recognised and upheld as due by all really civilised people.

> I repeat there is no law for the aborigine in this State. What law of justice can there be for people who are robbed and shot down or run into miserable compounds? What part or parcel have they in the land to which they have a right to live? It is true there are reserves marked on the maps, but what use are they to the natives when the squatter occupies every acre?
>
> Regarding massacres, heaps of human bones mixed with cartridge shells in different parts of this State are evidence of the fact of their having been shot down. Most people hearing of the dispersion of natives think that a few shots are fired over their heads to scatter them. The 'dispersion' takes a different form altogether.
>
> The educated Aborigines and half-castes in this state are about to form a protective union. As British subjects they claim, and mean to have, the protection of the same laws that govern the white man, not to be persecuted by the Aborigines Department and its officials.
>
> At Laverton we had the spectacle of natives in that district decoyed into the police station on the pretence of being served with food. The doors were closed on them, they were kept under lock and key until the train was ready to start, then taken under armed escort and locked in the train for Mogumber. I have since heard that the Laverton natives broke gaol and got away, except for one is blind. I don't think that anyone knows or cares if they ever got back ...

The editor's comments nicely illustrate Harris' point. Unashamedly casting aspersions on the credibility of Harris' statements, the editor was certainly one of those who did not know or care whether the Laverton events actually happened, let alone care enough to want to know whether the escapees got back home.

So, the editor certainly did not have first hand knowledge of the this event. How did Harris know about the Laverton 'spectacle'? There are no immediately apparent links between Harris, the spokesman for rights, and those he calls 'natives' from Laverton. A O Neville perceived a substantial difference in backgrounds and experience; he described the Laverton Aboriginal people as requiring 'pioneering' and as 'semi-civilised', and described Harris as raised as a 'white man'.[1]

Harris was born in Williams, had worked on stations in the north-west, owned a farm in Morawa, and had farming relatives in Toodyay. At the turn of the century, Harris had set out prospecting for gold around the Leonora district with his family, successfully setting up and working a small goldmine. Perhaps Harris was still in the Goldfields when the Laverton people were captured and sent away to Mogumber in 1921. Perhaps he had moved away,[2] but heard the story from friends still in Leonora. Or perhaps the story was simply very widely known among Aboriginal people, having been spread by the people who were at Mogumber at the time as they circulated through various communities on work assignments, or returned to their own communities.

Did Harris himself know the outcome of the story? The people's successful return may well have been known only within immediate and trustworthy circles. Or perhaps the lack of detail was deliberate. Harris and his informants may well have been fully aware of the outcome of the escape attempt but did not wish to make public the fact that the people had (nearly) all arrived home again. It would not serve his or their purpose to announce their success.

While Harris gives no dates in which to place the events, it is certain that they must have occurred between 1918 (the year of opening the Moore River Settlement) at the earliest and 1926 (when he wrote the letter) at the latest. I have concluded that these particular events in Laverton, as described by Harris, are the 1921 events.[3]

William Harris knew of the 1921 Laverton events. And in 1926 he cites this story in a published letter to one of Perth's major newspapers as a powerful illustration of the outrages committed by the Aborigines Department against the Aboriginal people. This particular event, to Harris, embodies the struggle of the oppressed people.

Absences in Contemporary Writings

Absences in Contemporary Writings documents those Writings of the contemporary society which might reasonably have been potential sources of evidence of the history of the 1921 events, but from which this history is absent.

Daisy Bates

Daisy Bates, a woman with a reputation as knowledgeable in Aboriginal Affairs, might have been interested in the Laverton events of 1921 if she had heard of them, but she was living in a tent in a distant desert and presumably did not hear.

Daisy May Bates lived in Western Australia from 1899 to 1910. During 1901 Bates visited the north of the state, spending some time staying at Beagle Bay Mission (particularly noteworthy in that the Mission prohibited the entry of females). From 1904 to 1910 she was supported by Western Australian Government grants to research the Aboriginal peoples of the State. Bates lived on the Maamba Reserve at the foot of the Darling Ranges for two years with the Bibbulmun people, then on other Reserves in the South-West of Western Australia for another two years, and then returned to Perth.

She accompanied the British anthropologist Radcliffe-Brown on his expedition to study the Aboriginal peoples of the North West in 1910. The principal destination of the expedition became the leprosy islands of Dorrè and Bernier near Shark Bay, but interestingly, Bates and Radcliffe-Brown deviated from their coastal journey to include the inland Sandstone district. Bates precedes her account of the expedition with a note about recent events in the Laverton district involving the Darlot people.

Before we left Perth, news came that the civilized and semi-civilized circumcised groups of Lake Darlot had descended in a raid upon a native camp at Lancefield, near Laverton, killing eleven men, women and children. The groups had scattered, and the police had found none of the murderers.[1]

The expedition sailed to Geraldton, and then despite, or perhaps due to, the news of the massacre, they

> went by rail to Sandstone ... A few miles from Sandstone, we pitched our tents among the natives gathered there ... We were surrounded by nearly 100 natives from near-by districts, and there was some obvious ill-feeling and friction among the groups ... It took some time to convince the natives that my companions were not policemen, of whom, for their own reasons, they lived in an unholy fear at the time ...
>
> After distributing generous rations and discussing family gossip, we were just beginning to make a little headway in questioning them regarding genealogies and customs when, to our surprise, a police raid was made upon the camps at dawn, and six of the natives arrested as the Laverton murderers. Several shots were fired by the police ... On the principle that 'one nigger is as black as another,' the constables had arrested one Meenya, whom I knew did not belong to Darlot, and who had only just arrived from his own country ...
>
> After the raid, our natives scattered, but returned to tell me that there was another policeman coming with a 'big mob'. This proved to be Constable Grey, appointed to inspect natives for symptoms of disease and to gather in half-castes from the camps. The natives were afraid to approach him until I explained that he was a doctor coming to look at us all. When I myself went into the tent, they followed with confidence.
>
> With Professor Radcliffe-Brown's assistance, Grey made his examinations, collected a few of the old men and women, and drove them away in his cart to join the unfortunates waiting in Sandstone. I shall never forget the anguish and despair on those aged faces. The poor decrepit creatures were leaving their own country for a destination unknown, a fate they could not understand, and their woe was pitiful. The diseased and the half-castes were housed in different sections of the gaol in Sandstone, and the grief of the Aboriginal mothers at

this enforced parting with their children was pitiful to see.

So turbulent and distressed was now the condition in all camps that it was useless for us to remain longer. Professor Radcliffe-Brown, Grant Watson and Louis the cook sailed for Carnarvon. I returned to Perth with my reports and notes. The Laverton murderers were travelling in custody on the same train, and my special commission entitled me to question them in private. For some hours I sat alone with the chained prisoners in the railway carriage, and learned the reason of the raid.

They explained that the Lancefield and Laverton camps had transgressed the bounds of every native law, that they were living in incestuous depravity with sisters and immature children to such an extent that the usual marriage exchanges were not possible. So the Lake Darlot tribes, unable to procure wives, took the law into their own hands, and planned to kill the men and seize the women. They had descended on the camp at dawn, and in the battle of flying spears some women and children were accidentally killed. I reported the circumstances to headquarters, and there was no trial. The natives were detained only until the departure of the next train.[2]

The expedition did not return to the Sandstone or Laverton Goldfields district, and neither did Daisy Bates. She sailed north and rejoined the expedition at Dorré and Bernier, and does not mention the Laverton or Darlot people again.

Bates' failure to explain the comment that the 'natives lived in unholy fear' of the policemen indicates a reluctance to criticise the system to which the people were subject. She demonstrates little remorse in having been personally implicated in the separation of the people from their families and country. She only regards them as 'poor decrepit creatures', and further, finds their grief 'pitiful'.

Bates' only interference with, and questioning of, the actions and rule of the police at Sandstone arises, not when shots are fired into the sleeping camp at dawn, not when children are torn from their mothers, not when the old and the sick are torn from their people, not when six men are arrested as murderers with little evidence of their guilt, but when one man who is certainly innocent is arrested. She arranges for his release. And then she interviews the other men on the train and arranges for the charges to be dropped. And that is the end of her involvement. Perhaps she thought it sufficient remedy.

Bates believed that she moved in 'sad sojourn among the last sad people of the primitive Australian race'.[3] She considered them 'the last', the 'sad' and dying out. Bates' life work focused more on easing the immediate physical suffering of the old and the sick than on political action for justice.

Bates later left Perth, left her husband, left her child, and left the 'natives' of Western Australia, and took up residence in the desert in South Australia, near Eucla in 1912. By July 1914 Bates was petitioning the Department of the Interior to appoint a local 'Protector of Aborigines', and recommending herself for the position, without success. In 1919 she relocated to Ooldea, an isolated siding on the Transcontinental Railway Line; she was still in the South Australian desert and still further away from possible contacts with the 'outside world'.

In 1921, then, Daisy Bates was living in a tent in the desert near Ooldea and cut off from all but the immediate happenings around her tent.

Mary Montgomerie Bennett

Mary Montgomerie Bennett was a woman with considerably more political impact than Daisy Bates. In October 1930 Bennett arrived in Perth, and in the same year successfully published in London *The Australian Aborigine as a Human Being*, which condemned the contemporary Aboriginal policy in Western Australia.

Bennett taught briefly at both the Forrest River Mission in the North-West and the Australian Aborigines Mission (AAM) Gnowangerup Mission in the South-West before seeking permission from Neville to join Schenk at the AAM Mount Margaret Mission in 1931, where she established a very successful education system. The school was revolutionary. Wongutha children were taught in English by the standard State

Correspondence School Curricula of the day — with great success.[4]

In her day, Bennett was well known as a writer and activist. A O Neville warned Schenk in 1931 that if Bennett moved to Mount Margaret she could create trouble for the Mission through her writings.[5] Undaunted by Neville, Bennett found a ready audience for her opinions; even the conservative *West Australian* discussed her views in 1932 under the heading of 'Allegations of Slavery'.[6] Bennett also roused the concerned interest of the Country Women's Association and the Women's Service Guild, two influential and active women's groups of the day — both groups sent messages to Parliament protesting the injustices of the current Aboriginal policy.[7]

Bennett's next major political action was to send to the 1933 conference of the British Empire League in London a paper which outlined her criticisms of the treatment of Aborigines in Western Australia. Her statements became widely discussed, drawing the attention of the British press and Perth parliamentarians alike.

The Western Australian Parliament at the time had plans to seek permission from the British Parliament to secede from the Australian Commonwealth, and due to concerns about the effect of Bennett's statements on Western Australia's reputation in Britain, the Western Australian Government appointed H D Moseley as Royal Commissioner into 'Aboriginal problems'. His 1934 report of the findings of the Royal Commission was used to quash international concerns sparked off by Bennett's accusations.[8]

Bennett presented evidence to the 1934 Royal Commission, and articulated again the 'radical' view that Aboriginal people were not intellectually inferior to Anglo-Saxons. Pressed by the Commissioners, Neville and Moseley, as to whether intellectual differences might exist between people of different races, Bennett replied, 'I suppose so. Atticus said that Cicero could not get his slaves in Britain because they all were too ugly and stupid.'[9]

Bennett was a strong agitator for Aboriginal Rights; she wrote of land, of the need to renew rights of access to land and to traditional game, and of education.[10] The arguments presented in her publications and books are often illustrated by reference to various events which took place in the Mount Margaret area.

Bennett had arrived at Mount Margaret in 1931, only ten years after Jidu's escape party had thwarted the repressive control of police, protectors and the department and returned home. A story with these elements would surely have appealed to Bennett. But no mention is made in her published works of the 1921 escape.

Goldfields Poetry Collection

> Nowhere else in the world is verse such an essential ingredient in local journalism. Most Westralians write rhymes it would seem and everybody reads them.[11]

So said the editor of one of Kalgoorlie's prominent newspapers in 1907.

The poems of this era, then, provide the accepted popular scope of opinion, given by a popularly accepted selection of society; they demonstrate clearly the approved, the published, the widely read view. This representative nature of the Goldfields poetry is testified to by a contemporary of one of the poets, who claims for the poet Dryblower the authority to express the opinion of the people:

> On important questions of the day he often said in verse what many people thought but could not find the words to say.[12]

Dryblower, the goldfields poet acclaimed as being able to perfectly represent public opinion, was a member of the White Australia League. He was apparently not censured for his views, nor for the public expression of them in his poetry. Dryblower was popular enough, and expressed popular opinion well enough, to be employed soon after 1910 by a large Perth paper, the *Sunday Times* — this newspaper evidently endorsed his writing and expected that their Perth readership would appreciate his views. He penned a poem entitled 'The Aliens', in which he clearly reveals his attitude towards any non-British person. He speaks of no individual aliens, he sees only masses. And the way that Dryblower advises the reader to ascertain an 'Alien' is by skin colour. His language is astounding:

The Aliens[13]

They come not as an open foe
    To loot the land with steel and fire,
No barricades to dust they blow,
    No landmark makes a lurid pyre.
They bear no bannerette of war;
    No trumpet forth a challenge yells.
From grim-built battleships to shore,
    They rain no hell-invented shells,
But still they war and still they win;
    They claim, and get, the victor's share.
Swarthy of heart as well as skin,
    The Alien comes —
              Beware! Beware!

Along the street no shrapnel shrieks,
    No rifle spits its venomed lead;
No hasty-dug entrenchments reeks
    With piles of disembowelled dead.
They bear no bayonet, lance, or sword,
    They blare no brass, they roll no drum;
When comes this irresistless horde
    From out its Mediterranean slum.
From where the stench of Lisbon's dock
    Pollutes the olive-scented air,
From plague-infected Antioch
    The Alien comes —
              Beware! Beware!

Along the Adriatic shore
    Where swarming beggars whine and weep
The tramp-ship shudders as they pour
    Into her vitals dark and deep;
From old Cadiz to Thessaly,
    From Montenegro down to Said,
They swarm across the Indian Sea
    To swell the beetle-browed brigade,
To cheat the Briton of his crust:
    To take what he and his should share:

To drag Australia to his dust
   The Alien comes —
                  Beware! Beware!

From Cairo to the Yellow Sea,
   The dusky pagan swells the flood,
The Ghan, the Kurd, and Atchinee,
   Are blending with Australia's blood.
Across a land once virgin-good,
   A trail of greed and lust he leaves,
And o'er its virile nationhood
   Degeneration's spell he weaves,
To tempt the fickle and the frail
   With many a tawdry, tinselled snare,
To buy where beauty is for sale,
   The Alien comes —
                  Beware! Beware!

In hovels never cleansed nor aired,
   On which the Law indulgent looks,
He serves you dainty meals prepared
   From filthy food by filthier cooks.
He laundries whatso'er you need,
   What he demands you promptly pay,
While women of a white man's breed,
   Barter their honour day by day.
He sells you fruits of Mother Earth
   That ripened in his loathsome lair.
To blast the land that gave you birth,
   The Alien comes —
                  Beware! Beware!

They come not as an open foe
   To loot the land with steel and fire,
No barricades to dust they blow,
   No landmark makes a lurid pyre.
They bear no bannerette of war:
   No trumpet forth a challenge yells
From grim-built battleships to shore,
   They rain no hell-invented shells;

But still they war and still they win,
  They claim, and get, the victor's share.
Swarthy of heart as well as skin,
  The Alien comes —
            Beware! Beware!

Britons such as Dryblower, it is clear from this extract, viewed Australia as the rightful property of Britons. Dryblower, in other poems, continues to declare the manifesto of 'freeborn sons of free born British blokes'[14] and panegyrises the virtues of 'men, by God! Who are British at heart — British and brave and white!' in his poem blatantly entitled 'White!'[15]

And this poetry was considered highly. As Bill Grono notes, an 'influential' critic and publisher of the day considered this poetry to be 'the best ... in Australia'.[16]

The inter-war years on the goldfields saw the closing of mines and woodlines resulting in 'most serious strikes',[17] in unemployment and unrest, and in the rising animosity of 'Britons' towards people of other cultural origins.

These inter-war years seem to have fostered a State-wide popular fear of an uprising by any group of people who might be opposed to the Britons — it is seen in Dryblower's 'The Aliens' published around 1924, it is seen in the rumour in Laverton of two hundred armed Aboriginal warriors gathering in the spinifex ready to attack the town in 1921. The attitude had taken visible form in the Kalgoorlie riots of 1919 where, fuelled by the simmering resentment of returned soldiers who didn't like foreigners working in their workplaces, a crowd of Anglo-Australians burned and looted Italo-Australian shops after the alleged stabbing of an English man by an Italian man. A decade later the ethno-centricity of the 'Britons' errupted into violence once again in the Australia Day Riots in Kalgoorlie in 1934 where the businesses and residential properties of the Italian and Slav communities were 'razed to the ground'.[18] It is worth noting that many of the Anglo-Australian men on the Western Australian goldfields had joined the rush to Western Australia from the spent Victorian goldrushes. They were called, and called themselves, 't'othersiders', and some may have brought with them prejudices learned in Victoria. One t'othersider poet elucidates this position in a poem published by the *Kalgoorlie Sun* in 1903, from which the following extract is taken:

> We have fought our fights and lost them —
> Given them battle and won.
> When Lalor led at Eureka,
> Witness the deeds then done.
> We drove the heathen before us,
> From 'Flat and Castlemaine,
> And what we have done aforetime
> We'll do in time again.[19]

In the paradigm expressed by the goldfields poets, any other-faith, other-language, dark-skin person was considered dangerous and was declared to be the enemy.[20]

Aboriginal people, being also non-Anglo, often experienced this hostility from those who considered themselves British Australians. At the same time, certain individual prospectors were friendly with the Wongutha. Wongutha trade dealings were conducted with such prospectors, and with the travelling Afghan camelleers.[21] Italians were also recorded as being kind.[22] These people were the exception in a prevalently antagonistic community.

Philanthropic and Church groups

A humanitarian view of the equality of all people has already been seen to be absent from popular goldfields opinion voiced around 1910. If humanism had not managed to find a foothold in the goldfields ground, it comes as no surprise to discover that philanthropic and church groups were rather rare in the 1920s.

The zealous missionary Schenk wrote in dismay to his friends in Victoria that he had discovered only one person in Laverton who was publicly regarded as 'a bit religious'. This lady's religious actions were limited to 'gathering up the children for Sunday School'[23] each Sunday; they did not extend to concern for Aboriginal people. The Laverton community made it clear that they did not share nor appreciate Schenk's concern for social justice for the Wongutha.[24]

Further afield, in July 1921, Schenk motor-biked two hundred miles around the mining towns in the vicinity of Laverton. In the towns and communities contained within those two hundred miles he found only one professing Christian, a 'dear old widow' who was 'regarded as eccentric' by her community. And he met one friendly elderly German couple who had arrived before the war and had 'suffered much persecution'. Schenk records his impression that his impromptu preaching in these towns was not overly appreciated and more often than not, aroused hostility.[25]

On the evidence of Schenk and the local verse, it appears that the members of the 'establishment' on the goldfields were quick to reject people on the basis of race or belief, quick to perceive enemies, even in old European immigrants, and were often heartless and ruthless to those who were not like them. Aboriginal people experienced less tolerance than Europeans and preachers.

While church groups were absent in the Laverton district, they did exist in the established goldfields cities. Canon Collick, 'the best known clergyman on the Goldfields' was an active Anglican priest with a well-developed social conscience.[26] Perhaps if he had heard of the Laverton events, he would have been moved to respond, to protest, to add his voice to that of Schenk.

Collick began his Goldfields career in Coolgardie in the mid 1890s, at which time the thriving city already boasted eight thousand (white) people, including four Roman Catholic priests, five Wesley ministers and three Presbyterian ministers. All of these churchmen, it seems, were busy. Willis observes that 'most clergymen of all denominations had decided that the needs of the white settlers were so great that the problems of the Aboriginal population would have to be set aside.' Collick, however, took an active pastoral interest in the local Aboriginal people: 'He procured medicine for the Aborigines, looked after their children and nursed their sick.' But his pastoral duties were firstly confined to the Coolgardie region, and secondly, generally stopped short of 'political involvement' on behalf of any particular group of society (although in 1899 he joined the miners' demonstrations against

Forrest's proposed amendments to mining legislation).

Collick moved closer to Laverton, to the new town of Menzies, in 1897 for 'pioneering church work' as the goldrush progressed further north. But his involvement in this region and the potential to follow the goldrush to the Laverton Goldfields was short-lived. In 1901 he was sent as a chaplain to the Boer War. He then spent three years in England, returning to Kalgoorlie in 1905, and was then made Anglican Archdeacon of the Goldfields in 1912. Collick continued to live and work in Kalgoorlie until 1924.[27] It appears that Collick was physically too remote from Laverton to hear about or act upon the events of the 1921 deportation.

Willis states that 'the Anglican Church was embarrassed at its inability to supply more priests to the goldfield's population'.[28] In fact, in 1921 there was no Anglican priest for the Laverton area, there was instead a non-ordained man (a 'lay reader'), 'Brother John', who was responsible for exercising pastoral care over the extremely large district north of Kalgoorlie. This area included Collick's old post of Menzies. Brother John travelled long distances between the numerous small townships, which necessarily made the frequency of visits to each town limited and his knowledge of local affairs minimal. It seems that Brother John visited Laverton in April 1921 and did not return until 1923.[29] It is hardly surprising, then, that Brother John did not hear of or protest the August 1921 Laverton events. In any case, according to Schenk, Brother John's stated 'hope for the Aborigines' was, in 1921, 'nil'.[30]

Mrs Boxall, of The Rectory in Boulder, was moved to question the Chief Protector on the standard of care for Goldfields Aboriginal people suffering from the drought in 1919.[31] It appears that Mrs Boxall entered into no further communication with the Chief Protector after the 1919 exchange of letters.

Publications of the Australian Aborigines Mission

Schenk, then, appears to have been a solitary voice of protest against the Laverton events; one of the few to observe and record the circumstances. How did his mission, the United or Australian

Aborigines Mission (UAM or AAM), respond?

The UAM published Schenk's book, *The Educability of the Australian Native* sometime around 1940. The book's intent is to demonstrate the scholarly aptitude of the Wongutha children; it does not mention the 1921 events.

The First ten years at Mount Margaret Mission, edited by a Mr Smith, was published in 1933 by the UAM in celebration of the work at Mount Margaret. Smith was supplied with all of Schenk's letters from which to extract the notable events of the first ten years of Mount Margaret Mission's existence. The events leading up to the formation of the Mission are skimmed in brief. Schenk's active social and political protests on behalf of the interests of the Wongutha are omitted; there is not even record of his comments about the 'drastic' actions of the police. Instead, Smith extensively quotes Schenk's comments on the price of land, goats and motorbikes. The 1921 deportation events which significantly influenced Schenk in his decision to establish the settlement are barely noticeable in Smith's text. The following is the only quote which refers to the event, and Smith offers no comment on the 'Moore River' aspect of its content:

> Laverton, November, 1921 — Just now I review the position:
> (1) Circumstances compelled me to remain in Laverton. (2) The natives sent to Moore River escaped, and are back in the bush here (3) Special contributions for goats and motor sale money make it possible to purchase about 300 goats, two old horses, two carts, harness, axes ...[32]

Smith quotes limited material from Schenk's August 1921 letter and September 1921 letters, but does not include Schenk's references to the deportation from these same letters.

Contextual background to Smith's selection of content is provided only by default. One glimpse of the political and social status of the Aboriginal people in the community occurs between the lines of a 'touching' testimony given by a 'reformed' Wongutha man, as documented in the letter of Mr Robert Powell:

> Bert, in his quaint broken English, said: 'Before time I go work

for white man. He tell me to do some work. I say, "All right, Boss." But I no do it, and he hit me on the head with a stick. Next day he tell me to do some more work. I say, "All right, Boss"; but I no do it, and he hit me again. Now I go work for white man, he tell me to go do some work. I say, "All right, Boss," and I go do it; he not hit me on the head any more.'[33]

State and Regional Newspapers

WEST AUSTRALIAN
Three weeks of the *West Australian*, on both sides of the date that the Mogumber archives recorded that the group had 'deserted', were painstakingly searched for any kind of public notice about the escapees, but nothing was found. In later years, Neville certainly used the *West Australian* as a medium for public appeals for information on the whereabouts of escapees from Mogumber,[34] but the large group of escapees in 1921 received no such attention.

SUNDAY TIMES
No public notices or other kinds of article requesting information or action were found at the time of the escape, nor for the next few months.

Six years later, the *Sunday Times* published William Harris' letter to the editor previously detailed in Writings 3.4. Harris' strong remarks about the Laverton events apparently did not draw forth public responses from the Aborigines Department, the police, nor the public concerning the events.[35]

GOLDFIELDS NEWSPAPERS
(*Kalgoorlie Sun, Coolgardie Miner, Kalgoorlie Miner, Western Argus*)
No public notices, or references of any kind to the 1921 events, were found in the prominent Goldfields newspapers at that time.

The newspapers did, at times, contain evidence of the serious and widespread effects of the drought.[36]

Interpretive Accounts and Absences in Recent Writings

Interpretive Accounts and Absences in Recent Writings is an examination of recently written sources, and potential sources, of information about the 1921 events. This history is predominantly absent. The 'invisible' nature of the events is sustained; the silence around the story has persisted in the pages of most Western Australian history. A selection of these 'absences' are documented here.

Discovering partial accounts of the events and passing comments on the story was a slow process. Every piece found is documented here.

Accounts and absences are mingled together, reflecting the process of discovery, recovery.

Account

In an ABC radio interview, Alice Nannup, an inmate of Mogumber after 1924, spoke to Bill Bunbury of the story of the escape of the Laverton people:

> There was a blind man. There were women and children. They were very shy, couldn't speak English, some of them! They just lived on the compound, and every now and again they'd move camp, just kept on moving camp. Each night they'd move to another place. And one night they made the escape and went back home.[1]

Bunbury refers to this escape as 'the biggest break-out in the history of Moore River'. He published his version of the story of the Laverton people in his book *Reading Labels on Jam Tins. Living Through Difficult Times.*

Bunbury traced two oral sources for the events in Margaret Morgan and Reggie Johnston. He begins his account with the following:

> Margaret Morgan was the daughter of missionary Roy Schenk who served at the Mount Margaret Mission in the North-eastern Goldfields in the years before World War Two. It was from nearby Laverton that in 1926 the police sent fourteen people down to Moore River, a thousand kilometres west of their own country.[2]

(Police records, Moore River records and Schenk's personal records provide evidence that 1921, not 1926, was the year in which the group deportation and escape occurred. Schenk's records also suggest that fifteen people were deported.)

From Morgan's interview about her father's experience of the event Bunbury included this one excerpt:

> He didn't know then. All he saw was that when he went down to the train he saw this cattle truck with the little notice, 'Fifteen Niggers for Mogumber'.[3]

Bunbury attributed the following statement to Reggie Johnston:

> They was glad when they went back. But some of the old people died when they returned, but many of them half-castes never returned.[4]

Bunbury provides more details of the event, mostly taken from Johnston's interview, supplemented with information supplied by Morgan; the sources are implied. Bunbury's text:

> The thousand kilometre journey back to Mount Margaret Mission was to take less than fourteen days. The group moved by night to avoid detection and steered by the stars. They had to leave the blind man behind in a paddock but he bawled for help. A kindly farmer picked him up, helped him trace his people and get home. Another, an old man, had to be left behind, sitting by the camp fire. Most

however, got back to their own community.⁵

This account, seen with the knowledge gained from the oral and archival evidence documented in the Writings and Speakings, clearly contains factual inaccuracies. It was this account, however, that provided my first contact with the story. I talked to Bunbury in 1996 when I started thinking about trying to research this story and he told me that he had no further sources of information than what he had quoted in the book and that he had found all the material there was to be found. Maybe I should try to find another story to research that wasn't, more or less, already 'lost', but I could refer to his interview with Reggie Johnston, held in Battye Library, if I liked. In 1999 Bunbury kindly gave me permission to reproduce his interviews with Reg Johnston and Margaret Morgan.

Extracts from the Transcript of Bill Bunbury's 1986 Interview with Reggie Johnston⁶

BUNBURY: [Tape ident.]* This is a conversation with Reggie Johnston recorded at Menzies on 10 November 1986 for the documentary on Moore River. Reggie Johnston's own father has memories of the Moore River incident and of harassment by police in that area, and we're going to be talking about those two topics on this tape. [End of tape ident.]
    Reggie, what are your own memories of the Moore River escape, because quite a number of people got away from Moore River, didn't they, in those early days and got back here?

JOHNSTON: Yes.

BUNBURY: Can you tell me how that happened?

JOHNSTON: Yes. Well, in 1926 I could recall, remember then because my father told me all these stories about police

---

* [Tape ident.] — *this square bracket formatting shows Bunbury's authorial insertions in the original interview transcript. (To avoid confusion, all inserts I make in the extract from Bunbury's interview will be formatted as* [italic]*.)*

harassment with the Aboriginal people. And in 1926 the seventeen niggers were sent to Moore River settlement and because the Government in — they were protected at the time [...]* the protector police is a protector and he's a protector and he had his law, and he put every Aboriginal people in gaol and sent 'em over to Government to the Aboriginal away from this area and so they can go out and die in the, down the Perth city, because they're not used to the city life. But they soon found their way back. They runned away from oh, about a fortnight after when they landed there they run away, they escape from Mogumber and they went through from Mogumber just out from Perth and they travelled north on foot.

They was in fear when they was travelling. They couldn't light a fire because they frightened because the police will follow 'em up and put them in gaol. So they had to walk and they had to make their own spears to catch rabbit and goanna and eat *[going]* long. They got to keep well away from the road because he know the police might be coming along any time to pick 'em up. And they had one old blind man there. They led him all the way from Mogumber; they was going to Mt Magnet through Wongan Hill, but this old bloke got tired. So they made a fire and he said, this old bloke said, 'I couldn't walk any further.' So the men he said, 'We'll make a fire and you stop and you die yourself out here.' And yet this old fella was, he's not far from the farm and he started to shout and shout and of course the farmer heard somebody was shouting. So he went and had a look and there's a poor old blind man ready to die. So the farmer being very sympathy, sympathetic to this blind man and brought him up to Yalgoo, just out from Morawa, and then tried to find out now, if this blind man got any relation and found out — they took him to Mt Magnet then and he found out his sister was there. So the sister had to walk all the way from Magnet through Sandstone, be about eight hundred kilometres she had to walk, this poor old blind man he couldn't but the old woman just picked up a little of bit of yams there, find the water.

---

* [...] — *formatting shows where some text from the original transcript has been omitted in this extract.*

But that old bloke went no — he went right through that area because, he had to follow, because he wanted to get back to his home at Laverton area. And there was people from all different — they was running away, some going towards and following the pipeline to Kalgoorlie. And all they could get there, them dozens and, about two or three dozen eggs the farmer give them to eat, because they used to eating — the Aboriginal people not used to eating eggs but they used to eating kangaroos and goannas and etcetera and ...* But they found their way through because in those times policeman, this Dave Hunter, he was a real hard man towards the Aboriginal people. And he cage 'em and he sent train-truckloads, some of them half-caste they sent up there they never returned back to see their parents. They went and got married and had family and their parents died out there and laboured in the bush and they never came back. Oh, it was very sad.

BUNBURY: How did they know their way back, Reggie? How did they make their way back across that country?

JOHNSTON: Well, I tell you the Aboriginal is a great man, he's just like an astronomer or astrologist, whatever it is, and they could read by the stars in the night. They travelled practically — they could read the stars; if they can find the star, the Seven Sisters, he know they're up north. So they make straight and follow the Seven Sisters every day and they follow the sun; when the sun [is] on your right you know that you're, if you go left you're right; you can get to that place where you're going to.

But they read the stars. A star becomes their guide for every Aboriginal. If I was to be lost one cloudy day and I just can see one star that I'm satisfied [—] when I see the Seven Sisters, I know where I am. And, see, the Aboriginals could read the stars and they look at the weather and they look at

---

* ... — *included in original transcript, probably signifying that the conversation tails off momentarily.*

the cloud and say, 'Oh well, this is the right track I'm going,' see, because he reads the trees too. Trees can tell you where north, south, east and west, just like a compass for the Aboriginal, you know, when he's travelling.

But this poor old fella, you know, he happened to come right back to Laverton. He had to travel with his sister and she was a very old woman at the time too, and brought him right back to Laverton.

Why the police were very bad towards the Aboriginal people because they found that a missionary came from Melbourne to establish a mission school for us Aboriginal. But the main, the white people of Laverton said, 'Oh, you'll never train a black fella. They're just like wild horses, you couldn't tame 'em.' But Mr Schenk had great faith in what he believes and he started this mission out there for school and we found out after that we had the best teachers came from all the way from England to teach us and gave us a real education. And they don't give it today because I was, in 1926 I went to the mission school and been there for fifteen years in the mission; we had to.

BUNBURY: When those people got back, Reggie, on that day did the people here expect them to come back?

JOHNSTON: Oh, people been expecting all the time. Oh people, you know they — you know the Aboriginal he's superstitious but [inaudible] ... nose cracks he know that somebody's on the way.

BUNBURY: I missed that, Reggie?

JOHNSTON: When the Aboriginal expecting somebody to come, when the nose crack, he know exactly that somebody's coming and that's what they're looking [for]. When they get down the sou'west they wanted to come back to their own home town.

BUNBURY: So the people here knew, they expected those folk back?

JOHNSTON: Yes. They're looking back, you know; they said, 'Well,'— when they get close up near enough from Laverton they burn a spinifex and smoke signal — 'Oh, somebody's coming.' You know, you can see for miles. Oh, they was glad when they went back but some of their old people died when they returned but many of them half-castes never returned.

BUNBURY: Why were they sent down in the first place? You told me that they put these fifteen people in a cattle truck and sent them there. Now, why did they do that?

JOHNSTON: Yes, well, to myself I think they want to do away with the Aboriginal people … [unclear] I couldn't use that word genocide because the Aboriginal people, you know — I believe in the early history days the white people in the town in there like Laverton — not like in the city or Kalgoorlie because you get a lot of people, see. But in the outskirts like Laverton they can do what they like with Aboriginal; they can shoot 'em, shoot their dogs and chase them. Policeman, Dave Hunter, he became the Commissioner of Police. After having all the Aboriginal people being sent down to Mogumber he became the Commissioner of Police in Perth. You know, you wouldn't believe that. Just doing, chaining Aboriginals, well, he made a name for himself.

BUNBURY: What was his name?

JOHNSTON: Dave Hunter. He was a — you can have a look at the record. But we had a native protector that time, his name Mr Neville. Oh, he was a very hard man and he's very prejudiced with the Aboriginal people and you know he'd go up to Mt Margaret to Laverton and all that area catching the half-castes and send 'em down to Mogumber. 'You go away,' that one, 'You have children. We take the children, you can have some more children,' because you know in those times you got to have a permit to live in the town like Laverton and Leonora, because the policeman a very hard man at the time of Hunter. I can just remember that police used to be stationed up there and the old police used to chase 'em on horseback. They had two policemen on horseback and one with them four-wheel sulky and they'd pick 'em all up and take 'em all chained up like real prisoners, and take 'em all, big chains on their necks.

[...]

BUNBURY: And the other thing that you were saying was that Mr Neville went round and picked up the half-castes. Why did he pick out the half-castes, not the full-blood people?

JOHNSTON: Yes. Well, he want the half-caste to go down to be integrated with the white and then he want the Aboriginal the dark, the black Aboriginal to die out. He said in time to come they going to die out sooner or later and that was his job, picking 'em up. He was a very hard man. He was against the mission; he was against starting school there and he cut all the ration depot which is, the policeman been issue rations for the Aboriginal people in Lyndon,* Morgans and Murrin and Leonora. And then they tried to cut that mission out because the Aboriginal people, when the mission got all the Aboriginal people coming here and he gave them a job pulling sandwood [?]† and they bring a lot of dingo scalp. That time — a few bob. So they can get flour and tea and sugar, and goats to live on. The main meat is goats because he has 400 head of goats in Mt Margaret and feed the Aboriginal people — with treacle [laughs] and dripping, and flour and tea and sugar and twist tobacco for chewing because there's no tobacco.

[...]

BUNBURY: Reggie, I wonder if you'd mind telling me about what life was like for Aboriginal people when your

---

*   Lyndon — Linden.

†   sandwood[?] — sandalwood.

parents were growing up in the Laverton area?

JOHNSTON: My mother used to work in the pubs ... Washing, washing woman. And I was a boy in Laverton and there nowhere to go for school but when my mother found out there was a school started at Mt Margaret Mission, they start to leave Laverton because they still in the fear of the police. Now, they had to — a mission becomes a real advocated to the Aboriginal people. They came in here in the night-time; you know, they travel in the night, way out from Mulga Downs, and way out from Warburton, from the desert they heard about this mission, so they said, 'Oh well, we're going to take our children and stay in the mission.' So we had this missionary as protector and because Mr Schenk, he was a man with plenty of brain and he had everything. He worked everything out and then [—] because the squatters didn't want the mission to be built at Mount Margaret Mission [...] then when he established a school [...] then my mother heard this mission and she brought me up to Mt Margaret.

When I got landed here Mr Schenk said, 'Hey, how about giving me that little boy there, Reggie? I want to teach him school.' And I was frightened, I didn't like to go but my mother turned and told Mr Schenk, 'You teach my boy very good,' and I think he done a great — you know, given us the education I would — I don't correspond in my time — we had a good schooling.* We had an Englishwoman, she sacrificed her life with the Aboriginal people. At Mt Margaret she gave all what she had and she taught us everything and she gave lot away to the people. I think Mrs Bennett was a great woman in teaching. We don't have teachers like Mrs Bennett today.

BUNBURY: You were saying earlier, Reggie, that your parents lived in fear round the Laverton area and therefore the move to the mission was a good one. Why did they live in

---

* *'I don't correspond in my time — we had a good schooling'* — Mt Margaret children had acess to an unusually high level of education for the time.

such fear in the Laverton area?

JOHNSTON: Well, they been harassed by police. Well, they can't walk out in the dark there to get away back to the camp. When policeman is issuing rations for the Aboriginal people come and he look at who the bloke look frightened, so when he come to get his flour, well, he put him in gaol, and that's the only way to catch an Aboriginal. But Aboriginal people still has a fear, you know.

[...]

BUNBURY: Reggie, you were telling me earlier that your father had some bad experiences with the policeman in Laverton. What sort of experiences did he have?

JOHNSTON: Oh well, they — when the Aboriginal people get on the booze, you know, they steal beer and then they drink and then they start a fight. And my father got speared in both legs, big wounds, so he couldn't run; so a policeman came up with the police trackers and they gallop him down and pick him up and put him in chain and took him away. Because the Aboriginal people, they still had that fear. You know, they don't like the — moreover they can't talk freely like as I'm talking to you because I'm used to talking to white people and 'cause I've, I have no fear. But some Aboriginal have fear now living in a place like Wiluna which is a remote area and they have fear [...] But today, now — because we got Department of Aboriginal Affairs to look after our people today, not like in those days. They run, run for miles. My mother run away once when she had a half-caste daughter, she's run away for about six years in the bush, out, a hundred mile out in the desert and then she had to come back to bring my sister to school and get 'em educated. But today now the Aboriginal people they're dying because through alcohol. Then the best thing the Government would say, 'Oh well, we give the Aboriginal real freedom now. They can go in the pub and have a drink.' [...] Today, now, they're dying through drinking plonk and drinking metho; whatever they can find to drink now that kill 'em. In Kalgoorlie, all these outback area people are dying. Some young blokes, the blokes I went to school with, they all died out. I'm lucky to be still alive. I think only by the grace of God through the mission that I'm living today now and I feel like a ball of muscle.

It should be taught in schools and so the white people would know. You see I've been around, I've travelled around through Canberra and through Alice Springs and I have an understanding about other people.

There was one bad time in Australia in the Skull Creek incident* in Laverton, when Aboriginal people came down from Warburton Ranges to go to have their law ceremonies at Waroona.† But I was at the time, there was no Aboriginal legal officer at the time, a policeman met them on the road here and jumped on the truck and pulled them by the hair and throw them and throw their tea and chook, and flour and everything, and the natives started to, Aboriginal people started walking back, because the police had put sugar in the carburettor. So, while I was working at the Aboriginal project at Wunga, the Wunga [unclear] at Laverton, the Department of Aboriginal Affairs said, 'Oh you'll have to take two busloads, one busload of Aboriginals and take them right through to Leonora because they couldn't be harassed by the police any more.' Oh, the little gaolhouse couldn't hold all the Aboriginal men all being belted and drunk. I walked in to see the Inspector of Police, and he said he was a great friend of the Aboriginal people but that day he turned out to be real hard. But when I went down to see him and all the young constables were there, that belted all these people, them all back, the kids and everything. So we had to finish up taking them to Waroona for their ceremony and we took them up there and left them and we'd pick them up later.

---

*   *Skull Creek Incident* — *occurred on 5 January 1975. (Skull Creek was also the site of an early contact massacre of Aboriginal people, hence the name. Bolton in Stannage 1981: 173,174.)*

†   *Waroona* — *presumably a transcribing error from the spoken 'Wiluna'.*

But that time was a real bad time, with the Skull Creek incident. You must have heard about the Skull Creek incident?

BUNBURY: I have indeed, and I'm curious to know why the police reacted in that way— Did they not understand what was going on?

JOHNSTON: They didn't understand because the Aboriginal people coming through that area had to pass by Laverton and the police, or someone sent the word, 'Oh,' he said, 'the Aboriginals are coming down with their spears and waddies and boomerangs, to come and fight the white policemen.' But they misunderstood, you know, and then big trouble started. And all the Aboriginals were running away. One man with one peg leg, he started to walk along. And I had just come out from church and I had my suit on and when I went down [...] I went and told the inspector, 'Look, see, what your officer has done to the Aboriginal people!' [...] And, you know what, the inspector agreed with the young bloke, and he said, 'They want to put you in. Agreed?'

'You're not putting me in gaol! Of course,' I said, 'you've got the power.'

I never committed any crime.

And then we started, of course all of those police had been taken up, one from Kalgoorlie, and there was a big motorload of policemen went over to Laverton to work.

But when we had our Commission there and they sorted out what to do with the police, well all them policemen at the time, they sent them out everywhere split 'em up, don't go down to Laverton because you get among the wild people that are coming in from the desert, you know, and you fight with them, because they don't understand. But now, the people understand now [...]

I used to be a Legal Aid officer one time and I started, er I didn't have the education but I know how to speak for the Aboriginal people because I had a bit of training in university in Perth. I studied about law events, and that helped me a lot.

But now we could talk to a policeman any time and say, 'Oh, well don't be so hard on the Aboriginal, let him go.'

So police are different today than in the thirties and twenties.

They even built a big prison. You wouldn't believe it, they built a big prison at, oh about eight hundred kilometres from Perth out in the real desert at a big place called Mt Gould.[7] They had a big prison built there with big chains, and they belted the Aboriginals and *[in later years]* they sent them over to Mogumber at that time, and that's where Mr What's-his-name, finished up there, this Dave Hunter became Commissioner of Police and everybody knew him around the Laverton area where he'd been putting the Aboriginal people, belting them and putting them in. But my father approached him with a waddy one day and they were going to have a go, see, and my father hit him on the elbow, and course that put him off the balance. Yes, them people in Laverton were real hard, even the town people [...] They didn't like that Mr Schenk going up there because they said he becomes a stirrer. But he taught us today, now, to live in this white man's environment.

BUNBURY: What sort of things did Aboriginal people have to do to get into trouble with the police?

JOHNSTON: Ah well, when they are going through sometimes, you know, and they might, they give the police trouble because they go into a paddock and frighten the sheep, see. And of course the Aboriginals used to get hungry and they used to spear one sheep, a whole ewe or something, and cook 'em and eat 'em, see. And that's why they'd get in gaol, they'd get twelve months for killing sheep, spearing sheep. And then they got into the prospector's camp and pinch a bit of tea, and a bit o' tobacco. Well, that's where it starts. But the Aboriginal didn't know at the time, they had nothing to support for their environment and so they had to steal, and then they'd get into trouble.

They've been running with the fear with their mothers and

they used to come to Mt Margaret Mission they used to come in the night-time there, get away from the police harassment, and they used to come in the night there, and when they got to Mt Margaret Mission at that time in nineteen thirties, twenty-six, a place of refuge. They were coming into a place that they would be well looked after, the Aboriginal people, you know, and they talk well of Mt Margaret today, you see, and, like the Aboriginal people had their own little area going — houses and everything, built up at Mt Margaret Mission. That is a milestone of my life, Mt Margaret Mission in 1921. I thank the mission for that.

BUNBURY: When you were at the mission, did Mr Schenk and the other missionaries try to make you people Christian, or did they let you have your own beliefs?

JOHNSTON: Yes. We were taught in the mission. He said, 'Oh well, you, now, you've got to make your choice.' He's a man of — he said, 'If you want to believe in God —'

[...] And the Aboriginal said, 'Oh you can't break my culture and my belief.' The Aboriginal was too strong at that time. You can't break our culture. Because the Aboriginal people in Australia before the white man ever came to Australia, they believed in a supernatural god, and because, the Aboriginal, when he goes to the bush he looks at the hills, he looks at the creek and he looks at the main trees, finds two big trees — if I was there I could show you two big trees because that represents that two great men came through from Fremantle, they came from Fremantle to our interior and wherever they've been they made a bit waterhole. I don't know how they do it, because they must have, er, well, they're supernatural. Well, supernatural is just like God himself, and that's what I believe, and I believe what the Aboriginal people say. You know, even the sky, if you were here at night time I'd show you all the stars you want, I can name all them stars for you.

Extracts from the Verbatim Transcript of Bill Bunbury's 1986 Interview with Margaret Morgan[8]

MORGAN: [...] They didn't go away when they were dispossessed of their [land] — and the squatters were the ones who really dispossessed them while the goldmining was going on.

All the land was free and they roamed around like they were used to doing and in those parts at that time there were wells every 200 miles that the Government had put there for prospectors so they had water, you see. Now when the squatters came they fenced in those lands and they fenced in those mills,* and they fenced in all that water and they didn't like the Aborigines being at their water where they frightened the sheep away with their dogs and themselves. They were in a bad way, so what they did was they just cadged all around town and they stole and they sold their women, and they were in a bad way.

You see, it was because of an outcry from the townspeople — the complaint would go down to Native Affairs Department or not Native Affairs, Aborigines Protection Board[9] was what it was called and he [Neville] had the police to implement his directions. He had the control and the police carried out his directives, so that when he took them down to Moore River that was to get them to go out bush. They would be so afraid, that they would all go out bush or else they'd do another exodus. That's what he [Schenk] heard — that there was going to be another exodus after that one.

[...]

BUNBURY: Can you tell me about that? How did that happen — this exodus you just mentioned?

MORGAN: Well, he found out from the people later what

---

* mills — windmills at the Government wells, or, transcribing error from spoken 'wells'.

had happened. He didn't know then. All he saw was that when he went down to the train he saw this cattle truck with the little notice on the outside of the truck — '15 Niggers for Mogumber' — and his heart sank, and he said all the people — it really did have that effect, they all just left and it wasn't until they all came back he found out what had happened. They used to have rations of blankets and that was once a year when that happened, so they were all in there in the police yard to get their ration from the police and while they were there 15 of them were popped into the cells and then the next day, or whenever it was — perhaps a day or two later, they were put in the cattle trucks and taken down to Moore River. [...] That's what I've written in the book here. You'd like me to say it?

BUNBURY: Yes, just to summarise what happened to that particular group.

MORGAN: Yes. That group went down. As I say I think they were all related in some way. When they got down there they found two of their people already there and one was a little fellow called Darbin* and he knew Sister Eileen, and he talks about Sister Eileen. The other one was a young man called Wuwaga†. They apparently, and this is what I haven't been able to find, were allowed freedom in a way. They weren't in the Government compound proper. They were allowed a bit of freedom as tribal people. What I haven't been able to ascertain is whether they were on the northern side of the river or the southern, but they had to get over the river and this is what they have told me. They've given me exactly how they did it. They got over it by looking at a big tree and using it as a bridge and dropping on the other side.

They had old people with them and they had a blind man with them, and this Wawuja, he was a strong young fellow, they tell me, helped get these old and blind across. He might

---

*   Darbin — a slip, Morgan means Mulga Joe, not Darbin.

†   Wuwaga — Wawuja.

have been a swimmer, I don't know, they didn't tell me that bit, but he got them across and all these 15 they got right across on the other side and travelled through the night. In the morning they woke up, I was told, and they looked to see where they were going to go and they looked at the sun and they worked out where they reckoned home was and they made a direct line and came to Wongan Hills.

When they got to Wongan Hills they sat down and wondered what they were going to do, and they split off in four directions. Some came down to the pipeline, C.Y. O'Connor pipeline, and followed that up to Kalgoorlie. Another little group went straight across the uninhabited land and struck Menzies. Others went north. They were going to come in the back way, Mulga Queen way. You see, that was their country, back up there, so they were going to go up there and come in that way, and on the way they left an old man who knew he was going to peter out. They left him with his fire and they never saw him again.

The blind one was holding them up so they just left him in a paddock, and that's the most incredible story of all because they said he sat in the paddock and he yelled for all he was worth. A farmer heard him and took him home to Yalgoo, of all places, which is further north and when he got there he sent a message around that he had this old man and did anyone know who he belonged to. Well, nobody could talk his language and then there was one woman up there who'd heard that her brother had gone to Moore River and so she came down to see him and sure enough it was her blind brother. She talked to him and found out, yes, it was him all right. So she took him up to —

BUNBURY: You were telling me that the woman who came down for her blind brother picked him up. Can you tell me where she took him?

MORGAN: She took him right up north, right up north to Meekatharra, tracked across east to Wiluna. Now she was miles and miles away up north of Leonora which is towards

Laverton and then she walked down with her brother. The way blind people usually help someone else is they carry a stick and the seeing person holds one end of the stick and the blind holds the other end of the stick in one long line, and they travel around like that. That's what they used to do. Then he just caught the train. All the rest, once they got to Leonora, just got on the cattle trucks and came home in the open cattle trucks, just took the train. [...] He *[Schenk]* found out that there were going to be more to go. He wondered what he should do, so he thought, 'Oh well, I'll change my place. I'll go to Wiluna.'

[...]

He thought, 'Oh well, I think I'll go to Wiluna.' He got his bike all ready — he had a motorbike — to go and just the next morning when he was going to go the rain came down. They had had about a five or six year drought. The rain came down and Skull Creek was a raging torrent and he couldn't get across it; so he thought, 'Oh well, I'll just have to wait.' [...] So he tried again the next morning to go to Wiluna and there it was — more rain during the night and he just couldn't go. Then 14 days later here they were all back again. He couldn't believe it, back again — even the blind man. That's what he couldn't quite believe. How did they get across? How did this blind one get back?

He never knew — I found that out from the people years later. He never ever found out just exactly how they got back.

Absence

Alice Nannup was sent as a young girl to Mogumber in 1924, three years after the Laverton people escaped. She writes, in her book *When the Pelican Laughed*, of other people's attempted escapes from Moore River over the years she was there, recalling primarily the inevitability of capture:

> If girls ran away they'd send the trackers after them and they'd be brought back and their hair would be cut off, then they'd do time in the boob.[10]

Nannup also writes with some horror of a time when a young couple attempted to escape, were caught by the trackers and brought back to the settlement, and the young man tarred and feathered. Nannup's interview with Bill Bunbury, as quoted previously in this chapter, would suggest that Nannup knew the story of the 1921 escape by the Laverton people, but there are no successful escapes, nor even rumours of successful escapes, included among her memories of Moore River as published in this book.

Account

Margaret Morgan's *Mt Margaret: A Drop in a Bucket* contains a detailed account of the capture of the Laverton people, their successful escape from Moore River, and their various return journeys. Material from her father's diary is referenced but the oral sources of other material relating to this story are unreferenced in the text. The account of the Laverton lockup experiences of the people prior to their deportation was told to Morgan by her mother, Mysie Schenk.[11] Mrs Schenk was not living in Laverton during August 1921 but she recollected conversations with people who had witnessed (parts of) the events.

Oral testimonies given by three elderly Wongutha people in the 1980s were the primary sources for Morgan's construction of the events.[12] Mr Lampi Turner (deceased) told Margaret Morgan an account of Blind Jinera and the group who took the northern-most route; Morgan calls this group 'Ngada's party'.* Mr Reggie

---

* It is not clear whether Turner or Morgan introduced that term, and whether implications of leadership are intended by it. Perhaps Ngada was the only person Turner named, or perhaps the only name which Morgan recognised or recorded when Turner was speaking to her of the events, or perhaps Morgan found it the most convenient descriptive method for her construction of the event. Similarly, it is unclear by whom and why 'Jidu's party' and 'Gadajilbi's party' were given such names.

Johnston (deceased) provided Morgan with a general escape account and with the detailed stories relating to the group that walked along the Kalgoorlie pipeline, 'Jidu's party' in Morgan's text. Mrs Doris Thomas (deceased) also told Morgan the stories relating to the pipeline group, and an account of the group which set their path through the central country to Menzies, 'Gadajilbi's party'.

The following is Morgan's published account of the 1921 events:

> Then came the fateful day, 15 August 1921, just four months after Rod's arrival in Laverton — a day that cast him into deepest despair the like of which he had not experienced before. On that day, fifteen Wongutha were caught and sent away to Moore River Government Settlement (also known as Mogumber).
>
> Under the *Aborigines Act 1905* the Chief Protector became guardian for all Aborigines and part-Aborigines to 16 years of age. He had power under the Act to remove people from one place to another as thought best for them, without reference to any other authority, with the Police Department to carry out his directives.
>
> Months later Rod learned from the people what happened that day in the police yard. The 'indigents' were all gathered around the Laverton police station to get their annual blanket and clothing issue. To their astonishment, the police popped fifteen of them into cells, parting husbands from wives and parents from children. One woman was kicked in the stomach. Next day they were bundled into a cattle truck, and marked on the outside of the truck was a stock notice which Rod read: '15 Niggers for Mogumber'.
>
> Months later Mysie met a white woman, in Hannan Street, Kalgoorlie, who began to recount to her how the 'niggers' were screaming and yelling in the cells that night — she thought it was hilarious. Mysie felt sick. She said quietly, 'Yes, and did you know that one of the men in the cells, separated from his young wife Nardie, anguished over her, wondering what had happened to her? And do you know what happened to her? She ran terrified into the bush with

her baby and was so shocked that she lost her milk and the baby died.' She never had another child.

The laugh changed to embarrassment as the lady listened, and she couldn't excuse herself fast enough. The tragedy was that the woman's unfeeling account of the incident merely reflected the prevalent feeling of the day. Many did not think that Aborigines had human emotions.

[Footnote text in original: Even in Parliament of the day it was said: 'When you take a child away from a native woman she forgets all about it in hours, and as a rule is glad to get rid of it.' Western Australian Parliamentary Debates 28:426 James Isdell, Pilbara.]

At the end of that awful day there was not one of the Wongutha left in Laverton precincts. They had all fled. It seemed that the policy had worked — to get the people out of Laverton into the bush.

[...]13

OVER THE RIVER
Mogumber, situated on the southern bank, is 105km north of Perth. Today it is an Aboriginal community under self-management. In 1921 it was not so. The names 'Moore River' and 'Settlement' were whispered in fear by the Goldfields people. This was the place to which their part-white children had been sent, never to be seen again. Others, minors among them, were sent there to serve penal sentences.

Mr A O Neville, Chief Protector of Aborigines, saw it as a place of training for part-whites. It was established during 1918 during the early part of his administration, and became a place of social isolation, both from their own kindred and from the white community. In practice it was a prison, with its own punitive enclosure within the fenced compound.

It was to that place that the bedraggled little group of Wongutha arrived after a rough trip in the cattle bogies — strangers in a strange land and among strange people.

[Footnote text in original: The group comprised JIDU, known as Jumbo, King of the Wongutha tribe. Tall and upstanding; BALDUL, one of Jidu's wives; MOONGOODIE, worked around the district. Astute man; THALBIN, one of Moongoodie's wives; JINERA, also known as Blind Charlie, Moongoodie's eldest brother; THIMBARN, nicknamed Gadajilbi (grey-headed);

THARNMOON, *Gadajilbi's wife;* WUNU; BIYUWARRA, *wife of Wunu;* ELYON, *Biyuwarra's baby;* NGANJUR, *known as Bill Carrigg;* THULYI, *known as Tom Harris;* GRARN, *known as Lame Charlie;* MUDARN, *an old woman;* NGADA.]

But not quite. They discovered two other captives there from their own country. One of them Wawuja, also known as Ginger, was a strong young man in his twenties, a nephew to Gadajilbi. He was an accomplished horseman at Cox's Find at Erlistoun north of Laverton. The other was Joe Mulgathunoo, known also as Mulga Joe. He was in his teens. Both he and Wawuja had committed some crime, probably stealing. Joe discovered his mother Thalbin among the new batch of deportees.

Because they were not housed in the compound the prisoners were allowed a certain amount of latitude on the north side of the river which formed a natural barrier to anyone planning escape. Fishing and catching jilgees was the pastime among the inmates, but not for the Wongutha. They were terrified of the fish. 'Don't go in the water, the fish will eat you,' they were told. They believed it.

While the other prisoners spent their time fishing, the Goldfields Wongutha, from the moment of arrival, spent their time planning escape. How could they get across that river? Fishing and swimming were unknown to them. They took particular note of a big tree with a bough leaning over the river like a natural bridge. The more they looked at it the more they could see that all they had to do was to climb along that bough and then jump into the water on the other side. Freedom was worth the hazard.

Wawuja, strong and enterprising, led the escape party after dusk, helping the old and the blind in their risky bid for freedom. Silently and fearfully the little group climbed the natural bridge and dropped into the shallower water on the other side. Once all were safe on the other side, they walked swiftly away through the bush all night — they dared not stop. They wanted to get as far away from Mogumber as they could.

Through thicket and trees they walked in a straight line east, following the stars, keeping out of sight. Next morning they wondered where they were. Someone said, 'Look at the sun. Which way is the sun coming up?' Reading the sun, they worked out the direction of Laverton, and so came to Wongan Hills.

Meanwhile, back in Laverton, Rod was so thoroughly dispirited and baffled he made enquiries around town to find out what was to happen to the people, and learned that the deportation was the first of many more to come, the reason being that the authorities thought the Aborigines were too numerous and troublesome around the township.

JIDU'S PARTY

After arrival at Wongan Hills the seventeen Moore River escapees sat down and consulted in the bush what their next move should be. They agreed that it was too risky to travel in a big group and it would be better to split up.

Jidu decided he would make for the Perth-Kalgoorlie railway; Gadajilbi headed a second party and Ngada another.

Jidu and his party made a straight line in a south-easterly direction for the C.Y. O'Connor pipeline, which ran alongside the Perth–Kalgoorlie road. Things went well for them. A farmer's wife gave them a 'feed of bread'. At the next farm they were given a bucket full of pullet's eggs.

That night — freezing cold — with a cadged box of matches, they dug a hole and lit a fire in it, cooked the eggs and broke their two-day fast. Huddling together around the fire, they slept well. They had been walking day and night. Before leaving at daybreak they covered the hole in and were on their way, keeping well off the road, out of sight.

At Southern Cross they decided they would rest a while, having walked almost non-stop. Here they met Thulyi and other members of the escape party who had forged ahead. All along the way they begged bread, and no one knocked them back. But those eggs! — they were the luxury item.

Reaching Bullabulling, they camped on the flat hill near the 'pub'. There was water there, and rabbits. When they came to Coolgardie they met friends who helped them with more food. From Kalgoorlie Jidu and company simply caught the train, riding free in the cattle trucks. Thulyi (Tom Harris) caught the train at Broad Arrow, alighting at Morgans, and walked the 32 km to Laverton via King's Well — which was later to become Mount Margaret Mission.

Gadajilbi's party

At the Wongan Hills planning meeting, Gadajilbi had decided against the Kalgoorlie railway route. In his opinion, it had too many risks. He felt safer in the wide, open bush, living off the land.

He set off with his party from Wongan Hills in a direction slightly north of east. Reading the sun, they walked steadily across a roadless, uninhabited landscape. Because of recent rains, they found water along the way, and catching goannas was no problem.

After walking about 400 km they hit Menzies dead on target. They too decided to take the train for the rest of the journey.

Ngada's party

Ngada's little party met with sadness and trouble after leaving Wongan Hills. He and his party headed north for Mount Margaret through farming country and back country roads. He thought it would be a lot safer to come in the back way to Laverton, via their own country: Mulga Queen, Cox's Find and Salt Soak.

They had just left Wongan Hills when old Wunu came to a standstill. He couldn't go another step. 'Leave me here,' he said to the rest. 'I will die here.' He knew the procedure. When a member of the tribe was too old or sick and became a handicap, the only thing to do was to leave that one to die. It was harsh reality in a nomadic life of subsistence. So they did as he asked. They made a big fire with plenty of wood beside him, and left him in the bush just out from Wongan Hills. They never saw him again.

Further on, the little party had more trouble. Old, blind Jinera was slowing them down, so they put him in the middle of a farmer's paddock and left him there, yelling his head off. He never did have a good temper at the best of times.

When Ngada's group reached Mt Magnet they turned eastwards to Sandstone, then walked cross-country to Mulga Queen. Helped on their way by their own people, they arrived back in Laverton, having walked a distance of well over 800 km. It was 18 days from the time they had been trucked out of Laverton.

BLIND JINERA
Jinera, a resilient old man, left to himself in the middle of the paddock was not dumb even if he was blind. His wailing and yelling attracted the attention of a farmer, who took pity on him and took him home to his farm near Yalgoo. However, nobody could understand what he was saying — his dialect was different from those in Yalgoo. The farmer rang all around the district of Mount Magnet inquiring whether anyone knew about a blind man.

An Aboriginal woman in Cue had already heard on the 'bush telegraph' that her blind brother Jinera had been sent to Mogumber. When her boss asked if anyone knew this 'blindfella' she decided to go to Yalgoo and find out.

When she arrived she recognised him immediately, and they had a quiet wail together as they greeted each other. After talking things over, she decided to take him back herself. They got a lift to Mount Magnet, then on to Cue and further north to Meekatharra, after which they went across country to Wiluna. From Wiluna they turned south and footed it down to Leonora, his sister leading Jinera with a stick. There they caught the Laverton train. At Morgans they parted company, the sister returning to her husband in Cue.

The fascinating question arises: how did that woman come to be living in Cue, hundreds of kilometres away from her own country? It transpired that the woman was one who had been taken captive by the Darlots in the early hours of that pre-dawn massacre a few years earlier and carried off to a strange country with a strange language. She was now part of that people.[14]

The names of those escapees who later became part of the community at Mount Margaret Mission are found throughout Morgan's book. She gives information about certain individuals' lives and momentous occasions. The stories she relates about individuals are based on her father's records and the personal reminiscences of her mother and herself.

One of Mysie Schenk's recollections of police treatment of Wongutha people (undated incident) is as follows:

> He saw it. Yes, and saw the boy that was shot. He told me all about that. He saw this native going to the Government dam, and the policeman riding up on his horse. Later, policeman rode away, then the boy came back and had wounds on his back put in with small shot, close up. Dad dressed his wounds and reported the matter. That was Thompson, maybe Hunter, and he was shifted and lost his stripe. Had some respect for Dad after that. Hated him.[15]

Mysie Schenk's comments pertaining to the deported Wongutha individuals who were the first to arrive and settle at the fledgling Mount Margaret Mission, as noted in the margins of Morgan's copies of Schenk's letters, are as follows:

> Ngunjurr — Bill Carrigg always stayed at Morgans, came from Kookynie side, talked English properly.

> The missionaries, out of their meagre assets, gave rations each to Old Charlie (Kardajilbe), Blind Charlie (Jinera), Nunjoor William, and Lame Charlie (Gooran).[16]

Mt Margaret: A Drop in a Bucket also records a number of instances where captured Wongutha on their way to sentencing or punishment managed to break free from police custody. One example follows:

> [Billy Ngarawanu] ... was finally caught at the Mission. The policeman was very pleased at catching him, and clapped a brand-new pair of legcuffs on him. Leaving him sitting in the motor car outside, he went in to Schenk's for a cup of tea. 'Are you sure he'll be all right out there?' asked Rod. 'Oh, he'll be all right. Those legcuffs are made of special steel,' he said, extolling their virtues. 'They can't be broken.'
> While they were talking there came a hue and cry: 'Billy's gone, Billy's gone!' They rushed outside, and sure enough there was no sign of Billy or the legcuffs. He could run like the wind, so Rod said to the constable, 'Look, he's gone over those hills. We'll never get him back now, and the others won't help you ... go back to Laverton ...'

Billy had had no trouble escaping. He had sent one of his mates to the woodheap to bring him back an axe, which he put under a link and then banged the link with the crankhandle. Away went the link, and away went Billy over the hills, with a legcuff dangling from each ankle. That escape was nothing new. The Wongutha were in the habit of escaping. When caught they could put on a dumb look, while all the time they were looking about to take advantage of any situation. With a great sense of humour, they always returned the mutilated legcuffs or handcuffs to the police as a keepsake.[17]

Absence

Doris Pilkington's *Follow the Rabbit-Proof Fence* is an account of a partially successful escape made in 1931 from Moore River by Doris' mother and two other young girls from the Pilbara region. Pilkington had access to the personal files of her relatives and found that by 1931, just ten years after the escape of the Laverton people, the Chief Protector of Aborigines was personally involved in directing the police to recapture escapees.[18]

Within the story, an inmate of Moore River says:

> You should have seen the other ones who were locked up for running away ... They all got seven days punishment with just bread and water. Mr Johnson shaved their heads bald and made them parade around the compound so that everyone could see them. They got the strap too ...
>
> They only got as far as Jump Up Hill ... The black tracker found them ... [and] whipped them with his stock whip ... He made them walk all the way back, without a break, while he rode his grey stallion like a white policeman.[19]

Pilkington does not refer to any successful escapes from the Settlement other than her mother's.

Account

Peter Biskup's *Not Slaves, Not Citizens* looks at, amongst other subjects, the various Mission and Church organisations that worked with Aboriginal people in Western Australia, their effects on the Aboriginal communities, and their participation in shaping the history of Aboriginal experience. He notes that Schenk was one of the more politically active missionaries. Biskup cites the following quote from one of Schenk's letters, and then interestingly, illustrates the statement with reference to the 1921 events in Laverton.

> 'My sincere love for the natives would lead me to ask big things for them, and I have a tendency to open my mouth too wide on their behalf.' *[Footnote reference in original to N.W.T. 6/1920.]* This faculty, which Schenk undoubtedly possessed, led him into immediate trouble.
>
> In September 1921 he accused the Laverton police of irregularities in the distribution of relief. Later in the year he sent Neville a somewhat undiplomatic letter in which he criticised the removal to the Moore River Aboriginal settlement of a group of Laverton aborigines.[20]

Schenk's correspondence with Neville in 1921 protesting the deportation of a 'group' to Mogumber is mentioned only in passing. Biskup quotes none of Schenk's 'undiplomatic' letter criticising the deportation; his text is less concerned with the deportation itself than with illustrating Schenk's character.

Absence

Pamela Rajkowski's *Linden Girl. A Story of Outlawed Lives* contains the account of the life of a Wongutha woman, Lallie, born in Linden (113 km from Laverton) in around 1908. Rajkowski had access to restricted personal files and her knowledge of the events is based on detailed Department records. Lallie spends her childhood eluding capture by the zealous protector/policemen of the area, as did so many Wongutha children. In 1926 Lallie becomes pregnant and seeks refuge at Mt Margaret Mission. Despite the pleadings of the Schenks, she is arrested under special warrant — Neville's Department had spent considerable effort tracking Lallie's movements in the past — and Neville arranges for Lallie's removal to Mogumber to occur less than a week after the stillbirth of her child.[21]

In early 1927 Lallie and another young Wongutha woman with three children attempt two escapes from Moore River, but they are recaptured by trackers. In October 1927 they make a third escape and are successful. The new Superintendent of the Settlement, Neal, corresponds by 'wire' with Neville on these occasions[22] and the statewide 'police network' is alerted. (Administration had tightened at Moore River since Campbell's time.)

The two women and the weary children take three months to walk home to Linden.[23]

Rajkowski provides context to these events. She cites oral evidence that the police used the occasions of ration distribution for their own purposes, and that arrests were made without trial and without reason:

> The Wongai's experience and perception of ration distribution was summarised by an elderly Wongai descendant. 'When the police issued rations they would look to see who looked frightened.' [Footnote reference in original: Interview, Reggie Johnston with Bill Bunbury.] When such a person approached the Constable distributing the flour he would have that person seized and put in gaol.[24]

Rajkowski cites a letter from Schenk to the Deputy Protector of Aborigines (Copping), written in June 1921, concerning the drought and lack of food for the Wongutha, noting that if 'three white men with good dogs and rifles took a three-day hunting expedition but did not get one kangaroo, how could the natives exist?'[25]

Rajkowski interviewed Ranji McIntyre, Reggie Johnston, and other Wongutha people in the Laverton/Kalgoorlie area in 1989; the stories she quotes from the 1920s are primarily to do with police harassment of the Wongutha, the methods by which the people hid their children in the bush and the spinifex country, and the people's great fear of the forced removal of their children by policemen. Rajkowski does not record any mention of the 1921 capture and escape story.

Absences

Other texts, broadly discussing aspects of Goldfields history and sporting titles such as *Colourful Tales of the Western Australian Goldfields*[26] make hardly any mention of the presence and existence of Aboriginal people. Colourful tales and daring adventures, in these histories, belong to white men of British background, and very occasionally, women with a British background. Occasionally, photographic collections contain some acknowledgement of the presence of Aboriginal people, but in these the Wongutha are portrayed primarily as outcasts and fringe dwellers of the white communities.

Absence

During the 1980s some 'Mount Margaret people' compiled their memories and published a book called *Recollections of Mount Margaret*. The book was edited by the Mount Margaret school headmaster of the time, Jim Heslop, for use as a teaching resource in that school. The events remembered are those in which the writers were themselves involved — consequently no mention is made of the escape events of 1921. Of the twenty Aboriginal contributors, most recall memories of early childhood life in the bush, of their arrival at Mount Margaret, and of school days.

Ranji McIntyre was the most senior contributor; the editor notes that McIntyre was an adult at the time of Mt Margaret's establishment. McIntyre tells of the history of the shooting of Tom James, of his bike ride back from Dumbleyung, his work with the prospector and sandalwood puller, and his work at Mt Margaret Mission.[27]

Ranji McIntyre:

I was born and spent my early years at Burtville which is about 16 miles from Laverton. I was a miner but mainly worked cattle.

... [McIntyre tells the story of the shooting of Tom James] ...

I stayed down at the Linden township for a couple of months before going back to Burtville where I went prospecting and sandalwooding. All this happened in 1920, just about the time when Mr Schenk arrived at Mount Margaret.

When Burtville town closed down, I went to the South West of Western Australia. It took a long time to travel to the Wagin/Dumbleyung area (9 days by horse and cart from Burtville to Kalgoorlie). The owner of the pub in Burtville had bought the railway tea rooms at Dumbleyung and invited me to go down there for a while. I stayed two years but got homesick for my country and decided to return home. My friends in Dumbleyung gave me a bicycle for the trip and I rode back to Burtville in 8 days. For example, I rode from Kalgoorlie to Menzies in one day, from Menzies to Malcolm on the next and then from Malcolm to Burtville on the third.

I spent a while longer working as a sandalwood cutter but then decided to shift to Mount Margaret where I have been ever since.

I worked for Mr Schenk building houses, the hospital and the school house, which was carted from Morgans in four pieces on the back of an old Chev truck.

... when I arrived at Mount Margaret there was only one well (King's Well) so Mr Schenk asked me if I could sink wells. I told him that I was a miner, so I would give it a go. I sank Pigeon Well 60 feet deep to find good water after a water diviner showed me the place. In all there were four wells at Mount Margaret, one at the Battery behind the hill, Pigeon Well, King's Well and another near Morrison's place ...[28]

Many contributors mentioned the childhood fear of being taken from their families by the police, and the constant running from the police that most families experienced in the 1920s, 30s and 40s in the Laverton area.

Phyllis Thomas remembers:

> I come from Cosmo Newbery. My parents got sick and tired of being chased by the police and having to hide because they had half-caste children and it was law, that all such children had to be put into homes.
> My parents used to burn sandalwood and rub me over in the grease to make me look black so the police wouldn't take me away. I was also hidden on the back of the truck under sacks. The police used to chase us a lot and burn our blankets and flour and sugar in order to make us come out of hiding.
> One day, Mr Shepherd, the manager of Ration Station at Mulga Queen told my parents that if they didn't hand over the children to the police, there would be no more rations for them ...
> So my parents handed us over ...[29]

Jean McKenzie's family came from the same station as Auntie Rosie:

> My parents were station hands living at Nambi Station, near Leonora. When I was three years old, my younger sister and I were placed in the hands of the missionaries at Mount Margaret. My older sisters and one brother were also at Mount Margaret ...[30]

Ron Bonney:

> I was born between Cosmo Newbery and Mulga Queen. My mother was at Cosmo Newbery and my father was at Cox's Find. In those days, when a half-caste child was born, they were taken to the Mission. So my mother was almost forced to take me to Mount Margaret Mission when I was a baby ...[31]

Cyril Barnes, the grandson of old Wunu, is another of the contributors. His memories go 'right back to grade one when my teacher gave me an apple for doing good work'[32] and focus entirely on his school years.

Francis Murray remembers that:

... half-caste children were rounded up by the police in the early days and sent to either Mogumber or Mount Margaret.

Once the police went up to the Government Well where my family was camped early in the morning when we were all asleep. The police tracker had shown them where we were. The police fired a shot and we ran away as fast as we could. I left my pet cat tied to a tree. When we finally came back to the Well when the police had left, I found that the police had shot my cat. We ran off to Cox's Find but the police chased us. They told two men that they had to bring the half-caste children into Laverton or they'd be put in gaol.

These men picked us up and we spent one or two nights in the gaol waiting for court. Mr Schenk and Mr Thomas went to court and asked [for] us to come to Mount Margaret. Mr Thomas spoke up in court for us and [said] if we were in Mount Margaret then our parents could come and visit us ...[33]

Bill Wesley recalls the long distance walk to take him to the safety of Mt Margaret, and the importance of knowing where water could be found in the land. And then there were the shocks of seeing white people, of adapting to their ways, of being put inside a building:

Before I came to Mount Margaret, I lived near Blackstone. We walked to Mount Margaret but it was a long way, so every 5 or 6 miles, I would ride on my old mother's back. There was no road, only a horse and cart track. My father and mother knew where the rockholes were, so we couldn't get lost. We would camp at the rockholes, stay there for a few days, and live off the land eating kangaroos, goannas and porcupines [echidnas].

It took my family about a month to reach Laverton. I was surprised at the large number of windmills there. I had never seen them before and they were in every backyard. I asked my mother 'What's this place?'

She said, 'This is a township, called Laverton.'

We stayed for about three days and then moved on to a place called Mount Margaret. When we arrived at the Mission, my mother saw the missionaries ...

I had never seen so many white people before and, being

very shy and frightened, I hid behind my mother's dress. I wondered what was going to happen now.

A missionary sent me up to a small dormitory ... I would climb out the window and go back to my mother's camp. I wasn't used to blankets, only the camp fire ...[34]

Account

Anna Haebich's *For Their Own Good: Aborigines and Government in the Southwest of Western Australia 1900-1940* contains, somewhat surprisingly given the geographic distance of Laverton from the South-West, two references to the Laverton people's escape from Mogumber.

The first reference appears in text discussing the fearfulness of Mogumber:

> Most Aborigines greatly feared the prospect of being sent to Moore River. One Aboriginal woman harking back to those days recalled that the people were 'terribly touchy about this Moore River. They was terrible frightened. No word of a lie. They was cruel frightened.' *[Footnote reference in original: Garlett, transcript of interview in Haebich 1985.]* People sent to the settlement were frequently wrenched from the rounds of their daily lives without any prior warning. In 1921 Aborigines at Laverton were decoyed into the local police station on the pretext of being served food by the police. Once inside, the doors were closed on them and they were kept under lock and key until the train that was to take them from Laverton to Moore River was ready to start. The police were later said to have acted entirely on their own initiative as they had decided that the Aborigines were a 'nuisance' around the town. *[Footnote reference in original: Sunday Times, 14/11/1926 William Harris' letter.]*
>
> The settlement became a final destination for adults, while for the children and young people it was supposedly a temporary stop before they were channelled into employment in the wider community. For all it meant a dramatic break with their former way of life and families.[35]

Haebich writes of the role of the trackers:

> The trackers at Moore River played a vital role in controlling the other residents by reporting on rebellious behaviour in the camp, tracking escapees, administering punishments and supervising inmates imprisoned in the 'Boob' ... A significant number of the trackers were originally from the north ... They were sent to Moore River after repeated convictions for alcohol-related offences or for challenging the role of the police. This reflected the intended reformatory role of the settlements, as did the practice of sending some Kimberly Aborigines to the Settlement after their release from Fremantle Prison or after their acquittal in Perth on such serious charges as attempted murder. These men usually had few ties with the predominantly south-west settlement population and this left them particularly dependent on the white staff. The trackers frequently administered unduly harsh punishments; they patrolled the settlement armed with truncheons and big sticks and one even carried a spear tipped with glass ... Clara Jackamarra recalls that they were 'one of the things I hated about the settlement ... They would flog a person who would not do what they were told and put them in the gaol house with only bread and water for food.' *[Footnote reference in original: Kelly, S.M. Proud Heritage. Perth 1980:73.]*
>
> Some men appointed to these positions refused to inflict such punishments and were removed from the job. Bob Allen, an Aboriginal originally from the Kimberleys who was sent to Fremantle Prison for bashing a policeman and then transferred to Moore River on his release, was taken off the job after he refused to whip a group of children for taking a walk without the matron's permission. *[Footnote reference in original: Kelly, S.M. Proud Heritage. Perth 1980:73.]*[36]

Haebich writes of rebellion against the institutional life at Mogumber; it is in this context that she refers again to the unusually successful escape of the Laverton people.

> There were also frequent attempts to escape from the

settlement. For example, the Aborigines sent there from Laverton in 1921 managed to escape en masse soon after their arrival. Charlie Sandstone recalls that trackers were sent out to bring them back 'but they were a little bit frightened to go there and find them. Because they was a mob. They'd say yes and no, but you wouldn't get them to go out there and track them up. They pretended to look that's all.' [*Footnote reference in original: Sandstone, transcript of interview in Haebich 1985.*]

Although some Laverton people reportedly made it back to their own country most were not so lucky and they were tracked down and thrown into the 'Boob'.[37]

Definitive elements of the event may be gleaned from this recollection. The first, that Charlie Sandstone, the storekeeper, remembers with clarity that there was a group large enough to be termed a 'mob' of people sent to Mogumber in 1921 from Laverton, and that they made a successful escape. Secondly, the settlement authorities were fully aware of the escape, for at some point in time they sent out trackers to pursue the escapees.

Furthermore, it was very unusual for the escape party to elude the trackers and to successfully escape. Sandstone recalls the event from an interesting perspective: the memory is in the context of an exceptional event in which the trackers, and the institution, were unable maintain their usual power and authority over those who opposed the institution.

Sandstone states that the trackers were 'a little bit' frightened of the Laverton Wongutha. Charlie Sandstone was originally from the Goldfields himself, from the Sandstone district.[38] The 'Laverton natives' were purported by various whites to be the 'worst'[39] in the state and 'very wild'[40] — perhaps the Wongutha were also regarded with some awe by other Aboriginal groups. (At that time initiated Wongutha men wore animal bones through their noses and wove select items into their hair to make head-dresses.)[41] In any event, Sandstone's understanding of the successful escape is based on a perception of unwillingness by the trackers to confront the large group of Wongutha — they 'pretended to look that's all.'

Haebich's text also includes a full copy of William Harris' letter to the *Sunday Times* previously documented in Writings, 3.4.

4

A New Account

Foreword

This story is not my story. The story belongs to the Wongutha people who experienced the events related in this account. In writing this, I wish to pay tribute to the people who lived through these events.

The 'New Account' brings together the various evidences and interpretations of the 1921 events in Laverton. It is an extrapolation based on all the evidence that has come to light. I am conscious that there are gaps and contradictions in parts of the evidence. However, this account does not seek to analyse these gaps and contradictions,[1] but rather, to document the accessible knowledge. I do not present this account as a 'full' or complete account of the events; while it is more 'full' than previous accounts, the true story in all its complexity is not fully known. This account is part of the journey towards the elusive truth of the historical event.

The new account relates one set of historical events, occurring within a fixed period of time. However, the experiences of the Wongutha people who lived through this event are not confined to one group, one place, one time, but are ongoing; the reality of the tragedies which befell people in 1921 can be vividly heard in the voices speaking of more recent events. The tragedies of an individual's life are simultaneously intensely personal and representational of the tragedies of a people.[2]

In this new account then, I also wish to honour those Wongutha who shared with me recollections of recent experiences.[3] I have incorporated their words freely into the account. I consider them vital, poignantly expressing a depth of experience which I cannot share and can only hope to vaguely grasp, sharply revealing the continuation of the past in the present. These words may or may not have been originally spoken about the 1921 story of exile and escape. Those quotes which relate to other stories and places are nevertheless deliberately incorporated into this account, for they powerfully illustrate the way in which the story expressed in this account also mirrors the experience of many other people.

I feel charged to communicate as much as I can of the history that they have shared with me. It was not for me alone that they sat down with me and talked of the past, telling me stories of their own experiences, of others' experiences. They were keen to ensure that their past was not forgotten.

The writing of this account of the 1921 events springs from the same impetus. This history is not lost; it should not become forgotten. In telling the story of the 1921 breakout from Moore River, I am following the tradition by which a story, another person's story, may be told by a non-participant in order to ensure that knowledge of the history is passed on. I have experienced this tradition when Uncle Fred told me the story of Auntie Queenie's brother, when Aunty Wyallie told me stories of Lampi, when groups of people told me of breakouts from the Laverton lockup, when I was told of various individuals who defied and outwitted police. Being told these stories, by one person about another person, has encouraged me in the writing of this book, which is almost entirely based on telling other people's stories, and similarly, this New Account.

'We wouldn't have told you if we didn't want you to know! Write it down, write it all down!' one of the women said to me when I asked, again, just to make sure.

Despite their assurances, I am still a little anxious — I am conscious that the process of writing the words on a page has not, until very recently, been part of the Wongutha storytelling tradition. A story which is told by an individual to a particular listener is told, framed, in such a way that the listener will make sense of it. A story is given different emphasis for different occasions and to illustrate different points. The telling is less about imparting information than promoting understanding; the listening, less about gathering information than about coming to terms with the past. In contrast, a written version of the story can take no account of the individuality of each receiver of the story. A written version is not variable, it is more or less fixed. There is no opportunity to vary the framing of the story on another occasion, nor to refine an expression, so that a spectrum of understandings is built up. A written account, despite these deficiencies, may speak with an usurped authority — in time, oral accounts may become endangered by the written 'history'. I am concerned that society often privileges written accounts over oral accounts; I was, for example, on a number of occasions referred to *A Drop in a Bucket* when I asked Wongutha people about the 1921 events.

I can only re-state that this 'New Account' of the story is not presented as 'The Authoritative Account'. My written construction of the historical events is only one possible construction. Since written accounts of (parts of) the 1921 story have already been constructed by two other writers, my hope is that this New Account may contribute to diversifying, rather than defining, knowledge of these events.

My aim has been to convey, powerfully, the reality of the story. Attempting to tell the historical account of this story as a narrative has posed some dilemmas.[4] Not all of the facts of the story are known. Some passages move beyond the formal rules of evidence for historical writing. For example, I know that it rained while they walked home, and before they walked home, but I do not know that it was raining on the actual night that they left the Settlement and crossed the river and walked off into the night — it is likely that it was raining, but it is not certain. I have interpreted the evidence, and I have suggested likelihood. The second dilemma was that my necessarily limited knowledge of Wongutha culture might compromise aspects of the account. I have, however, worked within the context of an over-arching human understanding of a cross-cultural nature, and within my understanding of Wongutha and Anglo-Australian culture. In order to enhance the prospects of the account's cross-cultural appropriateness, review and approval of the New Account text has been given by a Wongutha woman of high community regard.

The third dilemma is the question of my 'right', or rightness, to tell a version of the 1921 breakout. It is not my story. But I cannot contribute to the silence by keeping this story, this history, concealed. I feel that the book has received general community approval — the work has been done in the open, with the full knowledge and consent of all contributors. It has been known to many Wongutha people and I have received only support and encouragement to do it. More particularly, as previously stated, endorsement of the text as it stands underpins my confidence in presenting the New Account.

FORMATTING NOTE

Evidence, other than direct quotation, is not referenced as it has been identified in the earlier pages of this book.

A New Account

... it's still in my heart, you know ... it still remains with us. History, you know.[5]

Summer in Laverton, 1921, is seemingly unending. The heat is relentless; the ground is dry. Dust rises with every disturbance of the air and slowly re-settles, there is dust in the lungs of the people and in the empty creek beds. There is dust on the dead sheep that have drunk their water and muddied their drinking places. They have dug soaks in the dry creek beds, but the sheep are everywhere. They find another dead sheep lying submerged in the last muddy hole of the last creek. Any water seeping downstream will now be polluted. Water is scarce.

We come up the valley, you see, there's a windmill down the bottom! Big mob of sheep there too! ... Never mind, we went just like we owned the place, we sitting down by the tree there, big mob of sheep there![6]

They are harassed when they camp near the windmills that are draining the ground of water; the squatters or the police roughly move them on. They are harassed when they camp at the government wells; the policemen from Laverton come on their white horses before dawn and fire into the camp. The people are always ready and they escape into the bush, scattering into the pre-dawn light. The policemen do not catch any of the people. Instead they kick open their flour bags and tip out their water containers. Water is scarce, and food is becoming as scarce as the water.

The people are slowly starving, the marlu and the nganuti* for

---

marlu — red kangaroo.
nganuti — bush turkey.

miles around have been shot by the white people and the rabbits have vanished in the drought. *Native game is very scarce, in fact practically extinct ... They must either starve or steal, and naturally prefer the latter.*[7]

'Hey, what about we kill one of these lamb?'

'Ah! No way ... I don't want to be in strife now!!'[8]

They cannot kill a sheep unless they are willing for all the people to be treated roughly by the police until the police find and catch and chain a culprit, any likely-looking culprit, and then send him away on the train. *They might steal something, they might have gone to another place, and they'll follow it up, follow him up, and then, they chain all up, and put him in the train, and send him to Perth.*[9]

A policeman came up with the police trackers and they gallop him down and pick him up and put him in chain and took him away.[10]

Some of them come back, and some of them didn't come back. They stay there and they're all finish.[11]

The most viable option is not to steal but to request food and water from the white people. For about ten years, until quite recently, there had been large and thriving camps of the woodcutters and miners throughout the bush nearby — the cooks often gave the people left-over food and the day-old dry bread. But the mines have shut down, and the mining camps have disappeared. The woodcutting has stopped, and the woodcutters have also disappeared. The once flourishing towns of Burtville and Morgans are dwindling; Mt Margaret, the major town of the region only twenty years ago, is empty of all but one old prospector. Most of the remaining white people have put sheep onto the old townsites where there are wells and water. They are slowly taking up the rest of the land.

I come back, went back to Burtville, and Burtville finish. And, the squatter said, 'Put them, put the sheep in the paddock,' in that Burtville town, you see! That's, the town always all full, of everything, and they had the sheep, the sheep take it.[12]

Laverton and Morgans and Beria are dwindling. The police

station at Beria has just been closed. The Laverton draper is moving on, has packed up his business and taken it with him. Despite the reduction of their number, the white people in Laverton are less than generous with their water supply. There is a small reservoir of water at Laverton, but the white people do not allow the Wongutha to drink this water. One elderly woman, Nginjingil, has an arm broken by a policeman while he persuades her to leave the area. Every day at midday a policeman rides out on his white horse with his stockwhip in his hand and deals stringently with any Wongutha people who happen to be in the town.

The policeman is Dave Hunter. Dave Hunter and Tommy Thompson. Yeah. That's the old day police.[13]

Police Constable 'Tommy' Thompson 292 finds the Wongutha people *very troublesome*.[14]

The white community have also been causing him trouble, a number of them have been complaining to his superiors in Kalgoorlie about his style of policing the Wongutha. First the Sub-Inspector, and then the Inspector, at Kalgoorlie have questioned him about his leniency in allowing the Wongutha to camp and congregate near the towns. He has answered them patiently, reminding them that food and water is scarce out in the bush, that the five hundred or so people must starve or beg or steal to survive, that it is *only instinct*[15] to obtain available food and water rather than die.

Everything had been working quite well until a few years back when *a large influx of Spinifex Natives*[16] had taken place. It seems his superior officers do not understand about this spinifex country, for they have repeatedly questioned him as to why the Wongutha are not *driven out relentlessly*.[17]

He has made it clear, on a number of occasions that *the getting the whole of them out into the Spinifex is nearly impossible ... They cannot be got together and driven out like sheep, as soon as a move is made against them by the police they scatter like rabbits*.[18] Nor do his superiors seem to understand that many of these people are *purely wild*,[19] and difficult to police unless they are camped in one place where he can easily find them. The *large Camp of Natives* near Laverton is *practically under Police supervision*,[20] making it much easier for him to keep a watchful eye on their comings and goings, as he has told his superior officers time and time again. Additionally he can easily *effect early arrest*[21] should any given situation require him to take action, or to be seen to take action. Some years back the policy of moving the people away from the towns and into the outlying areas was strictly enforced with unfortunate results. *The camps of Woodcutters and Prospectors were robbed with impunity*, and he had suffered *no end of trouble*.[22] By the time word got in to Laverton, and he had a chance to organise supplies and leave town, and then find his way out to the right camp and get a sensible account of events from the angry men in the camp, the offenders would be *days and miles away*.[23] It was extremely difficult to maintain law and order in such a situation, for all three groups knew he would have little chance of catching the culprit. The woodcutters and prospectors were inclined to immediate action, and had threatened on numerous occasions that they themselves would deal with the Wongutha in a *drastic manner*.[24]

About, six year old then. And, we was in this bush, sitting down, under the tree.
    And our mothers, our aunties and their children — three, three kids was there ...
    We was playing around, then, next minute, I heard this shooting!
    'Chttoow, chttoow, chttoow!!'
    Then I looked, ooh, these white blokes all on the horse, three! Shooting!
    ...I was standing one side of a tree so they won't see me.[25]

The woodcutters and prospectors have carried out their threats on at least one occasion by shooting at parties of Wongutha. Thompson feels that his role as Protector of Aborigines in Laverton is compromised in such situations, as is his role as policeman.
    But, on the whole, his system has worked very well over the last few years. He has been able to report on a number of occasions

that the Wongutha people at Laverton *do not give any annoyance*.[26] Even the local JP, in the past, had *no complaints to make against the Natives*.[27]

But now, the mines had started closing down and his district had become difficult. He knew that the Wongutha were accustomed to *receiving a large quantity of waste food for doing odd jobs*[28] at the mining camps and woodline camps. He had seen these camps gradually shut down, and had watched with dismay as the people turned to the more permanent settlements and townships for food. Thompson then first began worrying about the *hordes of Natives*[29] who were *thieving from camps and infesting the towns begging*.[30]

The new work load was such that *a constable could be kept with horses doing nothing else but keeping Natives in check and following up Native offenders*.[31]

It was back in 1919 that the justice brokers in Laverton had begun to regularly sentence adult men to exile away from their land and people in the prisons at Rottnest or Fremantle, and youths to the settlement at Mogumber. Over these last few years, almost every month they had sent away one person. *Generally it was some misdemeanor, if you stole things from white people, for instance, you'd be caught. And if you came around the homesteads of the whites, and frightened them, you'd be caught and sent down there. They didn't want trouble around towns.*[32]

This year, in the first three months alone, he has already seen the sentencing of six Wongutha men who, it is presumed, have committed various *offences against the property & person*.[33] He has no clear knowledge of what these *bush natives coming in from the Spinifex*[34] go through when they are neck-chained and locked up, then sent days away on the lurching train to whatever systems of punishment the distant prisons and settlements can offer for six months or more, but he had thought that the experience would be enough to deter any of them from making trouble. But it did not.

And despite the policy of leaving those who completed their sentences to find their own way home from Perth, the men invariably returned to Laverton. And they returned bolder. Less chastised, less respectful, less law-abiding than he would have hoped. And this attitude was affecting the others, they seemed to be losing their respect for the white man's law. *Two natives made a daring escape from the Laverton platform, handcuffed and ready to be entrained for jail.*[35] They were also losing any respect they may have had for the white man's power. He was currently organising an armed pursuit party to go out looking for *one Aborigine who robbed a prospector of food, a revolver and cartridges.*[36]

The situation was becoming *most difficult.*[37] He had mentioned to the Kalgoorlie Inspector that the six-month or twelve-month prison sentence routinely given for alleged pilfering was too temporary to have much *of a good effect on the natives throughout the district.*[38] The man's response was likely to be unchanged by anything Thompson said; he would probably write back advising, yet again, that the solution was to keep the Wongutha strictly away from the places where white people lived.

Given *the recent drought, absence of water and native game,*[39] he can hardly do that. He cannot hope to keep the people away from the only reliable water source in the district. *There has been no rain for practically twelve months and the natives have been dependent on the towns for water.*[40]

He looks out at the troublesome town through the small, dust-smeared window of his one-roomed station and wonders again what can be done.

He looks at the harsh light outside and thinks of the vast stretches of dry bush beyond, of the miles and miles to Kalgoorlie, of the miles and miles to Perth. Distant Perth keeps coming to mind — in the last week he has received a telegram from no less a person than the Commissioner of Police in Perth, sent on to him by his Kalgoorlie superiors. The Commissioner has instructed him to deal stringently with the Wongutha.

The Laverton townspeople must have been complaining again. *They didn't want trouble around towns. In fact, that's what the townspeople used to say, they'd tell the police, tell the Native Affairs, 'Get rid of these people.'*[41] This time the highest authority has been invoked. He feels cornered.

To further complicate the situation, the whole district is reeling from the recent closing of the last big mine and the Woodline. More small townships will disappear. *All the principal mines throughout the district are shut down.*[42] Thompson rightly expects that the population of white men will continue to drop away and the six hundred men currently employed at Beria and on the Woodline will soon be gone, drifting down the train line to Kalgoorlie to join the big rallies of unemployed men. The ratio of white people to Wongutha people will level out, and he wonders, a little apprehensively, what changes might occur in the district. He is already having to quell rumours of attacks; the current word about town is of *a group of about two hundred natives some miles out, demanding food from settlers.*[43]

It is only twenty-five years ago that the first small parties of prospectors made their way from Coolgardie and Menzies up into this country, finding gold at Malcolm and Mt Margaret and Beria and Hawk's Nest, and finding that *the aboriginals in this locality were war-like and dangerous.*[44] The old prospectors still recounted stories of fearsome skirmishes between armed prospectors and armed Wongutha defending water supplies and camping places and women. Counted white men had been speared and countless Wongutha shot. The history is recent, and Thompson is not the only one who remembers. *The white folks and the natives have a wholesome fear of each other.*[45] Even this year, confidently armed parties of prospectors heading out into the unsettled spinifex country have limped back to the safety of Laverton with serious spear wounds.

The prospects of the district are anything but bright and the future looks dismal.[46]

He attempts to write a suitable answer back to Kalgoorlie for forwarding to the Commissioner. '... *as I have already mentioned the chief difficulty in keeping the natives well out is the absence of water.*'[47] But the time for ignoring instructions from his superiors has seemingly passed. He has already taken steps to effect the instructions. Constable 292 reports respectfully in his letter that the Wongutha people are now regularly *dispersed into the Spinifex, and although small parties of them keep coming back, they are again driven out.*[48]

Thompson finds a way to carry out the Commissioner's orders with minimal personal involvement and inconvenience: *through the closing down of Beria, the local police should have plenty of time to deal with the natives.*[49]

Constable Dave Hunter has plenty of time for such dealings. Constable Thompson generally leaves the unpleasant daily task of keeping the Wongutha people out of Laverton to Hunter. Hunter doesn't seem to mind.

The police took action to expel them and used stockwhips to flog them away with.[50]

Neither does Hunter mind chasing the people through the bush in attempts to find the children fathered by white men. Thompson also leaves this unpleasant task to Hunter.

Cooeyanbah, the people call him.

'Cooeyanbah' means Hunter the P.C. or any other bad man.[51]

He has earned his name.

Dave Hunter, he was a real hard man towards the Aboriginal people.[52]

Then the government took all the kids away.[53]

Water is scarce, food is scarce, and life is suddenly even more tenuous. The people live in fear and anger now. Some of their children have been *snapped up and taken away.*[54]

They have *been taken South,*[55] that much is certain, they saw that the children were bundled, screaming, onto the train that goes south. Where the train took them is not known. Why they have been taken is not known. *Anybody, doesn't matter what colour, the kids, got to send them away, or something.*[56]

Some children was a baby. Some children, some children was a baby.[57]

Hunter, the Cooeyanbah, took them away. And the children have not come back.

And he cage 'em, and he sent train-truckloads ... they never returned back to see their parents.[58]

Unlike the men caught and sent away before, the children have not returned. The people's fate and their vanished children's fate is uncertain, and it is the work of Cooeyanbah.

Joe Mulgathunoo arrives back in Laverton. He thrills to the blue of the sky, to the whisping clouds that streak thinly from one horizon to the next, to the sun. He walks on the red, red dust. He climbs to all the rocky outcrops and looks out over the changing land, he walks among the mulga-trees and mourns over the empty creeks. He exults in the moon-whitened trunks of the desert mulga trees, he sleeps under the open sky in the company of his people. The nights are cold; the people *get the fire and warm up the earth*[59] before sleeping each night.

Joe's return follows two long, cold years of exile at Mogumber, the Moore River Native Settlement. He is about sixteen. His mother Thalbin listens in horror to his stories of what has happened to him, of what he has seen happening to other people. He answers the questions of the mothers who have had their children snatched away, but he has not seen many of the children who were taken away by Cooeyanbah and put on the train. Dion Dirk, Jidu's deaf and dumb son, is one whom Joe has seen at Mogumber. And he has seen many, many unknown children, of many unknown languages, arriving at Mogumber. It is a fearsome place. Wawuja, another young man from the area, sent to Mogumber two years ago with Joe, is still imprisoned there.

Joe is fiercely angry at what he hears of Cooeyanbah.

The people's growing anger is tangible, and a white observer notes: *Mr Thompson ... would not think of entering in amongst them without being armed and mounted. I would feel the same if I were a policeman.*[60]

Their desperation is acute. They try to avoid going into the towns at all. They keep the children well away from the town. *Policeman always come in the bush, too.*[61]

> ... the police were after me! I was one of a lot of children listed to go to the Moore River Settlement. ... And when anyone came into the camp, we were warned to run for the trees!
>
> 'Run for the trees, hide!' We'd hide behind a trunk — stiff as a poker! Or we'd run for the culverts, and hide there until it was safe to move ...
>
> We lived in fear of the police. Every white man we saw, we thought was a policeman, coming to take us away.[62]

Soon it must rain, and then they will move, far away into the bush, far away from the town. In the meantime, they must stay where there is water and food. *About twenty of them are allowed rations and they come in from the scrub and vanish into it as soon as they get their flour.*[63] The people are slowly starving, *there is no game.*[64] They are desperate. Despite Cooeyanbah they come into Laverton almost daily, picking over the rubbish tip and *creeping around the houses on the outskirts to beg food.*[65]

There was a drought there, a big drought ... And we were starving. Each day we'd climb the trees, mulga trees, and collect these caterpillars ... We'd put them in a little Life guard milk tin ... We used to fill the tin up with the caterpillars, and we'd chew them! At least they were moist![66]

April turns to a dry May.

Young Joe Mulgathunoo is once more sent away south on the train. The police are finding some of the people particularly troublesome.

May turns to June, and still the rain does not come.

Went through the bush again, not where, where all the white people living. Through the bush ... Then we came to this water, Muggan. We call that place Muggan ... No more water there you know! It used to be good, cool water![67]

They are surviving on grubs, yilpa,* and begged food, supplemented by Government flour and stolen food. Occasionally they catch a remnant wild cat or a lone dingo, but not often enough. There are plenty of sheep dying in the drought, there is the stench of rotting flesh wherever they go. It is inconceivable that they may not kill one and eat the meat. It is inconceivable that the Wongutha should watch that meat source die and rot and themselves starve.

They give the police trouble because they go into the paddock and frighten the sheep, see ... And that's why they'd get in gaol, they'd get twelve months for killing sheep, spearing sheep.[68] Between April and the

---

* yilpa — goanna.

end of July six more men are captured by the Laverton police and convicted of stealing. They are sent away to Fremantle and Rottnest Prisons. *The Natives about here have always been a source of trouble.*[69]

Wawuja still does not return from Mogumber. The children still do not return from the south. Dion does not return. Joe does not return.

Cooeyanbah gets rougher. Schenk, the newly arrived missionary in Laverton, is horrified by what he sees of Cooeyanbah's treatment of the Wongutha: *On two or three occasions they have even been shot at and wounded by the constable.*[70] Schenk wonders whether to make a public protest *against the drastic measures taken by police,*[71] but thinks that to cause a stir about it would bring no benefits to the people, as *Mr Thompson is also the Protector(?) of Aborigines for the district*[72] and the police *act under orders.*[73]

Police is a protector, and he's a protector and he had his law.[74]

June turns to July and July eventually gives way to a dusty August. There is still no rain.

In mid August there will be another distribution of government flour and sugar and tea to those fifteen or so Wongutha whom Thompson and Neville have decreed are eligible to receive it. Only the old and the sick are eligible, and of the hundreds of people in the area, *only about fifteen old ones*[75] are on Thompson's list.

A party is formed to go into Laverton on 14 August 1921. It is not only the fifteen old and sick who approach the police station for ration collection. This party is unusual, for added to its ranks are those who are young and strong, who deplore the Laverton police, who avoid Laverton. They are not eligible for rations, they can have little reason to hope for kind treatment from Cooeyanbah and his colleague the Protector. And yet, on this day, they voluntarily come to the police station in Laverton.

Jidu, the leader of the people, is there.

(Perhaps he has decided to appeal to Thompson on behalf of his people; to ask for access to a water supply, a place that they may freely go to without fear of physical harm from Cooeyanbah until the drought breaks. Perhaps he plans to ask for a special allowance of flour for all the people. Perhaps he might request of the Protector that Cooeyanbah cease to whip and shoot the people. Perhaps he intends to ask where the children have gone, and when they will come back.)

Two young men who hold responsible positions as stockmen for squatters, and who have a mastery of English speaking, are also there. One is Thulyi, known as Tom Harris because he works for Tom Harris. The other is Nganjur, known as Nganjur William or Bill Carrigg because he works for Bill Carrigg.

(Perhaps they are accompanying Jidu in order to translate and to add to the delegation youth and strength and a tangible reminder of the reliability and trustworthiness of Wongutha people. Perhaps they are in town that day and turn up unexpectedly at the police station when they see that the others have come in from the bush.)

Baldul, Jidu's wife is there. Thalbin, Joe's mother, is there and her husband, George Moongoodie, an astute man, is there with her. Moongoodie's eldest brother, blind Jinera, is there. Jinera is probably entitled to rations. Wawuja's uncle, old Gadajilbi, is there. He is old and grey, and probably entitled to rations. His wife Tharnmoon is with him. Wunu, an old man, also probably entitled to rations, is there with his wife Biyuwarra, who has a baby. Old lame Grarn, who is dubbed Lame Charlie, is there. Old Mudarn is there. Ngada is there. Young Nardie, another of Jidu's wives, is also there, but she doesn't stay for long.

When policeman is issuing rations for the Aboriginal people, they come ... so when he come to get his flour, well, he put him in gaol, and that's the only way to catch an Aboriginal.[76]

A disturbance erupts at the police station: *At Laverton we had the spectacle of natives in that district decoyed into the police station on the pretence of being served with food. The doors were closed on them, they were kept under lock and key until the train was ready to start, then taken under armed escort and locked in the train for Mogumber.*[77]

Nardie escapes into the bush, running swiftly, bare feet silent in the soft dust, Jidu's baby heavy on her back. She stumbles, her shock is severe. Her husband, the leader of her people, has been taken captive by the police, treated roughly, appallingly, with dishonour and irreverence. He has acted in good faith and his faith has been violated. Nardie comes to the camp; she tells the people, Jidu's people, what she has witnessed. They are outraged. The promises of the policeman are seen to be hollow, treacherous; the policemen's actions ruthless and their conduct faithless.

Their leader has been captured. They are bereft. Their leader, their young men and their old men, their young women and their old women, and their children, have been captured.

I think it was because of what was happening around the district. It was drought, and they were stealing food. They were stealing food and killing sheep. And because of that, it was punitive: 'Send them off, get them out of the way.' And if they took one lot, it would speak to the rest. And, that's exactly what happened. They all just vanished.[78]

The remaining people flee from the vicinity of Laverton, they seek safety in the bush. The captured people — perhaps they still know hope, or perhaps now their last hopes of kindness, of peace and reconciliation, of acknowledged rights to water and food and land, of the return of their children, of equity — all these forlorn hopes are vanquished.

They are forced into the tiny gaol house.

(Old Mudarn, maybe, stares up at the rough metal spikes framing her view of the suddenly distant sky. A tall sheet-iron wall, taller than Jidu, taller than a mulga tree, wraps around the group of captives and confines them. Inset in the wall is a heavy metal gate. She can see through the hand-hole in the gate that the other Wongutha people who were in the town have vanished. She hopes they have time to warn the people at the camp that the policeman has gone wild, rougher than ever seen before. Old Mudarn, in her early nineties, bears the months-old welts of Cooeyanbah's stockwhip and knows well the fear of stumbling before his fury. Old Mudarn moves away from the gate, relieved that some have got away.)

One woman was kicked in the stomach by Cooeyanbah for attempting to resist capture. (She, perhaps, wonders how long they will be kept here in this dark place of punishment, she wonders what will become of them. Perhaps she expects that

Cooeyanbah will choose some men to send away on the train south as he has done in the past, and that any remaining men, along with the women, will be threatened, humiliated, and then let go.)

Others, too, are wondering what will happen. There are fifteen anxious, angry Wongutha in the tight confines of the Laverton lockup. Jidu tries to think, tries to calm them, tries to advise them. *They call him, old King Jidu.*[79]

The sun goes down. They do not see it cross the horizon from this place.

Night comes, and the tiny yard of the lockup becomes bitterly cold; there is no fire here to warm the earth. Neither do the three cramped cells of the lockup offer much protection from the cold; they grow only darker and smaller as the light fades. There is no word of what will happen to them.

Elyon is screaming and cannot be quieted. *Elyon was the baby, and her mother was Biyuwarra.*[80] One of the women begins to weep. The others cannot comfort her, nor reassure her. They have no words of comfort. She weeps for a long, long time.

The cold morning brings little hope.

There is still no word of what will happen to them. Jidu has prepared speeches of truce-making.

But when the police come there is no time for speaking. The yard gate is unlocked and dragged open and a revolver appears in the opening. Policemen are outside. A cell gate is unlocked and opened, and a small group, or perhaps the entire group at once, is taken away. Revolvers surrounding them, they are hustled away from the lockup, away from the police station, and down the street to the railway station.

They know with dreadful certainty that they will soon be gone from their Country. All of them are being sent south.

… gone just like a sheep.
On the truck and gone to Perth.
'Fifteen niggers to Mogumber.'
Mogumber, on the train, you know.

'Fifteen niggers to Mogumber.'
'Fifteen niggers to Mogumber,' on the truck.
Just like a little flock of sheep, or goats.
Truck them off.[81]

They are forced into a cattle truck at the front of the train by the gun-wielding policemen, the gate of the truck swings heavily shut despite the last angry efforts of the young men to push it back, a last desperate attempt for freedom despite the revolvers. Someone asks the now unseen policemen to listen, to explain, but there is no response. The policemen padlock the gate and walk away.

The people sit in the dusty cattle truck and gaze out through the wooden-slatted walls, they stand to look through the grills near the roof, hoping against hope for delivery from the dreadful prospect of exile.

Eventually the train engines are started. Smoke and ashes drift back on the cold wind. Someone knocks on the outside of the truck just as the train begins to move, someone is calling out to them in their language but they cannot quite catch what he says above the noise of the engines and the steam and the slow lurching of the wheels. It is Schenk, he has come down to the station and at the last minute has seen a sign on the outside of the truck that tells him the fate of these people. He too is bewildered, he cannot believe what he sees. And he too is helpless. His *heart aches for the distressed natives.*[82] The train pulls away, he watches it out of sight. Schenk goes in search of Mr Thompson.

In September 1921 he [Schenk] accused the Laverton police of irregularities in the distribution of relief. Later in the year he sent Neville a somewhat undiplomatic letter in which he criticised the removal to the Moore River Aboriginal settlement of a group of Laverton aborigines.[83]

Mr Thompson, unappreciative of Schenk's protest on behalf of the people, reports to Perth: *The Natives here at the present time, are giving no trouble and keeping themselves fairly scarce, this is principally through the recent deportation of a number of them to the Coast, this deportation, I might state is greatly resented by 'Schenk' and in consequence, I know he bears the Aborigines Dept and the police no good will.*[84]

The train moves off slowly towards the unknown, taking the fifteen captured people away to the unknown.

*I think there's some people come back,
but there's some of them didn't come back.*[85]

Sometimes the train pauses, they see the familiar towns of Malcolm or Morgans or Menzies, but no one sees them, no one answers their cries for help. And then, sending shock-waves along the length of the goods train, the steam-engine takes off, the sudden movement crashing each heavy carriage into the next and back again. The knifing winter air picks up speed through the slats again, and they huddle together in a vain attempt to conserve warmth.

Their Country, screened by the dust and ash and smoke of the train's progress, slips away from sight. They know that to follow the railway line in a horse and cart *take us, take us nine days to get to Kalgoorlie! We left Burtville there, and come all the way down the line, and got here, nine days.*[86] How long it takes in the train is unknown, but Kalgoorlie, they guess, must be the bustling town where the long stop occurs. The sickening sway of their small world slows and rights itself. The sudden silence is welcome after the continuous roar of the wheels on the tracks below them. Elyon falls asleep at last.

Their line, the Laverton line, ends at Kalgoorlie. Is this the end of the journey? But no one lets them out of the cattle truck and after some time they give up waiting. Night falls, a day has passed. Weary time slowly wears itself away.

At some stage in the night there is the unmistakable sound of an engine starting. And then they are flung without warning as the truck is roughly jolted around. Then all is still again. Old blind Jinera asks again what is happening, asks them to see it for him, but there is nothing much to see, nothing to say. And then the train whistles, and the truck lurches. They have turned west, they are leaving Kalgoorlie and dropping off the very edge of their Country.

> *Of course, there's some of them come back all right,*
> *and some of them didn't.*
> *Don't know what happened.*
> *Might have stayed there, and might have finished there.*
> *Don't know.*[87]

The train lurches on and on and on and on. The sun has set and risen and set again. And now pale chinks of light through the wood slats and the grill at the top of the walls are showing again. *Well. It's a slow journey from Mogumber. Taken away down there.*[88]

The train stops again, but they do not move. They have given up expecting anything beyond an endless, relentless continuation of the same patterns they have endured. Reality has become a deafening, head-splitting roar in the ears and a sickening sway in the mind and an endless, endless lurching of the box that closed them off from their Country. The wood at their backs is rough, the bitter wind unrelenting, the air in their lungs is full of ash. Their hopelessness is tangible. Soft dust underfoot and a clear distant sky are insubstantial and remote. And yet, the soft sky and the distant dust are constantly in their minds; their only certainty in the chaos. Knowledge of their Country and its firmness holds their hearts strong in the midst of their horror.

The train starts up again and moves away, taking them further into the endless darkness.

> *And I got off, at Mogumber ...*
> *They had all the people waiting there ... to see the new people come in.*
> *When I got there, big mob of people! I don't know any of them!*[89]

The Laverton mob stumble out of the truck on their numbed feet, faltering on the solid ground and before a strange world. There are a few white people waiting for them, impatient in the drizzling rain, they immediately begin talking at the new arrivals. Only a few of the Wongutha understand. They translate for the others, trying to soften the tone of the instructions and to pay the honour due to their senior people. Other people, not white but not Wongutha, watch them emerge — they begin speaking in languages unknown to the Wongutha.

Behind the people are strange trees with murky-brown thick trunks, dark-leafed, rough-limbed. They block out the horizon and shadow the ground. As for the ground, it is gritty and cold and wet. All the earth's colour has been washed away, and the country into which they slowly emerge is strange indeed.

They follow the people along a muddy road and enter a dreary place at the end of the road as if walking in a dream. It is too horrible for reality. All their consciousness is focused on trying to stay together.

They are lined up summarily and they are told that they must give their names to the white man sitting down behind the table. They are not sure whether he can understand their names at all, he makes faces at them and makes them say their names over and over again. Thulyi doesn't give his real name. The women are near the end of the line, the man loses patience and ignores what they say to him, he calls them Biddy and Polly and Annie.

It is his job to write something, anything on the page — names don't matter too much after this. He will match a number to each name, and will send them out to the compound. He won't have much to do with them individually anymore, they will just become a collective, the Laverton Natives, one more group to add to the collective of the Compound Natives. He briefly hopes that this lot will manage to keep themselves clear of the overcrowded makeshift hospital — the influenza epidemic has already caused him much inconvenience and his wife, the matron, is tired from much additional work — the routines of the Settlement have been disrupted, and he is unsettled.

At the very end of the line are some unknown children who arrived on the same train, he writes them down as Monday and Friday, and a white woman comes and takes the children away. Biyuwarra holds Elyon tightly, and the white woman signals that Elyon is only a tiny baby; that Biddy can keep her until she gets bigger.

The man finishes his writing and begins to talk to them severely. He tells them the rules of the Moore River Settlement, he talks of discipline and punishment. Most of the people do not understand what he says. As he talks they catch one familiar word; they understand that they have come to Mogumber.

The people are sent out of the compound to the camp near the river. They cause quite a stir, *they was a mob*,[90] and an unusual one. *There was a blind man. There were women and children. They were very shy, couldn't speak English, some of them!*[91] Jidu leads the others out, they walk along in the cold rain. Blind Jinera is asking testily, loudly, what place and what Country it is, what is happening, what will happen. His brother Moongoodie walks with him, keeping an anxious eye on Thalbin. Thalbin trails along behind, looking, looking, looking for her son Mulgathunoo Joe amongst the many strange faces turned their way.

Her son hears that some new goldfields people have arrived, he comes to find them, and Thalbin weeps in relief, in joy, in anguish to see him in this place.

And young Dion is found — for years Jidu has carried the face of his child in his heart; now they are face to face.

Wawuja joins them, he takes them to a sheltered place out of the rain. Some of the people fall asleep. Wawuja and Joe talk softly with Jidu and the other senior people. They speak in their language, they talk of their Country. And then they talk of their current situation. Joe and Wawuja are familiar with Mogumber life. They know the inevitability of Mogumber life, they have seen that those who have attempted to run away from Moore River are always *followed by the settlement trackers, given a beating and placed in the Boob … a square wooden room, covered in corrugated iron* and *kept there for up to a fortnight at a time, often in total isolation.*[92] They tell the others of the routine. They know of the *unduly harsh punishments*[93] meted out by the trackers. The trackers' eventual release from the settlement is dependent on their success in quelling *rebellious behaviour*; they are *armed with truncheons and big sticks and one even carried a spear tipped with glass*[94] and they are greatly feared by most of the inmates at Mogumber.

They talk for a long time. Some of them walk around the

boundaries of the Settlement. They inspect the river on the northern side, they look over the river to the scrub beyond, they look north and east to where their Country is. *At Moore River you are in another person's Country — that's not our Country. Your heart would be in your own Country.*[95]

They do not intend to stay imprisoned at Mogumber. The elderly people are desperate to return to their Country and their people, the young men keen to try anything.

In spite of the trackers and the 'Boob', a resolution is made. They will plan to escape. It is a dangerous plan.

Mulgathunoo Joe he run ... He ran away. He just went around, get the lay of the country.[96]

Mulgathunoo Joe is sent by the group to test an escape plan. He knows it is possible to walk home to Laverton; he has done it once already. He walked in the drought, on his own, only four or so months ago. He was a free man last time, though; he had finished his time at Mogumber and had been released, set free near Perth to make his own way home to Laverton.

People often try to escape — but they never get far. They are always caught by the trackers, brought back to the settlement, and humiliated and punished severely. It is not worth attempting a mass escape until they are sure of success. Mulga Joe is willing to take any punishments that may be incurred in unsuccessful escapes. He will try, at an opportune time, to get out of the Settlement's camp compound without being detected or apprehended. He will see if a carefully executed escape can be made. If it is possible to get out of the Settlement itself, he will then attempt *to see country.*[97] He will *get the lay of the country*[98] and then work out the safest route to get them away from Mogumber. He knows they have to head generally east and north, *he know where he come from.*[99] But if they are all to escape successfully they will need to know which way to go ... *where the road was ... where the farms are, and all this.*[100]

It is planned. They wait for the right time.

Their novelty value is high and the long term inmates are inclined to watch the Laverton mob: *They just lived on the compound ... they'd move camp, just kept on moving camp. Each night they'd move to another place.*[101] Their restlessness is accepted and their continual movements become commonplace. It is understood that they are from the bush, nomadic; they are not expected to remain for long in one place in the camp compound.

Joe soon makes his escape. He is successful. He returns to the camp without incident, having scouted through some of the surrounding country.

So when he went back ... he grabbed the whole lot and went away.[102]

On the right day, most of the Laverton people disappear into the dusk. Two men remain behind. They talk of the three children locked in the dormitory.

I have since heard that the Laverton natives broke gaol and got away, except for one who is blind. I don't think that anyone knows or cares if they ever got back.[103]

The Aborigines sent there from Laverton in 1921 managed to escape en masse soon after their arrival ... some Laverton people reportedly made it back to their own Country.[104]

Some of them run away! ... They were saved.[105]

We were waiting and the sun was going down, down, down. We were waiting and waiting, and it was getting dark.[106]

At the right time they silently gather at the Moore River. Their swift progress through the dripping undergrowth is, so far, unnoticed. They make their way to the place where they will cross over; Joe in the lead, Wawuja at the back obscuring their tracks. Even Elyon is silent.

They didn't know how to swim back. They couldn't get over the river.
So they had to cut the big long tree down, and climb up the tree and go, go over the river. Over the tree.[107]

The river appears even more menacing in the fading light. Such water is unfamiliar to the desert people. They are accustomed to sandy creeks that are wide and shallow and predominantly empty. This water is deep and fast-flowing, it foams at its edges and glimmers darkly, hungrily — they do not know what may live in its depths and lurk on its muddy banks. Noongar people have told Joe and Wawuja stories of the flesh-eating fish that live in the river, and they are inclined to believe them, having no evidence to the contrary. *You get frightened when it's not your own Country.*[108]

The fallen tree on which they are to cross the river doesn't quite reach to the other bank. Joe has told them that the last stretch of water at the other bank is not too deep or fierce to jump into and he demonstrates it now, followed by Wawuja. They remain standing in the water where the tree gives out to assist the elderly people. Jidu follows close behind them and makes it to the opposite bank, disappearing into the shadows. The others follow. Getting old, blind Jinera over the tree is slow and difficult, he does not like the feel of the slippery bark under his feet and very reluctantly and cautiously follows behind Moongoodie. It seems an eternity before they are all safely on the northern bank of the rain-swollen river. They immediately set off into the night.

Joe has already tested this route of escape, they know it can work if all the factors are right. They intend that the heavy rain will wash away any faint tracks that may be left, they anticipate that all the camp inmates will be huddling out of the rain around their campfires for the rest of the evening and night, that the trackers will be comfortably eating dinner at their campfire and will not be inclined to make an inspection round of the camp compound on such a wintery night. If so, they should not be missed in the camp until tomorrow morning, maybe even later. Their ploy of relocating their group within the camp compound for the few nights they were there should give them additional time before someone realises that they have gone. Their success depends on getting as far away as possible, leaving minimal evidence of their route, before the trackers are sent out after them.

Within a few hours they are out of the area reconnoitred by Mulga Joe, and all around them is unknown. They press on. They walk with the fear of being seen, followed, tracked, spurring them on and on. *Going along, along, away from the road.*[109] The pace is necessarily fast.

The ground is strange beneath their feet. The country is unknown, but the clouds break for a while and they carefully work out which way to travel from the almost familiar night sky over their heads: *See, night time, they look to where the stars coming from ... See all the stars. Don't know what to have a look, you better to read the star, where you going.*[110]

They walk all night, fast, confident, desperate. *They just read the stars*[111] when the stars are visible. They set a course for a small dark band of hills on the horizon. And then *when they watch the sun rise that way,*[112] they know for certain they have been travelling the right way. *Travel from Perth, to east! You get to Laverton.*[113]

They press on towards the hills. The pace has been fast, but now it picks up, for in the daylight they can see the ground beneath their feet and they can see the country stretching out before them more clearly. Despite the light, Old Wunu occasionally stumbles, his young wife Biyuwarra sees it with anxiety. Old Wunu is very tired, the mental shocks and physical demands of the last week have been almost more than he had strength to bear. Biyuwarra removes Elyon from his back and he gives her a grim look as he sees her concern. The morning wears away, the watery sun slips in and out of the clouds, they have not yet eaten or rested but they cannot afford to stop. At any moment their absence back at Mogumber may be noticed. And they are passing through farming land, cleared land, with only thin bands of bush in which to walk. There is nowhere to stop even if they wanted to.

Going along, and we come to ... Wongan Hills.[114] The eighteen escapees finally reach the relative safety of an uncleared band of hills sometime during the day. Climbing up a secluded valley, they find a breakaway where they can get out of the rain for a short rest. They stop, wearily, exultantly — they have covered a good distance and so far they have been unseen. This strange country has sheltered them. It is more than they had dared hope for. And already the land is changing, they have left behind them the gritty-grounded dirt with its washed-away colour, and have arrived suddenly in a place where the earth is a richer brown, a finer grain, where the rocks of the breakaway are tending towards red, where the country looks less hostile, if still alien.

They rest in silence for a few luxurious moments, and then they discuss the logistics of what next to do. The difficulties of walking speedily and stealthily in such a large group in unknown country have become evident to them all. It is hard to silently alert everyone at once, and they foresee many occasions when it will be necessary that the entire party instantly becomes motionless and noiseless. Noiseless signals are much easier in smaller, more compact groups. Splitting up will minimise the risk of the group being seen, and will also lessen the chances of immediate recognition of their party. A quick glance at their party now would be all that was needed to confirm their identity as the escapees: a mob of people with a blind man and a woman with a baby. If they break up into small groups, more than one glance will be needed to determine their identity if they are seen.

And, should trackers manage to follow them to this place, the trackers will also need to split up or follow only one group. A lone tracker will be easier to overpower than several trackers, a small group could easily deal effectively with one tracker. The trackers, after all, do not carry guns. If the trackers, reaching this place, decide to stay together and pursue only one party then the others will have additional time to get far away before the trackers can return to this place and start after them.

They sit in the shadow of the hill and look out to the east. Unknown Country, strange Country, cultivated and inhabited, stretches out before them. Beyond the limits of eyesight is more strange Country, miles and miles of it. They do not know where the sacred places are. They do not know where water is to be found, nor how to see water in these strange landscapes. Police and other Cooeyanbah are out there somewhere, in towns and on farms and in camps in the bush. It is perilous to walk through such unknown Country, even without enemies. But at the end of it all is their own Country and their own people. *They know where to go! ... They know where they going ... Some of them older ones, with them.*[115]

If I was to be lost one cloudy day and I could just see one star ... I know where I am. And see, the Aboriginal could read the stars and they look at the weather and they look at the cloud and say 'Oh, well, this is the right track I'm going,' see, because he reads the trees too. Trees can tell you where north, south, east and west, just like a compass for the Aboriginal, you know, when he's travelling.[116]

Some of the people, Jidu among them, decide on a route that will follow the water pipeline. They know the pipeline runs along next to the railway from Perth to Kalgoorlie, and that this railway is somewhere to the south of them. Once found, the pipeline offers a certain route, easily followed, and a guaranteed water supply all the way back to a known place, right on the edge of their Country. The unknown Country through which this route passes is heavily populated in parts, and so any sacred Country along the way will already have been disturbed by the white man. The biggest danger is that of being seen and apprehended by white people.

That danger is keenly felt by some. They would rather trust Country than white men. A number of them agree to head directly east, to walk through land that is uninhabited by white people. It is likely to be arid land, but if the rain that has followed them continues to do so it will provide them with water. They will walk east until they intercept the railway that runs north from Kalgoorlie to Laverton. And then they will follow the line back into their own Country.

Someone suggests a third option, a northern route through Yamathee and Darlot Country. The Country will not be entirely unfamiliar, its people are partly known. Ngada, old Wunu, and some of the others plan to travel north until they are far enough north, and then they will turn east, continuing to walk east until they arrive in known places, re-entering their own Country to the north of Laverton.

And then someone, maybe Jidu, declares that enough time has been spent here. If they are to elude the trackers, they must leave this resting place and travel with all possible speed. *They don't want to get caught by police.*[117] The eighteen people somehow divide themselves into three parties. They wish each other safety and success and turn their faces north, east, south-east.

A group, maybe six or seven people, sets off northwards, keeping to the cover of the bush-covered range of hills. Jinera is one of this party. *The others there, they'd lead him. Lead him with a, with a, with a*

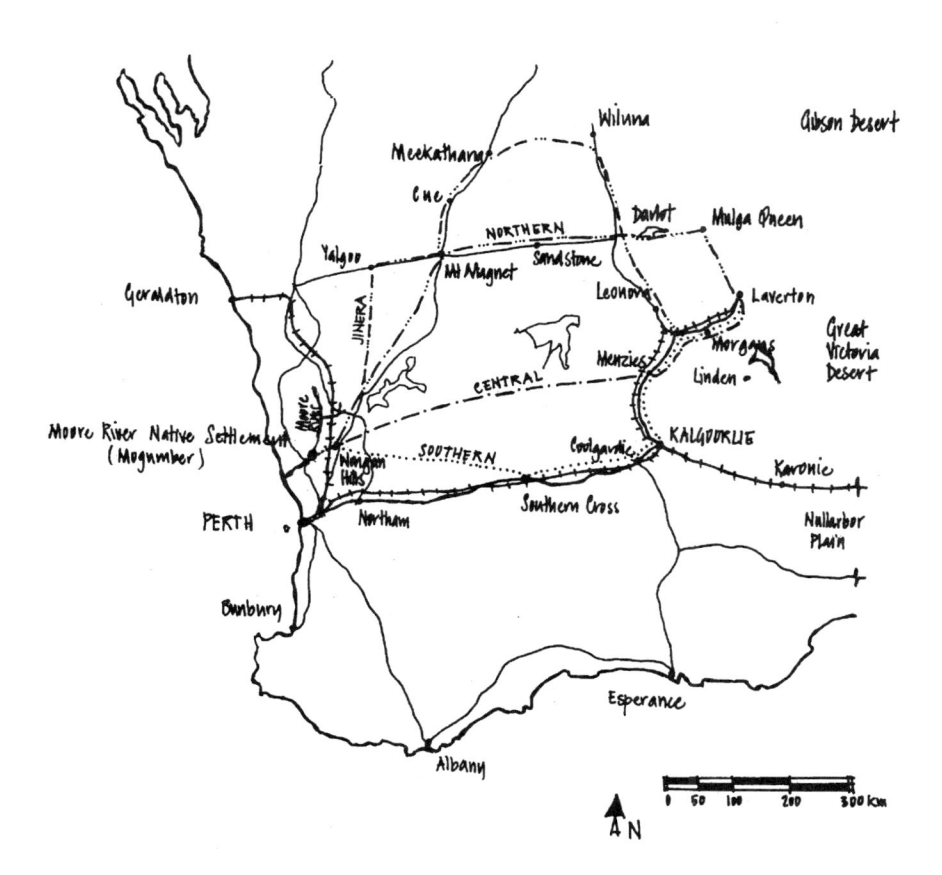

The Journeys

stick, you see? He'd carry a stick, and he'd, he'd come along behind there. They used to come along behind there, holding the stick there. And you go along in front of him, you see for him, you know.[118]

Jinera, accustomed as he is to being led, nevertheless finds the going hard and bewildering in this unfamiliar country, the ground is always falling away in some direction. Even on level ground wet mud gives way to firm ground only to return to slippery mud. The ground is difficult, the vegetation surprising. There are strange thickets of head high bushes that stick spines into their skin as they push through, there are low stringy plants that twist around the ankles.

Jinera mutters under his breath and jerks the stick every now and then when he is particularly displeased with the route that he is walking. He is known for being an impatient man, he has a *vile temper*,[119] and the restraints of blindness in this awful country do nothing to improve it.

Wunu is the only one who does not mind Jinera's hesitation when going through the prickly thickets and his reluctance to take downhill slopes at a run. Wunu is glad for any slowing of their pace, he is becoming more tired than he has ever imagined he could become. He has had a lifetime of walking for weeks on end without difficulty, he can feel that something is very different here. His Country is calling him, calling him home, but he somehow cannot *go another step*.[120] He can see the sky above and imagine it stretching out with ease to his Country, it is endless and timeless and without boundaries, unlike this place they are labouring painfully through. Biyuwarra walks behind him, silently. They are slowly falling behind the others, catching up only when the terrain forces the rest to go slowly, invisibly, across exposed hillsides or in the vicinity of farmhouses and the inevitable dog, or where consultation is held to determine the best route for traversing the landscape. Ngada glances at Wunu but presses on.

After a number of hours they come to the north-eastern end of the small range of hills. Flat farming country stretches out before them, they prepare to leave the sheltering bush and to head towards the tree-lined road which is snaking along on the horizon. They pause to drink where rainwater is running down the hill side in small cold rivulets, and Wunu stops. He has come to the end of his strength and he tells the others to go on and to leave him there to die. Biyuwarra draws a sudden, rasping breath.

It's just what they do; when they're out walkabout, if somebody gets too sick, and they're going to die anyway, they just leave them ... It's a fact of life. It's a fact of life in a subsistence society, and a walkabout society.[121]

Wunu finds a place on the hill, looking towards the north and east, where he will die.

There's some people come back, but there's some of them didn't come back.[122]

He sits down, and Biyuwarra and baby Elyon sit with him while the others gather firewood and soft bushes. They make Wunu a fire, and light it, and pile up a good stack of wood where he can reach it. And then they leave him.

He watches them go, and then, when he can see them no longer, he imagines their steady progress across the landscape spread out below him. He will follow them in his mind's eye for as long as he can.

Biyuwarra is carrying both Elyon and her grief for Wunu, her steps falter every now and then. Ngada, seeing her anguish, sets a brisker pace; it is the gift Wunu has given them and they must use it. Biyuwarra treads automatically in his footsteps, unseeingly. The road to Mount Magnet runs parallel to a tree-lined river, and they follow the river for some hours until it swings away to the west of their path. The road also veers away to the west. *Miling there somewhere.*[123] They consider whether to follow the road or to keep heading north across the farming country. The late afternoon light slips into long shadows while they debate it.

The light fades to the south of them, the sun sinks slowly behind Wunu's hill, the late afternoon light catches in the smoke from his fire and in the droplets of water in the trees and then it is gone.

The people have walked for a night and a day with only a brief rest at Wongan Hills, and they have not eaten.

Some of them old people they walked back, and,

> they come through the bush, I think.
> Yeah. I don't how they get on for tucker and things...[124]

The group travelling towards the pipeline are hungry. Their party has been keeping off the roads, skirting around paddocks and open places, and avoiding farmhouses, careful to keep their movements concealed as they move silently over the land. A line of trees leading away from a tree-lined road comes into view on a distant rise — a small farmhouse will be at the end of it, and the group begins to work out a route to take them around the house in the shelter of trees. They can see a small plume of smoke coming from where the house will be, it speaks to them of food, and the young men in the group propose to go and ask at the farm house for food. The others agree, reluctantly, that they must eat sooner or later, and to catch food in this unknown farming country will take more time than they can spare.

The best English speaker is sent off to try his luck at the farm-house, approaching from the road, and the others skirt around the house on the opposite side. They keep walking, they will not slow down until they have reached a tree-covered rise a considerable distance from the house, where they can see the farm-house and will wait for the young man for a short time. It is possible that he will be given no food and will leave the house empty-handed, and that the farmer will later ring the police to alert them to the presence of a stranger in the district. If the people are hostile, the young man will try to make confusing tracks before rejoining the waiting party. They will then have to make all haste to get clear of the area. If he does not leave the house within a certain time, they will press on without him and hope that he can escape and rejoin them along the railway later. It is a risky plan to approach white people. But he is willing to take the risk; he will not take long, he is sure, he will rejoin them before sunset.

The farmer's wife is kind, she gives the young man *a feed of dry bread*[125] and asks no questions. *Just somebody, unnamed, who was kind. They met kind people.*[126]

Their spirits and their hopes rise. *All the farmer gave them eggs and bread.*[127]

The small group of escapees heading east is also still untroubled by trackers. Gadajilbi looks back to the west from where they have come, he can still just make out the smudge on the horizon that is the Wongan Hills, blurry in the hazy light of the sinking sun. He checks their direction again; the sun is slipping over the southern edge of the hills, they have walked *slightly north of east.*[128] Soon the stars will come out and they will be more certain of their path. Night travelling has other good aspects: farmhouse lights are a warning beacon of white people and barking dogs and give clues about the proximity of roads, lights from small towns and camps are easily seen and the area skirted. They walk resolutely towards the darkening eastern skyline. *They knew what they were doing.*[129] They walk and walk and the darkness overtakes them.

Well, they didn't come back on the train, they, they cut across the bush. From Perth to somewhere. They cut across to Laverton.[130]

Long after the last glow of the sun has faded from the western sky, the party heading towards the pipeline are still walking. At this time of day no one else is about. They make good progress. *At night time we travel on the road!*[131] Late in the night, when all the farm lights have disappeared, they stop in a small clearing in some bushland. The rain clouds have gone, it is a bitterly cold night, a clear open sky stretches out between the branches of the big trees around them. Someone has cadged a box of matches along the way and the group is cold enough, hungry enough, or confident enough to light a small fire, concealed in a hole in the wet ground. They cook the eggs, and eat them with the dry bread; it is their first food since escaping. Some of the party are exhausted. They have been walking for a night and a day with only one break, they have endured beyond what they thought they could endure, they have persevered, they have kept up the pace. They can go no further without sleep.

Thulyi, for one, is dismayed. He is terribly afraid that the trackers may gain on them if they stop. They do not know how far they still must walk before they leave the farming country and arrive on the edges of the bush country, a place of relative safety — they may yet have a long, long way to go. Thulyi is young. He too is tired, exhausted physically and emotionally, but he is fiercely determined that he will not be caught again. Soon he will decide to leave the group and press on. (Perhaps he leaves them now, unwilling to stop and sleep and so possibly jeopardise his freedom.) When he goes, a few others go with him. *Some of our people go in front.*[132] Perhaps Thulyi and his companions plan to keep walking until they are out of farming country; to stop when they find a good hunting place and *make their own spears to catch rabbit and goanna.*[133] By the time the others reach them, the food will be cooked and ready; smoke will lead them to the place.

Some of the group sleep.

In the grey half-light before the dawn they wake. They fill the fire hole and obscure the camp site and start out east again, walking half asleep, long before the sun creeps over the horizon. The sleep has been short, but they are now revived in spirit if not in body, and the new day's pace is fast. Soon after dawn they find that they are almost on the edge of the farming country; the country around them is more often bushland than cleared land. A direct path, with no need for deviations around houses and paddocks and towns, can now be taken through the bush.

The group heading east left the last signs of white people's activities in the land during the early stages of the night. They had managed to dig up a yilpa near the place where they stopped to rest for the night, they had made a small fire and cooked it, and then they had slept well during the night. And now they are on their way again. They are almost certain that neither trackers nor police will pursue them into this roadless country; they are almost certain that they will find enough water along their way; they are almost happy.

They walk and walk until they are beyond tiredness, they walk unswervingly towards the eastern horizon.

Travelling. No breakfast.[134]

Somewhere to the north is the group heading towards Mt Magnet; they are having a hard time. *Ngada's party met with trouble.*[135]

Blind Jinera is becoming unpleasantly ill-tempered. They had expected, from knowledge acquired by long association, that as hard day followed hard day this elderly man would become tired and irritable, less rational, more prone to fits of rage. They had not expected that he would become so slow. They had not thought that he would allow his petulance to take such a form in such a desperate situation. It is only the second day, and already he is antagonising them, it seems, by going slowly. He refuses to walk faster, neither encouragement nor rebuke affect him; he steadily drops his pace until even his brother is angry. *It's still a long way from Mt Magnet ... Long way yet.*[136] The group are concerned about trackers. Theirs will be the easiest track to follow; Jinera's foot placement is hardly strategic and they do not have the time or materials to make feather or fur coverings for his feet. The smoke from Wunu's fire may have drawn attention from the local community, and someone may, given enough time, link the dying man with the escape party from Mogumber. They urge Jinera on, but he is stubborn.

Eventually old blind Jinera openly defies them all and refuses to move at the required pace. He is slowing them all down, he is putting them all at risk of being overtaken by the trackers and recaptured. They give up reasoning with him.

They find a good place, they make a fire, and they leave him there.

They do not look back. Hard-pressed, they walk away resolutely, swiftly, silently, towards freedom and their Country.

Those looking for the pipeline find it. Their route now runs alongside the railway and pipeline for as far as the eye can see. Their pace picks up.

At Southern Cross, Jidu and those walking with him catch up to Thulyi and the others who had forged ahead. They all rest there for a while.

And we have a feed.[137] There is little delay, they lose no time in hunting.

They set off again, and now they are moving steadily through a landscape that is not entirely unfamiliar to them. The soil is similar to their own Country's soil, the occasional outcrops of rocks are similar, the land is flat and the bush is generally low except where tall trees mark out occasional water courses.

Water is not a problem for this party, they travel along in the bush along side the pipeline. *Had water-tap everywhere! All along! ... They get plenty of water!*[138]

Gadajilbi and the people with him journey east through open country, under an endless sky. *They come through the bush.*[139] Familiar sounds wash over them as they walk; the wind in the desert sheok trees above them, the wind rippling through the knee high flowers all around them, the whirr of startled birds' wings, the twilight songs of insects.

It has rained recently, for which they are very glad. They now have a reasonably sure supply of water, if they can find the water places in this land, and tracking food is easier. *After the rain ... we seen a big goanna track going along.*[140] They follow the track, they dig the goanna out of its hole in the ground; this is familiar work. Some of the bigger racehorse goannas are almost as long as a person is tall; the big ones provide enough meat to keep them going.

You might be out in the bush, and the rain come along and fill the rockholes up and you're, you're right for water, you see.[141] But it is difficult to know where the rockholes might be in this vast nameless landscape. Sometimes they do not find water by the end of the day.

Some, if you going to another water rockhole,
some of them, a little bit, little bit, you know,
a bit too far to get to in one day ...
You go along and you camp, dry camp in the night
and you get up early in the morning.[142]

They start walking again, having had no water, hoping to find a rockhole before the end of that day.

The group that has lost Wunu and Jinera is pushing on northwards. They wonder whether the other groups are being chased, or have already been apprehended, whether Jinera will draw the trackers this way. Biyuwarra alone does not think about the trackers. She is still stricken with grief that Wunu should die so far from his Country, her Country. The harsh physical demand of the constant walking consumes all of her energy and concentration. *We walk all day, and half of the night.*[143]

They eventually, gladly, reach the edge of the farming country near Wubin. Uncleared station country, less populated, stretches out before them. Still no trackers have caught up to them.

And night-time comes, we go on the road, and then daytime, we off in the bush.[144]

Long cautious days are followed by weary nights of walking. They sleep for only a short time each night. There is always a long way to go.

The end of another day approaches as those following the pipeline reach a mining town called Bullabulling. They camp that night on *the flat hill near the pub.*[145] The town has a reservoir of water caught from a large granite rock; the permanent water supply attracts game: *I s'pose they get plenty of meat, you know, rabbits, and things like that ... No trouble there, be able to get them rabbits.*[146]

They watch the evening light gathering on the western edge of the land, it forms in the wake of the setting sun and spreads out across the sky, this sky that reaches out beyond the horizon to Laverton and their Country.

They sleep well. And then they are up early and making their way towards the horizon well before the sun crosses it.

The party travelling north watches the slow change of vegetation by day and the stars at night. They are walking in endless scrub; they are waiting for the right point to turn east.

Finally, large water tanks appear on the horizon, markers of a town. The small group of Wongutha people stop on a low rise in the head-high scrub and look eagerly to the north. It is the town of Mount Magnet. There is a dirt track going east to Sandstone from this town. As they skirt the town they come across the track and decide to follow it, walking off to the side, in the bush. They have finally turned east here. It is a great moment; their faces are towards their Country as they walk, and the edge of the Country is now surely only a matter of days away.

There is still some rainwater in small dips in the ground, but the surface water is generally beginning to evaporate. All around them stretches the unknown land, covered in bush that is becoming more like their own bush, but still alien. They do not know where this Country keeps its water, they have to hope for rockholes, they scan the horizon for outcrops of granite as they walk. *They mightn't ... know the, you know, the gnamma hole or something, the rockhole or something. They might keep going to rock, to a granite rock. They might get some water there, you see.*[147]

But sometimes, in this vast scrubby plain, they do not find any rocks within the day's walk. In the sandy stretches they look for water in little rain-fed creeks. Even empty creek beds are useful: *might be soak, you got to dig the soak out and get the water, you see.*[148]

Endless time and distance later, the people who have followed the pipeline arrive in Coolgardie. Coolgardie is a big town. All the stories of the old prospectors in the bush out from Laverton feature Coolgardie and perhaps the people feel some degree of home-coming as they arrive there. And in their progress around the edges of the town, avoiding the administrative centre, they find *friends*[149] who give them food and help them on their way. To come at last to a place where they have friends! Home, their Country, is suddenly almost within reach.

They strike out for Kalgoorlie.

Gadajilbi scans the landscape stretching out before him to the distant eastern horizon. From this rock outcrop, it seems as if they are walking through an empty land — they have not seen any people to whom this land might belong, nor the tracks of people, nor even old camp fires. No people have pursued them to find out what they, strangers to the land, are doing walking across it. There are no stations in this country, it is too arid for sheep and white men alike; there are not even signs of mining tenements or lone prospectors. They walk on and on under the empty sky.

They cross over a long, low range of hills, they map out their course from the highest point, steering south of a large salt lake that glimmers whitely in the sunlight for further than they can see against the glare.

They find small lizards when there are no yilpa, and chew on little edible plants and grubs when water and meat takes longer to find than they have time to spare. They press on.

The northern group begin to feel less anxious about trackers as they come closer to their Country; they allow a little more time for tracking and catching food. Deprived of their usual hunting implements, they must slowly and painstakingly stalk the game. *They hit him with a wooden stick. Knock him on the head. Kangaroo, and emu and goanna. Oh, they eat up everything! Wild cat.*[150]

They feel a little safer. They are almost on the edge of their known world. But the stakes are somehow higher, they become more desperate to arrive home as they come gradually closer to their Country. There are still, maybe, four or five days of walking in front of them. They do not slow down. *We're not going to stop now we've made it this far.*[151]

They are very wary when skirting station homesteads, they are worried about disturbing sheep at windmills where they sometimes draw water, they make their fires far away from the road. When they cross the little dirt roads that run through this mining country they try to leave no tracks at all. They are always on the look out for shepherds' camps and mining camps. They live with the fear that any person who sees their group might invoke the law of white men against them, *might ring the police and tell them, and they'd get punishment worse than ever. And if you're halfway to Mt Margaret, your own Country, you wouldn't want to get caught halfway. You'd be devastated. All that way and all that planning for nothing.*[152]

There is a new element of fear in this Country. *Most of the time they'd be on the alert.*[153] They scan the horizon for campfire smoke throughout the day. They carefully examine any footprints they come across. It is not the trackers that they now listen for around their campfire in the middle of the night. Somewhere here, north and west of Laverton, is the Country of their age-old enemies, the Darlot people, the *Wunmala ... the killers.*[154] It is only a few years ago that the aggressive Wunmala attacked, at dawn, a camp of Wongutha in the middle of Wongutha Country; they *descended in a raid upon a native camp at Lancefield, near Laverton, killing eleven men, women and children.*[155]

Sleeping, even for only a few hours each night, in the vicinity of Wunmala Country is difficult. Someone stays awake, to listen. *Because any little thing, you know somebody's around. Even a little twig! Wongutha pick that up! ... little twig! Or stone roll. You know somebody's around.*[156]

Thulyi is wary of towns, and the policemen in them. He has been very aware of the risks of travelling along the pipeline; he has consistently been alert for trackers, he has thought of search parties and policemen in all their planning, he has urged the others on faster when they lagged and he has left them behind when they could not keep up to his pace. He becomes more cautious as they come closer to home. It seems to him that the chances of policemen seeing them, and knowing who they might be, rise steadily as they approach the Kalgoorlie and Laverton goldfields. Thulyi is determined to avoid the region's biggest city and centre of administration, Kalgoorlie; he speaks to the others. And when the rest of the group decides to proceed into Kalgoorlie, Thulyi decides not to accompany them. Some distance after Coolgardie, Thulyi cuts off into the bush away from the road again, north-east, cross-country. He hopes to meet up with them again somewhere to the north of Kalgoorlie along the line.

The others walk into the city, keeping clear of the main street and the places where they will be conspicuous.

Perhaps they wait until night-fall, venturing into Kalgoorlie under cover of the twilight, or at the time that white people are preoccupied with eating an evening meal. Perhaps they stop in Kalgoorlie over night, camping with other Laverton people down near the railway station. Or perhaps they rest there for only a few hours, being anxious to be on their way.

I didn't went to town, I went down the railway station. And the old goods train was hooked up.[157] A goods train that looks and sounds to them as if it is about to leave Kalgoorlie is hooked up on the north-facing line, the Laverton line. A daring plan has been formulated, and the group is tired enough, footsore and bone-achingly tired enough, to attempt it. Or perhaps they are simply brave, emboldened by their successful journey so far, invincible in their nearness to home.

They can see that there are empty cattle trucks hooked up in the train. Some of them are quite accustomed to 'jumping' the train. Perhaps, on this occasion, they check that they can easily get out of any truck they get into. They move off the platform, onto the tracks: *I went round the other side. I went to another side, and, the guard blows the whistle.*[158] There are no padlocks on this gate. The escapees climb in. *The guard blows the whistle and the train was getting ready, and the train started moving.*[159]

The train steams its rough way northwards through the bushland, stopping, joltingly, at every siding to deliver the supplies to the various goldfields' communities, and then slowly picking up speed again, spitting ash and smoke as it goes. The Wongutha in the cattle trucks are content with its progress. The young men watch the ground race away beneath them through the gaps in the flooring of the carriage, exulting in the ease with which they are covering the distance. The triumph in converting these instruments of exile to their own purposes of escape is sweet indeed.

A day slides past. Some of them are lost in their thoughts and hardly notice the passing of time, others watch each landmark go past and feel as if this last day will never be ended. Eventually, however, even the town of Morgans is behind them. The train whistles one last time; they steam into Laverton. The people jump out quickly, on the side away from the platform, and disappear out of the town and into the bush.

They walk to where their central camping place had been. There is no one there. It takes only a glance to realise that there has been no one there for some time.

They fall silent, it is almost certainly the work of Cooeyanbah. But they do not despair, they quickly reason that their people would surely not have remained camping so close to Laverton after the recent events at the police station. They set off walking into the familiar, welcoming bush, away from Laverton, northwards, deeper into their own Country.

As they walk they scan the bush for signs of their people; they see signs of past campsites, recently abandoned. *They been camping around here, all around here, somewhere.*[160] It does not take them long to find the new camp; they see the smoke from campfires twisting up into the still air, and they make their way through the bush towards the place. *When they seen us coming, the dog barked, they all crying, them people.*[161] The Wongutha people, with great joy, welcome back these tired and jubilant exiles.

Schenk visits the camp after their return, and records in his diary of 30 August 1921: *Some natives back from Moore River.*[162] They may have been back for a few days already. On the day that Schenk sees them, it is only fifteen days since these people were loaded into the cattle-trucks and sent off to exile.

A few representatives of the group who have been walking the central route emerge from the darkening bush late one evening and cautiously approach the town of Menzies.

Then, then, we had to stop, and make our camps, because our people got to go and have a look at this place ... They went along, showed themself first. And we all sitting down waiting. Go to town, have a look. Then they came back. Everything okay.[163]

No white people take any notice of the advance guard, who find some Wongutha people, and are assured that Menzies is quiet, peaceful; that they will be safe in the town. They go back into the bush to bring out the few who are waiting, hidden.

So Gadajilbi's group *hit Menzies, spot on, and they finished on the train.*[164]

They find their people about seven miles north of Laverton.

Schenk: *September 2. Nearly all natives back.*[165]

But they are not all back. One group *went the long way round. They keep on the north. They keep on the north side.*[166] They are still walking, still uncertain of completing the journey, wary all day and all night, desperate for their Country.

They walk on and on. Morning after morning the wintery sun rises over them; they are already walking. Evening after evening the dusk falls over them, and they are still walking.

But now the country surrounding them, stretching every way they can see, is more familiar, and they map their course more easily. Signs of water in the land are becoming more evident to them: *they can find the water. They find a tree … water there.*[167] Or they look for water near places where they see a flock of *finches flying around.*[168]

They cross over various ranges of hills, they skirt many salt lakes. They keep walking. Almost every night they see small glows of light punctuating the safe darkness; the area is fraught with the potential danger of mining camps, parties of woodcutters and small mining towns. They walk, and keep on walking. They are still heading east, waking in the pre-dawn, and finally stopping long after sunset.

They reach a long lake in the shadow of what the white men in the area call Mt Carnegie, it is Lake Darlot, and from there they follow a freshwater creek which runs almost to Mulga Queen. Turning south near Mulga Queen, they walk past old Beria, Cox's Find and Salt Soak. And so finally they arrive[169] in their own Country, coming in through known places. They meet their own people again, they find that the other exiles have also returned.

The reality is almost too much to grasp.

They are re-united, restored; tears of joy and laughter overwhelm them.

They sleep with the scent of the wattle trees drifting around them, with their Country's moon and cloudless sky over their heads.

Some of the natives were taken to Moore River ... I thought of the distance ... The natives sent to Moore River escaped and are back in the bush here (intended re-capture is reported but I am believing otherwise) ... I feel that the first victory of a long battle has been won.[170]

They sit at night around their campfires and talk over their different journeys. *We heard when the people they came back.*[171]

The returned people speak, and all the people draw close to listen.

The story is told to others who haven't heard; the story is of *Jidu ... our King. He went down there ... to Mogumber, then he come back.*[172]

They *repeat it over and over ... It's history.*[173] They are still waiting for five to come back, waiting for the story to be completed.

The people mourn for old Wunu. *Lot of them people died when they went away. There's no people left now ... Lot of them never returned.*[174]

They mourn for their children who have not returned.

They mourn also for Blind Jinera. They wonder what fate might have overtaken him. They mourn for his exile from his Country, from his people, from those who speak his language and know his ways.

And then, to their astonishment, some months later *this blind man came back on his own!*[175]

He tells them his story, an *absolutely marvellous story.*[176]

Jinera had not wanted to go any further; they had left him. And when they had gone, *he started to shout and shout.*[177]

He had shouted for a long time. And then he had listened. He had heard nothing but the sound of the wind in his ears and the faint sound of sheep drifting along on the wind. Jinera heard no sound of his people in the land; they had gone and the land had already forgotten them. He suddenly knew for a certainty that they had gone. And now here he was, all alone in a strange unseen place, with a fire but no food and, and far, far from his Country.

He sat there for some time. A long time. The wind was cold, he could feel the sun move across the sky. And then, late in the day, drifting on the wind came a new sound — the sound of someone riding. Jinera stood up, and shouted again.

And of course the farmer heard somebody was shouting. So he went and had a look and there's a poor old blind man ready to die. So the farmer being very ... sympathetic to this blind man ... brought him up to Yalgoo, just out from Morawa, and then tried to find out now, if this blind man got any relation.[178]

Aboriginal people from all around Yalgoo had come to talk with him, but he had been unable to understand what they were saying. He had stayed at that place for days, comfortable enough, but lonely and isolated, unable to see, unable to communicate, unable to understand what anyone said.

The farmer had rung the stations all around the district, asking if anyone knew anything about this blind man, with no good result.

They took him to Mt Magnet then.[179]

And then he meets his sister up there![180]

Jinera's sister and her husband worked on a station near Cue — the station owner had passed on to them the unusual news of the unknown blind man, apparently abandoned on a farm near Yalgoo. She had previously heard that Jinera had been sent away from Laverton, down to Mogumber, she had wondered if this lost blind man might be Jinera, she had decided to go to where he was staying to find out. She had walked down from Cue.

It had been a few years since he had last spoken with his sister. Back at the time of *that massacre* when the Darlots *killed all the men off, and took the women off*[181] she had disappeared. She was now part of the Darlot people, her language was the Wunmala language and Wunmala Country was now her Country.

He had been amazed to meet with his sister again; she had told him of her new life. They had talked of the Laverton Wongutha also. And then she had offered to take him home to his people and his Country. It was the only thing to do.

So the sister had to walk all the way from Magnet through Sandstone, be about eight hundred kilometres she had to walk ... He had to travel with his sister ...[182]

Walking, just walking.[183]

They had taken their time. His sister knew people all along the way. And they had not been afraid of trackers so far to the north.

The old woman just picked up a little of bit of yams there, find the water.[184]

After days on end of holding the stick and following along behind his sister, they had reached the Wiluna area. They turned their faces to the south, and kept walking, heading for Leonora. After many days, they arrived in Leonora, he could hear the trains. They decided to catch the train from Leonora across to Laverton, but at Morgans, the last stop before Laverton, his sister left the train and *they parted company.*[185] Perhaps she didn't want to cause trouble between the Wunmala and the Wongutha.

She put him on the train, and back she went ... Well, she had to go home, you see she had a husband back there.[186]

And he had climbed off the train at Laverton, the end of the line. He had arrived safely. He was back in his Country. He had wondered how to stay out of sight of Cooeyanbah until someone came into town and found him. But he had hardly been in town half a day before someone had seen him, and had brought him out to the camp. And here he was, *home and dry.*[187]

Biyuwarra goes out walking, looking in her Country for some sign that Wunu's spirit might have come home.

I woke up, next morning ... daylight, and the morning star was up.[188]

Appendices

Notes on Transcripts

Layout note: The formatting of each transcript is intended to make the spoken pauses and breaks obvious in the written transcript, and so, if possible, to communicate some of the rhythm and nuance of the spoken conversation.
 Key to abbreviations and symbols used:

> ... — a section of the taped conversation has been omitted from this transcript at this point.
>
> _ — inaudible word.
>
> _ _ — inaudible words, phrases.
>
> _ _ [But we were safe at] — words in brackets are my best guess at inaudible words.
>
>> In some cases, the speaker has passed away and so the text could not be clarified (in which case relatives have kindly reviewed the transcript, made corrections where necessary and filled gaps where possible, and given permission for the text to be included in the book).
>> In most cases, during the review of the transcript, the speakers were not concerned with filling the gaps, preferring instead to retell that particular story. I have kept the original speakings' paragraphs and gaps in order to remain true to the flow and experience of the taped conversation, so gaps remain. Additional material provided by the speakers during the review of the transcript has been added where it provided clarification to the story and did not alter the flow and intent of the original conversation.
>
> [laughs] — laughter was an integral part of the experience of the Speakings.
>
> word — underlined words are words on which the speaker placed strong emphasis; such words were also elongated.

Glossary of Wongutha Words

baluga — get up!
doolgoor — singing
maku — bardi grubs
mamoo — devil
marlu — red kangaroo
mithithi — white person
nganuti — bush turkey
Wongai — abbreviation of Wongutha
yilpa — goanna

Note: Different sources offer different spellings of written Wongutha names words. I have, in all such cases, adopted the spelling suggested by the Wongutha people with whom I conferred on the matter.

Explanations of Process

This appendix contains the explanations of why and where and when the journeys took place, and how the book has evolved in its present form.

The Introduction alludes to fragments of the process and to the issues I have struggled with, as do the journal notes in Journeying and, more overtly, the Foreword to the New Account. Issues identified and discussed in these include the following: For what purpose did the people tell me the stories? Am I entitled to tell other people's stories? Am I entitled to write their stories in this book? How did I meet the people? Am I entitled to write about the people in this book? Am I, as a non-Aboriginal, and more specifically, a non-Wongutha person entitled to write about aspects of Wongutha history? Why have I presented the evidences with so little explication as to how they should be interpreted? Why did I not consider finding the archival material to be the end of the journey of discovery? Is it acceptable to ask people to remember the painful past? Why have I used the Speakers' words about their own past in the text for the New Account? Why does the New Account narrative move beyond the archival 'facts'? Will this written account endanger the fluid oral accounts? Must history, and history-writing therefore, be bound by a sense of linear progress, by chronology? How can I write to ensure appropriate communication of the histories? What does it mean to learn to live with the past?

Other issues which have not been discussed within the main text are raised below.

The Journeys

I have undertaken both physical and metaphysical journeys in the process of writing this book. The metaphysical is ongoing, revelationary, confronting and excellent! The physical journeys have been, and are, likewise.

The physical journeys were initially designed to re-cover the paths taken by the 1921 journeyers. I made two such journeys, in April 1997 (around Mogumber, the Moore River and to Wongan Hills) and October 1997 (Perth to Laverton and Mt Margaret via Kalgoorlie and Menzies, then Laverton to Perth via Sandstone, Mt Magnet, Paynes Find and Wongan Hills). Additionally, for five of the last seven years, I have travelled north from Perth in mid-August to the Lake Moore area south of Paynes Find, experiencing the feel of the landscape and the various climatic conditions at that time of year, looking, feeling, listening; some years walking, or more accurately wading, across granite outcrops running with still-falling rainwater, other years keeping to the shade by day and looking for emu prints on the dew-dried red dust at sunrise. And every year, sleeping cold under the night sky. And always, every year, in awe at the spectacular wildflowers, the striking colour, the lavishness as far as the eye can see — August would have been a glorious time to be travelling.

Following these journeys across the land, I was invited to return to Kalgoorlie to visit the people I had met while journeying in October 1997. The emphasis now was not so much on discovering aspects of the 1921 history, but on listening to the people's stories again and learning from them of their experiences of the past. This journey occurred in December 1997. This is the time at which most of the Speakings were recorded.

A number of contributors live in or spend considerable time in Perth, so I have also been able to spend time with these Wongutha people in Perth. Regular contact and discussion has taken place since 1997, throughout the formation of the text.

When the manuscript was completed, permission and approval was sought for the book's text generally, and from each Speaker specifically for the inclusion of the transcript of their conversation in the book. In October 1999 I travelled to Kalgoorlie to talk through the transcripts with the Speakers and their families — further discussion of this process occurs later in this section. As a result of the wide consultation, additional material was offered by one Speaker after prompting from family members, and so I travelled to Kalgoorlie again in November 1999.

The visits will continue. I will not forget about Next Time!

Permissions

The names of people who have passed away are used throughout this book.

I have sought and have been given permission by representative family members to print the names, photos and spoken contributions of those speakers who have passed on since I recorded their stories for this book.

A number of Wongutha people have given me permission to speak and print the names of the 1921 exiles.

The Speakings

All the texts of the conversations printed in the Speakings have been reviewed and approved for publishing by the speaker and/or a close relative of the speaker.

Recordings were made after numerous visits with each of the speakers (except where two individuals' health appeared to be precarious, in which case the recording was made on the first visit as suggested by other Wongutha people), with their permission, and only after the purpose for such a recording had been discussed. The interviews were originally recorded in the homes of the speaker, or in the home of a relative with whom I had a more established relationship. I met the extended family members of the speakers, and representatives (from various generations) of the speaker's family were present at all recording sessions. The process of meeting people and recording their stories was therefore known of and approved by the community, in addition to being approved by the individual speakers.

So, Speakings contains selected extracts from these tape-recorded conversations with people who have some connection to the 1921 events in Laverton. I am conscious that the process of extracting, of removing sections of the conversations, may alter the construction of the histories told, but after consideration I have decided that to present all the interviews in their entirety in this book is not appropriate. The final transcript construction has been approved by each Speaker, or by a relative where the Speaker has passed away or was unable to read the text. In some cases where a relative was reviewing the text for a Speaker who was unable to read it for themselves, I also read the transcript aloud to the Speaker to ensure an opportunity for corrections and clarifications to be made.

Much of the material presented in the Speakings may seem unrelated to the 1921 events. It is included in order that both the various historical experiences and the priorities of the individual speakers can be seen and comprehended. Ranji McIntyre, for instance, can remember back to the years before 1910, he has many years of stories and yet he has chosen to tell me one particular story each time I have visited him. He selected the story of the shooting of Tom James by ex-policeman Jack O'Loughlan in the 1920s as his starting story when I first visited him in October 1997, and then he told me that same story again in December 1997, and again in October 1999 — I have ensured that this story, so significant that it was communicated on each visit and on both occasions when the tape recorder was running, is presented in each of his Speaking sections. I consider the histories told when the tape-recorder was running to be deliberate constructions of the Speakers; the tape was understood to be for a wide and unknown audience, and the people spoke with that end in mind.

Releasing this Book

Explicit permission has been given by the contributing Wongutha people for this work to be publicly released. I have endeavoured to make known the material contained within the book to representative Wongutha people prior to publishing, in order to ensure that all material was culturally appropriate. In addition to ensuring that each transcript was approved by the individual Speaker or a family representative, the text for the Journal Notes and the New Account has been reviewed, and then, after corrections, approved by a Wongutha woman of high community standing. We are of the opinion that the text is now suitable. Any inadequacies we have overlooked, however, fall on my shoulders, not hers.

Forming the New Account as Narrative

Narrative was not what I intended for the compilation of the conclusions of my research and journeying. I began writing my account of the 1921 events in what might be described as a conventional historical manner; I was the omniscient author, I listed the essential facts of the events according to the gathered evidence and ordered them carefully with measured analysis. But the story, as told to me in fleeting bits and vivid pieces by the Wongutha people to whom I listened, seemed to be vanishing beneath the weight of the comparative discussion. This astounding story seemed to be rendered lifeless by a detached historical telling. The form seemed alien to the story. I felt that to tell this Wongutha story in such a form would not be true to the experience of listening to the Wongutha people who had told me so many Wongutha stories.

So I explored the possibility of writing the account in another way, in another form, through which I intended the reader to more readily experience the reality of the story. I embarked, for a second time, on developing a new account. I wrote some passages, and I then compared the conventional format with the narrative form. I discarded the conventional, alien account and began constructing a narrative account in earnest.

After much internal debate, I have concluded that the narrative-related problems expressed previously in the foreword to A New Account are of less significance than the beneficial value of an appropriate and effective communication of the story.

So Little Explanation!

I have taken to heart Deborah Bird Rose's insight:

> Consider the differences between an explanation of love, a love-story, a love poem and a love song. Consider too, the power and passion of ... multiple interpretations.[1]

Paradoxes and Discrepancies

The evidence presented in this text does not always concur. There are discrepancies. You can draw your own conclusions. Come to your own intuitive understandings of the people and the histories. Peter Read suggests that you already are familiar with this process — it is the same way by which you understand your friends, inconsistent though they are.[2] Some of my process of reconciling the various data for the 1921 events is presented in the following appendices.

'The past has, is and can be known in many ways ... history always has many tellings and never a single epic chronicle.'[3] Discrepancies and other variations are allowable.

Testimonies about other events, and other histories, are presented and not discussed in this book. Wongutha recollections of Neville's direct interference in their lives is particularly interesting. Healy writes of the way in which various histories of Captain Cook (at odds with the 'official' western account of Cook) were developed by Aboriginal people across Australia to deal with the 'social dilemmas bequeathed by the past'. He suggests that these 'Aboriginal histories of Cook deploy a much less ossified sense of social memory.'[4] Wongutha histories of Neville may be similar. Was it really Neville walking around in the bush telling the Wongutha women that he was taking their children away but, never mind, they could have other children? Regardless of the name of the individual man who took the children away at that time, the Wongutha histories tell us it was Neville who took the children. We need to ensure that we do not 'restrict the possibilities of historical imagination to that which is already known'.[5] Likewise, the histories about Donegan hint at much which is not yet known to the wider community.

Lastly

The past continues on into the present.

'The study of history has many justifications. Perhaps the most compelling are social necessity and self-knowledge. Just as a person needs a memory, so societies must be aware of their history. Without historical records societies and the individuals within them suffer a loss of identity.'[6]

It is my hope that this book will contribute to the process of discovering identity, and, if possible, will promote a 'transformative shift of values, perspectives and motivations'[7] of the wider community.

'Our nation must have the courage to own the truth, to heal the wounds of its past so that we can move on together at peace with ourselves ... Our new journey then begins. We must learn our shared history.'[8]

Escape and Pursuit

Why weren't they recaptured by the Moore River Settlement trackers?

'There were black trackers for policeman ... Their main job was to catch anyone who ran away.'[1] Their 'main' task was to track and capture escapees and escort them back to the Settlement. Successful completion of this task was the key to the tracker's eventual personal freedom — it is therefore unsurprising that very few successful escapes were made. The trackers were highly motivated to do their job well. But the Laverton people successfully escaped. The trackers did not find them.

Were trackers sent out?

The Superintendent did not record in his record sheets that the group was missing until 18 September 1921, by which time most of the people had safely walked back to Laverton. Schenk's diary record of 1 September states that the majority of the group were already home, only two weeks after their deportation.

The *West Australian* reported an influenza epidemic at the Moore River Settlement in mid to late August 1921.[2] Perhaps in the confusion of the epidemic none of the authorities at Mogumber noticed their escape until it was too late to send out trackers. Perhaps the delay in recording the people's escape was because the trackers stayed out for some time before returning to report that the group had eluded them.

Charlie Sandstone, in an interview with Haebich, confirmed that trackers were sent out after the escapees. He suggested that the trackers did not want to confront the group; that because they were afraid of this Laverton mob they deliberately did not pursue them.[3]

Why weren't they re-captured by police along the way?

There is evidence to suggest that the state-wide police network was thoroughly briefed, district by district, to search systematically for later escapees, but on this occasion there is no such evidence.[4] It seems that there was no specific or urgent correspondence from the Settlement Superintendent notifying the Aborigines Department of the people's escape. It appears that Campbell was in no hurry to tell his superiors, the Department in Perth was not informed until the end of September when they received the usual monthly letter report of admissions and departures from the Settlement. It was, by then, too late for the Department to set in motion plans to recapture the people along the way — but did the Department know this? No correspondence concerning this escape was found in Neville's files. Perhaps he was on annual leave. Or perhaps a 'closed' file somewhere in the State Archives contains information on the Department's response to the escape.

Why weren't they pursued in Laverton?

The police at Laverton must surely have had the best opportunity for recognising and apprehending the group of returned escapees. But they apparently remained idle; they did not recapture the people, and there are no records of attempts to recapture them.[5]

A letter written by Schenk to friends in Victoria indicates that the Laverton police knew of the return of the escapees, for Schenk anxiously reports that he had been informed that the police were intending recapture, and were also intending to continue capturing other people for the purpose of sending them to Moore River.[6]

However, Thompson, the police officer at Laverton, in his annual report for 1922 confidently states that his disciplinary measure of deporting some people the previous year had been successful in gaining control over the movements of the Aboriginal people in the district and that they had given little trouble since that time.[7] Thompson evidently chose not to pursue the Wongutha.

He had certainly known when, on other occasions, convicted Wongutha had returned to the area once their sentences had been served, as shown in his letter dated April 1921 where he suggests that a permanent prohibition of their return to their home district would have 'good effect' on the other 'natives'. But on this occasion he does not make such comments in any of the records, and the success of the deportation that is declared in his letter of October 1921 stands.

Perhaps, given his earlier sympathies towards the Wongutha, he was satisfied with the successful disciplinary effect of the deportation, despite the return of the deportees.

Or perhaps Thompson was feeling that there was no point continuing to send people away to Mogumber if they were to escape and return. Having such people outwit the system and flout State control would surely have some local consequences, and his reputation might suffer. Or perhaps an official from the distant Aborigines Department might notice such events and require him to take on extra work to find escapees. Thompson's letters indicate that he felt that the Perth-based Aborigines' Department and his Superior Officers in the police force had little understanding of the difficulties of pursuing individuals in the spinifex country surrounding his post.[8] It is likely that Thompson would have been reluctant to bring upon himself additional work.

And then, Thompson, like most white members of the Laverton community, had 'a wholesome fear' of the Aboriginal people.[9] Away from the Laverton township and from the safety of numbers, the power of the white people diminished. Most were afraid of the unknown Aboriginal people, as demonstrated by the events they chose to recount to Schenk. Laverton in 1921 was rife with stories of confident prospecting parties heading out into the spinifex country only to retrace their steps back to safer country after being speared.[10] An Aboriginal man had allegedly 'nearly flogged a white man to death with a waddy'.[11] Aboriginal people had successfully stolen firearms from prospectors; there was speculation in Laverton as to the number of firearms in the possession of 'very wild' Aboriginals. Rumours had recently been circulating of militant groups of up to two hundred Aboriginal people gathering in the spinifex, unafraid of white people.[12] Additionally, the Wongutha were purported by many to be particularly warlike. Evidences of fatal fighting between the Laverton-based Aboriginal people, the Wongutha, and the Darlots, from further north, were still frequent. It was clear to all that spears were effective, and that the people were fiercely brave, risking death in defence of their own.

All these events and rumours of events suggest that the feeling of the day in Laverton was that Aboriginal people met on their own ground away from the town were not powerless, even before the white man's gun, and were to be feared.

Thompson, as a police officer, perhaps also had reason to fear personal retribution. One of the officers in Laverton was widely known to have shot at Aboriginal people with the result of wounding them, to have used a stockwhip to drive the Aboriginal people out of Laverton, and to have broken an old woman's arm.[13] These actions were probably those of Hunter, Thompson's fellow officer, as he was the officer most feared by the Aboriginal people. Schenk notes that the people had a particular word which meant 'Hunter the P.C. or any other bad man'.[14] Thompson, wearing the same uniform and representing the same authority as did Hunter, may have feared that retribution may be exacted on him. Schenk recorded the conversational advice given to him within the first few days of his arrival in Laverton:

> Mr Thompson advised me not to go to far into the bush lest I be speared. He says that they are very wild and that he would not think of entering in amongst them without being armed and mounted. I would feel the same if I were a policeman.[15]

In order to preserve his safety, his reputation and his time, then, it is extremely likely that Thompson would have taken great care to avoid being required to pursue Aboriginal people through the lonely spinifex.

Or perhaps he merely wished to avoid the additional work which would be required of him if he decided to, or was directed by his authorities to, recapture the people. Thompson had stated on previous occasions that attempting to find certain people, and then to capture them, was very difficult work; and the Wongutha had since scattered into the bush.

Or perhaps Thompson was satisfied with seeing the people scatter into the bush. Maybe the permanent exile of that group of people was less important to the policeman than the immediate effect of that exile, in ensuring that all of the Wongutha avoided Laverton. Thompson's orders had been to take action to keep the Wongutha out of Laverton, and he had achieved this result. Law and order, along with his authority and power, were re-established in the eyes of the Laverton people. It may have been enough for Thompson.

Thompson evidently chose not to pursue the people who escaped in 1921.

This degree of local leniency was not to last long, as evidenced by the testimonies presented in Speakings. Thompson left Laverton during the 1920s.

The Department of Aborigines and Fisheries' request for more detailed information about certain Wongutha in the Laverton area from the local police in 1922 marks the beginning of a significant increase in the Department's centralised knowledge and control of Aboriginal people. However, the local police officer again does not comply with the request in full — whether the lack of detail is due to defiance of distant superiors, or to an inability to identify specific Wongutha people, or merely that police duties at the time took a higher priority than Protector duties, remains a matter of conjecture — but one senses the beginning of an administration where records will not merely state that 'some' people were deported, but will record names and numbers and see to it that the named and numbered people remain where they are sent by the administration.

By the 1930s, Neville had a comprehensive 'personal file' system detailing information about individual people from the Laverton region. More and more parents began to take their children to Schenk's Mt Margaret Mission, travelling by night to avoid detection by police-protectors and the inevitable exile of the children to Mogumber.[16] Schenk was required by the Department to provide to the Department the names and details of the children who were residing at Mount Margaret — for the purposes of obtaining Government rationing and blankets. Neville, on receipt of the requested September 1937 list, wrote an internal memo stating: 'When I return from the Murchison I would like to see the personal files for each of the natives mentioned at p29.' On this occasion, of the fifty-four children on Schenk's list, twenty-three already had files; even those aged four years old were already the subjects of Departmental interest.[17]

Schenk, obviously concerned by past precedents, wrote to Neville on a number of occasions requesting Neville's promise that children would not be removed from Mount Margaret Mission and sent 'south'. Neville refused to give any such promise.[18] So children 'unofficially' lived at Mt Margaret — they appeared on no Government lists, and the Mission paid their living expenses out of Mission funds rather than provide the Department with information about these children whose parents sought safety and education for them at Mt Margaret. These children would seek refuge in the nearby hills whenever visitors approached. Adults also camped unofficially at the Mission, and would move away temporarily when official visitors where due to inspect the Mission.[19] Neville, stumbling across a camp of people in the bush on one such visit to the area, was incensed to discover that they usually lived at Mt Margaret but that Schenk had asked them to head bush for a few particular days.[20]

Neville filed notes about this event, and reported:

> The Commissioner visited Mt Margaret Mission on the 5th, 7th and 8th September 1939. Unfortunately, the visits on the 7th and 8th were considerably marred by Mr Schenk's hostile attitude towards the Department generally and the Commissioner in particular. Mr Schenk did not hesitate to voice his criticisms in the presence of natives and made use of the utmost invective. His attitude was most unwarranted and disloyal.[21]

Neville's decision to demote Schenk from the position of protector, and to instate a 'loyal' manager at a new Government settlement somewhere else in the area, seemingly began around this time:

> The alternative is either to immediately establish our own centre where these activities can be carried on under a Departmental Officer, or appoint a Departmental Officer for the district to act as Protector, supervise the issue of rations, and generally attend to any matters in this area between Kalgoorlie and Wiluna as may be directed by the Commissioner. Further, I do not think that Missions ... should be permitted to be set up anywhere in this State until such time as they are compelled to conform with requirements of the Department in every way ... I want to add in fairness to Mr Schenk that the natives he has cared for have nothing to complain about, and that he is doing quite a lot of good in caring for some children and maintaining some who would otherwise need to be cared for by the Department, but the good he is doing is nullified by his general attitude, and the efforts being

made are not wholly in conformity with the principles laid down by the Department. In my opinion, the Government having adopted a policy should insist that its principles become effective even in Missions, as in its own institutions ... A united policy carried out by all ... is what is necessary to bring the solution of the native problem nearer. Lest it be thought that my remarks have been somewhat influenced by Mr Schenk's attitude towards myself personally, I have refrained from mentioning his insulting behavior towards me in the presence of the natives, but knowing Mr Schenk as I do, and having witnessed several similar outbursts previously, this only adds to my feeling that he is unfit to have any authority over our natives generally.[22]

1921 People: Who Were Exiled? Who Escaped?

The Moore River Settlement Records record the admission of nineteen people from Laverton at some time during August 1921. According to the Moore River Records, there are nine men and six women and four children who are admitted to Moore River.[1]

Schenk's diary records that fifteen Wongutha people from Laverton were sent away in the cattle truck of the train on 15 August 1921.[2] Margaret Morgan's book lists Elyon, a baby who also appears as one of the four children on the Moore River Records, as one of the fifteen exiles. Morgan notes, from oral sources, that nine men and five women and one baby were sent away.

The Moore River Settlement records attribute one extra woman and three extra children to the incoming Laverton group. There are a number of possible ways in which this discrepancy could be explained; two options seem most likely.

Perhaps fifteen Wongutha from Laverton were sent away in the train to the Moore River Settlement. The three children and one woman not acknowledged in Morgan's record of the oral evidence of the Wongutha people may have come from a different part of the goldfields. The Superintendent who, when the new arrivals spoke little English, made assumptions about their names, ages and descent for his records, was likely to have made assumptions about places of origin. His hastily written records are less likely to be accurate than oral records of the Wongutha people.

Or perhaps nineteen people were sent away in the train; fifteen adults and four children. Rod Schenk's record of fifteen people did not include the children, either deliberately or because he did not know of their presence. Mysie Schenk's recollection as told to Morgan is that Schenk's knowledge of the people about to be exiled was gained from the policeman's note attached to the cattle-truck at the railway station: 'marked on the outside of the truck was a stock notice which Rod read: "15 Niggers for Mogumber".'[3] Did the policeman count the children?

The Moore River Settlement records state that all but one of the twenty-two 'Laverton' people who were inmates in August 1921 escaped/deserted, but not all at the same time. There were two escapes. In September 1921, seventeen people are recorded as 'deserters' (fourteen of those who arrived in August plus three who were there already) and then later, in November 1921, the escape of three children and one man is recorded. Only one man ('Jimmy Tongona') has no record of escape — it is possible that the Superintendent overlooked one man. What the Superintendent records in his own books and what he tells the Department are at odds: the Department is notified in September that sixteen people escape. (Polly Tarnuga, 292, is not listed as one of the escapees in the September letter to the Department, but in the Settlement Register of Inmates her name is crossed off the register and the remark alongside reads 'Deserted 18/9/21'.[4] [See Writings 3.3, Figure 3.3-D.])

Morgan's account, constructed from oral evidence and her father's diary, is of seventeen escapees — fifteen who arrived at Mogumber in August 1921 plus two who were already at Mogumber. However, Morgan did not know that Dion Dirk was one of the 1921 escapees, so her account does not include him — Dirk is missing from Morgan's account. Similarly, Morgan does not refer to the five people who remained behind until November.

Moore River records state that there were twenty-one people from Laverton imprisoned in Mogumber at the time of the first escape. Sixteen escaped and they took with them a woman who was probably not from Laverton. Why didn't all of the Laverton people escape together? What of the five who did not escape with this main party?

Since the escape group did not fail to take with them an old blind man, a deaf and dumb youth, and a woman with a baby when they left Mogumber, they must have had good reasons to leave behind two men and three children. Children were segregated from adults at Mogumber. Children slept in locked dormitories, they ate their meals in the brand new dining room, there were routines, beds and matrons to keep them in place, they had a roll call and a school of sorts. They lived under watchful white eyes in the Settlement's 'compound'. The adults in the Settlement's 'camp' were watched primarily by trackers. It seems likely that the three Laverton children who were left behind were locked in a dormitory when the main group escaped. The two men perhaps stayed behind to keep an eye on the children, at the least, and maybe to keep watch for a potential time to escape with the children. Perhaps they sought also to maintain the impression of the group's presence at Mogumber, keeping cooking fires burning at night. One man is recorded as escaping a few months later, with all three children, in November 1921 (refer to Writings, Figure 3.3-D).

Morgan's informants told her who came back from Mogumber. And they told her the escape stories — in her account of the journeys she tells stories of all of these men, by name, except for two. The two who do not appear in her written version of these oral accounts are Nganjur (Bill Carrigg) and Gram (Lame Charlie). Morgan implies their escape with the others, but perhaps these were the two who stayed behind. They did not stay behind permanently, for both re-appear at Mt Margaret in Schenk's diary of 1922. All of the people returned home, except for Wunu.

I suggest, from an overview of oral evidence, Morgan's accounts and the various Moore River Settlement records, that there were seventeen Laverton people and one non-Laverton woman who successfully escaped in August/September, followed by two men and three children, all of Laverton, who escaped in November. The following tables attempt to show my comparisons of the various records.

Table A5-A
Archive Records from Moore River: Laverton admissions and escapes.

Admission to Moore River August 1921	Escape from Moore River August or September 1921
280 Charley 'Bunya'	280 Charley 'Bunya'
281 George	281 George
282 Billy	282 Billy
283 Jumbo Wills	283 Jumbo Wills
284 Billy Tindora	284 Billy Tindora
285 Jimmy Tongona	285 no record of escape
286 Dicky Coomtat	286 Dicky Coomtat
287 Billy Tomula	287 Billy Tomula
288 Annie Kadro	288 Annie Kadro
289 Biddy	289 Biddy
290 Maggie Yandorda	290 Maggie Yandorda
291 Jimmy Talati	291 Jimmy Talati*
292 Polly Tarnuga	292 Polly Tarnuga
293 Kitty Twinda	293 Kitty Twinda
294 Maggie Morrell	294 Maggie Morrell
295 Alyon Child	295 Alyon Child
296 Monday child	296 Monday*
297 Friday child	297 Friday*
298 Violet child	298 Violet*
Previously admitted:	
103 Ginger Cowager	103 Ginger Cowager
104 Mulgardoon Joey	104 Mulgardoon Joey
171 Dyon Duik	171 Dyon Duik

*   *These people escaped on 3 November 1921. (Refer to Writings, Figure 3.3-D.)*

Table A5-B
Matching Wongutha Names and English Names

Recalled by local people and told to Morgan c1980	Additional information from author's interviews and research (Source shown in brackets)
Jidu, known as Jumbo	Jeedo, alias Jumbo. Husband to Thaldool. (Marriage certificate of their son Kunjel. Original held by Morgan.)
Baldul, Jidu's wife	Thaldool, alias Maggie. Wife to Jeedo. (Marriage certificate of their son Kunjel. Original held by Morgan.)
Moongoodie	George Moongoodie. (Interview 1 with Ranji McIntyre. Refer Speakings 2.2.)
Thalbin, wife of Moongoodie	Dalphin. (R Schenk, Diary.)
Jinera, also known as Blind Charlie	
Thimbarn, nicknamed Gadajilbi (grey-headed)	Old Charlie, Kardajilbe. (R Schenk, Diary.)
Tharnmoon, Gadajilbi's wife	
Wunu	Woonoo, alias Billy. Husband to Biyoora. (Marriage certificate of their daughter Cissie. Original held by Morgan.)
Biyuwarra, wife of Wunu	Biyoora, alias Biddy. Wife to Woonoo. (Marriage certificate of their daughter Cissie. Original held by Morgan.)
Elyon, Biyuwarra's baby	Elyon.
Nganjur, known as Bill Carrigg	Nunjoor William. (Refer to Writings 3.6.) Nganjur worked for Bill Carrigg. (Margaret Morgan, Interview with author.) Also Ngunjurr. (M Schenk.)

Thulyi, known as Tom Harris	Thulyi worked for Tom Harris. (Margaret Morgan, Interview with author.)
Grarn, known as Lame Charlie	Lame Charlie — Gooran. (Mysie Schenk. Refer to Writings 3.6.)
Mudarn, an old woman	
Ngada	
Joe Mulgathunoo or Mulga Joe	Joe Mulgasunoo. (Refer to Writings 3.2. Schenk's Letter. 01/07/22.)
Wawuja, also known as Ginger	A Ginger Stokes used to work around the Laverton area. (Ranji McIntyre, Interview with author. Refer Speakings 2.2.)
Dion Duik	Dyon Dirk / Dion Duik. Jidu's eldest son. (Margaret Morgan, Interview with author. Refer Speakings 2.9.)

Table A5-C
Linking Moore River Records Lists with Oral Lists

Oral Sources	Moore River Archives
1. George Moongoodie	1. 281 George
2. Jidu or Jeedu or Jumbo	2. 283 Jumbo Wills
3. Baldul, or Thaldool, or Maggie	3. 294 Maggie
4. Elyon, the baby	4. 295 Alyon Child
5. Biyuwarra or Biyoora or Biddy	5. 289 Biddy
6. Wawuja, or Ginger	6. 103 Ginger Cowager
7. Mulga Joe, or Joe Mulgathunoo	7. 104 Mulgardoon Joey
8. Dion Dirk	8. 285 Dyon Duik
9. Tharnmoon (f)	9. 288 Annie Kadro or Kadoo?
10. Thalbin (f)	10. 292 Polly Tarnuga?
11. Mudarn (f)	11. 293 Kitty Twinda?
12. Thulyi or Tom Harris	12. 287 Billy Tomula?
13. Ngada (m)	13. 282 Billy?
14. Blind Charlie or Jinera	14. 280 Charley 'Bunya'?
15. Wunu (m)	15. 291 Jimmy Talati? (November escape)
16. Gadajilbe or Thimbarn (m)	16. 285 Jimmy Tongona? (no record of escape)
17. Nganjur or Bill Carrig	17 284 Billy Tindora?
18. Lame Charlie or Grarn	18 286 Dicky Coomtat?
No recognition of Yandorda	19. 290 Maggie Yandorda
No information	20. 296 Monday (November escape
No information	20. 297 Friday (November escape
No information	20. 298 Violet (November escape)

William Harris' Evidence

William Harris' statement about events in Laverton is undated. Is it the 1921 story, or some other story, to which he refers? There are a number of strong parallels between Harris' account and Mysie Schenk's account (as related by Margaret Morgan's *A Drop in a Bucket* text previously quoted) including: the innocence of the people; the deliberate scheming of the police; the capture of the people when they came in for rations (food or blankets); the locking up in the Laverton gaol; transportation by train; escape; the presence of a blind man.

While Harris gives no dates in which to place the events, it is certain that they must have occurred between 1918 (the year of opening the Moore River Settlement) at the earliest and 1926 (when he wrote the letter) at the latest.

Examination of Laverton police records[1] from 1915 onwards shows that prior to July 1921 a number of individuals were sentenced away from Laverton. The Constable does not refer to any deportation nor sentencing of a group of people until October 1921, when he writes of the successful effect of the 'recent deportation of a number of them'.[2] It seems that this is the only group exile between 1915 and 1921.

Schenk's diary record of Laverton events begins in April 1921. He records the exile of the group of people in August 1921. By the end of 1922 Schenk's Mount Margaret Mission was operational and the Wongutha people had begun making their homes there, almost free from harassment by the police. Rationing and water, the main attractions of Laverton to the Wongutha, were readily available at Mount Margaret. Three of the returned exiles (Mulga Joe, Gadajilbi and Ngunjur William) were the first to stay for any length of time at Mount Margaret, and after convincing themselves of its suitability and safety, they left to spread the word amongst the Wongutha throughout the district that there was now a safe a place to gather. They returned with a large group of people. By March 1923 Jidu, according to Schenk's personal diary, had announced his 'intention to stay at Mt Margaret until he died'. More and more people gradually settled at Mount Margaret.[3] Schenk thus over time became more and more acquainted with the dealings of the police with the Wongutha. Having recorded and publicly objected to the 1921 deportation of people he did not know, he would surely have had more reason to record any other deportation of a group large enough to be called a mob if such a group had been exiled between 1921 and 1926. Schenk's diary documents the many occasions on which he visited individual or pairs of convicted Wongutha offenders in Laverton before they were sent to Mogumber by train, but does not refer to any sizeable groups other than the 1921 group.

From Schenk's records we may conclude that only one large group of people was sent to Mogumber from Laverton between the years of 1921 and 1926. The deportation of a large group of people prior to 1921 has already been ruled out through examination of the police records. So, Harris' account, the only undated version of the event, also provides evidence supporting the 1921 events.

Notes from Neville's Files

This section contains notes and letters extracted from various archival files of the Aborigines Department — none of them mention the 1921 events, but they are, nonetheless, revealing.

Extract: Telegram to Schenk, 2 Dec 1938[1]

> Government of Western Australia
> Department of Native Affairs
> 57 Murray St
> Perth
>
> Mr R.S. Schenk,
> United Aborigines Mission.
> MORGANS
>
> Dear Sir
>
> ... I am not aware of any conflict of views between the Police and yourself regarding children. On other questions, I know, of course, that you have complained against the Police and I have had to send your statements on for investigation ... we all get criticism and recently I have had more than a fair share from you ...
>
> Yours faithfully
>
> Commissioner of Native Affairs

Numerous Escapes from Moore River by Laverton men

In 1924, the Deputy Chief Protector of Aborigines was troubled by the fact that people from the Laverton region were in the habit of escaping from the Moore River Settlement. He proposed a solution that might enable the Department to 'hold' them 'away from their country'. (See Figure A7-A.)

388   Appendices

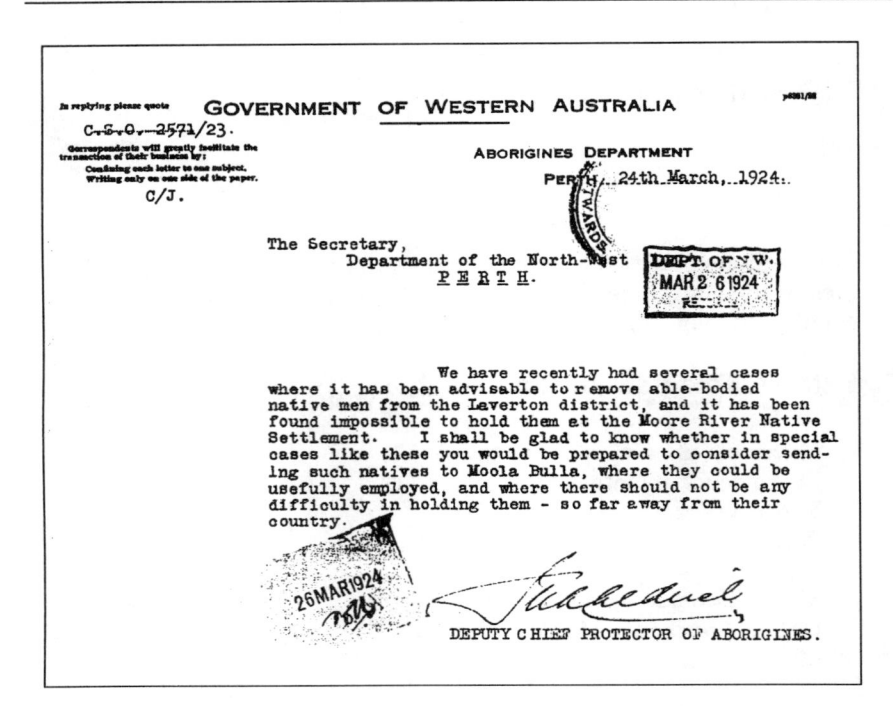

> **GOVERNMENT OF WESTERN AUSTRALIA**
>
> In replying please quote
> C.S.O. 2571/23.
>
> ABORIGINES DEPARTMENT
>
> PERTH, 24th March, 1924.
>
> C/J.
>
> The Secretary,
>   Department of the North-West
>   P E R T H.
>
> DEPT. OF N.W.
> MAR 2 6 1924
>
> We have recently had several cases where it has been advisable to remove able-bodied native men from the Laverton district, and it has been found impossible to hold them at the Moore River Native Settlement. I shall be glad to know whether in special cases like these you would be prepared to consider sending such natives to Moola Bulla, where they could be usefully employed, and where there should not be any difficulty in holding them - so far away from their country.
>
> 26 MAR 1924
>
> DEPUTY CHIEF PROTECTOR OF ABORIGINES.

Figure A7-A
(State Archives, AN 1 /4 Acc 653 File 166. 1924: 1)

Annual Report, 1921 — Deputy Chief Protector of Aborigines[2]

The Hon. Colonial Secretary

I have the honor to submit herewith my annual report for the year 1920–21.

During December, 1920, the control of the Aborigines was divided, and I was appointed Deputy Chief Protector of Aborigines in charge of Aborigines South of Parallel 25° South, with the exception of coastal towns North of Geraldton. I am dealing hereunder with the Southern portion of the State for the whole year ended 30th June 1921.

The condition of the natives generally has been very good and, apart from a little influenza, sickness had been no more prevalent than at normal times.

Employment has been plentiful, and the conduct of the natives good.

The native population totals 4,927. Compared with the population for last year, there is an increase of 564 ... The general increase in the figure may also be due, in great extent, to the fact that as the country is becoming settled the Police are able to gauge the number of aboriginals more accurately.

Of the total population, aboriginals, or half-castes deemed to be under the Act, number 4,520; adults 3,607 and children 913. Half castes not deemed to be under the Act number 407; of these 283 are adults and 124 children. Statement 'A' attached gives details of the population in various Police districts.
...

<u>Blankets and clothing</u>
The whole of the clothing required for natives throughout the State during the year was manufactured at the Carrolup River Native Settlement. The total number of garments manufactured was 4,000. The following were distributed in the Southern portion of the State:-
Dresses............................ 636
Shirts............................... 440

Undershirts.................... 652
Trousers........................ 440
Girls' underclothing.... 313

In addition, the following blankets and Military coats were issued:-

Blankets......................... 574
Military overcoats........ 210
Military tunics.............. 518

making a total number of blankets and garments issued 3,783.

...

Certificates of Exemption
Five applications were received from aboriginals for exemption under Section 63 of the Act. Three applications were granted, and two refused.

Moore River Native Settlement
Upon the transfer of Mr Mitchell to Carrolup River Native Settlement, Mr John Campbell was appointed Superintendent at Moore River, and took up duties in February 1921.

During the year a large children's dining-room was erected, also a store and office. Both of these buildings were very much needed. The buildings which are still required are a boy's dormitory, a kitchen or cook-house to be attached to the dining room, and a small structure to be utilised as a hospital. The want of a building to accommodate the sick has been keenly felt, but as other structures have been more urgently needed the erection of a hospital has had to be postponed.

Additional clearing has been carried out, and about 60 acres planted for hay. The land, generally speaking, at this settlement is very poor sand country, and practically useless ...

The well that was sunk during the previous year and collapsed, has been cleared out and re-timbered where necessary, and although information previously obtained indicated that the well would be a good source of constant and good water supply, the latest reports show that the supply of water is very limited, and it has therefore, been decided to rely on one of the river pools for supply of water for general settlement use.

...

The question of manufacture of clothing for other Government departments has been under consideration for some time past, but only carried out on a very limited scale until recently. Arrangements have now been made to carry on this work to a greater extent, and in order to allow for this a sewing factory has been commenced at Moore River Settlement. The native and half-caste girls make very good seamstresses, and the work already carried out has given entire satisfaction to the Departments concerned, a considerable saving in cost is effected.

Missions
At the beginning of the year there were three half-caste and native missions in operation, namely, the New Norcia Mission, the Salvation Army Girls' Home, Kalgoorlie, and the Swan Native and Half-cast Mission, each of which were subsidised. During the year the Salvation Army Girls' Home and the Swan Native and Half-cast Mission were closed. Those inmates who were old enough and suitable were placed out to employment, and others were sent to the settlements.

The total amount paid to the Missions as subsidies during the year was £202. Owing to the closing of two of the Homes the expenditure in this direction will be considerably reduced.

...

In conclusion, I wish to record my appreciation of the loyal support given me by the Office Staff, also the Staff at the two Settlements. The satisfactory work carried out at Moore River and Carrolup River Settlements is largely due to the hearty co-operation of the Superintendents and their Assistants.

The thanks of the Department are also due to the Commissioner of Police and his Officers, and the Honorary Protectors, for their assistance in the administration of the Act, and care of the Aborigines throughout the area under my administration.

(Sgd) F. Aldrich
Deputy Chief Protector of Aborigines
26/9/21

'Statement A' to the 1921 Annual Report mapped the official representation of the 'total' Aboriginal population as well as their characteristics of particular interest to the Protectors. Select extracts are reproduced in the following table.

Extracts from 'Statement A', attachment to the 1921 Annual Report

Place		Laverton	Lawlers	Leonora	Morgans	Perth
Pop. Est.	'Full-blood' M	172	26	8	34	1
	'Full-blood' F	197	30	6	32	1
	'Full-blood' C	53	3	1	15	0
	'Half-caste' M	3	2	2	4	6
	'Half-caste' F	1	0	0	2	0
	'Half-caste' C	2	1	1	6	0
Total		428	62	18	93	8
'Natives' increasing or decreasing		increasing	neither	decreasing	neither	neither
Condition and health		fairly good	good	good	good	good
Epidemics		colds and influenza	nil	nil	nil	nil
Conduct		bad in some cases	fair	good	—	good
Employment		plentiful	'natives' don't care to work	'natives' too old to work	'natives' disinclined to work	plentiful

'Statement B' to the 1921 Annual Report showed the extent of the provision of rations and relief. It did not refer to the total number of people in a locality, only to the number who received rations at that locality.

Extracts from 'Statement B', attachment to the 1921 Annual Report

Place	Supervised by	Average number of 'natives' fed per month		Total cost (£)	
		1919-20	1920-21	1919-20	1920-21
Moore River	Superintendent	135	167	1500.3.0*	1765.14.3*
Burtville	Police	0	1	0	3.2.11**
Kanowna	Police	1	1	0.15.6	6.2.2
Kookynie	Police	5	5	41.9.6	50.3.2
Lawlers	Police	11	10	142.16.7	146.10.9
Laverton	Police	15	15	137.2.5	149.8.4
Leonora	Police	6	6	3.13.8	10.9.6
Meekatharra	Police	11	10	91.17.1	109.18.4
Mt Magnet	Police	2	2	7.16.2	24.9.11
Norseman	Police	5	5	44.8.9	47.6.9***

* — Includes cost of white employees
** — Ceased. Temporary relief.
*** — Ceased. Indigents removed to Moore River.

File Case Study — The Goldfields Drought, 1919

The following pages contain a selection of material from one file of the Chief Protector of Aborigines.[3] The various extracts are written during the year 1919, and reveal aspects of the extent and effects of the drought at that time. This drought continued for another two years, breaking only in late August 1921 — many of the comments made about the conditions of the Aboriginal people in 1919 would have been equally, if not more so, applicable in 1921.

The *West Australian* ran a short article in June 1919 stating that the Goldfields Aborigines were reported to be starving and that the Department was taking no action. (Refer to Figure A7-B.) Neville made no file response to this article, and apparently no action was taken.

Mr Henry Harris of Edjudina wrote to the *Kalgoorlie Miner* in July 1919 about the 'Condition of Aborigines'. (Refer to Figure A7-C.) A Mrs Boxall, of the Rectory at Boulder, read his letter. She immediately forwarded a copy of the newspaper article to the Aborigines Department for Neville's personal attention, accompanied by a letter which politely inquired about the action the Department might be proposing to relieve the conditions. She implied that the Chief Protector in distant Perth might not be fully acquainted with the dire situation in the Goldfields.

Mrs Boxall's letter, intimating that Neville was not adequately informed on the matter, spurred Neville to make inquiries and make good his reputation. The following documents are revealing.

> **GOLDFIELDS ABORIGINES.**
>
> REPORTED TO BE STARVING.
>
> Kalgoorlie, June 22.
>
> It is asserted that many of the aborigines who have come into Kalgoorlie and Boulder from the back country in order to participate in the Government's distribution of blankets, are in a starving state, owing to the fact that the recent heavy rains have killed off the rabbits, upon which the natives depended largely for their food. The local bodies have requested the Aborigines Department to feed these unfortunate people, but so far the department has taken no action. The police now report that the aborigines are moving off to their own districts.

Figure A7-B
'Goldfields Aborigines' *West Australian*. June 1919.

(State Archives, AN1 /4 Acc 652, File 803, 1919.)

CONDITION OF ABORIGINES.

To the Editor.

Sir,—In your issue of June 28, under the above heading, I noted the substance of a report from Mr. Neville, Chief Protector of Aborigines, made to the Colonial Secretary, Mr. Scaddan, concerning the condition of the natives, and the issue of rations in the Kalgoorlie-Laverton district. I have waited in hopes of a more able writer than myself taking up the cudgel for these poor devils of blacks. From what I can see the officers at the head of affairs in the Aborigines Department don't care a tuppeny tinker's cuss whether the niggers live or die, so long as they refrain from doing the latter within the said officer's town boundary. Instead of seeing to it that the Government fulfils the obligations, both legal and moral, that are the due of these unfortunate people, Mr. Neville seems quite content to sit in his office and make inquiries per medium of his typewriter as to the true position of the goldfields blacks. Apparently he is quite content to trust to the charity of the public and the black's ability to provide for himself, for he airily states that "A black fellow never starves in the bush." Has he any idea to what lengths the black will go if he is hungry? I can assure Mr. Neville that he often is hungry, and darned hungry, too. Since pastoral leases have been let on the goldfields and the country has been stocked, the natural soaks and wells have been drained out, and now round all wells and dams the country is literally strewed with baits. There isn't a mile of country from Kalgoorlie northwards to Lawlers and Laverton, or from Pingin westward to Mt. Ida, that it is safe to take a dog across, unless on a chain. This being the case, how do the black hunter and his dogs get on? However, in the face of this Mr. Neville can rest assured that the native will never starve so long as there are prospectors' camps to rob. Driven to desperation for food the native robs the camps—who is to blame? I was always under the impression that the Protector's Office was created for the protection and care of these people, but apparently the yearly Government grant is insufficient to go far beyond office expenses, while the long-suffering and charitable public are called on to shoulder the department's responsibility. When one knows the number of natives that were in and around Kalgoorlie last June, the list of "gifts" is laughable. A whole 14 blankets and some dozen pairs of trousers and 36 shirts among some five hundred blacks. And to think that the kindness of the Department didn't stop at the infirm and old, but what was left over was given to the able-bodied. Cold comfort, 14 blankets among five hundred blacks. Is it any wonder that the native race is rapidly passing away? The police as a body do what they can, but the howl for retrenchment in all expenses is continual and insistent, with the exception of salaries. Only a fortnight ago I saw 18 rations issued to infirm natives at Yarri. The rations were issued by a police officer, and consisted of 10 lb. of flour, and a little tea and sugar. About 150 natives were present, including many young children, but apparently regulations or finance prohibited the issue of the necessities of life to them. Should they ever live to reach manhood and womanhood it will be small thanks to the Aborigines Department. That a large tract should be reserved in each blackfellows' district is acknowledged by all, but in the meantime depots should be established to issue weekly rations to all natives requiring them. These could be supervised by the police or an inspector appointed—not the Perth or armchair type—but a man who thoroughly understands the natives. At the same time a statement from the Aborigines Department as to what proportion of the sums annually voted actually reached the goldfields blackfellow in the shape of rations and clothes, would be of interest to those people who are interested in the preservation of the few remaining local blacks. From a taxpayers' point of view the cost of administration might also

> prove of interest. In conclusion, I will quote a further case of sheer neglect and apparent indifference of the Department. Some six weeks ago two very old gins, the one blind and the other unable to walk, crawled into a station close to Yarri for a drink of water. Both were quite naked and abandoned by their fellow blacks. Local charity was extended to them, and the Department written to for rations and blankets. After much delay authority to issue rations came to hand, but up to date there is no sign of any blankets. In the meantime the one gin is dead, and it is anticipated locally that the other one and most of the local residents will be in a like state before the Department bestirs itself sufficiently to carry out its function and duty in this particular case.—Yours, etc.,
>
> HENRY HARRIS, Edjudina, July 18.

Figure A7-C
Henry Harris — Letter to the *Kalgoorlie Miner* July 1919.
(State Archives, AN1 /4 Acc 652, File 803, 1919.)

(Copy)

Original on A. & F. 721/19.

THE CHIEF PROTECTOR.

Recently a large number of natives from various centres including Linden, Laverton and Norseman, have been camped in the vicinity of Kalgoorlie, but owing to the fear of an outbreak of influenza at this centre these natives were ordered by the Police to leave and return to their own country. They in consequence left, and are making back to their respective localities. Since leaving Kalgoorlie numerous complaints have been received as to their starving condition, and that they were looting camps, etc. This is not to be wondered at as the native food throughout the district is very scarce, but the difficulty is to know how to relieve their distress until they have settled down in their respective localities. A large number of them are strong, able-bodied men, but too lazy to work and to hunt for food is out of the question as the bush at present is devoid of game.

These natives on returning to their own localities will receive attention. I have already instructed Const. Lewis of Morgans to visit Linden and see to their welfare.

(Sgd) R. DUNCAN,

Inspector.

30/6/19.

Figure A7-D
Letter to Neville, Chief Protector of Aborigines, Perth, from Inspector Duncan, Kalgoorlie July 1919.
(State Archives, AN 1 /4 Acc 652, File 803, 1919.)

COLONIAL SECRETARY'S DEPARTMENT.

ABORIGINES AND FISHERIES.

THE UNDER SECRETARY.

Respecting my memo. of the 23rd June, hereunder, I have now received a report from Inspector Duncan, Kalgoorlie.

It appears that recently a large number of natives from various centres have been visiting Kalgoorlie, but owing to the fear of an outbreak of influenza were ordered by the Police to leave and return to their own country. This they did at once.

Since leaving Kalgoorlie complaints have been made as to the starving condition of these natives, and that they were looting camps. There is practically no native food available at the present time in this district, and owing to the roving disposition of these people it is impossible to follow their movements and supply their wants while they are travelling. Relief is available to them in the districts from which they come, and on their return to their own localities attention will be given to the matter.

As a matter of fact, a number of these natives are strong, able-bodied men who are too lazy to work.

I am asking Inspector Duncan to see that all natives in his district are supplied with relief as necessary while their natural food is scarce, and particularly during the influenza scare, when everyone seems to think it necessary to shun the natives, and drive them away from settlement.

A O Neville
CHIEF PROTECTOR OF ABORIGINES.

3rd July, 1919.
N/S.

Figure A7-E
Letter to the Under Secretary, Colonial Secretary's Department/Aborigines and Fisheries from Neville, Chief Protector of Aborigines. July 1919.
(State Archives, AN 1 /4 Acc 652, File 803, 1919.)

Neville's reply to Mrs Boxall

2nd August 1919

Madam,

I have to acknowledge receipt of your communication of the 24th ult. which came to hand during my absence in the country, enclosing copy of a letter written to the *Kalgoorlie Miner* by a Mr Edward Harris. I do not know who Mr Harris is, but his statements are so obviously incorrect that I have no intention of entering into a newspaper controversy with him. The public generally must know perfectly well that the Aborigines Department would never allow such a state of affairs to exist as portrayed by Mr Harris. His references to myself do not matter, except that he makes me use an expression which I never uttered and which on the face of it is absurd.

Mr Harris stated that he saw natives rationed at Yarrie, when there about 150 present. The information which I have is to the effect that 60 or 70 natives were camped at Yarrie on their way from Kalgoorlie to their own districts, and that of these the Police rationed 18 aged indigents, and one woman with children.

Respecting the two old women mentioned by Mr Harris later in his letter, these are probably two that I gave instructions to ration in May last. I was not aware that one of them had died, and no request was ever made to me for blankets, which would have been made available if they had been required.

In order that you may be aware of the system under which this Department rations natives generally throughout the State, I enclose for your information a copy of a circular sent to all Police Stations throughout the State in 1917. This outlines the procedures to be adopted, and as you will see by Clause 3, the Police have discretionary powers to ration any natives up to a period of one month without first seeking my approval. This circular also indicates the scale of rations allowed, and as you will see, there are special arrangements made for children. Rations are issued by the Police at the following places on the Eastern Goldfields: Wiluna, Leonora, Laverton, Menzies, Coolgardie and Kalgoorlie, while special temporary arrangements have been made to also feed the natives at Yarrie, Linden and Burtville. At Kookynie five old people have been regularly fed for a very long time past.
[...]

I am well aware that settlements such as we have on the coast should be established on the Goldfields, a fact which I brought under notice of the Government some years ago, and I am in hope that something may be done in this direction before very long. Generally speaking we must rely upon the Police to act in these matters for the Department, and I have never had cause to complain of any lack of attention or inhumanity on the part of these officers. On the contrary they have done all they could to assist us in every possible direction.

Apparently the whole present trouble has arisen from the fact that the Laverton, Linden, Morgans and Norseman natives recently made one of their periodical visits to Kalgoorlie, and during their return came up against hard times owing to the lack of natural food, whereas had they remained at their centres those requiring sustenance could have obtained it. It is, of course, practically impossible to ration tribes while making for some rendezvous or other to go through their annual rites and ceremonies.

I have to thank you for calling my attention to the matter, and hope as soon as I can possibly get away to personally visit the Goldfields.

I have the honour to be,
Madam,
Your obedient servant

CHIEF PROTECTOR OF ABORIGINES

Mrs A.E. Boxall,
The Rectory,
Boulder.

There is no further recorded communication between Mrs Boxall and the Department. Perhaps her mind was set at ease by Neville's statement that the 'Department would never allow such a state of affairs to exist', perhaps she believed Neville's assurances as to the attentiveness and humanity of the police who administered the Department's ready assistance, or perhaps she considered that Neville's personal attention to the matter might result in an improvement to the dire situation. Or, perhaps she considered it useless petitioning him further.

The extent of the Department's limited action to assist the drought-stricken people is documented in a short letter to Inspector Duncan of Kalgoorlie. Refer to Figure A7-G.

Western Australia

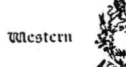

In replying please quote:
Circular 10/17.

ABORIGINES DEPARTMENT,
PERTH, 25th APRIL, 1917.

To the Officer in Charge

Police Station.

Rationing of Indigent Natives.

Please note that, in future, the following instructions are to be observed, and that all previous instructions in regard to the rationing of indigent natives are cancelled:—

1. Where natives are rationed by Police Officers, the day of issue is to be Monday, commencing as early in the morning as convenient. Rations are to be issued weekly, unless otherwise directed by the Chief Protector of Aborigines.

2. Only natives whose names appear on the ration list approved by the Aborigines Department are to be regularly supplied with rations. It is to be understood, however, that wherever conditions warrant the discontinuance of supplies to any natives such action may be at once taken by the Issuing Officer, who will subsequently notify the Chief Protector of Aborigines.

3. Natives whose names do not appear on the approved list may, in special or urgent circumstances, be supplied with rations over a period not exceeding four weeks, at the discretion of the Issuing Officer, but the facts must be immediately reported to the Chief Protector of Aborigines, whose approval must be sought if extended assistance appears to be necessary.

4. If it appears desirable to place any additional names on the approved list, the Chief Protector of Aborigines is to be communicated with and informed of the circumstances, but no names are to be added to the permanent list unless approval is first obtained.

5. In the event of natives wishing to leave the district in which they are usually rationed, either temporarily or permanently, and desiring to be placed on the ration list of the district in which they intend to reside, the Chief Protector of Aborigines is to be communicated with before further supplies are granted.

6. The following is the weekly scale of rations to be issued to each adult—10lbs. flour, 1¼lbs. sugar, 4ozs. tea, and 1 stick of tobacco to those accustomed to its use. The tobacco is intended as a comfort for the aged and infirm, and is to be given, not at stated periods, but at the discretion of the Issuing Officer. ⅞lb. meat daily may be supplied in special cases approved by the Chief Protector, and when so supplied the flour allowance is to be reduced to 8lb.

Children over 2 and under 12 years of age are to receive half the foregoing allowance, excluding tobacco, but the supply may be varied, at the discretion of the Issuing Officer, to include oatmeal, rice, sago, or tinned milk to an equivalent value.

For children under 3 years of age, 2lbs. of sago, rice, or porridge meal may be issued with not more than 2 tins of condensed milk.

No further variation of the ration allowance is to be made without the approval of the Chief Protector of Aborigines, or except upon the written authority of a medical officer.

7. All accounts for rations must be sent forward monthly, and Issuing Officers are requested to see that this is done.

A O Neville

Chief Protector of Aborigines.

Figure A7-F
Copy of Aborigines Department's Circular 10/17, 'Rationing of Indigent Natives' (as sent to Mrs Boxall by Neville).
(State Archives, AN 1 /4 Acc 652, File 803, 1919.)

803/19

INSPECTOR DUNCAN, POLICE STATION,
KALGOORLIE.

. . .   .

I enclose herewith for your information a copy of a letter which I have today addressed to Mrs. Boxall, of the Rectory, Boulder, and also put up a letter written by Mr. Henry Harris to the "Kalgoorlie Miner" for such comments as you care to make.

So far as Linden is concerned, I approve of the arrangements made by Constable Lewis for the feeding of the old woman ▓▓▓▓▓, and trust that any others requiring sustenance will be induced to remove to Burtville for it, the course which was formerly decided upon.

As to Yarrie, I have today wired Constable Lewis asking him to continue to have rations issued at that place so long as it is necessary.

Constable Thompson of Laverton asks permission to supply rations to five natives at Burtville every month. He states he visited there recently and found these badly in want of rations. In this connection I would point out that arrangements were made in 1916 for the Laverton Police to ration natives twice monthly at Burtville, vide Constable Thompson's minute of the 23rd November, 1916. This arrangement has never been cancelled that I am aware of, and can be continued on account of any indigents who may require sustenance there.

I have passed vouchers in favour of William M. Jones of Morgans for £2, and Constable Lewis for £4:13:-, for payment.

2nd August, 1919.   CHIEF PROTECTOR OF ABORIGINES.
N/S.

Figure A7-G
Letter to Inspector Duncan, Kalgoorlie Police Station, from Neville, Chief Protector of Aborigines August 1919.
(State Archives, AN 1 /4 Acc 652, File 803, 1919.)

NOTE: Name obscured for reasons of privacy.

Rosie Green — Escape Documentation

The following extracts[1] from records made by police, the Superintendent of the Moore River Native Settlement and the Department of Native Affairs provide collaborative evidence and additional historical information for the events related by Auntie Rosie in Speakings 2.5.

A Warrant for Rosie's Potential Arrest and Removal

27 August 1940. The Commissioner of Native Affairs sends a warrant to the Commissioner of Police:

> Attached is a warrant for the removal of a half-caste woman named Rosie from the Laverton District to the Moore River Native Settlement. Rosie is out at Hootanui, about 100 miles from Laverton ... She is said to be very white and for this reason it is thought that she might be deserving of removal to the Settlement.

The Commissioner adds that the 'execution of the warrant' is to be left to the discretion of Constable Gravestock of Laverton and Mr Donegan of Cosmo Newbery; 'they may decide on her removal to the Settlement as set forth on the warrant ... if she appeals to them as a likely subject for training' for 'domestic service'.

Donegan and Gravestock attempt an execution of the warrant almost immediately.

Unsuccessful Attempts to Capture Rosie, 3–10 September 1940

Extracts from a report by Constable Gravestock, Laverton:

> Inspector Clements,
>
> I respectfully report leaving Station at 10.30am 3/9/40 and returning to Station at 11.30am 5/9/40, from Hootanui and

Mulga Queen off Inquiries for Halfcaste Rosie ... and report that on 3/9/40, P.C. Gravestock, Mr A.J. Donegan, and Trackers Jimmy, Pannican and Jacky, arrived at Hootanui in the Cosmo Newbery Ration Station Motor Truck at 5pm and after making inquiries found that Halfcaste Rosie [was] ... at Biddy's Flat about 20 miles from Hootanui towards Darlot. Party proceeded there arriving at about 5.45pm and found about 20 Natives camped at this place.

Inquiries were made and Natives stated Rosie [was] ... not camped there but Native Trackers found her Tracks where she had run away. The Tracks were followed for about 3 hours, and as they did not get too far away from the camp Party returned and P.C. Gravestock kept watch all night for Rosie ... to return for food and water. Rosie ... did not return through the night and at Daylight on the 4/9/40, Horse was obtained from an Halfcaste at the camp and Rosie's Tracks were again found and followed and Tracks led Party to the Breakaways a few miles from the camp where Trackers could not follow them and Party returned to the Native camp at about 5.30pm after travelling many miles Tracking Rosie. Several of the Natives from the camp tried to get Rosie to come from the Breakaways by Native Signals but she failed to respond and Party went back to Hootanui after dark ...

Party made further attempt to get Rosie by sending her Native father Old Tom who is now King of the Darlot tribe out to bring her in but he failed to find Rosie ... so Party had to return back to Laverton arriving at Laverton at 11.30am 5/9/40.

Party travelled 250 Miles in Ration Station Motor Truck in an endeavour to get Halfcaste Rosie ... Further endeavour will be made to get Rosie ...

P.C. Gravestock visited Cox's Find on 8/9/40 and again on 10/9/40, on Inquiries and whilst there made further inquiries as to the whereabouts of Rosie ... but so far there is no trace ... and no word has been received ...

Should Mr A.J. Donegan of Cosmo Newbery make a further visit to Hootanui Police will accompany him and give him every assistance to get Rosie ...

P.C. 1373 Laverton 11/9/40

Rosie's Imprisonment and Transit to Moore River

11 September 1940. Rosie is apprehended and detained by Leonora

Police. The Laverton Police instruct the Leonora Police by telegram to 'await Warrant and forward Rosie to Settlement, Native Affairs.' Rosie is held in the Leonora lockup for three nights.

14 September 1940. Rosie is taken under police escort, by $8^1/_2$ hour train journey, from Leonora to Kalgoorlie and is 'detained' in the Kalgoorlie Police Station overnight.

15 and 16 September 1940. Rosie's exile journey continues. She is taken by train, with police escort (Constable Mohr and Mrs Mohr) to Perth.

16 September 1940. Rosie arrives in Perth and is taken to the 'East Perth Natives' Receiving Depot' while arrangements are made by the Commissioner of Native Affairs as to where she should go next.

By this time, one week had elapsed since Rosie was first detained and locked up. Records viewed did not provide the date of Rosie's transfer from the 'East Perth Natives' Receiving Depot' to the Moore River Native Settlement.

The First Escape, 9 October 1940

The Department of Native Affairs is notified by Mr Paget, the Superintendent at the Moore River Settlement, that Rosie 'absconded and then returned voluntarily to the Settlement on the 9th inst.'

In the same letter, Paget proposes to the Department that Rosie be given the surname of Green, as he has already given her two brothers that surname.

The Second Escape, 17 March 1941

Mr Paget writes to the Commissioner of Native Affairs:

> I have to advise that three girls have absconded from this Settlement. Rosie Green, Ivy Wiluna, and Bessie Carnamah. Two have absconded before.
>
> The trackers are out after them and the Moora Police have been notified. These girls got away late last night.[2]

The Commissioner of Native Affairs Checks the Records, May 1941

20th May 1941

The Superintendent.
Moore River Native Settlement
Mogumber

On 17th March last you advised me that Rosie Green, Ivy of Wiluna and Bessie Carnamah had absconded from your Settlement the previous night.

Bessie Carnamah went to Yalgoo and is being employed by Constable Kay's wife in her house. However, Bessie is to be returned to the Settlement.

Have Rosie Green and Ivy of Wiluna been returned to the Settlement? If not, have you heard of their whereabouts? Action will have to be taken for their apprehension and return to the Settlement if they have not yet been secured.

Commissioner of Native Affairs.

The Commissioner of Native Affairs Alerts Police and Protectors, June 1941

6th June 1941

I wish to advise you that Rosie Green, a half-caste woman aged about 22 years [...] absconded from the Moore River Native Settlement on the 16th March Inst. She was accompanied by a half-caste girl named Ivy, aged about 15 years, who also absconded on the same date, and they are believed to be heading for Wiluna, as they originally came from the district between Wiluna and Leonora.

If you can locate Rosie and Ivy they are to be apprehended and returned to the Moora Police Station where they will be charged with absconding from the Moore River Native Settlement. If any natives at your centre know the whereabouts of these natives, would you kindly advise me as early as possible so that I can arrange to have the girls picked up and returned to Moora.

Commissioner of Native Affairs.

Addressed to Protectors of Natives at —
> Leonora,
> Wiluna,
> Meekatharra,
> Cue,
> Mt Magnet,
> Yalgoo,
> Mullewa,
> Geraldton,
> Lawlers.

Responses to the Commissioner's Request for Information, June 1941

Schenk of Mt Margaret Mission promptly replies. He attempts to secure domestic service employment for Rosie with the station-owner who employs her family:

> We find out that Rosie is at Nambi Station. Mr Fitzgerald ... would like Rosie to help his wife, and as that would satisfy his desire for the help that he has been wanting for so long, we hope that you will agree to give him a permit for her ...[3]

The response from Constable Kay at Yalgoo:

> In reply to yours of the 6th inst I have to advise that the half-caste woman Rosie Green and the half-caste girl Ivy Wiluna escaped from the Moore River Settlement together with Bessie Carnamah.
> They travelled on foot and on reaching Thundelarra Station (about 50 Miles south-east of Yalgoo) Bessie left them and came into Yalgoo.
> Bessie informs me that the other two were making their way back to Wiluna.[4]

The Commissioner Arranges for Rosie's Second Capture and Exile, June 1941

11 June 1941. Procedures established for Rosie's arrest. Refer to Figure A7-A, Memo from the Commissioner of Native Affairs to the Deputy Commissioner of Native Affairs.

12 June 1941. Extract from a letter from the Commissioner of Native Affairs to the Commissioner of Police, D Hunter.[5]

> I should now be pleased if you would arrange for Rosie to be apprehended again in accordance with the Hon Minister's Warrant, and returned to the Moore River Native Settlement.

D.C.N.A.

        Detective-Sergeant Cameron telephoned me from the Detective Office this morning to the effect that Rosie Green had been located at the Nambie Station, 45 miles from Leonora. Detective-Sergeant Cameron would like instructions as to the action to be taken for Rosie's return to the Settlement. So, far as he knows, no complaint was lodged at the Moora Police Station against her, and the only information that he has is that she was reported as a Missing Friend.

        Please take action to ascertain whether or not Mr. Paget lodged a complaint at Moora against Rosie for absconding. If not he should do so straight away, and so facilitate Rosie's arrest and return in due course under escort from Leonora. Immediate action should be taken.

C.N.A.
11/6/41.

Figure A8-A
Memo from Commissioner of Native Affairs, 11 June 1941.

Recapture, June 1941

12 June 1941. Constable Savage at Leonora Police Station, Protector of Aborigines, receives instructions by telegram 'to apprehend Rosie Green at Nambi Station via Leonora'.

13 June 1941. Rosie is arrested, removed from Nambi Station and taken to Leonora Police station.

Constable Savage makes a Belated Request for the Brokenhearted, June 1941

14 June 1941. Constable Savage writes to the Commissioner of Native Affairs:

> I have to report that ... I left on the morning of the 13th inst, and apprehended Rosie and ... brought her into Leonora Police Station.
>
> At 9.15a.m. 14th inst Constable Mohr & Wife as Matron left Leonora to escort Rosie ... to Kalgoorlie en route for Moora Police Station.
>
> Mr Fitzgerald of Nambi Station via Leonora, Who notified Me re Rosie's arrival at His Station, and at My request kept Rosie helping His Wife at the Homestead there, until I arrived out, Has requested Me to inform You that His Wife would very much like to employ Rosie at the Station, if You would approve of it ...
>
> Mr Fitzgerald is of the opinion that Rosie would be content at His Station, and His Wife thinks a lot of Rosie. And Rosie Herself seemed broken hearted when I had to take Her away from there, and stated She would not stop at the Settlement ...

Second Exile, June 1941

16 June 1941. Rosie Green, 'native woman prisoner' arrives in Perth after travelling for three days under police escort by train via Kalgoorlie. She is initially 'detained at Central Station', however, as 'it is felt that Rosie may abscond' the Commissioner of Native Affairs and the Commissioner of Police arrange for her to be 'held at the Central lock-up pending her transfer to Moore River Native Settlement'.[6]

19 June 1941. Rosie arrives back at the Settlement 'under Police escort'.[7] A week has elapsed since Rosie was removed from her family at Nambi Station.

25 June 1941. Rosie Green is taken before the Moora Police Court and receives a 'severe caution'. Refer to Figure A7-B.

6 September 1941. Wiluna Police, apparently not realising that Rosie is currently imprisoned at Moore River, are still looking for Rosie and Ivy in the Wiluna district. Refer to Figure A7-C.

The Overturning of the Warrant for Rosie's Detention, July 1942

25 July 1942. Letter from the Commissioner of Native Affairs:

The Honourable Minister for the North West,

In August 1940 you approved at p26 of the removal from Hootanui in the Laverton district to the Moore River Native Settlement of a halfcaste woman named Rosie Green. At the time, I expressed doubt as to the wisdom of Rosie's removal, and advised that the matter might be left to the decision of Constable Gravestock and Mr Donegan. In some cases it is useless removing halfcastes of tribal habits. Nothing can be done with them at the Settlement and as usually they are beyond training they more often than not are a source of trouble as invariably they abscond. For disciplinary reasons it is necessary to recapture them but there is a limit to this sort of thing since the absconders cause a lot of expense to the taxpayers in the shape of mileage, fares, escort fees etc.

Subsequently Rosie absconded and we were involved in an expense of £26.19.6 in bringing her back from Leonora.

As I am sure Rosie will abscond again I made some inquiries as to whether employment could be found for her in the district and have ascertained that Mr Fitzgerald of Nambi Station is willing to employ her as a house-girl. He also guarantees that she will not be allowed to go into the native camps ...

I think the commonsense course is to accept this offer and place Rosie in Mr Fitzgerald's care and employment.

I recommend, therefore, that you allow this course to be taken. Rosie is under your Warrant for detention at the Moore River Native Settlement; therefore she must remain there until you determine otherwise.

29 July 1942. Rosie's release from detention at the Moore River Settlement, and future employment by Mr Fitzgerald, is approved by the Minister for the North West, A M Coverly.

410 Appendices

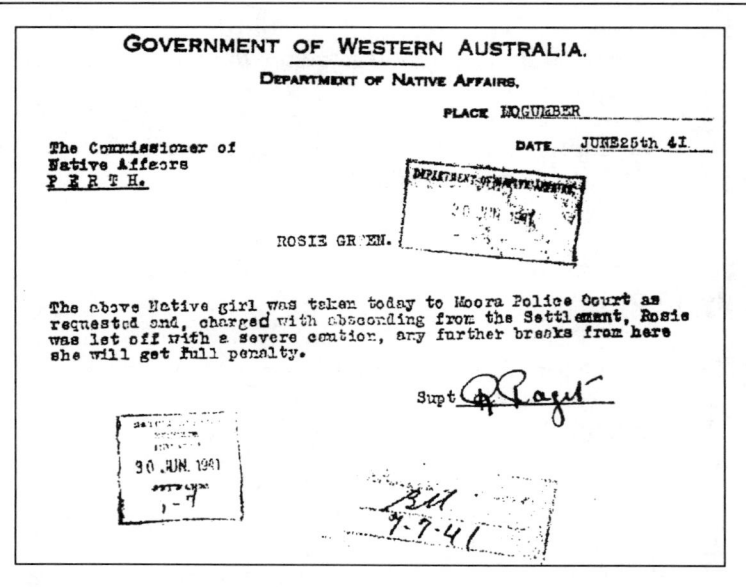

> **GOVERNMENT OF WESTERN AUSTRALIA.**
> **DEPARTMENT OF NATIVE AFFAIRS.**
>
> PLACE MOGUMBER
> DATE JUNE 25th. 41.
>
> The Commissioner of
> Native Affairs
> P E R T H.
>
> ROSIE GREEN.
>
> The above Native girl was taken today to Moora Police Court as requested and, charged with absconding from the Settlement, Rosie was let off with a severe caution, any further breaks from here she will get full penalty.
>
> Supt.

Figure A8-B
Letter from the Commissioner of Native Affairs, 25 June 1941.

> COPY, ORIGINAL ON D.N.A. FILE NO. 1266/38
>
> The Commr. Native Affairs,
> 57 Murray Street,
> PERTH
>
> Re Rosie Green, and Ivy halfcaste women
> abscondees from the Moore River
> Native Settlement.
>
> Dear Sir,
>
> Inquiries have been made throughout this district for the above mentioned women, but so far no trace of them can be found.
>
> Wiluna Station.   (sgd.) E.J. POLLETT.
> 6.9.41.   Sergt. 1189

Figure A8-C
Letter to the Commissioner of Native Affairs, 6 September 1941.

Notes on Cosmo Newbery, 1930s and 1940s

Wongutha people spoke to me of many undocumented aspects of the history they had experienced. One of the frequently occurring themes was that of Cosmo Newbery.

The people I met spoke to me with great horror in their voices of Cosmo. Wongutha people died there. Government rations were cut to a half-supply even in a time of severe drought and people starved. People were shot when they attempted to escape from Cosmo. The people were forced to undertake hard labour and were subject to verbal abuse and humiliation from Donegan.

Cosmo Newbery was established as a rations depot and reserve by Neville in January 1940. Wongutha people were removed from the Laverton district and from Mt Margaret Mission and placed under the dubious protectorship of A J Donegan. Donegan was consistently described as 'rough' by Wongutha people, even by those who had been inmates at the Moore River Settlement.[1]

> There was a story going round when I was a girl, that when the people escaped from Cosmo and were walking back to Laverton, Donegan saddled up his horse and chased them, then he sat on his horse and horse-whipped them all the way back to Cosmo. That's what people used to say.[2]

Another party of people who attempted to escape from Cosmo in order to return to Mount Margaret were shot at with blank cartridges and chased from the Cosmo area to the 'Ida H' mine area.[3]

Schenk's evidence corroborates with the oral testimonies that Wongutha people certainly died at Cosmo Newbery. Morgan quotes a December 1940 entry from Schenk's diary: 'Since Cosmo opened about 14 natives have died'.[4]

In February 1941 another escape party returned to Mount Margaret from Cosmo. The people at Cosmo had been told that 'they were never to leave there'. They 'received only half-rations'.[5]

According to Morgan, Neville ordered the removal to the Cosmo reserve of 'old people who had been at the Mission for over 15 years'. Also, 'full-blood children were ordered to be taken out of the school and sent there.' The group removed by the Department from Mt Margaret

Mission to Cosmo Newbery included financially independent people who owned their own camels.[6]

Mt Margaret Mission was no longer a certain safe haven. Refer to Figures A9-A and B for two memos of the Native Affairs Department.

Neville retired in March 1940, and F Bray became the Commissioner of Native Affairs.

Regional controls over the Wongutha were tightening: six remote mining centres scattered through the area, where they had once received rations and were accustomed to seeking and finding employment from the white population, were declared as 'prohibited areas' for Aboriginal people in 1941 and 1942. Burtville, Linden, Kookynie, Murrin Murrin, and Malcolm — Wongutha were prohibited from remaining in the vicinity of these small but vital trading and transportation centres.[7] (Refer to Figure A9-C.)

Schenk visited the Minister for Native Affairs, A M Coverley (who was also the Chief Secretary in Willcock's Labor Government) in November 1940 in Perth to discuss the situation at Cosmo. Coverley threatened to remove all the children from Mt Margaret if Schenk carried out his intention of publicising that the Department was removing children from Mt Margaret to Cosmo, despite the absence of a school at Cosmo, and removing the sick from Mount Margaret to Cosmo, despite there being no hospital at Cosmo.[8] Mt Margaret had both facilities. The Medical Officer who reported on Mt Margaret to the Department in 1942 stated that the hospital facilities were:

> without question equal to similar conditions in most country white hospitals. The dormitories were clean, neat, ODOURLESS and well lit. Psychologically the natives are well cared for and as a result all appear quite happy ... From an educational point of view, the work carried out by the native pupils, as shown on the walls of the well-ventilated, pleasant and well-lit school room, reflect great credit on them.

In the same report he comments on Cosmo Newbery, noting that Cosmo's 'real service' is in 'keeping the indigent and unemployed natives out of the township of Laverton, thus preventing them making nuisances out of themselves in and around Laverton'. These 'unemployed' people consisted of 'many young boys and men who should be given an opportunity later on to earn their own living'. And 'according to Donegan, the natives are of the bush type and, as yet, not quite used to civilisation.'[9]

The doubtful civilisation offered at Cosmo Newbery, and other matters relating to the history of the Cosmo area at this time, require further investigation and documentation which is, unfortunately, beyond the scope of this book.

D.C.N.A.

        Mr. Schenk makes reference to children, and I suppose there is correspondence about them somewhere, but I have not time to look for it. I believe I refrained from answering some of his communications in this regard because he wanted me to promise that the children would not be taken South at any time after their admission to his institution, and that promise I was not prepared to give.

        Please let somebody look up the references to these particular children.

[signature]

C.N.A.
10/5/38.

MR. BISHOP.

        Will you kindly tie up the relative papers?

        I recollect writing to Carlisle and Schenk respecting two children but I cannot now remember their names.

[signature]

11th May, 1938.
B/B.
D.C.N.A.

D.C.N.A.

        Please see files 39/38, 705/37 and 477/35(P.54) for correspondence re ▓▓▓▓ ▓▓▓▓ and ▓▓▓▓ respectively We have no separate file for ▓▓▓▓ but he is referred to at page 62 of this file.

31/5/38.

[signature]
RECORDS.

Figure A9-A
Memo regarding children who might be removed south.
(AN 1/7 Acc 993 1939. State Records Office. Western Australia.)

NOTE: Names obscured for reasons of privacy.

> D.C.N.A.
>
> I do not propose to give Mr. Schenk any information about Lorna and Thelma until we have dealt with the matter of the mother, as we would only disturb our chance of securing a conviction against the whites concerned.
>
> As to Myrtle, she is an orphan, and for very good reasons we are removing her to our Settlement.
>
> As to the position generally, the new Regulations define that, and they will be abided by as far as I am concerned. I am not prepared just now to give any ruling as to children generally in the Laverton District, as there are many considerations which govern the matter, such, for instance, as :
>
> 1. Our intention to establish a depot in the district.
>
> 2. The wisdom of taking in purely native children to a home of any sort, and thus depriving the parents of them. Such a policy, if adopted, must be State-wide. There is every probability that if handed over to Mr. Schenk these children would become inmates of a Mission for all time.
>
> C.N.A.
> 4/6/38.

Figure A9-B
Memo. Native Affairs Department.
(AN 1 /7 Acc 993 1937. State Records Office. Western Australia.)

NATIVE ADMINISTRATION ACT, 1905-1941.

PROHIBITED AREA. MUIRIE MURRIN.

PROCLAMATION.

WESTERN AUSTRALIA
To Wit

James Mitchell

LIEUTENANT-GOVERNOR.

By His Excellency Sir James Mitchell, K.C.M.G. Lieutenant-Governor in and over the State of Western Australia and its Dependencies in the Commonwealth of Australia.

WHEREAS by Section 42 of the Native Administration Act, 1905-1941, the Governor may by Proclamation, whenever in the interests of the natives he thinks fit, declare any municipal district or town or any other place to be an area in which it shall be unlawful for natives not in lawful employment to be or remain : NOW, THEREFORE I, the said Lieutenant-Governor, by and with the advice of the Executive Council, do hereby declare an area at Murrin Murrin, more particularly described in the attached Schedule, to be an area in which it shall be unlawful for natives not in lawful employment to be or remain.

Figure A9-C
Declaration of Prohibited Area.
(AN 1 /7 Acc 993 File 972 1941. State Records Office. Western Australia.)

Notes on Mt Margaret Goldfields Contact History (1890s)

The following notes reveal aspects of the 'first contact' history of the Mt Margaret and Laverton Goldfields. Europeans first passed though the area in 1869, the goldrush of the 1890s brought a rush of prospecting Europeans and Afghan cameleers to the area, and then the 1920s saw pastoralists settle there on a more permanent basis.

The notes are made up of extracts from the published writings of explorers and prospectors,[1] and from 1890s newspaper articles. These sources provide insight into the prevalent attitudes of the writers and the society for which they wrote, against which the 1921 events may be viewed.

A government surveying team under the leadership of John Forrest were the first Europeans to enter the Mt Margaret region. During the winter of 1869 they set out from Perth and headed east, looking for new pastoral country for the expanding Western Australian colony and for inland rivers that might promote overland communication with the colonies in the east. Forrest did not consider that he had found any useful pastoral country, but he named a prominent hill Mount Leonora (after his two children, Leo and Nora), and recommended to the Governor that geologists investigate the area's mineral potential.

From Forrest's diary (as published in his book), an extract dated 23 June 1869[2]:

> Started this morning, in company with Tommy Windich ... After travelling three miles towards Mount Lenora, saw a native's fire bearing N.E. about three miles, to which we proceeded, and surprised a middle-aged native. Upon seeing us, he ran off shouting, and decamped with a number of his companions, who were at a little distance. The horse I was riding — Turpin, an old police-horse from Northam — evidently well understood running down a native, and between us we soon overtook our black friend and brought him to bay. We could not make him understand anything we said; but, after looking at us for a moment, and seeing no chance of escape, he dropped his two dowaks and wooden dish, and climbed up a small tree about twelve feet high. After securing the dowaks, I fired my revolver

twice, and showed him the effect it had on the tree. The report had the effect also of frightening all the natives that were about, who no doubt made off at a great rate. I began to climb after him, but he pelted me with sticks, and was more like a wild beast than a man. After discovering we did not like to be hit, he became bolder and threw more sticks at us, and one hitting Tommy, he was nearly shooting him, when I called on him to desist. I then offered him a piece of damper, showing him it was good by eating some myself and giving some to Tommy. He would not look at it, and when I threw it close to him he dashed it away as if it was poison. The only way of getting him down from the tree was force, and, after considering for a moment, I decided to leave him where he was. We accordingly laid down his dowaks, and bade him farewell in as kindly a manner as possible.

David Carnegie's exploration and prospecting party arrived in the newly 'discovered' Mt Margaret Goldfields in May 1894. Carnegie's book records his surprise at finding Europeans prospecting in that area. He also notes the various forms of resistance fighting taken by the indigenous people attempting to force the early Europeans to leave or perish:

On the 22nd day we were surprised at cutting a freshly made dray-track, along which it was clear that many had passed — and the next day arrived at the Red Flag, an alluvial rush that had 'set in' during our sojourn in the sand. This came as a great surprise, as we had no idea that gold had been found so far afield. This camp, some twelve miles north-east of Mount Margaret, consisted then of only forty or fifty men, though others were daily arriving. These were the first white men we had seen for seven weeks, and they were greatly astonished to see us, when they learned what direction we had come from ...

We heard that hundreds had started for the rush, but this camp represented all who had persevered, the rest being scared of the distance. This reads funny now when Mount Margaret is as civilised as Coolgardie was then, and is connected by telegraph, and possibly will soon be boasting of a railway ...

The blacks had been very troublesome, 'sticking up' swagmen, robbing camps, spearing horses, and the like. It is popularly supposed that every case of violence on the part of the natives, may be traced to the brutal white man's interference in their family arrangements. No doubt it does happen that by coming between man and wife a white man stirs up a tribe, and violence results, but in the majority of cases that I know of, the poor blackfellow has recklessly speared, wounding and killing, prospectors' horses, because he wanted food or amusement. A man does not travel his packhorses into the bush for the philanthropic purpose of feeding the aboriginals, and naturally resents his losses and prevents their recurrence in a practical way.[3]

Stanton quotes further evidence of widespread resistance by the Wongutha people:

Early in 1895, the diggers at Mt Margaret were brought close to starvation by the repeated loss of provisions and draught animals to the local Aboriginal groups. A wagon-load of food was dispatched from Coolgardie by one of the shopkeepers as soon as the news reached the town, and this ensured the survival of the prospectors over the summer.[4]

The reminiscences of prospector Norman Sligo, as published in his book *Mates and Gold*,[5] further illuminate certain aspects of life on the Mt Margaret goldfield in the goldrush days of the 1890s. The book contains certain inaccuracies of chronology,[6] but it reveals much that is independent of time — Sligo's book provides graphic insight into the publishable attitude of an 1890s prospector towards the Aboriginal inhabitants.

Sligo's text also contains an account which testifies to the high speed that Wongutha people could sustain when undertaking long distance journeys on foot:

'TIGER'

When 'Tiger' or Wimbah — his native name — was found dead near the Kensington Hotel about three miles east of Menzies on 14 October 1898, Sergeant Duncan, Constable Hoy and Johnny Rowe immediately set off to investigate.

Tiger and Johnny Rowe had been shepherding for the butchers Whitford & Co., and Tiger, a north-west native, was aware that the local tribe were after him.

When found no injury was visible but a slit in his waistcoat revealed a small puncture wound under the left shoulderblade. A reconstruction by the native trackers showed that he had been working on a boomerang while waiting for his billy to boil and had been speared from about 20 to 30 feet. It was thought that the killing was either revenge for his stealing a Pendinnie tribe gin or his finding and reporting that the man McInnes had been killed by natives ... Two trackers Nimbool and Bingee with Sergeant Hoy trailed the killers through hard and hilly ground via Cane

Grass, Bardoc, Broad Arrow and to Kanowna.* There Hoy arrested Caldari, Yilberi, Woollie and Moodigur. Caldari the dwarf claimed to be the killer. They had covered a little more than 140 miles on foot in very little of 48 hours.[7]

Sligo's book contains many accounts of attacks made by Aboriginal people on prospectors, and much description of the landscape and his discomfort in it. His language at all times is revealing — he uses phrases like 'to conquer and settle the waste lands' — and contextually interesting. The extracts following have been selected for readily apparent reasons:

> In February 1894 ... two prospectors Gilbert Harry Swincer and the writer were camped at a small soak about thirty miles south of Mt. Margaret in the North Coolgardie goldfield.
> In those days water was scarce, and gold seekers often bestowed as much time and energy looking for water, as they spent in search of the precious metal ... In the year mentioned the aboriginals in this locality were war-like and dangerous[8]

> ... before 5 a.m. I was on the track to Pendinnie.† All that day we travelled through auriferous country, but not a trace of water and knowing I would have a dry camp that night, I selected the best patch of feed I had seen for some miles, and camped for the night. The night passed without incident, and after breakfast I yoked up and was soon following up the track ... At sunset I arrived at the soak, which can be described as a small hole scooped out in the middle of a sandy creek ... I was surprised to find a fire burning, and a hasty glance showed dozens of naked footprints, men, women and children's ... I made a virtue of necessity and resolved to make a bold bid for possession of the soak and camp. After short hobbling the horses, I cut down boughs and built a regular stockade round the cart, firmly lashing the saplings together, leaving only one small opening, leading under the cart; then after loading the rifle and revolver, I raked together the blacks' camp fire and prepared tea. As soon as darkness set in I commenced firing occasional shots into the nearest clump of bush, then after a brisker cannonade, I crept under the cart and vainly

---

* *Kanowna is approximately 10km northeast of Kalgoorlie. Distance covered was 225km in less than 48 hours (and this journey was taken directly after a similar journey to get to Menzies).*

† *Approximately 50km south-southwest of Mt Margaret.*

trying to keep awake fell asleep.

Whether it was the effects of a badly cooked damper or nervousness I cannot tell but my sleep was anything but peaceful. I could see blacks creeping from all directions, while numberless twinkling eyes seemed to be watching and peeping through the bushes of my stockade. I noted in particular one old black fellow with an enormous beard walking slowly round the stockade and digging a spear through each opening. Nearer and closer he came to the space leading under the cart and good heavens he dropped on his knees to creep in. The sweat poured off me while I made herculean efforts to reach my revolver. I could almost feel the barbed spear touching my flesh as he leaned backwards to put weight into the thrust. With a yell of horror, I sprang up, bumping my head so hard against the axle of the cart that I went down just as quickly. Grabbing my revolver I blazed through the bushes, pulling the trigger as fast as my fingers would allow. By this time I was thoroughly awake and at the fifth shot a yell some yards distant told me that I had either wounded a native or the bullet had gone close enough to singe him ...

Next morning I could see sufficient evidence to prove that the natives had been round the cart in large numbers and unless I had awakened at the right moment would have had a poor chance with this tribe, who numbered over half a thousand and were a dangerous lot. Nothing eventful occurred during the day while through the night I was extremely wakeful and vigilant, firing off my rifle or revolver at intervals.[9]

...

When we rode over the diorite ranges on the east side of the valley the blacks were chasing two prospectors half a mile south of the soak, one of whom repeatedly turned and menaced the blacks with his rifle. We did not care about butting in at this juncture as strange witnesses are not wanted in any fights with the blacks.[10]

The following extracts relate to a resistance fighter named Culgul (Tommy) who was active in the country to the west of Leonora. Interestingly, the passages also note the introduction of stock into the goldfields, and draw attention to the pastoralists' influence on government policy and police action towards Aboriginal people:

In April 1898 the Granite Creek tribe led by Culgul, alias Tommy, raided a camp on Stuart Meadow station taking firearms and ammunition. Constable Breen from Lawlers encountered them but due to the nature of the country they got away. Many horses were speared ... at one place 15.[11]

> ... At about 3.00 a.m. on 24 January 1895 a shower of spears was thrown. One transfixed Kellas through the breast ... He lived until 31 January, dying in great agony. This was at 'Maunn' or 'Manna' some 40 miles NNW of Menzies ... A few weeks later Ebsary and mate were attacked by the same tribe at Granite Creek.
>
> The killer was Tommy ... Hayden was also speared by him in August 1895. He had been seen in Coolgardie shortly after killing Kellas and there were many complaints that he was not arrested. The view was that the government was prepared to harass prospectors for defending their lives, but not control the natives — until of course stock entered the area, when police raids would start. But then, to a bucolic government, bovines evidently had a higher market value than prospectors. It is no wonder that some vigilantes took care of their problems without recourse to the absent authorities.
>
> Tommy and Billy (Merrin) were finally captured at Mt. Ida in late May 1898 and both received twelve months imprisonment and twelve strokes of the cat of nine tails.[12]

The following extracts relate to a resistance fighter whom the prospectors and police called Jimmy. The incidents related by Sligo occurred in an area about 100km from Mt Margaret, to the south of Murrin Murrin:

> Harry was standing with his arm thrown over the grey mare's neck and seemed to be looking down into the soak; looking further ahead where the Mulgas fringed the edge of the valley, I could discern scores of blacks creeping towards Harry, some of them being within eighty yards and several had their spears fitted into the wommeras ready to throw. I jumped on my hack and galloped down the steep slope; reaching the level ground I fired haphazardly into the nearest fringe of Mulga. As my rifle rang out, Harry startled from his reverie, took in the situation, and without more ado took cover behind his mare's shoulder while the long barrel of his Martini Henry glided across her withers and the skirr of the bullet ended in a shout from the blacks, drowned by the long hiss of scores of spears. Our rifle fire had disconcerted their aim, but peering into the scrub, we could see their leader encouraging them to attack, while the women seemed anxious for a retreat. In a short time they again mustered courage and about four hundred strong made a forward move, the men leading while the women with fresh relays of spears brought up the rear.

Their leader, afterwards known as Jimmy ... rarely showed himself but one herculean fellow fully six feet three inches high, was conspicuous in the front rank of the attackers.

The situation now became serious and once more our rifles spoke while the black leader met with an accident to his leg, but squirming behind a tree was immediately assisted by the blacks to a safe position. While waiting for further eventualities Harry recounted having met some camel men from the Hawk's Nest country who were stuck up by blacks at this soak and among other stores were robbed of eighty sovereigns. It was hastily decided that we would endeavour to collect these sovereigns, and as I had previously met Jimmy, the leader, it was arranged that I would endeavour to coax him from the main body. With this object in view we placed our rifles between the two horses, and covered by Harry's revolver and my own handy, I walked into the bush a short distance, calling on Jimmy and holding out a plug of tobacco, Jimmy took the bait and slowly approached, glancing alternately at Harry's revolver and the stick of tobacco. Finally holding out his hand for the tobacco, he was made a prisoner, and alternately led or hauled, arrived alongside Harry. We now showed Jimmy a sovereign and he explained that a fellow tribesman had plaited them in his hair and had gone westward. At this juncture the black was squirming and I asked Harry to give me a spell. Just as he relieved me a black gin, coming from nowhere, darted between the horses, picked up both rifles, and ran for the scrub. Harry let Jimmy go, and fired a shot from his revolver which so frightened the gin that she dropped the rifles and disappeared into the thicker scrub, while Jimmy's tail end could be seen like a black streak disappearing in the same direction. Immediately we retrieved our rifles the blacks commenced a hasty retreat while we, chagrined at being nearly outwitted and out-generalled. We mounted our horses and galloped in pursuit. Revolver in hand we chevied them for about six miles, in our rear over one hundred women were running screaming directions to the pursued and as we made no attempt to injure them they became bolder and one black damsel more warlike than her fellows rushed at me when we were passing some thick bush, armed with a log almost as thick as herself she aimed a heavy blow at my head as I trotted past ... After pursuing them to within a mile of the Wallaby Rocks, we returned to their camp near the soak and broke up all the spears and war implements stored at their whurlies ... I will add before closing that notwithstanding all the spearing and shooting nobody was badly injured ...[13]

> ... about seventy blacks could be seen running towards us. Quickly unslinging our rifles we closed up the horses and waited results: as they came nearer we could distinguish several of the blacks including our old friend, Jimmy. On they came, apparently without weapons, and making every demonstration of peace. Their leaders now commenced to crowd close, while a large number spread out in a semicircle about forty yards distant. Looking keenly round, I noticed several spears which the natives were endeavouring to keep out of our sight, and drawing Harry's attention to this old trick, we moved on threatening to shoot anyone who followed.[14]

The *Western Mail* carried the following report of Jimmy in 1898:

> Mount Malcolm, August 12. The notorious Stone Creek native, Jimmy, who was found guilty at Mt Margaret of camp robbery, and who is suspected of having murdered several prospectors, was escorted to Mt Malcolm on Tuesday by Constable Topliss, preparatory to being taken to Rottnest. Jimmy gave the Mt Margaret police a lot of trouble, breaking away from the log to which he was chained.

These events provide a contextual background against which the events of 1921 may be viewed. It is unfortunately beyond the scope of this book to further investigate the histories of indigenous resistance in the Mt Margaret/Laverton region — it is clear that such history is waiting to be written.

By 1899, the Mt Margaret township, the one-time centre of the Mt Margaret Goldfields, was dwindling. Extensive flooding from Lake Carey made the mines too expensive to maintain — they were abandoned and residents of Mt Margaret moved to Mt Morgans and to Laverton. Laverton was rapidly becoming the central 'town' for administrative purposes, although in 1899 a townsite had not yet been declared. The turn of the century saw the removal of the post and telegraph office, and also the hospital, from Mt Margaret to Laverton, signalling the end of Mt Margaret's prominence. Twenty years later Schenk purchased the abandoned buildings at the already 'old' Mt Margaret townsite for use at his fledgling mission.

By 1921, pastoralists were actively engaged in enclosing Wongutha land.

Wongutha people spoke to me of undocumented massacres that occurred during the 1920s — a number of informants stated that groups of Wongutha people had been shot by pastoralists in reprisal for sheep spearing. They named many locations, including Lakewood and Edjudina; the knowledge of these events had been passed on to them by grandmothers who had run away and escaped the shooting. These stories were not part of the taped constructions of their own stories, but were told to me later. Learning to live with the past perhaps is facilitated by a slow accumulation of knowledge.

Legislation: Review of Development of Legislation in Western Australia Affecting Aboriginal People in 1921

The *Aborigines Protection Act 1886*, passed by the British Parliament, established the 'Aborigines Protection Board' in Western Australia in order to provide legal protection to Aboriginal people in Western Australia. The Board exercised supervision of 'all matters affecting the interests and welfare of the "aboriginals"'.[1] The provisions of the Act included the following:

- 'Aboriginals' could be prohibited from entering or remaining in towns.
- The Board could appoint honorary local protectors (usually policemen) to oversee rationing and medical care of 'aboriginals' and to report on the condition of 'aboriginal' children.
- The Board was to prepare recommendations for the Governor regarding 'the care, custody and education' of children of 'aboriginals'.
- Aboriginal children and 'half-caste' children (of a 'suitable age' if younger than 21) could be apprenticed out only by permission of Resident Magistrates acting under the instruction of the Board, and only if provisions were made to ensure the child's 'proper and humane treatment' in addition to clothing and maintenance.[2]

Guardianship of children was first removed from Aboriginal parents and vested in an institution under the *Industrial Schools Act 1874*. Children under the age of twenty-one who 'voluntarily surrendered' themselves, or who were surrendered by 'any parent or apparent guardian or friend', to a school or institution would be compelled to remain under the legal and exclusive guardianship of the manager of that institution until they reached the age of twenty-one.

This Act, then, gave local protectors the potential to remove children from their families, either by attempting to persuade Aboriginal parents to relinquish their children in order to have them educated, or by persuading children to leave, or by forced removal if, in the protector's view, the child was 'apparently' an orphan.

The *Aborigines Act 1897* created the State-managed Western Australian Aborigines Department and abolished the British Parliament's Aborigines Protection Board. The Department's duties were similar to those of the former Board, with the major change being that it now was to 'provide' for the care, custody and education of children of 'aboriginals', in place of advising the Governor about such matters. The Department was therefore more autonomous and less accountable.

The Act allocated the Department an annual budget of £5,000, thereby intentionally replacing the 1% of annual Government revenue which the Western Australian Constitution of 1889 specified as the amount to be annually allocated to providing for Aboriginal Western Australians. However, in 1904 it was realised that this provision made the Act invalid due to its inconsistency with the Western Australia Constitution which had been enacted by the British Parliament. *The Aborigines Act 1905* validated the previous invalidity, and repealed both the *Aborigines Act 1897* and the *Aborigines Protection Act 1886*.

In 1904 a Royal Commission, headed by W E Roth, inquired into the condition of Western Australia's Aborigines. Roth criticised police and employer exploitation of Aborigines. The Commission found that the treatment of Aboriginal prisoners was harsh, that the arrests of Aboriginals were 'brutal and outrageous',[3] that the Chief Protector had no power to enforce the *Aborigines Protection Act*, and that Aboriginal people were employed without employment contracts despite legislative requirements. Roth's recommendations were not adopted in full, but those relating to the regulation of the conditions of employment of Aborigines, the establishment of local protectors, prohibitions of inter-racial marriages, and the guardianship of the Chief Protector over children formed the basis of the 1905 Act.

The *Aborigines Act 1905* increased the control exercised over Aboriginal people in Western Australia by the Chief Protector, reducing considerably any opportunities for personal and community autonomy, and imposing severe restrictions on personal freedoms. Haebich describes the Act as:

> the basis for the development of repressive and coercive state control over the state's Aboriginal population. It set up the necessary bureaucratic and legal mechanisms to control all their contacts with the wider community, and to enforce the assimilation of their children and to determine the most personal aspects of their lives.[4]

This Act defined 'aboriginal' as follows:

— 'an aboriginal inhabitant of Australia';
— 'a half-caste who lives with an aboriginal as wife or husband';
— 'a half-caste, who otherwise than as wife or husband, habitually lives or associates with aborigines';
— 'a half-caste child whose age does not apparently exceed 16 years'.

'Half-caste' was defined as including any person born of an

'Aboriginal' parent on either side and the child of such a person.
The Key Provisions of the Act were as follows:
— The Board could appoint honorary local protectors (usually policemen) to oversee rationing and medical care of 'aboriginals' and report on condition of 'aboriginal' children.
— Such protectors were empowered with authority to grant permits for employment of 'aboriginal' males under 14 years of age, and 'aboriginal' females.
— Written permission of a protector was required if any 'aboriginal', any male 'half-caste' under 16, or any female 'half-caste' was to 'remove' from a district by their own choice, or to be removed for purposes of employment etc.
— The Minister for Aboriginal Affairs was empowered to arbitrarily remove 'aboriginals' from one reserve or district to another.
— The marriage of an 'aboriginal' woman and a 'non-aboriginal' man would require permission from the Chief Protector.
— The Minister could exempt 'aboriginals' from the Act. Such an exemption was not permanent and could be cancelled.
— Regulations could be made pertaining to the 'care, custody and education of the children of aborigines and half-castes', and could be made for the purpose of 'enabling any aboriginal or half-caste child to be sent to and detained in an aboriginal institution, industrial school or orphanage'.

And such regulations were made. The Aborigines Protection Regulation 1909 empowered police, other local protectors and Justices of the Peace to remove any 'half-caste' child to a mission or institution.

The *Aborigines Act Amendment Act 1911* caused Aboriginal mothers to lose their rights to their 'illegitimate half-caste' children. The Chief Protector was made their legal guardian, 'to the exclusion of the rights of a mother of an illegitimate half-caste child'. As 'mixed marriages' were forbidden (unless permission could be gained from the Chief Protector) any child except a 'full-blood' child would be considered illegitimate by the State.

Mary Montgomerie Bennett stated to the Moseley Commission in 1934 that, under these laws, 'they are captured at all ages, as infants in arms, perhaps not until they are grown up, they are not safe until they are dead.'[5]

Hasluck notes that during the 1920s the Chief Protector was increasing his reach:

> Some persons hitherto unnoticed were classified as Aborigines. This tendency spread during the 1920s ... Anyone with an Aboriginal ancestor must be treated as an Aboriginal and regarded as being different in nature, in entitlements and in way of life from all other Australians and human beings.[6]

The power of the Chief Protector to exert control over Aboriginal people was extended at various times, most notably in 1936 when the definition of an Aboriginal person who came under the Act was expanded. The 1905 Act and the 1909 Regulation were not repealed until the *Native Welfare Act* in 1963.

So then, in 1921, the autocratic power of the Chief Protector of Aborigines was formally established, and his guardianship of 'every Aboriginal and half-caste child' set in place. Local 'honorary' protectors were often policemen, and were more likely to act in their authoritative capacity as a policeman and from their allegiance to the white community, than as a protector of the personal rights of Aboriginal people. Protection of Aboriginal people generally meant protection from exploitation and abuse by the white community. In a situation where there was a conflict of interest between his role as protector of Aboriginal people and that of maintaining white law and acceptable order, in addition to popularity with his peers, he was 'first and foremost a member of the white community and a policeman'.[7]

Furthermore, a local protector was required to refer 'protective' matters to the Chief Protector in distant Perth. A policeman was not required to refer matters to the Protector, and could also carry out the removal of Aboriginal persons to an institution, as the Act specified, without referral and without delay. A policeman could act rapidly and decisively. One critic noted that 'Mr Neville seems hand-in-glove with the police.'[8]

For more detail of relevant Legislation and its effects on Aboriginal people, refer to:

A Haebich. *For Their Own Good; Aborigines and Government in the Southwest of Western Australia, 1900–1940*. University of Western Australia Press. 1988.

Bringing Them Home. Report of the National Inquiry into the Separation of Aboriginal and Torres Strait Islander Children from Their Families. Human Rights and Equal Opportunity Commission. 1997.

P Biskup. *Not Slaves, Not Citizens*. University of Queensland Press. 1973.

G Bolton. 'Black and White after 1897' in CT Stannage (ed.) *A New History of Western Australia*. Nedlands, University of Western Australia Press. 1981.

A Haebich. 'On the Inside: Moore River Native Settlement in the 1930s' in B Gammage and A Markus (eds) *All that Dirt: Aborigines 1938*. Canberra. 1982.

P Hasluck. *Black Australians; A Survey of Native Policy in Western Australia 1829–1897*. Melbourne University Press, 1942; 2nd ed, 1970.

Task Force on Aboriginal Social Justice. *Report of the Task Force*. Vol. 1. April 1994.

Endnotes

INTRODUCTION
1. Chris Healy. *From the Ruins of Colonialism. History as Social Memory.* Cambridge University Press. Cambridge, United Kingdom. 1997 p7.
2. Bill Bunbury. *Reading Labels on Jam Tins. Living Through Difficult Times.* Fremantle Arts Centre Press in association with the Australian Broadcasting Corporation. 1993.

2. SPEAKINGS

Introduction to the Speakings
1. Refer to Appendix A3 'Explanations of Process' for details of the process of hearing the stories, recording the stories, speakers' reviews of the transcripts, permission to publish and other explanations.

Rosie Meredith
1. Refer to Appendix A8 'Rosie Green — Escape Documentation' for collaborative records compiled by the Aborigines Department.

Margaret Morgan
1. Morgan, Margaret. *Mt Margaret: A Drop in a Bucket.* Margaret and Keith Morgan. 1986.

3. WRITINGS

3.0. Introduction to the Writings
1. At around this time I found another record of the exile and escape story in Margaret Morgan's book about Mt Margaret Mission. Morgan, quoting evidence from her father's journal and letters about these events, also dated the story in 1921. I traced Mrs Morgan and she was willing to be interviewed, but was initially not willing to allow me access to her father's diary and letters. Subsequently, Mrs Morgan kindly allowed me access to Schenk's personal documentation.
2. Material that examines such topics as the Moore River Native Settlement, or the Chief Protector Neville and his ideas, actions and effects on State policy and Department practice has been previously published. The history and experience of Goldfields Aboriginal people, however, is almost entirely undocumented, and the daily events of small Goldfields towns have similarly been overlooked. Thus it has been considered important to establish a context in which to view the events in Laverton in 1921.

Refer to Appendix A11, for a brief overview of legislation affecting Aboriginal people in 1921, to Appendices A7 and A8 for examples of Neville's dealings.

3. Refer to:

A. Haebich. *For Their Own Good; Aborigines and Government in the Southwest of Western Australia, 1900–1940.* University of Western Australia Press. 1988.

Bringing Them Home. Report of the National Inquiry into the Separation of Aboriginal and Torres Strait Islander Children from Their Families. Human Rights and Equal Opportunity Commission. Sydney. April 1997.

P. Biskup. *Not Slaves, Not Citizens.* University of Queensland Press. 1973.

G. Bolton, 'Black and White after 1897' in CT Stannage (ed.) *A New History of Western Australia.* Nedlands, University of Western Australia Press. 1981.

A. Haebich. 'On the Inside: Moore River Native Settlement in the 1930s' in B. Gammage and A. Markus (eds). *All that Dirt: Aborigines 1938.* Canberra. 1982.

P. Hasluck. *Black Australians; A Survey of Native Policy in Western Australia 1829-1897.* Melbourne: Melbourne University Press, 1942; 2nd ed, 1970.

S. Maushart. *Sort of a Place Like Home: Remembering the Moore River Native Settlement.* Fremantle Arts Centre Press. 1993.

For a wider overview of the general political context of Western Australia at the time, the reader is referred to the following:

C T Stannage (ed.). *A New History of Western Australia.* Nedlands, University of Western Australia Press, 1981.

Bobbie Oliver. *War and Peace in Western Australia: The Social and Political Impact of the Great War 1914-1926.* Nedlands, University of Western Australia Press. 1995.

3.1. Laverton Police Letter Books

1. As stated previously, certain records such as the Charge Books and Occurrence Books from the Laverton Police Station were not able to be located by the State Archivist, although currently only the Charge Books are officially listed as missing. Permission to access other archives, in particular those records relating specifically to the 'Protection' of Aboriginal people by the Local Protector, and his correspondence with the Aborigines Department (AN5/3 ACC430, 4763 Laverton Police Protection) was unobtainable from the Department of Aboriginal Affairs; these files are 'closed'.

2. Haebich, Anna. 1988:87.

3. 'aggressive times' — for some background accounts of the contact history, refer to Appendix A10 — Notes on Contact History (1890s).

4. Even as late as 1947 this sentiment was still keenly felt; the quote is from a police officer who described Laverton as 'the most Easterly outpost of civilisation in the State'. (Anderson, A F. 'A Bush Patrol'. Laverton Police Station, Western Australia. 1947 unpublished).

5. Thompson's role as Protector/defender would have been compromised

by his role as Police/prosecutor in charging the Wongutha. This was inherent in the system. The provisions of the 1905 Act would suggest that sentences for offences against the Act could only be passed by either two local Justices of the Peace (white men of Laverton) or a travelling Magistrate (John Elton Geary, of Menzies — Acting Stipendiary Magistrate for North Coolgardie, Mt Margaret, East Murchison Magisterial Districts; Acting Magistrate of Local Courts in Menzies, Leonora, Laverton, Lawlers and Wiluna; and Warden for North Coolgardie, Mt Margaret Goldfields and Wiluna and Lawlers Districts of the East Murchison Goldfields. [*Government Gazette* No 43, Tuesday September 13, 1921]). Local courts could only impose sentences of up to six months duration, with or without hard labour. (Haebich, A. *For Their Own Good. Aborigines and Government in the Southwest of Western Australia 1900-1940*. University of Western Australia Press, Nedlands, for the Charles and Joy Staples South West Region Publications Committee. 1988 p87,88).

6. Refer to Appendix A4 — 1921 Escape and Pursuit for discussion on whether or not Thompson knew they had returned, and why they were not eventually recaptured by Laverton police.
7. (July 1921) Annual Report — The report date is obscured by a document pasted over it, but can be assumed to be the 1921 July annual report due to the following:

    The page pasted over the top of the report/attached to same page in book is dated 27/6/21, and contains instructions about the details to be supplied in the Annual Report.

    The next record entry is dated 1/10/21; the previous record entry is dated 11/4/21.

3.2. R S Shenk's Letters and Diary

1. AN 1/ 4 ACC 653 File 6/20, State Archives, Battye Library, Perth
2. AN5/Laverton ACC 3354/1 2 July 1919.
3. Moved from Laverton to the common at King's Well near the old Mt Margaret mining town, along with Jim Jago, also of the Australian Aborigines Mission.
4. Mt Margaret Common.
5. Schenk was given an honorary Protectorship in 1928. However, ten years of criticism of the actions of the local police, the Chief Protector and the Department did not escape Neville's notice and displeasure. Neville wrote a telegram to Schenk in 1938, saying pointedly, 'We all get criticism and recently I have had more than a fair share from you.' *(AN1/7 Acc993 File905 1939 p106)*

    In Neville's report on Mt Margaret Mission in September 1939, he wrote: 'The Commissioner visited Mt Margaret Mission on the 6th, 7th, and 8th September 1939. Unfortunately the visits ... were considerably marred by Mr Schenk's hostile attitude toward the Department generally and the Commissioner in particular. Mr Schenk did not hesitate to voice his opinions in the presence of natives and made use of the utmost invective.

His attitude was most unwarranted and disloyal.' *(AN1/7 Acc993 File905 1939 p7)*

Neville was so displeased with Schenk that he withdrew Schenk's Protectorship, and in 1940 transferred the title and the duties of Protector to the Department's employee Mr A J Donegan at Cosmo Newbery Native Settlement. Government rationing was also withdrawn from Mt Margaret and transferred to Cosmo.

3.3. Moore River Settlement Records

1. For contextual material relating to the Moore River Native Settlement (Mogumber), refer to Part 2: Speakings, and to Writings 3.6.
2. G Bolton 'Black and White after 1897' in CT Stannage (ed), *A New History of Western Australia*, University of Western Australia Press, Nedlands. 1981:138,139. (Hereafter Bolton in Stannage, 1981.)
3. Correspondence, Moore River Native Settlement, Mogumber. AN 1/6 ACC 1326. (See Also Figure 3.3-A)
4. Refer to the Department's Annual Report of 1920–21 in Appendix A7.
5. Haebich, A. 1988: 203.
6. 17 June 1921. Secretary to Campbell. Correspondence, Moore River Native Settlement, Mogumber. AN 1/6 ACC 1326 (p70)
7. Comparison of the various lists of names can be found in Appendix A5.
8. The Secretary was constantly entreating Campbell to be more efficient and accurate. In May 1922 the Secretary advised him that his April records showed multiple inmates with the same allocated numbers, and that one of the inmates not yet recorded as discharged on his records had died — the Department had received a death notice for this inmate in 1920.

    Further, Campbell's 'list of names, numbers etc for the inmates of this Settlement' for May 1922 was sent back to him with the following message from the Secretary: 'Will you please let me have a fresh type written copy as early as possible, the copies you sent me up are useless.' (AN 1/6 ACC 1326)

    Appendix A5 compares the lists of names of admitted Laverton people with those who escaped.
9. Dion was the elder brother of Kunjel, who was about ten years old in 1923. (Morgan, private communications, and Morgan, 1986:57, 149.) His age is not listed by the Superintendent at Moore River Settlement at the time of his admission (listing age was the usual practice for any child admitted), which might suggest that the Superintendent considered him an adult. However, his transfer to Moore River Native Settlement from a children's mission home (refer to Figure 3.3-F) suggests that he had recently been considered a child.
10. Refer to Speakings, also to Morgan, 1986:23, 96.
11. For example, AN5/Laverton ACC3354/1 p 214, 216, 228 and as documented in Writings 3.1.
12. As previously stated, access to the 'Protection' Records of the Laverton

Protector of Aborigines, Constable 292, (AN5/3 ACC430 4763) was withheld by the Aboriginal Affairs Department. The Occurrence & Charge Books of the Laverton Police are 'Missing' from the State Archives. Therefore, it has not been possible to ascertain for how long or for what reasons Joe and Ginger were sentenced. The 1919 Annual Report of Constable 292 of Laverton records 12 'native' convictions, with an unspecified number of those offenders receiving sentences of two-and-a-half-year duration. (Refer to Writings 3.1)

13. Morgan, 1986:149, 150.
14. Swan Mission — the 'Anglican Swan Native and Half-caste Home'. Opened in 1871, children living there received education according to the State School curriculum as well as training for domestic and farm work. Between 1915 and 1920 the government halved expenditure on missions and from 1915 all children under the legal guardianship of the Chief Protector were sent by the Department to the Moore river and Carrolup Settlements instead of the mission homes. The Swan Home, along with Dulhi Gunyah Orphanage, the Ellensbrook Mission, and the Salvation Army Girl's Home in Kalgoorlie, all closed as a result of these practices — Ellensbrook in 1917, Dulhi Gunyah in 1919, the Swan Home late in 1920 (Haebich 1988:8,168), and the Salvation Army Home in 1921 (Aborigines Department Annual Report 1921 — Refer to Appendix A7).
15. Letter to Inspector Duncan, Kalgoorlie from Constable 292, Laverton 11/4/21. Refer to Writings 3.1.
16. Schenk, Letter to friends, July 1922. Refer to Writings 3.2.

3.4. William Harris' Letter to the *Sunday Times*

1. Neville: 'pioneering' quoted in Schenk's letter home (Laverton, April 24, 1921); 'semi-civilised' quoted in P Biskup *Not Slaves Not Citizens*. University of Queensland Press. 1973:122 (reference in original text: N.WT 6/1920); 'white man' quoted in A Haebich *For Their Own Good; Aborigines and Government in the Southwest of Western Australia, 1900–1940*. University of Western Australia Press. 1988:276 (reference in original text: A 94/1928).
2. When Harris led the first Aboriginal Deputation to the Premier of Western Australia in 1928, the *West Australian* described him as from the 'North-West'. In 1927, however, Harris was campaigning for the Native Union (which he had founded the previous year) in several places in the south of the state, 'drumming up support' and visiting Aboriginal groups in various areas. (Haebich, 1988:272)
3. Refer to Appendix A6 for the analysis that led to this conclusion.

3.5. Absences in Contemporary Writing

1. Daisy Bates, *The Passing of the Aborigines: A Lifetime Spent Among the Natives of Australia*. London John Murray (1938), 1944 p94. (Hereafter Bates 1944).
2. Bates 1944:95–6.
3. ibid:96.

4. Report of Inspector Mitchell to the State Education Department, noted by Neville as a 'glowing report'. State Archives AN 1/4 Acc 993.
5. Morgan 1986:136
6. *West Australian*, 17 May 1932
7. G Bolton 'Black and White after 1897' in C T Stannage (ed.) *A New History of Western Australia*. Nedlands, University of Western Australia Press 1981 p147. (Hereafter Bolton in Stannage 1981.) (Referencein original text: Premier's Department 166/1932)
8. Bolton in Stannage 1981 p147.
9. Moseley Commission evidence (10 March 1934, qn 315) quoted in Bolton in Stannage 1981 p147.
10. M M Bennett *Teaching the Aborigines: Data from Mount Margaret Mission* W.A. Perth, 1935 (Hereafter Bennett 1935).
11. Quoted in Grono, William (ed). *Margins. A West Coast Selection 1829–1988.* Fremantle Arts Centre Press 1988:18.
12. Bennett, Arthur. *Dryblower Murphy: His Life and Times*. Fremantle Arts Centre Press (Community Publishing Project) 1982:1.
13. 'The Aliens' in Murphy, E.G. (Dryblower). *Dryblower's Verses.* Perth undated circa 1924 p42
14. 'A howl for a holiday' *Kalgoorlie Sun*, Kalgoorlie. 28 January 1912.
15. Murphy c1924:14,15.
16. Grono 1988:18.
17. Telegram from Governor Newdegate to Lord Milner, 21 January 1921. Archbishop Clune Papers, St Mary's Catholic Church Archives, Perth. Quoted in Oliver 1995:208
18. Stanley Davidson in Bill Bunbury *Reading Labels on Jam Tins. Living through Difficult Times.* Fremantle Arts Centre Press 1993. p120. Also Stella Villa: 'You could feel this undercurrent of hostility towards the foreign element, particularly Italians.' [p101] A few pages later Bunbury notes that 'Australia in the 1920s and 1930s was British Australia and all peoples not British were not only less fortunate but less tolerated.' [p106].
19. Frederick William Ophel ('Prospect Good') 'The Prospectors', in the *Kalgoorlie Sun*, Kalgoorlie. 1 February 1903.
20. Laverton police correspondence during WWI also evidences hostility towards the 'enemy' found in miners of German and Italian background. (AN5 Acc 3354/1)
21. Wyallie in Speakings 2.6, Ranji McIntyre in Speakings 2.2 and 2.3.
22. May O'Brien in Speakings 2.7
23. Schenk. Letter, 24 April 1921. Unpublished. Refer to Writings 3.2.
24. Refer to Writings 3.1 and 3.2.
25. Schenk. Letter. 1 July 1921. Unpublished. Refer to Writings 3.2.
26. Elizabeth Wills 'Canon Edward Collick. The Priest' in Lyall Hunt (ed.) *Westralian Portraits* University of Western Australia Press, Nedlands 1979 p122. (Hereafter Wills in Hunt 1979).

27. Wills in Hunt 1979:120–123.
28. ibid. :120.
29. Schenk. Letter, 24 April 1921. Unpublished. Refer to Writings 3.2.
30. ibid.
31. Refer to Appendix A7.
32. H P Smith (ed.) *The First ten years of Mount Margaret Mission, WA: as given in a letter, following a visit to Mt Margaret by Mr Robert Powell and extracts of prayer letters, written during the years by Mr R. S. Schenk.* United Aborigines Mission, (Keswick Book Depot) Melbourne, c1933 p18. (Hereafter Smith c1933.)
33. Smith c1933:13.
34. For example, when three young girls escaped from the Moore River Native Settlement in the winter of 1931, the *West Australian* contained the following article:
    'Missing Native Girls'
    'The Chief Protector of Aborigines, Mr A O Neville, is concerned about three native girls, ranging from eight to fifteen years of age, who a week ago, ran away from the Moore River Native Settlement, Mogumber. They came in from the Nullagine district recently, Mr O' Neville said yesterday, and, being very timid, were scared by their new quarters, apparently, and fled in the hope of getting back home. Some people saw them passing New Norcia, when they seemed to be heading north-east. The children would probably keep away from habitations and he would be grateful if any person who saw them would notify him promptly. 'We have been searching high and low for the children for a week past,' added Mr O'Neville, 'and all the trace we found of them was a dead rabbit which they had been trying to eat. We are very anxious that no harm may come to them in the bush.' (From the *West Australian* 11 August 1931. Quoted in Doris Pilkington/Nugi Garimara. *Follow the Rabbit Proof Fence.* University of Queensland Press, St Lucia. 1996 p102.)
35. No responses were found in editions of the *Sunday Times* published over the next months, however, Haebich (1988:208) implies a later response to Harris' letter. (Refer to Section 3.6, Interpretive Accounts and Absences in Recent Writings for Haebich's text.)
36. Refer to Appendix A7.

3.6. Interpretive Accounts and Absences in Recent Writing

1. Bill Bunbury, 'Out of Sight, Out of Mind. Aboriginal Internment' in *Reading Labels on Jam Tins. Living Through Difficult Times.* Fremantle Arts Centre Press in assoc. with the Australian Broadcasting Corporation. 1993 p182. (Hereafter Bunbury 1993.) This book was based on the ABC radio documentary 'Out of Sight, Out of Mind (Moore River 1916-1950)' produced by Bill Bunbury.
2. ibid.:180.
3. ibid.:182.
4. ibid.

5. ibid.
6. Recorded in 1986 for the ABC radio documentary 'Out of Sight, Out of Mind (Moore River 1916–1950)' produced by Bill Bunbury.
7. prison ... at Mt Gould — A police camp was established at Mt Gould in 1888 by a Constable Christmas who arrived there with two horses from Geraldton. By 1896 three mounted constables with four 'native assistants' were stationed at this camp patrolling the Mt Gould & Peak Hill area. In 1903 the police camp at Mt Gould was closed. ('Distribution of the Police Force,' Appendix, in the Annual Reports of the Commissioner of Police, various years. Battye Library.)
8. Recorded in 1986 for the ABC radio documentary 'Out of Sight, Out of Mind (Moore River 1916–1950)' produced by Bill Bunbury.
9. Aborigines Protection Board — the Victorian equivalent of the Western Australian Aborigines Department.
10. Alice Nannup, Lauren Marsh and Stephen Kinnane. *When the Pelican Laughed*. Fremantle Arts Centre Press. 1992: 74. (Hereafter Nannup 1992).
11. Morgan conducted interviews with Mysie Schenk in the 1980s.
12. Margaret Morgan, interview with author. 22 March 1997.
13. [...] — some of Morgan's text is omitted at this point.
14. Margaret Morgan. *Mt Margaret: A Drop in a Bucket*. Margaret and Keith Morgan. Perth. 1986. (Hereafter Morgan 1986.)
15. Personal communication M Schenk to M Morgan. c 1980. Private Collection.
16. ibid.
17. Morgan 1986:118.
18. Neville to Jigalong Police (21/10/31 File 175/30) quoted in Doris Pilkington *Follow the Rabbit Proof Fence*. University of Queensland Press. 1996:126. (Hereafter Pilkington 1996.)
19. Pilkington 1996:71.
20. Peter Biskup. *Not Slaves, Not Citizens*. University of Queensland Press 1973:123. Biskup does not cite his specific sources for Schenk's accusation of the Police nor the letter to Neville about these events. I was unable to find these two documents in the Aboriginal Affairs Department's files that were 'open' for research in 1997-1999.
21 Pamela Rajkowski. *Linden Girl. A Story of Outlawed Lives*. University of Western Australia Press. Nedlands. 1995.
22 ibid.:152-157.
23. ibid.:158.
24. ibid.:169.
The quote about flour is actually referenced: Letter from Police Constable Warren to Chief Protector of Aborigines, 1923 Acc 993, File 484/26. However, this seems unlikely. Rajkowski's footnote reference numbering appears to be mixed up. The previous quote is attributed in the text to Constable Warren and this reference probably applies to that quote. This quote is attributed in the text to an 'elderly Wongai', and matches the next

footnote reference to an interview with Reggie Johnston by Bill Bunbury in December 1986. This statement about flour is definitely made by Johnston to Bunbury in 1986, as seen in the extracts of the interview reproduced earlier in this chapter.
25. Quote is referenced: Letter from R Schenk to Copping, 27 June 1926, Acc 993, File 484/26. Rajowski 1995:117.
26. Norma King. *Colourful Tales of the Western Australian Goldfields.* Rigby Publishers Limited. 1980.
27. The details as told to me in 1997 in all cases corroborate this written account recorded fifteen or so years earlier. Some phrases, despite Heslop's editorial input, are almost identical to those I heard.
28. Ranji McIntyre in Jim Heslop (ed.) *Recollections of Mount Margaret.* Aboriginal Education Branch. [Undated, c1980s, no page numbers]. (Hereafter Heslop c1980.)
29. Phyllis Thomas in Heslop c1980:no page numbers.
30. Jean McKenzie in Heslop c1980:no page numbers.
31. Ron Bonney in Heslop c1980:no page numbers.
32. Cyril Barnes in Heslop c1980:no page numbers.
33. Francis Murray in Heslop c1980:no page numbers.
34. Bill Wesley in Heslop c1980:no page numbers.
35. Haebich 1988:208.
36. ibid.:205,206.
37. ibid.:218.
38. ibid.:113.
39. As quoted (unnamed source) in Schenk's Diary. (Unpublished) 10 July 1921.
40. As quoted by Schenk, Letter, 24 April 1921.
41. Interview with Margaret Morgan, 22 April 1998.

4. A New Account
1. For omparative analysis of evidence refer to Appendices A4, A5, A6.
2. Diane Barwick 'Writing Aboriginal History. Comments on a book and its reviewers.' *Identity.* Vol 4, No 7, June 1982:7–14; also Peter Read, 'What oral history can't tell us: the role of the CD-Rom' *Oral History Association of Australia Journal* . No. 16 1994: 87–90; also Neil Gunson. 'Proud Shoes: Black Family History in Australia.' *Aboriginal History.* 5(2) 1982.
3. Their recollections are documented in Speakings.
4. Refer to Appendix A3, Explanations of Process, for discussion of the process that led to construction of a narrative account rather than a conventional historical account.
5. Ngunnu. Refer to Speakings 2.6.
6. Rosie Meredith. Refer to Speakings 2.5.
7. AN5/Laverton Acc3354/1 p174, 5 June 1915. Refer to Writings 3.1.

438 Endnotes

8. Rosie Meredith. Refer to Speakings 2.5.
9. Ranji McIntyre (1). Refer to Speakings 2.2.
10. Reggie Johnston to Bill Bunbury. Interview recorded in 1986 for the ABC radio documentary 'Out of Sight, Out of Mind (Moore River 1916–1950)' produced by Bill Bunbury.
11. Ranji McIntyre (2). Refer to Speakings 2.3.
12. Ranji McIntyre (1). Refer to Speakings 2.2.
13. ibid.
14. AN5/Laverton Acc3354/1 p214, 2 July 1919. Refer to Writings 3.1.
15. ibid. p174, 5 June 1915. Refer to Writings 3.1.
16. ibid. p214, 2 July 1919. Refer to Writings 3.1.
17. ibid. 11 April 1921. Refer to Writings 3.1.
18. ibid.
19. ibid.
20. ibid. p174, 5 June 1915. Refer to Writings 3.1.
21. ibid.
22. ibid.
23. ibid. 11 April 1921. Refer to Writings 3.1.
24. ibid. p174, 5 June 15. Refer to Writings 3.1.
25. Wyallie. Refer to Speakings 2.6.
26. AN5/Laverton Acc3354/1, p201, 1 July 1917. Refer to Writings 3.1.
27. ibid. p174, 5 June 1915. Refer to Writings 3.1.
28. ibid. 11 April 1921. Refer to Writings 3.1.
29. ibid. p214, 2 July 1919. Refer to Writings 3.1.
30. ibid. 11 April 1921. Refer to Writings 3.1.
31. ibid. p214. 2 July 1919. Refer to Writings 3.1.
32. Margaret Morgan Refer to Speakings 2.9.
33. AN5/Laverton Acc3354/1, 11 April 1921. Refer to Writings 3.1.
34. ibid. 1/7/1922. Refer to Writings 3.1.
35. Schenk, Annual Report for 1921. Refer to Writings 3.2.
36. Schenk, Letter 24 April 1921. Refer to Writings 3.2.
37. Schenk, Annual Report for 1921. Refer to Writings 3.2.
38. AN5/Laverton Acc3354/1, 11 April 1921. Refer to Writings 3.1.
39. ibid. p226, July 1921. Refer to Writings 3.1.
40. ibid. 11 April 1921. Refer to Writings 3.1.
41. Margaret Morgan. Refer to Speakings 2.9.
42. AN5/Laverton Acc3354/1 p226, July 1921. Refer to Writings 3.1.
43. Schenk, Letter 24 April 1921. Refer to Writings 3.2.
44. Sligo, N K. *Mates and Gold: Reminiscences of the Early Westralian Goldfields, 1890–1896*. Hesperian Press, Perth. 1995: 165.

45. Schenk, Letter, 1 August 1921. Refer to Writings 3.2.
46. AN5/Laverton Acc3354/1 p226, July 1921. Refer to Writings 3.1.
47. ibid. 11 April 1921. Refer to Writings 3.1.
48. ibid.
49. ibid.
50. Schenk, Letter, 24 April 1921. Refer to Writings 3.2.
51. ibid.
52. Reggie Johnston to Bill Bunbury. Interview recorded in 1986 for the ABC radio documentary 'Out of Sight, Out of Mind (Moore River 1916–1950)' produced by Bill Bunbury.
53. Reggie Johnston. Refer to Speakings 2.1.
54. Schenk, Letter, 2 May 1921. Refer to Writings 3.2.
55. ibid.
56. Rosie Meredith. Refer to Speakings 2.5.
57. Wyallie and Ngunnu. Refer to Speakings 2.6.
58. Reggie Johnston to Bill Bunbury, op.cit.
59. May O'Brien. Refer to Speakings 2.7.
60. Schenk, Letter, 24 April 1921. Refer to Writings 3.2.
61. Wyallie and Ngunnu. Refer to Speakings 2.6.
62. May O'Brien. Refer to Speakings 2.7.
63. Schenk, Letter, 24 April 1921. Refer to Writings 3.2.
64. ibid.
65. ibid.
66. May O'Brien. Refer to Speakings 2.7.
67. Wyallie. Refer to Speakings 2.6.
68. Reggie Johnston to Bill Bunbury, op. cit.
69. AN5/Laverton Acc3354/1 p227, 1 October 1921. Refer to Writings 3.1.
70. Schenk, Annual Report for 1921. Refer to Writings 3.2.
71. Schenk, Letter, 9 May 1921. Refer to Writings 3.2.
72. ibid. 24 April 1921. Refer to Writings 3.2.
73. ibid. 9 May 1921. Refer to Writings 3.2.
74. Reggie Johnston to Bill Bunbury, op. cit.
75. AN5/Laverton Acc3354/1 p226. July 1921. Refer to Writings 3.1.
76. Reggie Johnston to Bill Bunbury, op cit.
77. Harris, in *Sunday Times*, 14 November 1926. Refer to Writings 3.4.
78. Margaret Morgan. Refer to Speakings 2.9.
79. Ranji McIntyre (1). Refer to Speakings 2.2.
80. Margaret Morgan. Refer to Speakings 2.9.
81. Wyallie and Ngunnu. Refer to Speakings 2.6.
82. Schenk. 26 September 1921. Refer to Writings 3.2.

83. Biskup 1973:123.
84. AN5/Laverton Acc3354/1 p227, 1 October 1921. Refer to Writings 3.1.
85. Ranji McIntyre (2). Refer to Speakings 2.3.
86. ibid. (1). Refer to Speakings 2.2.
87. ibid. (2). Refer to Speakings 2.3.
88. Queenie Donaldson. Refer to Speakings 2.4.
89. Rosie Meredith. Refer to Speakings 2.5.
90. Sandstone in Haebich 1988:218.
91. Nannup in Bunbury 1993:182.
92. Haebich 1988:210, 211.
93. ibid. 205.
94. ibid.
95. May O'Brien. Refer to Speakings 2.7.
96. Fred Meredith. Refer to Rosie Meredith, Speakings 2.5.
97. ibid.
98. ibid.
99. ibid.
100. Fred and Rosie Meredith. Refer to Speakings 2.5.
101. Nannup in Bunbury, 1993:182.
102. Fred Meredith. Refer to Rosie Meredith, Speakings 2.5.
103. Harris, in *Sunday Times* 14 November 1926. Refer to Writings 3.4.
104. Haebich 1988:218.
105. Queenie. Refer to Speakings 2.4.
106. May O'Brien. Refer to Speakings 2.7.
107. Reggie Johnston. Refer to Speakings 2.1.
108. May O'Brien. Refer to Speakings 2.7.
109. Rosie Meredith. Refer to Speakings 2.5.
110. Ranji McIntyre (2). Refer to Speakings 2.3.
111. ibid. (1). Refer to Speakings 2.2.
112. ibid. Refer to Speakings 2.2.
113. ibid. Refer to Speakings 2.2.
114. Rosie Meredith. Refer to Speakings 2.5.
115. Queenie Donaldson. Refer to Speakings 2.4.
116. Reggie Johnston to Bill Bunbury, op cit.
117. Reggie Johnston. Refer to Speakings 2.1.
118. Ranji McIntyre (1). Refer to Speakings 2.2.
119. Morgan 1986:72.
120. ibid.:26.
121. Margaret Morgan. Refer to Speakings 2.9

122. Ranji McIntyre (2). Refer to Speakings 2.3.
123. Rosie Meredith. Refer to Speakings 2.5.
124. Ranji McIntyre (1). Refer to Speakings 2.2.
125. Morgan 1986:24.
126. Margaret Morgan. Refer to Speakings 2.9.
127. Reggie Johnston. Refer to Speakings 2.1.
128. Morgan 1986:26.
129. Margaret Morgan. Refer to Speakings 2.9.
130. Ranji McIntyre (2). Refer to Speakings 2.3.
131. Rosie Meredith. Refer to Speakings 2.5.
132. Wyallie. Refer to Speakings 2.6.
133. Reggie Johnston to Bill Bunbury, op. cit.
134. Rosie Meredith. Refer to Speakings 2.5.
135. Margaret Morgan. Refer to Speakings 2.9.
136. Rosie Meredith. Refer to Speakings 2.5.
137. Wyallie. Refer to Speakings 2.6.
138. Ranji McIntyre (1). Refer to Speakings 2.2.
139. ibid.
140. Rosie Meredith. Refer to Speakings 2.5.
141. Ranji McIntyre (2). Refer to Speakings 2.3.
142. ibid. (1). Refer to Speakings 2.2.
143. Rosie Meredith. Refer to Speakings 2.5.
144. ibid.
145. Morgan 1986:25.
146. Ranji McIntyre (1). Refer to Speakings 2.2.
147. ibid.
148. ibid.
149. Morgan 1986:25.
150. Reggie Johnston. Refer to Speakings 2.1.
151. May O'Brien. Refer to Speakings 2.7.
152. ibid.
153. Ngunnu. Refer to Speakings.
154. Sadie Canning. Refer to Speakings 2.8.
155. Bates 1944:94.
156. Ngunnu. Refer to Speakings 2.6.
157. Ranji McIntyre (1). Refer to Speakings 2.2.
158. ibid.
159. ibid.
160. Rosie Meredith. Refer to Speakings 2.5.

161. ibid.
162. Schenk, Diary. Refer to Writings 3.2.
    Note: Of those 15 days, some were spent in captivity in the train and some in captivity at Moore River. In 1940, it took over a aweek for Rosie Green to be transferred from Leonora to the Moore River Settlement. In 1941 this transit time was again one week. (refer to Appendix A8.) I have estimated a minimum of five days for transit and period of captivity at Mogumber for the 1921 group. Trains were more frequent in 1921 than in 1940.) This group probably spent less than ten days travelling home, including the day on the train from Kalgoorlie to Laverton. They covered a distance of 1000km, of which they walked about 700km, along a well-defined route. (They walked about 80km per day if they walked for the longest possible time span of nine days, or faster and further per day if they had more time at Mogumber and less time walking, and faster and further again per day if they had arrived back some time prior to allowing Schenk to see them on 30 August.) Their speed, compared to the other groups, may have been due to the fact that they could walk on a cleared road or track by night and that they were following a clearly marked route with a ready water supply close at hand. (Whereas, the central route walkers were making their way through scrub and uncleared bushland.) Perhaps the people who chose to take this potentially risky pipeline route were the fastest and most able of the escapees (whereas the Northern route walkers who might also have taken advantage of walking on roads at night included the elderly Wunu and Jinera.) They may also have 'jumped' the train for some of the journey to Kalgoorlie. As early as the 1890s, Wongutha people were jumping the trains. (Refer to Appendix A10.)
163. Wyallie. Refer to Speakings 2.6.
164. Margaret Morgan. Refer to Speakings 2.9.
165. Schenk. Diary. Refer to Writings 3.2.
    Note: Those who took this route walked a total of about 550km through roadless, unmarked, bush-covered country, their route set by the stars and the sun alone, and then caught the train for the next 200km of their journey. They walked about 50kms per day if they walked for the longest time span of eleven days, or faster and further per day if they had more time at Mogumber and less time walking, and faster and further again per day if they had arrived back some time prior to Schenk seeing them on 2 September.
166. Reggie Johnston. Refer to Speakings 2.1.
167. ibid.
168. May O'Brien. Refer to Speakings 2.7.
169. Note: This group covered a distance of 830km, walking all the way, along both moderately defined routes and cross country.
170. Schenk, Letter, 30/12/1921. Refer to Writings 3.2.
171. Reggie Johnston Refer to Speakings 2.1.
172. ibid.
173. Ngunnu. Refer to Speakings 2.6.

174. Reggie Johnston. Refer to Speakings 2.1.
175. Margaret Morgan. Refer to Speakings 2.9.
176. ibid.
177. Reggie Johnston to Bill Bunbury, op. cit.
178. ibid.
179. ibid.
180. Margaret Morgan. Refer to Speakings 2.9.
181. ibid.
182. Reggie Johnston to Bill Bunbury, op. cit.
183. Margaret Morgan. Refer to Speakings 2.9
184. Reggie Johnston to Bill Bunbury, op. cit.
185. Morgan 1986:27.
186. Margaret Morgan. Refer to Speakings 2.9.
187. Ranji McIntyre (1). Refer to Speakings 2.2.
    Note: Blind Jinera's journey covered approximately 1300km, of which he walked about 820km.
188. ibid.

APPENDICES

Notes and Glossary

A3. Explanations of Process

1. Deborah Bird Rose. *Nourishing Terrains: Australian Aboriginal views of landscape and wilderness.* Australian Heritage Commission, Canberra, 1996: 1.
2. Read, Peter. 'A phantom at my shoulder. The final draft of Charles Perkins: a biography'. in Ian Donaldson, Peter Read, James Walter (eds.) *Shaping Lives: Reflections on Biography.* The Humanities Research Centre Monograph Series 6. ANU Canberra 1992: 169.
3. Healy, Chris. *From the Ruins of Colonialism. History as Social Memory.* Cambridge University Press, 1997: 14.
4. ibid. 7.
5. ibid. 14.
6. Stannage, Tom. 'Introduction' in Diane Barwick, Michael Mace and Tom Stannage (eds.). *Handbook for Aboriginal and Islander History.* Aboriginal History, Canberra, ACT. 1979.
7. Wadley, Ian. 'Worlds Apart: A Proposal for Frame Reflective Discourse in International Environmental Negotiations' in Lawrence E Susskind, William Moomaw, Kevin Gallagher (eds.). *International Environmental Negotiations: An Integrative Approach.* Papers in International Environmental Negotiation, Vol. 9, PON Books (Program on Negotiation at Harvard Law School), Cambridge Massachusetts, 1999:131.
8. Extract from the 'Draft Declaration for Reconciliation' in the *Draft Document for Reconciliation.* Council for Aboriginal Reconciliation. 1999.

Supplementary Text

A4. 1921 Escape and Pursuit

1. Alice Nannup, Lauren Marsh and Stephen Kinnane. *When the Pelican Laughed*. Fremantle Arts Centre Press. 1992: 63.
2. *West Australian* August 1921 (after 15th August — notes lost.) Left hand side of page.
3. Haebich. 1988: 218.
4. For example, see Doris Pilkington/Nugi Garimara's *Follow the Rabbit Proof Fence*. University of Queensland Press, St Lucia. 1996.
5. Refer to Writings 3.1. Also, note that the file of correspondence between the Chief Protector and Constable Thompson, the Protector at Laverton, remains closed.
6. Schenk, Letter to friends, 30 December 1921. Unpublished. Refer to Writings 3.2.
7. Refer to Writings 3.1
8. ibid.
9. Schenk, Letter to friends, 1 August 1921. Unpublished. Refer to Writings 3.2.
10. ibid. 2 May 1921. Unpublished. Refer to Writings 3.2.
11. Schenk. Annual Report 1922. Unpublished. Refer to Writings 3.2.
12. Schenk. Letter to friends, 24 April 1921. Unpublished. Refer to Writings 3.2.
13. Schenk. Annual Report 1922 and Letter to friends 24 April 1921. Unpublished. Refer to Writings 3.2.
14. Schenk. Letter to friends, 2 May 1921. Unpublished. Refer to Writings 3.2
15. ibid. 24 April 1921. Unpublished. Refer to Writings 3.2
16. Refer to Writings 3.6, Interpretive Accounts and Absences in Recent Writings.
17. AN 1/7 Acc 993 File 487. 1937: 36, 29, 54.
18. ibid.: various.
19. Morgan 1986:83, Speakings 2.7, also AN 1/7 Acc 993 905 1939.
20. AN 1/7 Acc993 905 1939. Report on Mt Margaret by the Comissioner of Native Affairs, A O Neville Esq, 26 September 1939.
21. AN 1/7 Acc 993 File 487. 1937: 7.
22. ibid.: 12.

A5. 1921 People

1. Refer to Writings 3.3.
2. Refer to Writings 3.2.
3. Morgan 1986: 21.
4. Inmates Register Record Book, Moore River Native Settlement AN 1/6 ACC 1326. p10.

A6. William Harris' Evidence

1. Refer to Writings 3.1 for relevant records.
2. 1 October 1921 Laverton Protector of Aborigines to the Deputy Chief of Aborigines, Perth. AN5/Laverton ACC3354/1.
3. Refer to Margaret Morgan's *Mt Margaret: A Drop in a Bucket*. 1986: 32–43.

A7. Notes from A O Neville's Files

1. Telegram from Neville, 2 December 1938, AN 1/7 Acc993 File 487. 1937: 106.
2. Source: State Archives, AN 1/4 Acc 653 File 479, 1921. The Annual Report for the year ending 30 June 1922 was unavailable for viewing.
3. ibid., AN 1 /4 Acc 652, File 803, 1919.
4. Refer to Figure 2.6-F for the Circular Attached.
5. 'settlements such as we have on the coast' — the Moore River and Carrolup Native Settlements.

A8. Rosie Green — Escape Documentation

1. Extracts — Some details have been omitted at the request of Rosie Meredith.
2. Letter. R Paget, Superintendent at Moore River Native Settlement (Mogumber), to the Commissioner of Native Affairs, Perth. 17 March 1941.
3. R S Schenk, Mt Margaret Mission, Morgans, to the Commissioner of Native Affairs, Perth. 10 June 1941.
4. Constable Kay, Yalgoo Police Station, to the Commissioner of Native Affairs, Perth. 12 June 1941.
5. Dave Hunter, the Commissioner of Police, was a police constable in Laverton earlier in his career and in 1921 was known to the Wongutha as 'the bad man'.
6. Letters from the Commissioner of Native Affairs to Superintendent Paget, Mogumber, and to the Commissioner of Police, Perth. 17 June 1941.
7. Letter from Superintendent Paget, Mogumber, to the Commissioner of Native Affairs, 19 June 1941.

A9. Notes on Cosmo Newbery

1. Rosie Meredith's mother was taken to Cosmo Newbery by Donegan; Rosie had been at Moore River Settlement. (Refer to Speakings 2.5). Corroborative statements were also made by Ranji McIntyre. (Refer to Speakings 2.2). Numerous other people spoke of Donegan's reputation, but 'off the record'.
2. Informant's name withheld at their request.
3. Morgan 1986: 250.
4. Schenk, December 1940, Diary. Quoted in Morgan 1986: 251.
5. Schenk, February 1941, Diary. Quoted in Morgan 1986: 251.
6. Morgan 1986: 249.
7. AN 1/7. Acc 993 various files, 1941, 1942.
8. Morgan 1986: 250. (No further reference cited in Morgan's text.)
9. Medical Officer to the Commissioner of Native Affairs AN1/7 Acc993 File 487 p173, 4 February 1942.

A10. Notes on Mt Magaret Goldfields Contact History

1. Few sources are available relating to the history of contact between pastoralists and the Wongutha, however Schenk's records, as presented in Writings, provide some context.
2. Forrest, J. *Explorations in Australia*, Manston and Searle, London, 1875 (Facsimile edition 1969): 49–50.
3. Carnegie, D. *Spinifex and Sand: a narrative of five years pioneering and exploration in Western Australia.* London: Arthur Pearson. 1898. Ringwood, Vicoria: Penguin facsimile. 1973: 58–60.
4. Reid, A. *Those Were the Days.* Perth: Barclay and Sharland. 1933: 189. Quoted in John Stanton. 'Conflict, Change and Stability at Mt Margaret: an Aboriginal Community in transition.' PhD thesis, University of Western Australia, 1984: 92.
5. Sligo, N K. *Mates and Gold: Reminiscences of the Early Westralian Goldfields, 1890–1896.* Perth: Hesperian Press. 1995.
6. Sligo's introduction acknowledges that his chronology may not always be correct, and that some people's names have been misspelled or altered (Sligo. 1995: vi).
7. Sligo, NK. 1995: 231–232.
8. ibid.: 164–165.
9. Sligo, NK. 1995: 99–100.
10. ibid.: 113.
11. *Western Mail*, 13 May 1898.
12. Sligo, NK. 1995: 140–144. Sligo makes reference to the *Coolgardie Pioneer*, 28 May 1898 and the *Western Mail*, 27 May 1898 in connection to these passages.
13. Sligo, NK. 1995: 112–113.
14. ibid.: 178–179.

A11. Legislation Review

1. *Bringing Them Home. National Inquiry into the Separation of Aboriginal and Torres Strait Islander Children from Their Families.* Human Rights and Equal Opportunity Commission. Commonwealth of Australia. 1997: 629).
2. ibid.: 630.
3. Task Force on Aboriginal Social Justice. *Report of the Task Force.* Vol. 1. Perth. April 1994: 36.
4. Anna Haebich. 1988: 83.
5. Quoted in *Bringing Them Home.* op. cit. p109.
6. Paul Hasluck. *Mucking About. An Autobiography.* University of Western Australia Press, Nedlands. 1994: 244.
7. Hasluck. 1994: 245.
8. Schenk, quoted inMorgan. 1986: 223.

Figures and Illustrations

Introduction
Map 1: Western Australia. (C Wadley Dowley.)
Map 2: Laverton area. (C Wadley Dowley.)

Journeying
Photographs. (C Wadley Dowley.)

Writings
Section 3.1: Laverton Police Records
   Figure 3.1-A: Letter of appointment of Constable EP Thompson, Laverton, as Protector of Aborigines. (AN 1 /3 Acc 652 75 1915.)
Section 3.3: Moore River Native Settlement Records
(AN 1/6 Acc 1326 State Record Office. Perth.)
   Figure 3.3-A: Correspondence April/May 1921, Superintendent of the Moore River Native Settlement (MRNS) and Secretary of the Aborigines Department.
   Figure 3.3-B: August 1921. Correspondence, Superintendent of the MRNS and Secretary of the Aborigines Department.
   Figure 3.3-C: Admissions and Departures List, September 1921. MRNS.
   Figure 3.3-D: Register of Inmates, MRNS. 1921.
   Figure 3.3-E: List of Admissions and Departures, May 1919. MRNS.
   Figure 3.3-F: List of Admissions and Departures, October 1919. MRNS.
   Figure 3.3-G: List of Admissions and Departures, undated, 1921. MRNS.
   Figure 3.3-H: Register of Inmates. MRNS.
   Figure 3.3-I: List of Admissions and Departures, March 1922. MRNS.
   Four photographs (Battye 12227P/12222P/12238p/12246P.)

A New Account
Map 3: Routes of the Escapees. (C Wadley Dowley.)

Appendices

Appendix A5 : 1921 People: Who were exiled? Who escaped?
  Table A5-A: Archive Records from Moore River: Admissions and Escapes.
  Table A5-B: Matching Wongutha names and English names.
  Table A5-C: Linking Moore River Lists with Oral Lists

Appendix A7: Notes from Neville's Files (State Archives AN 1/3 Acc 652 File 803 1919 unless otherwise noted)
  Figure A7-A: Laverton men escaping from the Moore River Native Settlement. (State Archives AN 1/4 Acc 653 File 166 1924.)
  Figure A7-B: 'Goldfields Aborigines' *West Australian,* June 1919.
  Figure A7-C: Henry Harris: Letter to the *Kalgoorlie Miner,* July 1919.
  Figure A7-D: Letter to A O Neville, Chief Protector of Aborigines, Perth, from Inspector Duncan, Kalgoorlie. July 1919.
  Figure A7-E: Letter to the Under Secretary, Colonial Secretary's Department/Aborigines and Fisheries from A O Neville, Chief Protector, July 1919.
  Figure A7-F: Circular Attached to a Letter to Mrs Boxall, Boulder, from Neville, Chief Protector, August 1919.
  Figure A7-G: Letter to Inspector Duncan, Kalgoorlie, from Neville, Chief Protector, August 1919.

Appendix A8: Rosie Green — Escape Documentation *(Rosie Green's personal file. Used with permission.)*
  Figure A8-A: File memo regarding procedure to secure Rosie's arrest for escaping from Mogumber. Commissioner of Native Affairs to Deputy Commissioner, 11 June 1941.
  Figure A8-B: Mogumber Superintendent to Commissioner of Native Affairs: Notification of Moora Police Court's charges against Rosie Green. 25 June 1941.
  Figure A8-C: Wiluna Police to Commissioner of Native Affairs: Notification of unsuccessful search for Rosie Green. 6 September 1941.

Appendix A9: Notes on Cosmo Newbery, 1930s and 1940s
  Figure A9-A Memo regarding children who might be removed South. Native Affairs Department. (AN 1/7 Acc 993 1939.)
  Figure A9-B Memo. Native Affairs Department. (AN 1/7 Acc 993, 1937.)
  Figure A9-C Declaration of Prohibited Area. (AN 1/7 Acc 993, File 972 1941.)

Bibliography

Published Sources

Aboriginal Legal Service of Western Australia. *Telling Our Story: a Report by the Aboriginal Legal Service of Western Australia (Inc) on the Removal of Aboriginal Children from their Families in Western Australia*. The Service, Perth, Western Australia, 1995.

Barwick, Diane. 'Making a Treaty: the North American Experience. For the Aboriginal Treaty Committee'. Published posthumously as Barwick, Diane. 'Making a Treaty: the North American Experience'. *Aboriginal History*. Vol. 12, 1988: 9–26.

Barwick, Diane, Isobel White and Betty Meehan (eds.). *Fighters and Singers. The Lives of some Aboriginal Women*. George Allen & Unwin, Sydney, NSW, 1985.

Barwick, Diane E and R E Barwick. 'A Memorial for Thomas Bungeleen'. *Aboriginal History*. Vol. 8, No. 1/2, 1984: 9–11.

Barwick, Diane E. 'Writing Aboriginal History. Comments on a book and its reviewers'. *Identity*. Vol. 4, No. 7, June 1982: 7–14.

Barwick, Diane. '1939–88 Aboriginal History. Questions and suggestions for research and coverage'. *Australia 1939–1988: a Bicentennial History Bulletin*. No. 3, May 1981: 29–35.

Barwick, Diane. 'A response to Dr Hirst's suggestion of a Biographical Approach to the 1939–1988 Vol.'. *Australia 1939–1988: a Bicentennial History Bulletin*. (Unpublished. Source: C T Stannage, private collection).

Barwick, D. 'Equity for Aborigines? The Framlingham Case'. In Patrick Troy (ed.). *A Just Society? Essays on Equity in Australia*. George Allen & Unwin. Australia 1981.

Barwick, Diane. 'Memorandum on a Proposed Dictionary of Aboriginal Biographies'. 19 April 1979. (Unpublished. Source: C T Stannage, private collection).

Barwick, Diane, Michael Mace and Tom Stannage (eds). *Handbook for Aboriginal and Islander History*. Aboriginal History, Canberra, 1979.

Barwick, Diane, Nan Philips and Tom Stannage. 'Biography: writing a life story'. In Diane Barwick, Michael Mace and Tom Stannage (eds.). *Handbook for Aboriginal and Islander History*. *Aboriginal History*, Canberra, 1979.

Barwick, Diane and W E H Stanner. 'Not by eastern windows only: anthropological advice to the Australian Governments in 1938'. *Aboriginal History*. Vol. 3, No. 1, 1979: 37–61.

Barwick, Diane and James Urry. 'A select biography of Aboriginal history and social change: theses and published research to 1976'. *Aboriginal History*. Vol. 1, No. 2, 1977: 111–169.

Barwick, Diane. 'And the lubras are ladies now'. In Gale Fay (ed.). *Woman's Role in Aboriginal Society*. Australian Institute of Aboriginal Studies, 1974: 51–63. (Citations refer to 1974, 2nd edition. First published in 1970).

Barwick, Diane. 'Outsiders: Aboriginal Women'. In Julie Rigg (ed.). *In Her Own Right: Women of Australia*. Sydney, Nelson, 1969: 85–97.

Barwick, Diane. 'Economic Absorption Without Assimilation? The Case of Some Melbourne Part-Aboriginal Families'. *Oceania*. Vol. 33, No. 1, 1962–1963: 18–23.

Bates, Daisy, (Isobel White [ed.]). *The Native Tribes of Western Australia*. National Library of Australia, Canberra, 1985.

Bates, Daisy. *The Passing of the Aborigines. A Lifetime Spent among the Natives of Australia*. John Murray, London, 1944 (1938).

Bennett, Arthur. *Dryblower Murphy. His Life and Times*. Fremantle Arts Centre Press (Community Publishing Project), 1982.

Bennett, Mary Montgomerie. *Human Rights For Australian Aborigines: How Can They Learn Without A Teacher?* Brisbane, 1957.

Bennett, Mary Montgomerie. *Teaching the Aborigines: Data from Mount Margaret Mission W.A.* Perth, 1935.

Bennett, Mary Montgomerie. *The Australian Aboriginal as a Human Being*. Chance and Bland Ltd., Gloucester, London, 1930.

Bird, Delys and Dennis Haskell (eds). *Whose Place? A Study of Sally Morgan's My Place*. Angus & Robertson/Harper Collins, Australia, 1992.

Biskup, Peter. *Not Slaves, Not Citizens: The Aboriginal Problem in West Australia 1898–1944*. University of Queensland Press, 1973.

Blackburn, Julia. *Daisy Bates in the Desert*. Martin Secker and Warburg, London, 1994.

Bolton, G C. *A View from the Edge: An Australian Stocktaking*. Boyer Lectures 1992, Australian Broadcasting Corporation, Sydney, 1992.

Bolton, G C. 'Black and White after 1897'. In C T Stannage (ed.). *A New History of Western Australia*. Nedlands, University of Western Australia Press, 1981.

Bolton, G C. 'Mary Montgomerie Bennett'. In *Australian Dictionary of Biography, 1891–1939*. Vol. 8, 1981.

Braddon, Russell. *Images of Australia*. Collins Australia, 1988.

Brady, Veronica. *Can These Bones Live?* Federation Press, New South Wales, 1996.

Brett, Judith. 'Breaking the Silence: A Gift to the Reader'. *Australian Book Review*. No. 93, Aug 1987: 9–11.

Bringing Them Home. Report of the National Inquiry into the Separation of Aboriginal and Torres Strait Islander Children from Their Families. Human Rights and Equal Opportunity Commission, Sydney, April 1997.

Bunbury, Bill. 'Out of Sight, Out of Mind: Aboriginal Internment'. In *Reading Labels on Jam Tins. Living through Difficult Times*. Fremantle Arts Centre Press in assoc. with the Australian Broadcasting Corporation, 1993.

C F. 'Questions of Collaboration: An interview with Jackie Huggins and Isabel Tarrago'. *Hecate*. Vol. 16, No. 1/2, 1990: 140–147.

Carnegie, D. *Spinifex and Sand: a Narrative of Five Years Pioneering and Exploration in Western Australia*. London: Arthur Pearson. 1898. Reprinted Harmondsworth: Penguin facsimile, 1973: 58–60

Carroll, John (ed.). *Intruders in the Bush: the Australian Quest for Identity*. Oxford University Press, 1982.

Carter, Jan. *Nothing to Spare: Recollections of Australian Pioneering Women*. Penguin, Ringwood, 1981.

Clark, Manning. *A Short History of Australia*. Heinemann, London, 1964.

Clendinnen, Inga. *True Stories*. Boyer Lectures 1999, Australian Broadcasting Corporation, 1999.
Climo, Jacob. 'Transmitting Ethnic Identity through Oral Narratives'. *Ethnic Groups*. Vol. 8, No. 3, 1990: 163–79.
Council for Aboriginal Reconciliation. *Draft Document for Reconciliation. A Draft for discussion by the Australian people*. Australia, 1999.
Curthoys, Ann and Andrew Markus (eds). *Who are our enemies? Racism and the Australian Working Class*. Hale and Iremonger, NSW (in association with The Australian Society for the Study of Labour History. Canberra), 1978.
Darian-smith, Kate, Liz Gunner and Sarah Nuttall (eds). *Text Theory Space: Land Literature and History in South Africa and Australia*. Routledge, London, 1996.
Davis, Jack. *John Pat and other poems*. Dent, Melbourne, 1988.
Davis, J. *The First-born and other poems*. Dent, Melbourne, 1983. (Angus and Robertson, Sydney, 1970.)
Davis, Jack, Stephen Mueke, Mudrooroo Narogin and Adam Shoemaker (eds). *Paperbark: a Collection of Black Australian writings*. University of Queensland Press, 1990.
Docker, John. *Postmodernism and Popular Culture. A Cultural History*. Cambridge University Press, 1994.
Donaldson, Ian, Peter Read and James Walter (eds.). *Shaping lives: Reflections on Biography*. Chapter 11, 'A phantom at my shoulder. The final draft of Charles Perkins: a biography'. The Humanities Research Centre Monograph Series 6, Australian National University, Canberra, 1992.
Doncaster, E W and Elizabeth Willis. 'Edward (Henry) Mallan Collick'. In Nairn, Bede and Geoffrey Serle (eds). *Australian Dictionary of Biography, 1891–1939*. Vol. 8, 1981: 68.
Douglas, Louise, Alan Roberts and Ruth Thompson. *Oral history. A handbook*. Allen & Unwin, Australia, 1988.
Doyle McCarthy, E. *Knowledge as Culture. The New Sociology of Knowledge*. Routledge, NY, 1996.
Eades, Diana. 'You Gotta Know How To Talk: Information Seeking in Southeast Queensland Aboriginal Society.' *Australian Journal of Linguistics*. Vol. 2, 1982: 61–82.
Eades, Diana. 'They Don't Speak an Aboriginal Language, or Do They?' in Ian Keen (ed.) *Being Black: Aboriginal Cultures in 'Settled' Australia*. Aboriginal Studies Press, Canberra, 1988:97–115.
Elkin, A P. *The Australian Aborigines*. Angus and Robertson, 1938 (1974).
Facey, A B. *A Fortunate Life*. Fremantle Arts Centre Press, Western Australia, 1981.
Forrest, John. *Explorations in Australia*, Manston and Searle, London, 1875, (Facsimile edition 1969): 49–50.
Fox, Charlie. *Working Australia*. Allen & Unwin, Sydney, 1991.
Fox, Charlie and Marilyn Lake (eds). *Australians at Work: Commentaries and Sources*. McPhee Gribble, Fitzroy, Victoria, 1990.
Frost, Lucy. *No Place for a Nervous Lady. Voices from the Australian Bush*. McPhee Gribble in assoc. with Penguin, Victoria, Australia, 1984.
Fullerton, M. *The Australian Bush*. The Outward Bound Library. J M Dent & Sons, London (undated, post 1914).
Geertz, Clifford. *Works and Lives: The Anthropologist as Author*. Stanford University Press, Stanford, California, 1988.
Geertz, Clifford. *The Interpretation of Cultures: Selected Essays*. Hutchinson,

London, 1975.
Gooneratne, Yasmine. 'Australian Biography as History: You can't put lies in a book'. *Meridian*. Vol. 7, No. 1, May 1988: 3–12.
Grieve, N, and A Burns (eds.). *Australian Women: New Feminist Perspectives*. Oxford University Press, Australia, 1986.
Groen, Fran de. 'Healing, Wholeness and Holiness in My Place'. In Delys Bird and Dennis Haskell (eds). *Whose Place? A Study of Sally Morgan's My Place*. Angus & Robertson/Harper Collins, Australia, 1992.
Grono, William (ed.). *Margins. A West Coast Selection 1829–1988*. Fremantle Arts Centre Press, 1988.
Gunson, Niel. 'Diane Barwick'. *Aboriginal History*. Vol. 9, No. 1, 1985: 4–5.
Gunson, N. 'Proud shoes: Black family history in Australia'. *Aboriginal History*. Vol. 5, No. 2, 1982.
Haebich, Anna. *For Their Own Good: Aborigines and Government in the Southwest of Western Australia, 1900–1940*. University of Western Australia Press, 1988.
Haebich, A. 'On the Inside: Moore River Native Settlement in the 1930's'. In B Gammage and A Markus (eds). *All that Dirt: Aborigines 1938*. Canberra, 1982.
Halbwachs, Maurice. *On Collective Memory*. The University of Chicago Press, Chicago, 1992. (Translated by Lewis A. Coser from *Les cadres sociaux de la memoire*. Presses Universitaires de France, Paris, 1952; and from *La topographie legendaire des evangiles en terre sainte: etude de memoire collective*. Presses Universitaires de France, Paris, 1941).
Hasluck, Paul. *Mucking About. An Autobiography*. University of Western Australia Press,s, 1994.
Hasluck, P. *Black Australians: a Survey of Native Policy in Western Australia 1829–1897*. Melbourne University Press, Melbourne, 1942 (2nd ed 1970).
Healy, Chris. *From the Ruins of Colonialism. History as Social Memory*. Cambridge University Press, Cambridge, United Kingdom, 1997.
Heslop, Jim (ed.). *Recollections of Mt Margaret*. Publishing details not listed, undated.
McShane, Ian. *History and Cultural Resources Project*. Committee to Review Australian Studies in Tertiary Education. Part 1: Report. Part 2: Seminar Papers. Canberra, May 1896.
Holden, Colin. *Ritualist on a Tricycle. Frederick Goldsmith. Church, Nationalism and Society in Western Australia 1880–1920*. University of Western Australia Press, 1997.
Huggins, Jackie and Judy Skene (interview). 'Experience and Identity: Jackie Huggins and writing history'. *Limina*. Vol. 2, 1996: 1–7.
Huggins, J, Rita Huggins and Jane M Jacobs. 'Kooramindanjie: Place and the Postcolonial'. *History Workshop Journal*. Vol. 39, 1995: 165–181.
Huggins, J. 'Pretty Deadly Tidda Business'. In *Second Degree Tampering*. Sybylla Feminist Press, Melbourne, 1992.
Huggins, J. 'In My Terms'. *Hecate*. Vol. 17, No. 2, 1991.
Huggins, J. 'Writing My Mother's Life'. *Hecate*. Vol. 17, No. 1, 1991.
Huggins, J. 'Firing on in the mind: Aboriginal Domestic Servants'. *Hecate*. Vol. 13, No. 2, 1988.
Huggins, J. 'Black Women and Women's Liberation'. *Hecate*. Vol. 13, No. 1, 1987.
Huggins, Rita and Jackie Huggins. *Auntie Rita*. Aboriginal Studies Press, Australian Institute of Aboriginal Studies, Canberra 1994.

Hunt, Susan Jane. *Spinifex and Hessian. Women in North-West Australia 1860–1900.* University of Western Australia Press, Western Australian Experience Series, 1986.
Kimberley Language Resource Centre (ed.). *Moola Bulla. In the Shadow of the Mountain.* Magabala Books Aboriginal Corporation, Broome, 1996.
King, Norma. *Colourful Tales of the Western Australian Goldfields.* Rigby Publishers Limited, 1980.
Layman, E and T Stannage. *Celebrations in Western Australian History. Studies in Western Australian History No. 10.* Department of History. University of Western Australia, April 1989.
Malouf, David. *An Imaginary Life.* Pan Macmillan Australia, 1994. (Chatto & Windus, London, 1978.)
Malouf, David. *Remembering Babylon.* Vintage, 1994. (Chatto & Windus, London, 1993.)
Malouf, David. *Conversations at Curlow Creek.* Chatto & Windus, London, 1996.
Malouf, David. *A Spirit of Play. The Making of Australian Consciousness.* Boyer Lectures. Australian Broadcasting Corporation, Sydney, 1998.
Markus, Andrew and M C Rickefs (eds.). *Surrender Australia? Essays in the Study and Uses of History.* George Allen and Unwin, Australia, 1985.
Marshall, John. *Battling for Gold, or Stirring Incidents of Goldfields Life in West Australia.* Facsimile edition Hesperian Press, Carlisle, Western Australia, 1984. (E W Cole, Melbourne, 1903).
Maushart, Susan. *Sort of a Place like Home: Remembering the Moore River Native Settlement.* Fremantle Arts Centre Press, 1993.
Mediansky, F A (ed.). *Australia in a Changing World.* Maxwell Macmillan Publishing, Australia, New South Wales, 1992.
Miller, Constance. *Paved with Gold.* Hesperian Press, 1994.
Morgan, Margaret. *Mt Margaret: A Drop in a Bucket.* Keith and Margaret Morgan (printed by Mission Publications of Australia), 1986.
Morgan, Sally. *Aboriginal Experience: My Place.* Learning Materials Production Centre/Open Training and Education Network. Redfern, New South Wales, 1994.
Morgan, Sally. *My Place.* Fremantle Arts Centre Press, Fremantle, 1987.
Mudrooroo. *Us Mob. History, Culture, Struggle: an Introduction to Indigenous Australia.* Angus and Robertson: Harper Collins, 1995.
Murphy, Edwin (Dryblower). *Dryblower's Verses.* Perth, undated (circa 1924).
Nannup, Alice, Lauren Marsh and Stephen Kinnane. *When the Pelican Laughed.* Fremantle Arts Centre Press, 1992.
Narogin, Mudrooroo. *Writing from the Fringe: A Study of Modern Aboriginal Literature.* Hyland House Publishing, Victoria, 1990.
Newman, Joan. 'Race, Gender and Identity: *My Place* as Autobiography'. In Delys Bird and Dennis Haskell (eds.). *Whose Place? A Study of Sally Morgan's My Place.* Angus & Robertson/Harper Collins, Australia, 1992.
Pederson, H and Banjo Woorunmurra. *Jandamarra and the Bunuba Resistance.* Magabala Books Aboriginal Corporation, Broome, 1995.
Pilkington, Doris/Nugi Garimara. *Follow the Rabbit Proof Fence.* University of Queensland Press, St Lucia, 1996.
Rajkowski, Pamela. *Linden Girl. A Story of Outlawed Lives.* University of Western Australia Press, 1995.
Randall, Margaret. 'Reclaiming Voices: Notes on a New Female Practice in

Journalism'. *Latin American Perspectives.* Issue 70, Vol. 18, No. 3, 1991: 103–113.

Read, Peter. 'The Return Of The Stolen Generations'. The Trevor Reese Memorial Lecture, 30 January 1996, London. In Tom Griffiths (ed.). *Public Lectures in Australian Studies 1995–1996.* Sir Robert Menzies Centre for Australian Studies, Institute of Commonwealth Studies, University of London.

Read, Peter. *Returning to Nothing; The Meaning of Lost Places.* Cambridge University Press, 1996.

Read, Peter and Valerie Chapman (eds.). *Terrible Hard Biscuits: A Reader In Aboriginal History.* Journal of Aboriginal History, St Leonards: Allen & Unwin, NSW, 1996.

Read, Peter. 'My Footprints are Here: Oral History and the Attachment to Place'. *Oral History Association of Australia Journal.* No. 17, 1995: 40–47.

Read, Peter. 'What oral history can't tell us: the role of the CD-Rom'. *Oral History Association of Australia Journal.* No. 16, 1994: 87–90.

Read, Peter. 'A phantom at my shoulder. The final draft of Charles Perkins: a biography'. Chapter 11 in Donaldson, Ian, Peter Read, James Walter (eds.). *Shaping Lives: Reflections on Biography.* The Humanities Research Centre Monograph Series 6, Australian National University, Canberra, 1992.

Read, Peter and Jay Read (eds.). *Long Time, Olden Time. Aboriginal Accounts of Northern Territory History.* Institute for Aboriginal Development Publications, 1991.

Read, Peter. 'Oral History Interviewing'. In Diane Barwick, Michael Mace and Tom Stannage (eds.). *Handbook for Aboriginal and Islander History.* Aboriginal History, Canberra, 1979.

Reece, R H W and Anna Haebich. 'Auber Octavious Neville'. In Geoffrey Serle (ed.). *Australian Dictionary of Biography, 1891–1939.* Vol. II, University of Melbourne, 1988.

Reece, Bob and Tom Stannage (eds.). *European-Aboriginal Relations in Western Australian History. Studies in Western Australian History,* No. 8. Department of History, University of Western Australia, 1984.

Rose, Deborah Bird. *Nourishing Terrains: Australian Aboriginal Views of Landscape and Wilderness.* Australian Heritage Commission, Canberra, 1996.

Schenk, Rod. *The Educability of the Australian Native.* United Aborigines Mission, Melbourne, undated (c1940) (Perth: Service Print).

Shaw, George (ed.). *1988 and All That. New Views of Australia's Past.* University of Queensland Press, 1988.

Sheils, Helen (ed.) and W E H Stanner (Convenor). *Australian Aboriginal Studies: A Symposium of Papers Presented at the 1961 Research Conference.* Oxford University Press, Melbourne, 1963.

Sheridan, Susan. 'Different Lives: Two Aboriginal Women's Stories'. *Antipodes: A North American Journal of Australian Literature.* Vol. 3.1, Spring 1989: 20–3.

Shoesmith, Brian. *Media, Politics and Identity. Studies in Western Australian History,* No.15. Department of History, University of Western Australia, 1989.

Sligo, N K. *Mates and Gold. Reminiscences of the Early Westralian Goldfields. 1890–1896.* Hesperian Press, Carlisle, Western Australia, 1995 (1980).

Smith, H P (ed.). *The first ten years of Mount Margaret Mission, W.A: as given in a letter, following a visit to Mt Margaret by Mr Robert Powell and extracts of prayer letters, written during the years by Mr R.S. Schenk.* Keswick Book Depot, Melbourne, 1933.

Somerville, Margaret. 'Life (Hi)Story Writing: The Relationship Between Talk and Text'. *Hecate*. Vol. 17, No. 1, 1991.
Stannage, C T (ed.). *A New History of Western Australia*. Nedlands, University of Western Australia Press, 1981.
Stannage, C T. *The People of Perth: A Social History of Western Australia's Capital City*. Perth City Council, Perth, 1979.
Stannage, C T (ed.). *Local History in Western Australia: A Guide to Research: Papers Read at the Local History Seminar held at Subiaco on 29 August 1974*. Local History Seminar, Subiaco, 1974.
Stanner, W E H. *After the Dreaming*. 1968 Boyer Lectures, Australian Broadcasting Corporation, Sydney, 1969.
Thomas, Sue. 'Connections: Recent Criticisms of Aboriginal Writing'. *Meridian*. Vol. 8, 1989: 39–46.
Tully, James. *Strange Multiplicity. Constitutionalism in an Age of Diversity*. (John Robert Seeley Lectures, 1994) Cambridge University Press, Great Britain, 1995.
Wadley, Ian. 'Worlds Apart: A Proposal for Frame Reflective Discourse in International Environmental Negotiations' in Lawrence E Susskind, William Moomaw, Kevin Gallagher (eds.). *International Environmental Negotiation: An Integrative Approach. Papers in International Environmental Negotiation*. Vol 9. P O N Books (Program on Negotiation at Harvard Law School), Cambridge Massachusetts, 1999.
Ward, Glenyse. *Unna you fullas*. Magabala Books, Broome, 1991.
Ward, G. *Wandering Girl*. Magabala Books, Broome, 1987.
Whittington, Vera. *Gold and Typhoid. Two Fevers. A Social History of Western Australia 1891–1900*. University of Western Australia Press, 1988.
Wright, Judith. *A Book of Australian Verse*. Oxford University Press, Melbourne, 1968.
Wright, J. *Preoccupations in Australian Poetry*. Oxford University Press, Melbourne, 1965.
Yudice, George. 'Testimonio and Postmodernism: Whom does testimonial writing represent?' *Latin American Perspectives*. Issue 70, Vol 18, No. 3, 1991,

Unpublished Sources

1. Manuscripts

POLICE DEPARTMENT RECORDS
AN5/3 ACC 430 4092 Annual Report to 30 June 1922, Laverton Police.
AN5/Laverton ACC 3354/1 Letterbook + Reports on Locality, Laverton Police.
AN5/Coolgardie ACC 463 Occurrence Book Vol. 38, Coolgardie.
AN5/Gingin ACC 411 Occurrence Book Vol. 10, Gingin.

MOORE RIVER NATIVE SETTLEMENT RECORDS
AN 1/6 ACC 1326 1108/21 Register of Inmates.
AN 1/6 ACC 1326 622/21 Accounts, and General Correspondence.
AN 1/6 ACC 1326 1610/23 Annual Report of Superintendent for year ending 30 June 1923.

AN 1/6 ACC 1326 74/21 Application for Position of Superintendent.
AN 1/7 ACC 993 509/26 Miscellaneous Correspondence.
AN 1/7 ACC 993 351/28 Register of Inmates.
AN 1/7 ACC 993 459/33 Register of Inmates.

Department of Native Affairs/Department of Aborigines and Fisheries
AN 1/7 ACC 993 364/26 Missions.
AN1/7 ACC 993 560/26.
AN1/7 ACC 993 97/27.
AN1/7 ACC 993 273/27.
AN1/7 ACC 993 487/37 'Mt Margaret Mission – Native Matters'.
AN1/3 ACC 652 75/15 'CPA Aborigines Act Section 7 – Appointment of Constable E P Thompson, Laverton'.
AN1/3 ACC 652 803/19 'Newspaper Report re: Natives Starving in Kalgoorlie'.
AN 1/4 ACC 653 6/20 'R Schenk, Victoria, Letter'.
AN 1/4 ACC 653 479/21 'Chief Protector of Aborigines Annual Report 1920–21'.
AN 1/4 ACC 653 462/23 'Chief Protector of Aborigines Annual Report 1921–22'.

Personal Records, Rod Schenk
Monthly letters to friends/financial supporters in Victoria. 1921–1933. Unpublished. (Private collection – Margaret Morgan.)
Annual Report to United Aborigines Mission, Victoria. 1922. Unpublished. (Private collection – M Morgan.)
Diary. 1921–1933 Unpublished. (Private collection – Margaret Morgan.)

Miscellaneous
Anderson, A F. 'A Bush Patrol by Constable A F Anderson, Laverton Police Station' Laverton, 1947. (Battye Library.)

2. Theses, Dissertations and Unpublished reports

Barwick, Diane. 'A Little More than Kin: Regional Affiliation and Group Identity among Aboriginal Migrants in Melbourne'. Ph.D., Australian National University, 1964.
Stanton, John. 'Conflict, Change and Stability at Mt Margaret: an Aboriginal Community in Transition' Ph.D., University of Western Australia, 1984.
Task Force on Aboriginal Social Justice, 'Report of the Task Force'. Vol. 1. Perth. April 1994.

3. Newspapers

Goldfields Distribution
Kalgoorlie Weekly, Kalgoorlie Sun, Western Argus, Goldfields Courier, Kalgoorlie Miner, Coolgardie Miner.
Western Australian distribution
West Australian, Sunday Times.

Index

Aborigines Act 1905, 192, 225, 300, 425–6, 428, 431
Aborigines Act 1897, 425–6
Aborigines Act Amendment Act 1911, 427
Aborigines Protection Act 1886, 424, 426
Aborigines Protection Board, 245, 295, 424–5, 436
Aborigines Protection Regulation 1909, 427
Afghans, 141, 276, 417

Baldul, 301, 333, 382, 384
Bates, Daisy, 207, 214, 240, 267–70
Bennett, Mary Montgomerie, 270–2, 289, 427
Biyuwarra, 89, 206, 302, 333, 335, 339, 344, 348–9, 355, 364, 382, 384
Burtville, 76, 80–1, 84, 93–5, 97, 100, 141, 159, 228, 233, 311, 323, 337, 393, 398, 412
Bush (as location of traditional Aboriginal lifestyle), 43, 46–7, 51, 54, 56–8, 61, 66–7, 88, 91, 100, 102, 105–6, 108, 134, 140–2, 149, 151, 154, 160–2, 170–2, 175, 178, 185, 188, 190, 192, 202, 211, 227, 229, 234, 238–9, 241, 243, 279, 285, 290, 294–5, 301, 304, 310, 324, 326, 329, 330–1, 333–4, 342, 345, 352, 354, 356, 360–2, 372, 375–7, 412, 416

Canning, Sadie, 26, 28, 192–203
childhood, 47, 70, 140, 172, 192, 308, 310–1
children, being taken away, 41, 44–45, 47, 50–1, 72, 74, 105–6, 110–4, 136–7, 140, 157, 166–7, 172, 186–7, 192–3, 239, 311–2, 329–30, 327, 402–10
disguised, 46, 148–9, 161
hiding, 47, 142, 144, 146, 163, 169, 188, 312, 330–70, 140
Christians, 37, 50, 57, 100, 105–1, 277, 294
Cosmo Newbery, 63, 103–4, 110, 137, 141, 321, 402–3, 411–2, 432, 445
Country, 14, 141, 157, 172, 185, 196, 199–200, 258, 335, 337–8, 340–3, 345–6, 348, 353–8, 360–4
Culture, Aboriginal, 172–3, 294, 320

Darlot/Darlots *(also see Wunmala)*, 56, 108–9, 132–3, 200–1, 207, 216, 267–9, 305, 346, 358, 361, 363, 375, 403

deportation, 71, 75, 140, 222–3, 225–6, 232, 241, 278–9, 282, 299, 302–3, 306, 308, 336, 370, 374, 376, 385–6

Donaldson, Queenie, 40, 56, 64, 105–7, 319

Donegan, A J, 63, 103–4, 108–10, 137, 402–3, 409, 411–2, 432, 445

drought, 34, 189, 212, 230, 237, 240, 278, 280, 298, 309, 323, 327, 331, 333–4, 341, 394–8, 411

Dryblower Murphy, 272–5

Edjudina, 142, 145–6, 154, 394, 424

education, 41, 72, 193–4, 247, 270–1, 286, 289, 292, 377, 412, 425–7, 433

Elyon, 75, 89, 206, 302, 335, 337, 339, 342, 344, 349, 379, 381–2, 384

escape, 14, 19–21, 24, 29, 39, 41, 43–5, 52–4, 59, 70–1, 73, 80, 86, 94, 108, 170, 198, 204, 209, 212, 216, 222–3, 243, 245, 248, 252, 255, 257–8, 264–6, 272, 279–84, 298–300, 302–3, 305, 307, 309–10, 314–6, 318, 322, 327, 333, 341–5, 350–1, 353, 359, 362, 373–85, 387, 402, 404, 406, 411, 416, 424

exile, 14, 18, 21, 27, 29, 222, 255, 257, 318, 326, 330, 336, 359–62, 369, 376, 379–85, 386, 404, 406, 408, 429

featherfoot man, 178, 181–2, 200

food, 21–3, 25, 31, 34, 44, 45, 50, 65, 73, 76, 102, 116, 118, 120–1, 124, 130, 132, 141–2, 144, 154, 161, 185, 189, 211–2, 224, 226–7, 229–30, 237–8, 240–1, 243, 265, 271, 274, 288, 303, 309, 314–5, 322–4, 326–9, 331, 333–4, 350–2, 354–7, 363, 385, 398–9, 403, 418–9

gaol *(also see lockup)*, 35–7, 40, 110, 113, 135, 151, 230, 245, 258, 265, 268, 284, 290–3, 309, 313, 315, 331, 333–4, 342, 385

Grarn, 244, 302, 333, 383

Government, 14–5, 35, 37, 72, 106, 130, 134, 136, 176, 192, 222–4, 227, 246, 264, 266, 271, 284, 290, 295–6, 300, 306, 313–4, 322, 329, 331–2, 376–8, 387, 391, 399, 411–2, 416, 420–1, 426, 428, 432–3

Harris, William, 223, 264–6, 280, 314, 316, 385–6, 431, 435

Hunter, P.C. Dave/'Cooeyanbah', 80, 238–9, 285, 287, 293, 306, 324, 329–35, 345, 360, 364, 375, 407, 445

Index

Jackson, Mrs, 176–8, 180, 186, 188
Jidu/Jumbo, 20–1, 50, 57, 72, 74, 87, 94, 96, 134, 140, 205–6, 216–7, 244, 246–7, 255, 272, 299–301, 303, 330, 332–5, 340, 343, 346, 353, 362, 381–2, 384–5
Jinera, 58, 84, 206–7, 215, 299, 301, 304–6, 333, 337, 340, 343, 346, 348, 353, 355, 362–3, 381–2, 384, 442–3
Joe Mulgathunoo/Mulga Joe, 41, 63, 85, 136, 198, 210, 244, 255, 258–9, 296, 302, 330–3, 340–3, 381, 383–5, 433
Johnston, Reggie, 25–6, 28, 48–9, 51, 72–4, 106, 208, 214, 219, 282–4, 300, 309

Kalgoorlie, 13, 23–5, 28–9, 31–2, 35, 41–4, 49, 51–3, 55, 58, 61, 64, 72, 75, 81, 83, 95, 100, 105, 108, 140, 148, 152, 209, 224, 226–7, 232, 272, 275–6, 278, 280, 285, 287, 291–2, 297, 300, 303–4, 309, 311, 324, 327–8, 337–8, 346, 356, 358–9, 377, 368–9, 391, 394, 396, 398–9, 401, 404, 408, 442
Karonie, 46, 64, 105–6, 141, 147, 151, 209

Laverton, 13–5, 27, 32–41, 44, 47, 50, 59, 71, 79–80, 83, 87–8, 96–7, 100, 103–4, 107–8, 112, 167, 170, 173–4, 181, 186, 192, 196–200, 204, 207, 210, 214–5, 217, 220, 223–49, 252, 255–9, 264–9, 275–82, 285–7, 289–93, 298–309, 311, 313–6, 318–39, 341–2, 344, 346, 351, 355–6, 358–64, 368, 370, 373–6, 379–81, 383, 385–7, 391–4, 398–9, 402–4, 409, 411–2, 416, 423, 429–32
Law, Aboriginal/Wongutha, 178, 201, 269, 291–2
law, 224–5, 264–5, 274, 284, 312, 325–7, 332, 358, 376, 428
Leonora, 15, 26–9, 32, 40, 42–3, 56, 58, 60, 63, 108, 110, 132, 135, 192, 194–5, 197, 202, 215, 237, 266, 287–9, 297–8, 305, 312, 364, 393, 398, 403–9, 416, 420
legislation, 193, 278, 425–8
Linden, 142, 154, 209, 245, 308–9, 311, 398–9, 412
lockup *(also see gaol)*, 37, 40, 66, 110, 196, 198, 299, 319, 335, 404

McIntyre, Ranji, 49, 53, 63, 75–104, 309–11, 370
Menzies, 25–6, 56, 74, 83, 208, 217, 278, 283, 297, 300, 304, 311, 328, 337, 360–1, 368, 398, 418, 421, 431
Meredith, Fred, 42–3, 45–6, 56–8, 61–6, 108–10, 112, 114–5, 117, 134, 136–8, 319
Meredith, Rosie/Rosie Green, 29, 32, 42–6, 54–9, 61–6, 108–139, 170, 184–5, 312, 400–10

missionaries, 29, 48, 157, 172, 174, 176, 180, 193, 294, 306, 308, 312–3

Moongoodie, 88, 244, 301, 333, 340, 343, 381–2, 384

Moore River Native Settlement/Mogumber, 29, 41, 43–6, 50, 52, 56–7, 62, 70–1, 73–5, 85, 89–90, 94, 97, 102, 107–8, 110–1, 113–5, 135, 137, 140, 144, 157, 170, 172, 184, 188–9, 198, 204, 206, 210–1, 222, 225, 242–3, 248–66, 279–84, 287, 293, 295–303, 305, 307–9, 313–6, 319, 326, 330, 332–6, 338, 340–2, 344, 353, 360, 362–3, 368, 373–4, 376, 379–83, 386–7, 390–1, 393, 402–11

Morgan, Margaret, 21, 24, 26, 37, 39, 50–1, 55, 184, 199, 202–20, 238, 244–7, 282–3, 295–307, 379–80, 385, 411

Morgans, 39, 96, 173–4, 243, 288, 311, 323, 337, 360, 364, 387, 399

Moseley, H D/Moseley Royal Commission, 271, 427

Mt Margaret Mission, 29–31, 33, 38–40, 46–7, 51, 57, 64, 68, 72–4, 84, 86–7, 90–1, 93–6, 105–7, 140, 148, 152–3, 155–9, 163–4, 166, 172–7, 183–8, 190, 192–4, 200, 202, 204–5, 207, 225, 231, 246–7, 259, 280–9, 291, 294, 297, 303, 305–6, 309–10, 312–3, 323, 328, 358, 368, 376–7, 385, 406, 411–2, 423

Mudarn, 29, 34, 87, 302, 333–4, 383–4

Neville, A O, 105, 135, 223, 236, 239, 247–8, 265, 270–1, 280, 287–8, 295, 301, 308–9, 332, 336, 372, 374, 376–7, 387–412, 428–9, 431–3

New Norcia, 44, 112–3, 391, 435

Ngada, 58, 215, 217, 299, 302–4, 333, 346, 348–9, 353, 381–4

Nganjur/Bill Carrigg, 89, 302, 333, 343, 381–2, 384

Ngunnu, 46–9, 54–5, 61–2, 140–1, 146–9, 156–171

O'Brien, May, 31–2, 55–6, 172–91

pipeline, Goldfields water, 20, 22–3, 53, 74, 82–3, 93, 198, 285, 297, 300, 303, 346, 350–1, 353–6, 358, 442

police, 34–5, 37, 41, 45–6, 58, 64–6, 70, 73, 79–80, 93–4, 97, 107–8, 110–1, 117–21, 132, 137, 141–2, 144–5, 152, 157, 160, 166–8, 185, 188, 197, 210–1, 222–36, 238, 240, 246–7, 255, 258, 265, 268–9, 272, 279–80, 282–4, 286, 290–6, 300, 305–15, 317, 322–5, 327, 329–37, 345–6, 350, 352, 358, 360, 373–6, 385–9, 391, 393, 398–9, 401–5, 407–9, 420–1, 423, 426, 430–1, 433, 445

Protector, 35, 104, 109, 223–4, 229, 231–2, 234, 236, 238, 240, 255, 270, 278, 284, 287, 289, 300–1, 307–9, 325, 332–3, 376–7, 387, 389, 391, 384, 396–7, 399, 401, 408, 425–33, 435–6

rations, 35–5, 151, 224, 226–8, 238, 268, 288, 290, 296, 306, 309, 312, 331–3, 377, 385, 393, 398, 411–2
Roth, W E/Roth Royal Commission, 1904, 426
Rottnest, 41, 326, 332, 423
Royal Commissions, 271, 426–7

Sandstone, 44–5, 58–60, 125, 129–30, 132, 267–9, 284, 304, 316, 356, 364, 368, 373
Schenk, Mysie, 204, 299–300, 305–6, 379, 385
Schenk, Rod, 50, 84–5, 87, 91, 93, 96, 104, 172, 174, 190, 204, 231–2, 236–47, 270–1, 276–9, 282, 284, 289, 293–5, 298–300, 303, 306, 308–9, 311, 313, 332, 336, 360–1, 373–9, 385–7, 406, 411–2, 423, 429, 431–2
school, 96–7, 105–6, 146, 174–5, 178, 181, 203, 216, 270–1, 276, 286, 288–91, 310–2, 411–2, 425, 427, 433
sheep, 33–4, 45, 70, 93, 119, 131, 169–70, 212, 229, 242, 293, 295, 322–4, 331, 334–6, 357, 363, 423
shooting, 34, 47, 70, 79, 98–9, 102, 121–2, 145–6, 154, 227, 242, 245, 265, 268–9, 287, 306, 310–1, 313, 323, 325, 328, 332–3, 370, 375, 411, 417, 419–20, 422–4
Skull Creek, 291–2, 298, 353
squatters, 289, 295, 322, 333

Thalbin, 88, 301–2, 330, 333, 340, 381–2, 384
Tharnmoon, 88–90, 302, 333, 381–2, 384
Thimbarn/Gadajilbi, 26, 88–90, 93, 300–4, 333, 351, 354, 357, 361, 381–2, 384–5
Thomas, Doris, 219, 300
Thompson, P.C. E P, 80, 223–35, 238, 306, 324–30, 332, 336, 374–6, 430
Thulyi/Tom Harris, 90, 302–3, 333, 339, 351–3, 358, 381, 383, 384
trackers, 31, 44, 108, 114, 116, 290, 299, 309, 315–6, 323, 340–1, 343, 345–6, 351–3, 355, 357–8, 364, 373, 403–4, 418
train, riding the, 23–4, 64–5, 82–3, 110, 135, 170, 208–9, 265, 269–70, 282, 285, 296, 298, 303–5, 314, 323, 326, 329–31, 333, 335–9, 351, 359–61, 364, 379, 385–6, 404, 408, 442

tribe, 238, 241, 245, 269, 301, 304, 399, 403, 417–8, 420–2
Turner, Lampi, 30–1, 41, 51, 207, 215–6, 218, 299, 319

Warburton, 30, 47, 196, 289, 291
water, 14, 21–3, 25, 33–4, 44–5, 59, 73, 82–3, 91–3, 98, 101–2, 107, 112, 114, 117, 119–22, 128–31, 154–5, 181–2, 185, 227, 229–30, 232, 234, 239, 249, 284, 294–5, 302–4, 307, 311, 313, 315, 322–4, 327–9, 331–2, 334, 342–9, 352, 354–7, 359, 364, 369, 385, 390, 403, 419
Wawuja/Ginger, 85–6, 210, 255, 258, 296, 302, 330, 332–3, 340, 342–3, 381, 383–4, 433
white people, 24, 34, 47–8, 54, 62, 70, 80, 97, 141, 143, 150, 154, 156, 161, 169, 173–4, 179, 188, 195, 211, 224–6, 232, 237, 241, 242–3, 245–6, 264–6, 272, 274–5, 277, 280, 286–8, 290–4, 300–1, 307, 309–10, 131, 315–6, 323–31, 338–9, 346, 350–2, 357–9, 361–2, 375, 393, 402, 412, 417, 428
Wiluna, 56, 115, 200, 207, 236, 238, 290, 297–8, 305, 364, 377, 398, 405–6, 409
Wongai/Wongutta, 13–5, 19, 22, 31, 34, 39, 45, 50–2, 56, 59, 61, 63, 67, 70–1, 89, 104–5, 120, 126, 140–1, 146–9, 153, 163, 172–3, 176, 200–1, 204, 222, 224–6, 228–9, 247, 255, 270, 276–7, 279, 299–302, 305–10, 316–21, 324–29, 331–5, 339, 356, 358–61, 364, 367–72, 374–6, 379–82, 385–6, 411–2, 418, 423, 431, 436, 442
Wongan Hills, 117, 284, 297, 303–4, 344, 349, 351, 368
Wunmala *(also see Darlots)*, 200–1, 358, 363–4
Wunu, 89, 217, 302, 304, 312, 333, 344, 346, 348–9, 353, 355, 362, 364, 382, 384, 442
Wyallie, 13, 29–32, 41–3, 45–50, 53–8, 60–5, 67, 108–9, 111, 140–158, 162, 164–71, 319

Yalgoo, 206–7, 284, 297, 305, 363, 405–6
Yamathee, 185, 200–1, 346